Habitus and Field

Pierre Bourdieu

Habitus and Field

General Sociology, Volume 2

Lectures at the Collège de France (1982–1983)

Edition established by Patrick Champagne, Julien Duval, Franck Poupeau and Marie-Christine Rivière

Translated by Peter Collier

polity

First published in French in *Sociologie générale. Volume 1. Cours au Collège de France (1981–1983)* © Éditions Raisons d'Agir/Éditions du Seuil, 2015

This English edition © Polity Press, 2020

Polity Press
65 Bridge Street
Cambridge CB2 1UR, UK

Polity Press
101 Station Landing
Suite 300
Medford, MA 02155, USA

ISBN-13: 978-1-5095-2669-7

A catalogue record for this book is available from the British Library.

Library of Congress Cataloging-in-Publication Data
Names: Bourdieu, Pierre, 1930-2002, author. | Bourdieu, Pierre, 1930-2002.
    Sociologie générale. Volume 2. English
Title: Habitus and field / Pierre Bourdieu ; [translated by] Peter Collier.
Description: Cambridge, UK ; Medford, MA : Polity Press, [2019] | Series:
    General sociology ; volume 2 | Includes bibliographical references and
    index.
Identifiers: LCCN 2019010410 | ISBN 9781509526697 (hardback)
Subjects: LCSH: Sociology--Study and teaching (Higher)--France. | Habitus
    (Sociology) | Sociology.
Classification: LCC HM578.F8 B68213 2019 | DDC 301--dc23 LC record available at
    https://lccn.loc.gov/2019010410

Typeset in 10.5 on 12 pt Times New Roman by
Servis Filmsetting Ltd, Stockport, Cheshire
Printed and bound by CPI Group (UK) Ltd, Croydon, CR0 4YY

The publisher has used its best endeavours to ensure that the URLs for external websites referred to in this book are correct and active at the time of going to press. However, the publisher has no responsibility for the websites and can make no guarantee that a site will remain live or that the content is or will remain appropriate.

Every effort has been made to trace all copyright holders, but if any have been overlooked the publisher will be pleased to include any necessary credits in any subsequent reprint or edition.

For further information on Polity, visit our website: politybooks.com

Contents

and conformism – Critique of the economic discourse – The
economic conditions of economic practices

Contents

Editorial Note

With this book, we continue the publication of Pierre Bourdieu's lectures at the Collège de France. A few months after his final lecture in this institute in March 2001, Bourdieu published a condensed version of the last year of his teaching (2000–1), entitled *Science of Science and Reflexivity*.[1] Since his death, a further two volumes have been published: *On the State*, in 2012, and *Manet: A Symbolic Revolution*, in 2017, corresponding to his lectures for 1989–92 and 1998–2000 respectively.[2] The present volume is the second in the 'course of lectures on general sociology' that Bourdieu had chosen for the first five years of his teaching at the Collège de France.[3] It presents the lectures for the second year – that is, thirteen two-hour lectures given between October 1982 and January 1983. Further volumes will collect the lectures from the three following years.

Our edition of this 'course of lectures on general sociology' follows the editorial conventions that were defined for the publication of the lectures on the state, in order to reconcile fidelity with readability.[4] The text published here is a transcription of the lectures as they were actually delivered. However, in transposing from the oral to the written mode we have introduced some minor revisions, while respecting the approach that Bourdieu himself adopted when he revised his own lectures and seminar papers: making stylistic corrections and smoothing the rough edges of oral delivery (such as repetition, and other linguistic tics). Only on exceptional occasions have we suppressed the development of an argument, sometimes because it was too hastily improvised, but more often because the sound recording was not clear enough for us to establish a convincing text. In general, we have placed inaudible words and passages, or interruptions to the recording, where we were unable to obtain a secure reading, between square brackets [. . .].[5] The division of the text into paragraphs is the work of the editors, as are the subheadings and the punctuation. The 'parentheses' where Bourdieu digresses from his main argument have been handled in different ways, according to their length and their relation to the context. The shorter ones have been placed between dashes. When these digressions acquire a certain autonomy and imply a break in the thread of the argument, they are placed between brackets, and when one is really too long it may be given the status of a separate section in its own right. The endnotes are mostly of three different kinds. Some mainly indicate the texts to which Bourdieu refers explicitly or implicitly, when it has been possible to identify them; in those cases where it seemed helpful, short quotations from these texts have been added. Others aim to indicate to the reader those writings by Bourdieu, whether predating or postdating the lectures, that develop the points under discussion. The third kind of note provides contextual information, for example explaining allusions which might escape the contemporary reader or a reader unfamiliar with the French cultural context of the period.

We have reproduced in an appendix the summaries of the lectures as published in *L'Annuaire du Collège de France – cours et travaux*.

Acknowledgements

The editors would like to thank Bruno Auerbach, Donald Broady, Christophe Charle, Johan Heilbron, Thibaut Izard and Remi Lenoir for their contributions to this book.

Lecture of 5 October 1982

The retrospective illusion and the unreality of theory in research –
A work of axiomatisation – Scientific concepts – The fundamental
questions – Realist definition and interactionist definition – Metaphysical
requirements for sociology – Iron filings

I ask you to bear with me while I outline my aims for this course of lectures. In defence of this preamble, I would first point out that one of the
advantages of an oral delivery over the written is that it can generate
a metanarrative on the aims of the primary discourse, which can help
counter the misunderstandings inherent in any act of communication.
The metanarrative that I intend to create here will not resemble those
that generally accompany self-styled 'theoretical' narratives, the sort
that I would call 'self-important' metanarratives, designed to argue in
favour of the importance of the narrative and the narrator.[1] It will be
more of a critical metanarrative. And, indeed, faced with the task of
presenting sociology to an audience so diverse and with such different
academic backgrounds, I feel somewhat overwhelmed by the responsibility. So I would like to admit one problem straight away: the fact that
there are some things which these lectures are not designed to convey,
in particular the techniques of research, but also my own personal and
professional limitations. My role here is subject to conflicting constraints on account of the variety and diversity of my audience.

First and foremost, I shall offer a series of arguments that I shall
develop in their logical sequence over a longish period of time, for I see
my teaching as a series of demonstrations connected by a certain logic,
within the framework of an academic year, or perhaps several. Given
this plan, I have to face the problem, among others, that the division
of the course into separate lectures runs the risk of obscuring the overarching logic of my enterprise. At the same time, my determination

to provide such an overarching logic deprives me of the liberty that I would otherwise assume, to treat each lecture as a self-contained unit and take the opportunity to comment directly on the problems of the moment that seem most pressing, as I would have liked to do this morning, for instance. Like many among you, no doubt, I learned the results of an opinion poll on French authors, and I thought that I could do you a favour by analysing the logistics or perhaps the sophistry at work in the production of opinion polls and their exploitation by the press. That said, I think that I shall often have to refrain from this kind of commentary (although it would serve a useful purpose) in order to maintain the logical structure of my argumentation. I shall most likely have to compromise between a sustained narrative, with its virtually extra-temporal logic, and occasional interruptions or digressions inspired by the events of the day or my ongoing reflections.

The second problem, which I find even more decisive, is that an exercise in teaching at any level (and remember that in this institute I am supposed to be accessible to everyone, from whatever background, which is clearly an impossible mission) must satisfy two kinds of quite incompatible requirements. On the one hand I should satisfy those who want me to 'shed light on all subjects', as they said in the Grand Siècle; on the other hand I should also satisfy those who want to gain access to in-depth information on specific topics and walk away with a sheaf of notes. These two functions are not automatically compatible. It is often said that the most elementary teaching is best provided by the most eminent scholars. I willingly agree, but I think that the most elementary instruction is often the most difficult to provide, perhaps precisely because of its apparent simplicity. This is another of the problems that I shall have to face. I shall then be offering neither a chapter for an encyclopaedia of sociology nor genuine insight into research techniques. Nor shall I be able to transmit my experience of the latest research in progress.

The retrospective illusion and the unreality of theory in research

I think that one of the difficulties facing the teacher who wants to transmit the results of some research in progress is the fact that it is very difficult to reconstitute the experience of the process of research, which is that, as long as you have not found what you are looking for, you have not found anything. Conversely, as soon as you have found what you are looking for, it is impossible to forget that you have found it, and the simple fact of having obtained a result profoundly modifies your exposition of the sequence of procedures involved in the research. Everyone who records their scientific research encounters this problem and knows very well how, depending on the stage of research they have reached when they report, they write about different things and write them very differently, even if the truth of the subject they are describing has not changed. However hard, for example, you try to reconstitute the state of the problem at the moment when you started to work on it, or try to reconstitute the different stages of research to show how you proceeded, epistemological studies show that all these narratives bear the marks of a retrospective illusion; they are in general reconstructed artefacts produced by someone who knows the story and adapts the whole plot to anticipate the happy ending. Whether the research is conceptual or empirical, no attempt to teach that research can possibly tell of all the hesitations, interruptions and changes of mind that are the very stuff of research, and which by definition disappear from the finished, written accounts and even oral presentations, subject as they are to the constraints of scholarly scruples, scientific rigour or the formal occasion.

So although I am the first to regret it, this finalist illusion means that, in order to avoid indulging in a rather melodramatic restaging of the discovery of the results of my research, I shall be able to render only a very imperfect impression of the research experience itself. In a sense, then, my teaching will be a failure in my own eyes. I am saying this out loud in advance, because admitting the danger predicted can help me avoid it. (In sociology, the very fact of formulating a pessimistic prediction helps to prevent it from coming true, thus rendering the statement optimistic. So there is no point in wondering whether a particular sociologist is an optimist or a pessimist; they are always both at once.) My teaching includes an implicit therapeutic function, and I hope that my discourse, even on the rare occasions where it may sound polished and conclusive, will betray all the signs of the uncertainty, indecision and vagueness that are one of the virtues of scientific discourse.

Another difficulty, another contradiction: I could present what I have to say as a very general and universal account of sociology, and even imagine it to be so. But in fact, as will become obvious, what I have to offer you is my personal vision of sociology, although I do experience this as a universal vision, since it is scientifically based and offered up for public debate. I shall express my feelings of universality all the more confidently since I shall be led to show that this universality is not universally recognised. I shall offer a general theory of the social world, understanding 'theory' in its etymological sense of a method of thinking, a system of rigorously controlled means of perception of the social world. I shall therefore be exposing a method of thinking that is obviously the product of my research, and rooted in that research, but which, being presented outside the framework and situations of research, will inevitably take on a theoretical aspect. The very fact of speaking of sociology in an academic arena, detached from the actual practice of sociology, tends to give our discourse a bias towards what we traditionally call 'theoreticism', which is the discussion of theoretical mechanisms for their own sake, independently of the conditions of their production and usage, which happens when we speak of theories in the abstract without reference to their real function and practical applications.

Throughout these lectures I shall of course attempt to overcome the difficulties and contradictions that I have enumerated both for myself and now for you. For example, in order to counter the effect of theoretical unreality that I have just formulated, I shall seek an antidote in examples drawn from my own research or borrowed from other sociologists; these examples will help to show how the analyses that I formulate work in reality. That having been said, there will often be cases where this will only be effective if those of you who really want to learn are brave enough to go out and consult the particular research work cited, and even repeat the experiments yourselves. You should not, as too often happens, skip the empirical stages and just read the conclusions, for this would radically distort the work of the researchers by turning the hypotheses that they were trying to verify into 'theses' ready and waiting to be countered by alternative 'theses'. For me, sociology is a science, or at least makes every effort to be one, and it merits the respect of being subjected to the process of validation or falsification. We should not respond to a sociologist as we would to an essayist, by merely suggesting a contrary thesis. A sociologist who fails to welcome the process of validation is virtually abdicating responsibility for what is most specific to their enterprise. This is then another difficulty for me, and I shall often have to resign myself to the occasion and refrain from explaining the procedural details, which I shall regret all the more since, as I have often argued, there is more theoretical and scientific benefit to be had from working with concepts than in working on concepts, especially on those that do not relate to actual scientific research. So I shall often fall into the traps that I have exposed, and which I have alerted you to.

I have not told you all this in order to prevent others from saying it to me; on the contrary, I expect and shall welcome this. People usually listen to these preambles with the feeling that they have to resign themselves to the inaugural ritual, but what I have been saying is not intended as an exercise in ritual, or even good manners. And if I allow myself to continue further, it is because these remarks are part of my ongoing argument. If I could, I would even repeat them all over again at the start of every lecture.

A work of axiomatisation

That having been said, there is a virtue in doing what I am trying to do, which is a kind of work of axiomatisation; this may sound grandiloquent, but you will see that the reality is much more modest. I shall start out from research that has already obtained results and from scientific propositions that have been more or less validated, but I shall also comment on the operations used to produce these results, and I shall dwell less on the results themselves than on the instruments that produced the results, in order to check and test them. A theoretical apparatus or corpus comes into being through a succession of accretions, adjustments and connections that transform the whole system. We construct the thing rather as we would build a house, brick by brick. We do not turn everything upside down on every occasion, except precisely in those retrospective accounts where we claim that we have called everything into question, taken a blank sheet and started from zero. In practice, no researcher has ever done this, except possibly in a few rare cases of scientific revolution, which I may perhaps come to discuss. Scientists have only had to undertake such radical reappraisals two or three times in the history of science.[2] In their everyday practice, they more or less live in harmony with their conceptual system and constantly retouch both its details and its overall pattern. It may seem obvious, but it is important to say that you cannot work on one particular concept without affecting the whole system. By focusing my reflection on the relations interlinking the whole set of concepts, I hope to generate some positive results, not merely in pedagogical terms (which I would find insufficient) but also in the scientific domain. For instance, I think that I shall be able to reveal some hidden relations. To anticipate my argument, I may say that while I was preparing these lectures I brought to light a connection between the different kinds of capital and the notion of relative autonomy, which had been simmering on the back burner of my mind. When notions that have been functioning separately start to communicate with each other, they all benefit each other.

Another advantage of axiomatisation, recognised by all historians and theorists of science, is that, by foregrounding the relations between concepts, it 'exposes' these concepts in both senses of the word: it renders them visible and, in so doing, lays them open to all kinds of challenge, which from a scientific point of view is the greatest benefit. This is probably one important difference between scientific work and essay writing; the essay makes a display of itself, but scientists lay bare their concepts and take risks, and the more they lay their concepts open for transformation or modification by the critical community, the more scientific they are.

But how do we go about expounding a method of thinking? I shall be led to rehearse certain fundamental concepts that I have already elaborated, such as 'habitus', 'field' and 'capital', to show how they function and help us understand and construct the social world. To set out these concepts we may adopt an approach that I call genealogical or historical. This is a common pedagogical technique; when we want to explain a way of thinking we look for its ancestry and we find out how it came into being. I could go into greater detail, but for the moment I shall just say that these genealogies are very often fictitious; they are reconstructions after the event, even when their author is the author of the concepts that are the subject of the genealogy. As a sociologist, I shall adopt a systematically suspicious attitude towards any philosophical genealogy that a thinker may offer for their own thinking in so far as the main function of these genealogies is a social one – that is, to constitute a social capital: we fashion our own ancestry. It is no accident that we speak of the *founding fathers* of sociology. Choosing the founding fathers or ancestors from whom we inherit the eponymous names of our tribes – Marxist, Durkheimian, Weberian, etc. – is a way of affirming our symbolic capital, of appropriating the capital of all these prestigious ancestors, to affirm ourselves as their heirs and in so doing to appropriate the heritage. Of course, those who declare themselves inheritors thus expose themselves to the attacks of all those who envy them the heritage or wish to destroy it – in general their relation to the heritage is described in formulae such as 'You are nothing but a Weberian' or 'I'm the true Durkheimian'.

Such strategies nearly always haunt our genealogies, whether we are trying to trace our own or someone else's. The genealogy of our rivals' thought can be drawn up in order to undermine their originality (as defined by information theory).[3] If you manage to show that a concept used by X has already been used by Y, you discredit his capital. All these things are often brought into play at an unconscious level in the practice of analysing thought. Being well aware of this, you can well imagine that I am not going to go down that route and play games exposing all my sources and everyone else's. Of course, in the case of the notion of the habitus, I use it because I need to, but without wishing to refer either consciously or unconsciously to the whole tradition of previous users. It may be useful, however, to say a few words about its previous usage (by Aristotle, Thomas Aquinas, Weber, Durkheim and Husserl) for those who would like to refer to them, if only in order to discover the differences. But I think that these genealogical associations do not bring much enlightenment, and their main benefit is to warn us to be careful how we handle them. When we speak of the habitus, it is useful to know that the concept has already been used by this or that thinker so as to avoid unwise attributions, but it is more important to know that a concept takes on its meaning within the context of a system.

Scientific concepts

It is not in relation to more or less mythical ancestors that I would like to situate my usage of the concepts of habitus and field – perhaps the concept of capital too, although that is much more difficult – but in relation to the space of intellectual positions within which the concept is situated. In fact the true function of a scientific concept (and here once again I am saying something that is quite unremarkable in the Anglo-American epistemological context, whereas things are quite different in the French epistemological tradition) is not at all what is taught in the French tradition of logic; it is much more a kind of materialisation of a 'theoretical line' (using 'theoretical line' in the sense that we use 'political line'). In fact, if I wanted to derive a helpful definition from my own experience of using the concepts of habitus or field, for instance, it would be that a concept is the objectification or materialisation of a theoretical habitus, or more exactly of a theoretical direction or stance, in language. The concept materialises a series of distinctions within the space of rival contemporary positions and, in so doing, reveals a series of differences or rejections. I shall try to show, for example, that the concept of habitus takes shape in opposition to a philosophy of mind or a philosophy that we might call 'liberal individualism'. It materialises a series of oppositions and consequently takes its place within a whole field of positions manipulated consciously or unconsciously by the author or user of these notions and his audience. The slippage between the field of references inhabited by the speaker and the field of references inhabited by the listener being one of the major causes of misunderstanding in the communication of a discourse with scientific ambitions, I shall take pains to make explicit the space of positions in relation to which I have found it important to say 'habitus' rather than 'subject' or 'mind'.

A concept, then, is a position in a space. It is also a kind of shorthand for a series of practical operations. Here I must insist again on the difference between a scientific discourse and an essay. The essay writer – without necessarily seeking to do so – will play on the polysemy of the concept. Yesterday, for instance, someone asked me for my opinion on the consumer society. Obviously I refused to reply, because all a researcher can do in that situation is demolish the question. In fact, of all the concepts used by those who are licensed to comment on society and whom we call 'sociologists' (inverted commas obligatory), those that enjoy the greatest social success are precisely those such as 'the consumer society', which would not stand up to the type of argumentation to which I intend to subject my concepts. These popular concepts are designed to appear to transcend all the pertinent oppositions of a well-constructed theoretical space as if they were crossing the boundaries between the oppositions that are there in reality. This means that they owe their success to this kind of hybrid appearance, as Socrates said of the Sophists[4] – and bad sociologists inevitably bring the Sophists to mind. These are all-purpose concepts, which are not even falsifiable in Popper's terms – in fact, not even false.[5]

Concepts that claim to be scientific are not simply a sort of materialisation of theoretical flair; they are also the mnemotechnical representation of a series of scientific operations. I shall take an example that will oblige me to anticipate my argument, but it will help you understand what I intend to argue: you can say that you have understood the basics of the notion of the field (which I shall come to explain in considerable detail, since a half or even three-quarters of my time this year will be devoted to this notion) when you have understood the operations that it comprises, and you do not need to know everything that I am going to say about the concept of the field in order to act in conformity with its requirements in a given scientific situation. For instance, if you think in terms of fields when you are studying the *grandes écoles*, it means that you have a kind of automatic professional reflex; you know that the truth of each individual school lies not in the separate, individual school but in its relations with all the others, and that consequently it is preferable to study the whole set of schools superficially rather than make an in-depth study of one *grande école*.[6] This is what I implied when I said just now that I understood the word 'theory' much more in the sense of a method of thinking or even a method of perception than in the unfortunate sense the French give to 'theory', where the 'theoretical' is the opposite of the 'empirical' and, in designating everything that is not empirical, designates everything that is nothing to do with anything. The word 'theory', however, if used as I suggest, to designate a series of schemas for constructing reality (or for a scientific construction of reality), is a kind of scientific battle cry. I think in fact that we can follow the remit of the theory of the field without using the word 'field', so I intend to provide examples of empirical studies published in the review *Actes de la recherche en sciences sociales* that follow the model implied by the words 'habitus' and 'field', without mentioning the actual words.

Nonetheless, it is useful to make explicit what thinking in terms of a field or a habitus means, because it enables us to operate more efficiently than if we rely on a sort of theoretical instinct. There is a scientific virtue in being explicit; if we believe that a scientific habitus allows us to develop rigorous scientific practices, it is better to make explicit the practices of the habitus in order to transform the habitus into a method. This is the gist of what I want to say.

This time my preamble really has come to an end and I shall turn to the topic itself, but I think that I have already started to do so.

The fundamental questions

The subject of the teaching that I have to offer is very ordinary. It is a question basic to any course in general sociology that claims to discuss whether sociology has a specific object of study, and, if so, what it is. In formulating things this way, we immediately think of a whole series of works with the title 'Sociology . . .', and this is discouraging. Among such books there are some excellent ones written by the great masters who founded sociology and some lamentable ones written by vulgarisers. If my lectures should enable me at least to describe the foundations of sociology, this is not only in the interests of reaching a wider public but also because examining these fundamental issues will require me to return to problems that a still immature science such as sociology often pretends to have solved, whereas it has never fully formulated the questions. In fact, if I am able to deliver these lectures without feeling ashamed at repeating myself, it is because I have the profound conviction that enquiring into the nature of the specific subject of sociology is more than a merely academic and scholarly response. I think that sociology, like all the sciences, is defined by the laws specific to the construction of its object, which distinguish it from the other sciences and distinguish the object of its studies from those of the neighbouring sciences, and that sociology is in fact characterised by a certain manner of constructing its object. To answer the question 'What is sociology?' is therefore to answer the question 'What is its object?' and 'How does it handle social reality in order to turn it into an object of study?' The usual reply to the question 'What is sociology?' is that 'Sociology is the study of society.' If you look into encyclopaedias or books for the general reader you will find variants of this reply. But, if we are not satisfied with these questions, we can go a little further and ask: 'What society?' 'Where is that society?' 'How does it exist?' 'Does it exist in things? In people? In collectives? Is it a sum of individuals?'

Couched in such terms, these questions can seem academic or meta-physical, but we only have to return to the basics of linguistics to see that Saussure put the question of language in the same terms and, in so doing, immediately threw up a whole new set of questions: Does language (which he established by constructing it in opposition to speech, as I'm sure you are aware)[7] exist in the brain of the individual speaker, in the brains of all speakers, or in society as a whole? Does it exist in the dictionary or in the corpus of the library, in which case it transcends the individual brain and even the whole collection of all our brains? If you take another look at the *Course in General Linguistics* and the lecture notes by Saussure that have been added since,[8] you will see that these issues, despite their academic or metaphysical appearance, are obsessively reworked by Saussure – who talks of language as a collective or an individual treasure. I think that, if Saussure considered this question from every possible angle, it is because it is a genuine question. I have presented the argument rather abruptly, but I could regale you for hours with perfectly apposite quotations from the *Course in General Linguistics*. Those of you who want to would do well to refer to the text. What I really want to point out is the fact that these questions have been almost obsessively raised by linguists, and also by specialists in culture and the founders of ethnology: Where does culture exist? For it is 'culture' that ethnologists have devised in order to account for social reality, contrasting it with behaviour and using it as a code enabling us to assign the same meaning to the same behaviour and the same behaviour to the same meaningful intentions. Is there a *locus*, a place where we can locate culture? There is a well-known debate on the status of culture, echoed in a kind of imaginary Platonic dialogue between Kluckhohn and Sapir,[9] where we can find all the traditional philosophical positions on the subject of ideas and concepts: Does the intelligible exist as tangible reality? Does culture exist above and beyond its individual incarnations? These questions have been raised obsessively in linguistics and in the domain of ethnology.

Sociologists pretend to believe that they are rid of these problems, for example by implicitly assuming sociology to be the study of the collective. If, as has been done for psychoanalysis, we were to study ways in which the educated public uses and represents sociology, the most common definition would be one that we frequently hear: the sociologist is someone who studies the masses, the collective, the greater number. Hence the surprise when a sociologist such as Luc Boltanski produces a monograph on Amiel's *Journal*, for instance,[10] which in my opinion is eminently sociological but which does not fall under the usual definition of sociology. The spontaneous definition that most people have in mind often makes it difficult for them to engage in dialogue with historians, literary historians and art historians. Many sociologists too have this mindset, and they are not sure how to react when they handle both statistical information on large numbers of people and data associated with individuals.

This common definition is based on an absolutely realist representation of the social object, and to illustrate this I shall quote a famous definition by Ralph Linton in *The Study of Man*, which seems to me to be the most banal and trivial but at the same time the most common expression of this common representation of society and of sociology: 'A *society* is any group of individuals that has lived and worked together long enough to be organised and to think of themselves as a social unit with well-defined limits.'[11] In other words, it takes three or four conditions to create a society. First, there has to be the plurality of an aggregate or a sum of individuals. Second, there needs to be persistence in time – persistence in time being the condition for establishing the forces (although we do not know very well how they function) for integrating individuals 'who have lived and worked together long enough to be organised'. If we say 'forces for integrating', we are ascribing intent. This would be the difference that we commonly make between a genuine group and a public that is a temporary, ephemeral juxtaposition of individuals. We are assuming, third, that the individuals modify each other mutually, instantaneously, as billiard balls knocking against each other instantly change course, but we fail to consider what long-term changes might occur. Fourth, perhaps, we might postulate the existence of a group consciousness, of a feeling of unity, of what is often called an 'esprit de corps'.

I shall not spend much time discussing this definition of society as a group of individuals endowed with the properties in question. But before launching into my own representation of what I see as the proper object of sociology, I simply wanted to mention the common representation of the object of sociology and make the point that this

common representation haunts the unconscious minds of the majority of sociologists, who consider the debate to be closed and content
themselves with this common-sense representation. I would like to
add a very basic comment by Bachelard, which is that, as long as fundamental ideas are not called into question, a science can happily be
grounded in common-sense ideas, and it takes a very serious scientific
crisis to shake the implicit assumptions that the scientist shares with
people's common representations.[12]

Realist definition and interactionist definition

However, this common-sense definition, which treats the sociologist
as a specialist in groups and the collective, with their relations and
interactions, is entirely hostage to two obvious limits. There is, on the
one hand, the evidence of the biological individual: in fact, what we
see as social is composed of individuals, and, even more obviously, the
social is composed of masses (I don't mean 'the masses' in a political
sense),[13] of large numbers of individuals more or less juxtaposed in
a space. On the other hand, the aspect of society that we see deriving from the 'social' is the interaction between individuals reacting
with each other. What I propose is a break from these two definitions
that are well established in the social sciences: one consists in treating
groups as aggregates of individuals susceptible to a strictly statistical
analysis, and the other, which has given the name of 'interactionism' to
a school of sociological thought, reduces sociological phenomena and
social relations to a visible and directly observable interaction between
individual social agents.

I wish to develop this last topic, interaction, which I have not fully
explained. The so-called interactionist school has definite virtues and
has contributed to the advance of the social sciences in recent times.
It has been developed above all in the United States, in Chicago. It
undertakes to describe social relations as relations of interaction. For
example, Goffman, the leading figure in this school, describes the relations between two strangers who meet in the street: they know nothing
of each other but will obey more or less ritual rules. For example, they
will avoid contentious issues which might introduce distance or offence,
since neither knows where the other is coming from, so to speak. They
will not mention politics or religion but talk of the weather, which is
a frequent topic of conversation because it is one of the few neutral
meeting grounds where all social groups can share their opinions –
except in the sort of test case where tourists and farmers might have

conflicting interests in the matter [*laughter*]. Goffman's work consists in describing the interaction of two individuals studied in isolation and the strategies that they employ to avoid conflict and seek consensus. For example, he analyses what he calls the 'working consensus' – that is, the sometimes desperate efforts made by people to find something to say, to find some common ground.[14] This sort of analysis is a kind of objective phenomenology of interactions between individual agents. It does come very close to the definition that I shall give of sociology, since it takes as its object not individuals, but their relations – which is an advance over the more simple definition that studies individuals or aggregate masses of individuals divided into classes that are as homogeneous as possible. That having been said, these relations are interactions – that is, visible relations that anyone could observe or film. There would be no problem in illustrating Goffman's notion of interaction or finding an illustration for the cover of one of Goffman's books: you would just need to go down the road and take a picture of two housewives returning from market. One puts her shopping bag down, and then you take a photo of their interaction.[15]

In my opinion, what sociology should describe is something quite invisible, relations that you cannot photograph. To use a simple analogy, interactionist sociology follows a logic analogous to that of Cartesian physics, which describes the contacts between bodies and can imagine no way for one body to influence another except by striking it. What I shall suggest, with the notion of the 'field', is something that we might think of by analogy with Newton's or Einstein's physics, which analyses spaces that are not visible, that have to be constructed in order to account for practice, and within which the forces exerted can only be grasped through the modifications that they cause to individuals and their behaviour. I believe that, until now, sociology has never completely achieved this essential break, although in a way it has repeatedly attempted to (Durkheim worked towards this goal, but following a different logic). In my opinion sociology can have a truly scientific object only if it avoids visible objects such as individuals, groups of individuals and the overt relations between them. Relations involving communication, interaction, exchange and cooperation are indeed an object for sociology, but their basis does not lie in anything made visible. We must therefore move beyond this visible aspect of the social world and tackle complexes of things quite unseen, of relations existing independently, or even outside, of any practical rendition. To use a simple image, the two strangers whose gestures I could film and analyse may be enacting mechanisms that quite transcend what is happening in the actual encounter. If for example they are both French, but one is native-born and the other of Portuguese descent, the spirit of their interaction may depend on objective relations (of domination, of colonisation, and so on) between the two languages or the two countries. And the interactions that I can observe and measure may be only the superficial manifestation of hidden structures that are not present in the encounter, except as effects. This is a first, purely negative, argument.

Although social science repeatedly falls back on this realist representation of the social object, despite frequent attempts to escape it, I believe that our science must import a kind of reasoning that is normally used in the world of philosophy. I often advocate this form of thinking – and my critics think that my philosophical training has warped my mind – because I am convinced that it produces real scientific results. One of the techniques that a young sociologist can learn in order to achieve scientific results in their work could be to call into question things that seem to be self-evident. As I shall go on to argue later, one of the effects of socialisation, of concord between habitus and field – I am anticipating for those who understand the terms, but I will explain later for the others – is to produce a kind of orchestration of habitus and field: the person who has the typical habitus for the field is like a fish swimming in water or someone breathing the air around them, meaning that they have no awareness of gravity; and if these rhythms, rules, forces, laws and objective relations are so difficult to analyse, it is precisely because they are incorporated, existing at once objectively and subjectively, and are therefore not experienced in their own right. The work of objectification that consists in extracting them, so to speak, in order to see, construct, describe and analyse them, is difficult because their very efficiency disguises them. The deepest structures of the social world are at one and the same time in my mind and in objective reality, and this impacts upon my social experience: the social world is self-evident; it presents itself as self-evident. This makes social science particularly difficult.

Durkheim, to whom I often refer, said that the crucial difficulty for sociology is precisely that we think we know the social world because we live in it effortlessly, like fish in water. This illusion of transparency and spontaneous mastery of the social world is, according to Durkheim, the main obstacle to a scientific knowledge of the social world.[16] My argument will be more convincing when I have given a fuller account of the nature of the habitus and the field, but this kind of harmony and objective orchestration of a habitus and a field, needing no musical director, which means that some people are in their element in their universe, like fish in water, is the main obstacle to the double objectification that science needs to accomplish the objectification of objective structures (those relations that are not reducible to their manifestations and interactions) and the objectification of incorporated structures (those mental structures that are produced by the social, and through which we think the social). I am anticipating considerably what I shall be arguing later. We think the social with mental schemas that are largely a product of the social world. It is the social world itself that provides the spectacles through which we see it. And this means that we do not see it; we see everything except the spectacles, which are inside our minds and out there in reality at one and the same time.[17]

Metaphysical requirements for sociology

I want to insist on this appeal for sociology to adopt the kind of techniques of questioning usually reserved for metaphysics. Because the social hierarchy of objects of thought rates the social world as one of its least worthy objects (I shall often return to the important topic of how to undertake a socioanalysis of one's own thinking), it is very rare for people to apply to the social world the techniques of thought that they would apply to God or to Being, or to the difference between Being and Time. But, in order to account for the social world adequately, I believe that we should apply to it those manners of thinking that are usually reserved for the highest objects of thought, those of metaphysics, because we are lacking in the techniques of thought needed in order to grasp this extremely obscure object. To put it simply, we should think of the social world in Heideggerian terms – although those who know their sociology of the intellectual field will judge this to be impossible, for the two seem as incompatible as fire and water – and confront the social world with questions along the lines of: What is thinking?[18] What does it mean for a social thing to exist? What does it mean for an institution to exist? What is it that is instituted, and who is it that institutes the instituted? How is what is instituted instituted in the world? How is the instituted instituted in the mind? What is an act of institution? The word 'institution' is absolutely crucial, but it has been blocked once for all time by the Durkheim school's use of it.[19] And yet we owe it to Durkheim and his followers to have drawn attention to this absolutely central term – if I had to designate the social with a single word, I would choose the word 'institution'. However, if we conducted a rapid poll among ourselves to ask 'What do you understand by "institution"?' the replies would associate the word with a kind of old-fashioned Durkheimian philosophy. We don't think of the act of institution, or the words 'I institute my son as my heir' that we see in a contract or a will. We don't think of it at all in the sense that Merleau-Ponty conjured up in one of his lectures when he said that primitive societies institute their dead, in the sense that 'They make them exist despite everything by a social act that is stronger than death, stronger than truth or falsehood, stronger than reality.'[20] We see another remarkable act of institution in the declamation 'The king is dead, long live the king!' in Kantorowicz's book *The King's Two Bodies*.[21] If we consider the word 'institution' in its strongest sense, we realise that it is something dauntingly mysterious and as complicated as the question of Being. But we are accustomed to applying to the social no more intellectual horsepower than we would apply to reading *Le Figaro*, *Le Matin* or *Libération*.[22]

We need to ask pertinent questions of the social world, especially in order to see through a certain number of screen-words that masquerade as foundations. At present, the foundations of what sociologists have at the back of their minds when they perform sociology are a certain number of crystallised words that are a particularly dangerous unconscious magma; and, with this unconscious locked up inside them, these words take on the aura of thought, and in so doing they stop thoughts in their tracks and produce nothing. Our ultimate aim should be to interrogate and demolish these alien words that prevent us from seeing the social world, so that we may at last be able to put a new set of questions to that world.

After this somewhat abstract preamble, I shall now take a concrete example, following the principle that I announced just now. If I were to ask all the sociologists present here or living elsewhere to tell me what the Church is – and I could do the same with the State – I think this would provide empirical evidence that what I have argued is not mere rhetoric. We think we know what the Church is, and every day we use formulae such as 'The Church has said . . .'. Recently, when the bishops issued a statement on some social problem, you may have heard phrases such as 'The Church, the bishopric, has made a stand' repeated ten times a day. However, this begs a key question: whether the Church, whose real nature I have yet to grasp, can be identified with the bishopric. What does this identification imply? Is it an identification like 'The Bororó people are araras', in the famous quotation?[23] So is the Church its bishops in the same way that the Bororó people are parrots? May we conclude that the Church is everything that can be designated by the word 'Church'? Or rather that it is all the people who can speak with authority in the name of the Church – which would be a theologian's definition? You can find texts affirming that 'the Church is its bishops' or that 'the Church is the pope', which raises the question of papal infallibility. If a person is mandated to speak on behalf of the Church, that person becomes the Church. But the thing in whose name the pope speaks also exists, although it is not included in the definition: since the pope is speaking in the name of something, that something has to exist. Is there a definition that covers both the thing in whose name the pope speaks and the pope himself? How can a thing subsume both the signifier and the signified? I hesitate to continue, because this is not what you would expect from a lecture on sociology, and you might get the feeling that you have strayed into the room next door [*laughter*]! And yet we should continue this exercise, and I would like to be socially authorised to continue it at great length. So I shall continue for a while. Among sociologists there is a whole debate as to whether the Church is the whole set of the clergy and lay members (which is the general opinion of the Durkheim school),[24] or if it is only the clergy (this is the tendency among followers of Weber; when Weber says that the Church is the ensemble of those who hold the 'monopoly of the manipulation of the goods of salvation',[25] he is clearly designating the clergy, and only the clergy – that is, those who are the statutory guardians of the right of access to sacred goods). So we may ask the question Is it one or is it the other, or is it both? The texts of canon law show that there is a long history of debate over this definition.

This discussion may seem superfluous or theological to you, but we find exactly the same problem in the field of art: we can ask ourselves what is art, an artist and an artistic institution, or even why is there art rather than nothing at all. The question is of the same order: is art just the whole of the clergy – that is, the set of professional producers of the objects that we treat as art? There is a very fine article by one of the best specialists in the sociology of art, an American sociologist called Howard Becker. In describing the artistic institution, Becker says that there are 'art worlds', and that in these art worlds there are cliques, artists, salons, galleries, exhibition spaces, but never the public.[26] Which leads to a very simple question: Could there be any art if there were no consumers of art? In other words, can we conduct a sociology of something like art or the Church without considering the congregation, the public? We can imagine a Church with no congregation, but I think that we can only imagine it because we know that there has been a Church that had a congregation. We may be moving towards a Church with no congregation [*laughter*], but there has to have been a historic Church with a congregation. We could discuss this at length. It is a question which has real significance from a practical and, almost, from a metaphysical point of view.

So, is the Church the clergy or the lay members, or is it the clergy and the lay members? We could of course allow a syncretistic definition because, when we start to ask questions like this, the temptation is to finish with a definition – Gurvitch used to give fantastic lectures like that which finished in definitions two pages long that included every-thing.[27] Of course, I don't think that we should go down that route; I must close down that solution in order to make things more difficult. There are the clergy and the lay members, but also the churches, in the material sense of the term: the Church is also its buildings, consecrated places of worship that we must describe. For these places to be con-secrated, there must be people to consecrate them. Could the Church function without bishops to consecrate these places? There cannot be a Christian congregation without people to baptise and bless them. In asking these questions, we can already see a network of relations: perhaps it all exists only in these relations. We may take things further and involve a whole 'social technology', although it is not an elegant term. We can say of a review that it is 'Christian' or of an intellectual that 'he has a typically Christian style'; we recognise types of what I call a 'Christian habitus', Christian styles, Christian philosophers (we might say: 'Saint-Exupéry could well have been a Christian', and people often believe that he was [*laughter*]).[28] That is all part of the Church: without the Church, these effects that are expressed in phrases or life styles would not exist. The Church is obviously its material paraphernalia (cassocks, crucifixes, and the like), but also its intellec-tual trappings – its manners of thinking, as in canon law or matters of style (think of the Jesuit styles of architecture or rhetoric). Of course there are also legitimate spokesmen who are authorised to speak in the name of the Church (I admitted when I started just now – but I did not think that it would happen so soon – that there are cases where knowing the plot disturbs the order of the narrative). These people are more the Church than others, because when they speak it is the Church that speaks, and they may even contradict the opinions of the faithful. It frequently happens that members of the congregation say: 'I don't feel that the Church expresses my views, I shall go to the services at the church of Saint-Nicolas-du-Chardonnet.'[29] There can be some of the faithful who, although they are members of the Church, do not feel at home in the Church. If the sociologist has a realistic definition of the Church, he will say: 'Since the lay members do not feel at home in the Church, they are not members of the Church', but if he has a relational definition – here again I am anticipating my argument – the fact that they complain that they do not feel at home in the Church will incite him to include them in a definition of the Church. I could go on. The spokesmen, those representatives who claim to be the Church, with little likelihood of being contradicted – nobody will go up to the pope and say: 'You have no right to speak in the name of the Church', which would not be the case with the spokesman for a political party such as the PSU[30] – provide information on the group and on the relations between these spokesmen and the truth of the social world that these spokesmen express. How can we include all of this? I have to anticipate a little here. I have used this example to try to answer as best I can all the objections that I raised in my preamble: I am trying to introduce a concrete problem, to make it as real as possible for you. Of course it is a problem that I have lived with in depth for two or three years of my working life, reading canon law, calculating statistics and studying bishops, whereas for you it is a problem that I have only just mentioned in a few sentences, adding in a few jokes to make it feel more real. In fact, it is when you laugh that things start to move, because we have touched on something sacred.

Iron filings

I would now like to anticipate briefly my whole message for the year in the form of a parable, to use a religious metaphor. Using this example, I shall set out the schemas that I apply to the social world, with all the risks inherent in my approach. I shall obviously not attempt to give a definition of the Church, the State or the artistic institution. (And I would like to say in passing that we should always beware of definitions, because they lead us to believe that the problem has been solved.) If I had to answer the question 'What is the Church', I would first say that there is a field – I am using this word, although I should not because I have not defined it yet – or, more precisely, a social space, a set of objective relations between people who . . . what should I say? [*silence*] I am very embarrassed to try to explain without using the words which would allow me to name what I want to name, but since I haven't defined these words, I cannot use them [*laughter*] . . . Let us say that, if I wanted to say what the Church is in France today, I would not say that it is the bishops, or all the clergy, or even all of them together with the theologians and the Catholic intellectuals. No, the Church is the sum of the objective relations between all these people – it is by and large what I call a 'field'. These relations are such that a Church-space is formed, and the position in the space held by Mr So-and-So includes a lot of information on his strategies, positions and stances. In other words, the Church would be a sort of diagram in which we would situate not individual agents but positions defined by objective properties (such as the power to excommunicate, the power to exclude, or, on the contrary, the duty to attend mass every Sunday, and so on) that are themselves defined by their relation to the space as a whole, which I have defined in an objectivist way as if it were basically a physical world.

One of the properties of this space is that the behaviour of whoever enters it – a worker priest, or a young seminarist who wants to become a worker priest, for instance – will be modified by the whole set of these forces before they even realise it. He will be obliged for instance to resist or to rebel. One of the most dramatic effects produced by being introduced to a field is that the very efforts used to escape the forces of the field help to make the field exist. I can quote countless examples; for instance, certain left-wing Christians – and this is one of their con-tradictions – experience the force of the field, as incarnated at some time or other in the bishops or different representatives of these forces, precisely through their inability to act as if it did not exist. This field of forces is so powerful that, if you launch a little seminarist into it, as you might launch a billiard ball, these forces will modify his behaviour. He is not going to wander about in a pure, empty space where anyone can do whatever they like. That is how it is in the social world: it is a uni-verse where you cannot do just whatever you fancy. I have described it rather crudely, and for the moment I shall not enter into detail because it is complicated enough already, but these are not linear spaces at all; they intertwine and overlap. When we read in a book that 'The Church in France' has done this or that, it is shorthand for the result of the effects of the whole set of these activities. In fact, what the bishops of France declare is the result of everything that happens in this field of forces. It is important to remember this when we are faced with the spontaneous philosophy of history with its individual subjects that we all have in mind – which does not mean that individual subjects do not act at all, only that they do not act at all in the way that they think they do.

Secondly – and I will finish here – these iron filings (the people who wish to enter the field) are of a very particular type: they are social subjects endowed with memory. I must remind you that I am using the model of the parable, for as I speak I am suddenly afraid that I may one day hear: 'Bourdieu says that men are iron filings endowed with memory' [*laughter*]. These parables are designed to help us understand; later I shall destroy them, not because they are actually false – they are true in the way that a parable is true. The iron filing enters the field, it has a memory, it will be submitted to forces and will suffer the effects of those forces, among other things; at every moment it will be modified by the forces that it suffers and tries to resist. This memory is what I have called the 'habitus': it is the inertia of all the past experience that we have accumulated in our biological bodies. But, in order to understand what the little iron filing will do, it is not enough to know what forces affect it at one point in time (t), as in a case of pure physics. We have to know its whole trajectory: where it has come from, how it happened to arrive here, and so on. And everything that it has previously experienced will contribute, through the mediation of the habitus, to shape its response to the stimulus at this point in time (t); the momentary stimulus is important, but only in so far as it acts on the individual. This habitus also has a second property, that of constituting the stimulus itself – it does so in the sense that it perceives or defines or thinks the stimulus – which immediately modifies the power of the forces exercised by the stimulus. The Church, then, will be this space, together with this collection of iron filings wandering around inside it. And it will be not only these two things existing serially, *partes extra partes*, but also the relations between these two spaces of relations; it will be the Church, not as something dead but as a living reality, as something that responds, acts and transforms, that asks for subsidies and obtains them, that establishes churches, and so on. The Church as living reality will be a permanent dialectic between these fields, which are spaces of constraint, and the various habitus that encounter these given fields while trying at the same time to transform them, although in trying to transform them they will themselves be transformed, and so on and so forth.

After this little parable, I could deliver a sermon [*laughter*], for there is much more to say. I could for example say how simplistic are those philosophies of history couched in terms of 'all is change / nothing ever changes' or 'in favour of change / not in favour of change'.[31] It is so easy to see that these alternatives, which structure our everyday political debate, are one of the greatest obstacles to social thinking. They are really out of date. Which is why we need the concept of the field as a space of constraint that is itself a perpetual focus of conflict and is transformed by the outcome of the constraints that it imposes on the agents within it. I'll leave it at that.

If I were to offer a provisional definition to sum up what I have been saying, I would say that the Church could basically be 'defined' – in inverted commas – as a field of struggle between agents disposed, or indeed accustomed, to vie with each other for the right to define the Church and for the monopoly of the representation of the Church. If we were to nuance or complicate this rather simplistic definition, I believe that you would not only find it self-explanatory but also find that it explains very well why all the other definitions that I ran past you just now are deficient. This would also be the case for political parties and other institutions, and I might just as well have asked: 'What is the Communist Party?' or 'What is the Socialist Party?' These questions are very easy to transpose in so far as, at any given time, the whole set of the field of forces, struggles and rivalry is virtually crystallised in the person of a legitimate representative or spokesman for that intangible thing the Church, given that this monopoly of representation is one of the possible configurations of the logic of this field that I call the Church. This approach enables us to understand one of the profound effects produced by all social institutions: the 'organisation illusion', which I believe to be the fundamental obstacle to thinking the social world, and which we encounter when we accept phrases such as 'The Church thinks that . . .', 'France considers that . . .' or 'The president of the Republic thinks that . . .', and so on. These magical phrases must be interpreted as we would interpret magical thinking: we must take into account the extremely complex world of social relations within which are sketched the thousands of apparently Brownian movements and interactions which result in something assuming the likeness of a personal intention. Since we often see the world in terms of the logic of legal proceedings ('Who is responsible?', 'Who did this or that?'), we are most often satisfied with surface appearances ('The Church has decided'), whereas the whole point of scientific research is to find a language adapted to this virtually nameless reality. My own verbal hesitations at the end of this lecture give an idea of how extraordinarily difficult this research is. I think that social realities are so complex that it is very difficult to designate them using ordinary language. Yet ordinary language is what we speak all the time, and, the more confidently we do so, the greater the margin for manipulation. This is why one of the aims that I have set myself is a kind of mental re-education and political gymnastics.

Lecture of 12 October 1982

The double life of the social – The process of objectification and incorporation of the social – Moving beyond the opposition between subjectivism and objectivism – Scholarly understanding and practical understanding – The examples of reading and the work of art – Programme of future lectures and questions from the audience

In my last lecture I was asking what the object of sociology is, or, in other words, what the sociologist is supposed to study. In so doing I used the model of the parable to run through the questions that we might apply to the Church as an institution, since we could see the Church as the archetypal institution. I attempted to show how, as soon as we enquired into the nature of the existence of something like the Church, we were faced with a flood of extremely difficult problems, similar to those facing metaphysicians when they study the question of Being.

I shall pick up the argument here, but I want to clarify a point that has been put to me and avoid a possible misunderstanding. When I emphasised that, in the last resort, the Church exists only in so far as it manages to make people believe that it exists, I meant that each and every institution – the Church, but also the State or the family – tends to hide the fact that it is an object of belief; the key to the study of institutions is the grounding of the existence of these institutions in the minds of social agents. In other words, in the case of the Church – that is to say, the institution charged with organising belief – we run the risk of being misled if we forget that the deep structure of the organisation charged with organising belief is itself grounded in belief; ultimately, behind the mysteries generated, maintained and preserved by the ecclesiastic institution, there lies the mystery of the institution itself. I wanted therefore simply to make you aware of the difficulties and problems encountered by the sociologist by explaining that the mysteries of the institution itself are no less mysterious than the mysteries nourished and preserved by the institution.

(I would, however, like to draw your attention to something that I said in my lectures last year, which is that the theologians of the Middle Ages spoke of the mystery of the divine ministry assumed by the pope and bishops, and others.[1] The Church then, as the particularly mysterious institution charged with the management of mystery, is no less mysterious in its social existence than the things of which it speaks. For example, as I said last year, I was very struck on re-reading canon law or commentaries by historians on canon law to see that the theologians discussing their theological problems suggested a peculiarly refined and highly modern theory of the social world, projecting onto their institution the modes of thought that they were accustomed to use when thinking of their theological topics. I close this parenthesis, which I think is important because it helps me to avoid offering a somewhat Voltairean representation of sociology: I think that, if there is a sinister attitude in sociology, it is the Voltairean sneer, which refuses to understand what it doesn't understand, and thus understands nothing. What I am saying may seem mysterious, but, for those who do understand what I mean, I needed to say it. [*laughter*])

The double life of the social

To return straight away to my question What does the existence of something social entail? How does the social exist? How does it come to exist? How does it continue to exist? Do things social have a life of their own? I took the example of the Church because it suited me, but a more instructive example, and one much easier to understand, would be the book or the work of art. I think that we can admit without hesitation that a book or a painting or a musical score is a social thing, which can exist only as a product of human work objectified. Does this social thing really live on as long as it is physically in existence, or, to put it differently, is a book a complete social thing? We can see straight away what the familiar term 'a dead letter' expresses so well: a letter that nobody reads is a 'dead letter' – that is, a mutilated letter, which does not have a complete social existence. We could say the same of a painting (in a moment I shall try to show the errors that forgetting this double reality of the social thing can introduce into the study of art). Like the dead letter, the book that nobody reads or that nobody is able to read any more in the way that it should be read – although not exactly the same problem – is a dead book or one on artificial life support. It happens that archaeologists find objects whose function completely escapes them. These completely indeterminate objects imply a function, but nobody can replicate it: we are not accustomed to the object; we lack the appropriate 'habitus' to make the object function. In such cases we have come across customs or costumes that we are unable to inhabit. What I call the habitus is something that is solicited by these social things and turns these social things from being lifeless objects into living realities: they become like a suit that we wear comfortably because it is the right size. This leads us to a simple definition of the institution, the word which the other day I said had several meanings: the social institution or thing exists in two different ways. In the particular case of the book, it exists as a physical object, but a book that nobody reads is just another physical object like any other: you can burn it, destroy it or conceal it, use it as a blunt instrument to hit your enemy on the head, and so on. The book as physical object becomes a social thing only when it meets up with its other half, the half incorporated in the reader, or, more precisely, in the social agent endowed with the dispositions that incline them to read it and enable them to decipher it (these are the two dimensions of the habitus: the 'inclination to' and the 'ability to').

We could say the same thing of a rule when it is no longer applied, when it has become obsolete. Law is one of those social things that are full of dead letters: they exist, they are written down somewhere and could be unearthed by a scholar (who will say: 'In the nineteenth century, they used to cut off the right hand of people who . . .'), but these one-time social facts are rules and norms that are no longer habitual – the habitual, like the habitus, implies a permanent disposition, acquired through repetition. An even better example of the theory of the social that I am proposing would be that of some game we have lost the habit of playing. For example, if you re-read Huizinga's *The Autumn of the Middle Ages*, you will notice the place that tournaments took in the social life of the Middle Ages.[2] So many things, such as honour, life and love, were invested in the tournament. The fact that nobody nowadays would be prepared to die in a tournament means that the institution does exist, that it can be historically located, but that nobody will invest in it. Here I think that the word 'invest' matters: it can have an economic as well as a psychological sense, and it is characteristic of a living institution to persuade agents to invest in it, for in so doing they give it life and make it function. I think then that this simple analysis leads to a first definition.

(The other day I rather rashly said how suspicious I was of

definitions, and I have been criticised for this. All I wanted to say was that definitions are often a fool's game, for they use the artificial rigour of concepts to mask vagueness and sterility; that is why I issued a warning. But if we use the process of axiomatisation to reach a rigorous definition, there is no problem, and I shall do all that I can to choose my words rigorously and, when the need arises, to offer definitions.)

According to this first, provisional, definition, the social institution or the social is instituted, materialised and accomplished in 'reality' in two ways. (I often place the terms that I use between inverted commas, because they don't seem quite adequate enough.) On the one hand it is instituted in things, in objects such as the book, or mechanisms such as the game, which are not necessarily visible things: what I shall call a 'field' designates the rules that govern the working of a social space, the rules of the game. On the other hand the social is objectified in what I call the habitus, by which I mean dispositions that are permanent life styles resulting from learning, training and incorporation – for the moment I shall ask you to be satisfied with this definition. Briefly, I shall say that the social exists both in things and in bodies. But, as my argument has been suggesting, the social really exists as a living social – as opposed to a dead, 'archaeological', fossilised social, reduced to the state of a physical object – only when its two halves meet to mix and match their functions and relations. Thus a habitat ceases to be an archaeological site and becomes a human habitat when people who have the appropriate habitus inhabit it. For example, some years ago I analysed the structure of the space of the Kabyle house. I shall not repeat the demonstration here, but I did show that this apparently unremarkable rectangular space was organised around a whole system of complex oppositions, where we could identify the four points of the compass, as well as oppositions between wet and dry, masculine and feminine, and so on.[3] But this Kabyle house could only be inhabitable or inhabited by someone endowed with the appropriate habitus and able (quite unconsciously – I shall return to this point) to make the space function properly, in fact in such a natural manner that the owner was surprised when we asked him 'Where do you keep the water?' – although it was apparent that the water was placed to the right of the door as you entered, beside the animal fodder and other damp goods, without the opposition between fire and water being explicitly mentioned. This is a good example of how a living institution finds fulfilment in the relation between a thing or mechanism and a system of dispositions. I shall now give more precise details.

The process of objectification and incorporation of the social

In defining the social institution in this way, I simultaneously define the
work of the sociologist, which is my project for today. If the social is
fulfilled in these two forms, one of the sociologist's first tasks will be to
study the work of objectification – that is, the process through which the
'social' becomes instituted in the material nature of things (such as mon-
uments, documents and writings) or in the logic of mechanisms (such
as games, or phenomena such as the market). This initial aim consists
in studying the process of objectification and discovering what it signifies, how it works and the effects that it produces. What for example
are the social effects of passing from a vague, implicit feeling, say of
embarrassment, to the state of expressing it in speech or in writing? The
fact of saying something that was previously unspoken produces a very
powerful social effect. Sartre says somewhere – I quote from memory
– 'Words wreak havoc, and when a sentiment like love, that was only
vaguely felt, is motivated to confess and speak its name, everything
changes.'[4] This kind of elementary objectification that makes something
verbally explicit, *a fortiori* in writing, in a written discourse endowed
with authority, like the law, has an amazingly powerful effect. There
are also people whose profession and social function is to be specialists
in objectification: these are the people we call 'creative'. As always, the
ideological representation often has foundations in reality: the creator
is a professional exponent of this work of objectification, which is far
from being automatic. Whether in politics or psychology, the passage
from the diffuse and confused lived experience of badly formulated individual or social feelings to their declaration, display and public objectification, with the officialisation that this implies, is a social act of the
first importance, although it does not really constitute an action, since it
expresses something that already existed – 'Thou wouldst not seek Me
if thou didst not possess Me',[5] 'The prophet preaches to the converted',
etc. But the prophet who says the things that the converted were waiting
to hear performs an action that is absolutely capital and extraordinary
by telling people things that they both knew and did not know, since
they did not know how to say them. We need to study this phenomenon
of objectification; I shall discuss it later at greater length.

The second process is much more complicated and is unfortunately
much more difficult to approach, since it requires experimental techniques that the sociologist is not always able to handle: this is the
process of incorporation, the mechanism or logic whereby objective
structures and conditions become transformed into permanent dispositions. I shall explain this point in depth: one of the postulates of

sociology – at least as I view it – is that there is always a correspondence between the objective structures within which any given social individual lives and the mental structures that they draw on to conceptualise the social world and everything they see as an object. One of the mysteries that social science should use genetic sociology to explore is the process of apprenticeship through which these objective structures are incorporated.

Here, then, we already have two aims for the social sciences. But since the institution has two forms and exists as a live entity only through the relations between these two forms, social science also has as its object the relations between these two forms of existence. So, if you have followed me so far, you will see that, in place of the spontaneous opposition between individual and society to which we all subscribe (and I'm afraid this also includes a number of sociologists), I am tending to substitute the opposition between two modes of social existence: the social that exists in mechanisms and things, and the social that exists in bodies. To some extent, when a social agent enters into a relationship with the social – by taking the bus, buying a ticket or paying their taxes – it is in a way not a biological individual entering into relation with a social institution, it is one social institution entering into relation with another social institution. I don't intend to reduce the whole individual in all his aspects to a social institution, but the sociologists who construct their object should see that the relationship they should study is the meeting of one social institution with another. The social that is instituted in the incorporated and individuate biological body (because the body individualises – which does not mean that we are talking about 'an individual') enters into relation with the objectified social. This is one of the paradoxes that Durkheim studied, but without drawing all the conclusions from his reflections: the social is partly borne by individuals – that is, by bodies that are separate from one another – and, as Durkheim argues, all social groups attempt to solve the sometimes intractable problems that the effects of this individuation present.[6] Social groups attempt to transcend this fate of individuation, particularly through socialisation, which produces objectively harmonised individuals. I must say straight away, in order to follow the logic of my reflection, that there is a whole set of further properties linked to the incorporation of the social. The fact that the social has to be incorporated in biological bodies that are mortal, isolated and prone to all the calamities to which the flesh is prey (dementia, for instance), is of prime importance, and one part of the work of the sociologist will be to study the means employed by social groups to transcend everything that happens to social groups because they have to be incorporated. In the splendid book that I have already quoted, *The King's Two Bodies*, Kantorowicz reflects on the paradox of the formula that I mentioned in passing: 'The king is dead, long live the king!'[7] How does it come to pass that kingship survives the biological king? How does bureaucracy survive the bureaucrat? How can the Church be eternal and be able to survive everything that affects the biological bodies of those who are charged with incarnating it? These are questions that sociology must ponder.

In place of the commonly given opposition between individual and society, I have then constructed an opposition between the incorporated social, which I call a habitus, and the objectified social, which I shall call a social thing or mechanism, or field. I believe that one of the consequences and important advantages of this substitution is to dismiss the problem of the relation between individual and society that gives rise to so many treatises but which seems to me to be one of the major epistemological hindrances both to creating a social science and to researching into the social dimension of the individual. The opposition between social psychology and sociology that sociologists find so tempting seems to me to be the archetypal false model for scientific study. There can be no place in the scientific world for such ready-made oppositions and commonplace intuitions once we realise that the social world exists at one and the same time in the shape of social mechanisms and socialised bodies, both of which need to be studied by the sociologist.

The habitus, then, defined for the time being as a system of dispositions – I shall give a more precise definition later – is the incorporated and therefore transindividual social. Another consequence that I find highly significant is that there are different classes of habitus, and also a class habitus, which means that statisticians, even if they fail to understand why, may rightly treat a set of individuals as if they were identical, as long as the statistical classes have been correctly constructed in order to group together individuals who, having been conditioned by the same influences, have a homogeneous habitus and are therefore homogeneous through the incorporated social features that they share.

(I have perhaps rather rushed through this argument, but what I am trying to say here is both the basis and a provisional summary of what I shall be arguing throughout the year to come, and if I were sure of being perfectly clear and perfectly understood, I could stop here, now that I have stated my case. And yet I do intend to continue to speak [*laughter*], for I think that there are quite a few implications for me to unravel as my argument develops.)

I am going to propose a sort of model that I shall first sketch fairly simply but which I shall go on to develop at length. Do not be surprised if some of what I have to say appears obscure: what I want to do is suggest the overall logic, because I believe that you need to grasp the model as a whole and then take it to pieces. The habitus, being the social incorporated and therefore transindividual, can be constituted in terms of classes. There are classes of habitus, whereas biological individuals can be infinitely different according to Leibniz's principle of continuity: no two individuals are alike.[8] Using the hypothesis that the same causes produce the same effects, sociology can posit classes of habitus considered as homogeneous. Biological individuals subject to the same social conditioning will be homogeneous to a certain extent. I must point out straight away that no two habitus are alike, quite simply because the social conditioning is never identical. Even supposing that two individuals had experienced exactly the same individual adventures, the simple fact they had not experienced them in the same order changes everything; the probability that two individuals might live out exactly the same experience in the same order is practically nil, and there are no two identical individuals. That having been said, we may suppose that there are classes of habitus, in so far as there are classes of social conditioning. This provides a basis for statistical analysis without having to make sociology the science of the collective: there is also a sociology of the individual habitus and, for example – this is important for the division of labour in sociology – we can take an individual biography as an instrument to enable us to grasp the singular logic of a singular habitus. Enough said.

Moving beyond the opposition between subjectivism and objectivism

At this point, it seems to me that I have described the essence of the institution, but I would like to add in a first example, for, as I said I would, I intend to proceed throughout the year by alternating abstract analyses and semi-concrete analyses – because it is not always possible to give a discursive account of all the information that would be required for a complete statistical or ethnographical analysis. To illustrate the fact that these analyses have nothing purely theoretical about them but give rise to practical applications, I propose to take the example of the analysis of a work of art. If what I have said so far is true, we can conclude that social science should place itself beyond the ordinary distinction between the subject and the object in order to construct an object that includes the relation between the subject and the object. For example, to understand a specific artefact, work of art or book (or institution, or market, etc.), which itself includes a relation between the subject and the object, social science must place itself beyond this relationship. In other words, there is in the object studied by the sociologist a subject–object relation: the object studied by the sociologist is not only a book as a social fact but also a relation between the reader and the book, between a subject and an object. I shall perhaps draw a little diagram on the wall chart, although I am always wary of diagrams [*laughter*].

The case of the artistic, archaeological or ethnological object that you might see at the Musée de l'homme is I think extremely interesting because it obliges you to question the relation of the subject to the object. [*Bourdieu tries unsuccessfully to roll down the wall chart to draw his diagram, which makes his audience laugh.*] That's a very good illustration of my argument, you see: when you don't have the right habitus for your object, you fail.

I shall sketch it rapidly: here on one side we have a habitus; there, a field – in fact I should have put the book, the painting, the museum or the plough or whatever, there . . . But obviously, by putting 'field', I am adding something extra: I am implying that none of these really exist outside of a network of mechanisms that enables them to function. If we were talking about money, you would immediately understand: it's obvious that a coin cannot function all alone . . . but it is the same for a book or a piece of music: they need readers, composers, authors, and the like. The aim of sociology, then, will be to study all of that – both the habitus and the field, since both the habitus and the field are social. We are entirely immersed in the social even if in one case the social is engaged in the biological and in the other it is lodged in the physical – and not even exclusively, because there are cases where it exists outside these parameters, in the shape of mechanisms that are not objectified.

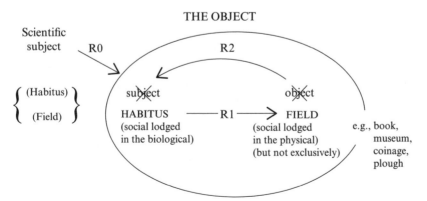

To continue what I was saying just now about the example of the book: one of the first things for sociology to study is the constitution and formation of the habitus; it will also study the constitution and formation of the field. How does this formation and objectification occur in the case of a book? This question leads on to another question: 'How are the producers of books produced? How are the material and symbolic producers produced?' I had started just now to say in abstract terms that social science should situate itself beyond the distinction between the subject and the object in order to construct an object that includes the subject–object relation. To anticipate: the scientific subject will itself be defined by the fact that it has a habitus and exists in a field. And this field is of a specific nature that has its own logic.[9] I have started to make things too complicated; let us leave that for later. For the time being, we have the scientific subject who finds in the object of study a relation of the subject–object variety – which we may call 'Relation R1', but we should not think of it as a subject–object relation, and we may well question the nature of this relation. However, another important relation is that linking habitus and field. This was implicit just now when I explained that a habitus is produced by the incorporation of objective structures, and that among these structures we find, for example, the structures of social spaces such as the fields of social class or religion. Part of what we will find in a habitus will therefore derive from the objective structures of the social world that it has incorporated. These two relations are not at all of the same kind: the relation 'R2' will be a relation of conditioning, while that of 'R1' will be one of knowledge. Here I am running ahead of myself, and I repeat what I said just now, to avoid misunderstanding: I am setting out the main lines of a model, but during the following lectures I shall elaborate at length on what now seems rough and ready. You will just have to trust me.

We could say, then, that this relation (field → habitus) is a relation of the kind 'habitus determined, conditioned by field'. But the habitus is also included in the field – and that too is a very complicated relation. One problem will be to know how the latter relation will be determined by the former. What are the implications of trying to comprehend a world of which we are part? Here I am deliberately exploiting the two senses of the word 'comprehend', as Pascal did in his time ('By space the universe encompasses and swallows me up like a mere speck: by thought I comprehend the universe.'):[10] the social world comprehends me, but I comprehend it. In fact that sums up rather well the elementary paradox which we doubtless have to enter into fully in order to found a sociology. This has often been said, but in a form that seems to me to be anti-scientific: people have insisted on this relation in order to argue that sociology or the social sciences in general are sciences of comprehension, sciences of the mind that have a logic irreducible to that of the other sciences.[11] In fact, I think that we need to take note of the existence of this dual relation, not in order to deny sociology or the social sciences in general the status of a science, but to oblige us to establish this relation in scientific terms. Let us consider the relation [R 1] for a moment. It is a relation of knowledge: when faced with a hammer, the appropriate habitus is one that is able to hammer – as Heidegger notoriously remarked;[12] a habitus is something that responds appropriately to the solicitations of a social object. In this way the habitus is linked with the object in a relation of knowledge, but – and this is the question – is this relation of practical knowledge of the same nature as the relation of scholarly knowledge? Here we have a relation that I shall call 'R0', and I think that one of the fundamental errors of the social sciences – which I shall constantly reflect on – consists in confusing R0 with R1: when the scholars conducting the research fail to constitute their object as including a 'subject'–'object' relation different from a relation of scientific knowledge, they project this scientific model into their relation and proceed as if the relation of practical knowledge were the same as the relation of scholarly knowledge.

This will again seem abstract to you, but, in order to help you understand it, I shall step right outside the logic that I was following and refer to a famous literary example that has often been commented on, particularly by Auerbach. I shall read you a passage from the chapter of *Mimesis* that he devotes to Flaubert, where you will hear something quite analogous to what I have been saying:

> But it was above all at meal times that she could bear it no longer, in that little room on the ground floor, with the smoking stove, the creaking door, the oozing walls, the damp floor-tiles; all the bitterness of life seemed to be served to her on her plate, and, with the steam from the boiled beef, there rose from the depths of her soul other exhalations as it were of disgust. Charles was a slow eater: she would nibble a few hazel nuts, or else, leaning on her elbow, she would amuse herself making marks on the oilcloth with the point of her table-knife.

And Auerbach comments that Flaubert presents us not only with Emma as physical object but also the world as seen by Emma.[13] Flaubert presents Emma as a physical object in the world that can be described as precisely as the oilcloth, but he also and at the same time

presents Emma's vision of the world. In other words, he presents us
with an object, but at the same time he reminds us that she is a knowing
subject. He presents us simultaneously with an object involved in a
situation and its (her) comprehension of that situation. He reminds us
that Emma is part of the picture that she paints and that she experiences this tableau as something that is liable to be described. It was
Georges Poulet, in *Les Métamorphoses du cercle*, who said: '[Flaubert]
presents as an object of contemplation a being who, in her turn, has
the contemplation of reality as her object.'[14] This can be mapped onto
a rigorous sociology. To complete the analysis, we should contrast this
vision, which has moved beyond the distinction between subject and
object, with two types of description: a description of a strictly objective or, as has been said of the Nouveau Roman, objectal type,[15] which
would describe Emma in exactly the same terms and language used to
describe the plates and the oilcloth; or totally subjective descriptions,
like those to be found in Joyce's Dedalus or in Virginia Woolf, where
we would find only glimmerings of consciousness as they ebb and
flow through the fictional subject. Flaubert, however, gives us both
at once, without making the mistake of being simultaneously inside
and outside, which is what the theoreticians of objectal literature have
reproached traditional novelists with. I refer you to a most interesting
book on the subject by Maxime Chastaing, *La Philosophie de Virginia
Woolf*.[16] Maxime Chastaing quotes a populist-style novel by Ramuz
which corresponds exactly to this mixture of the internal and the external, with observations by people who are outside the event but believe
they are inside. Ramuz describes a man digging with a pick who suddenly sees mud spurting up into his face.[17] Chastaing points out that
there are two possibilities: either you are hacking away and you see the
mud spurt up into your face – which is not a spectator's viewpoint –
or you are watching the digger dig and then you don't see the mud in
your face, but you could say – as Ramuz does, by the way – that the
farm hand was bent double and panting and covered in sweat. Maxime
Chastaing quite rightly draws attention to the fact that novelists have
accustomed us to this sort of divine vision: they describe the outside of
the prison and are at the same time beside the prisoner within; they are
inside the mind of the subject, making him talk to others or himself,
for instance, but they are also outside. They become not a mere human
spectator but also a divine spectator, who sees not only the walls of
the prison but also the inside of the prison cell, with its bed and other
objects. This totally subjective and totally objective narrative of the
total novelist is a logical monstrosity that relies precisely on this lack
of distinction: it is the work of someone who does not know what he

is talking about and does not realise that he is in fact on the outside all the time.

I think that a certain number of sociologists are almost inconsolable when they find that these two relations are so different. This gives rise to a certain number of misguided scientific enterprises: participatory sociology, for example – or one of its variants such as the sociology of action, where the sociologist is immersed in the movement he studies, for the same things are reborn under different names in every age.[18] It is the total novelist's dream to be at the prisoner's side and at the same time to be outside the prison to tell us that his fiancée has married somebody else, and so on. Think about it, and you can project it onto the sociology of the working classes; it works perfectly. One of the most important things to bear in mind is that these two relations are essentially different. There is a fundamental epistemological distinction, and if we fail to observe it we commit what seems to me to be the cardinal error of all social science – that is, the act whereby scholars project their minds into the experience of the external subject and thereby substitute themselves as subjects of the actions of those whom they are also studying as objects. Ethnologists very often fall back on this impossible, as it were magical relation, as they try to reconcile opposites.

I would like to take Flaubert's text and use it as another of my paradigms or parables. Flaubert makes us realise that, when faced with a social fact (such as looking at Fragonard's *Girl Reading*, watching a girl reading, or studying a lecture hall with a view to making a scientific study of it), we can adopt different postures, which run the risk of being confused if we attempt to reconcile the opposites that I have mentioned. The first posture is the type of objectivist posture that consists in describing Emma as being part of objective reality, as one object among others, and therefore to paint her from the outside in the same style as the stove, the wall or the plates. This posture, which is quite justifiable, is a kind of radical behaviourism perfectly conceivable in the social sciences. Alternatively, we may adopt a subjectivist posture: this would be *Mrs Dalloway*,[19] or Bloom in *Ulysses* – that is to say, that we would present the social subject through their own experience, their inner monologue, their life as they live it. This is also a viable way of speaking of the social world, the only obstacle being – and here we must accept Wittgenstein's radical critique[20] – the fact that, with the ordinary techniques of social science, it is almost impossible to have access to the subjective experience of other people. If it is true, as I said just now, that you would have to be a professional objectifier to make your own subjective experiences explicit, all that a sociologist conscious of his relation to his object could do would be to act as midwife and be the Socratic assistant at the birth of the expression of a lived experience which is not his own, it being understood that he could only have any chance of success if he knew that he was situated outside this experience and must never identify with it.[21]

A third posture would be a false synthesis or false transcendence of this opposition, which means the projection of the scholarly subject into his object, imposing a relation of scholarly knowledge. The question 'What is the social?', for instance, is already a question that is not social: when you are inside the social, the one thing you don't do is ask yourself what the social is; you just buy your ticket and hop on the tube or the bus. The questions that I raised just now are typically not the sort of questions that you ponder when you are filling in your tax return. One of the fundamental errors made by scholarly subjects is thus to project their scholarly experience and representations into the imagined mind of their objects and to generate questions that the thinking subject being studied does not encounter as practical issues. This is of the first importance. I said just now that the sociologist could become the social subject's assistant in the work of making explicit and objectifying experience; the Socratic metaphor of the midwife that I used is, I believe, well founded and very adequate.[22] I think in fact, *pace* Wittgenstein, that it is not impossible for the sociologist to work at objectifying experiences that they have not had themselves, as long of course as they are aware from the outset of the constant danger of identification, of 'putting yourself in their place'. If you re-read Husserl's texts on comprehension,[23] you will see that they are basically variations on the theme of 'putting yourself in their place', even if he phrases it in less mundane terms. Now if there is a scientific error in sociology, it is that one: you cannot put yourself in the place of the other, and for good reason; you are not in the same place. By definition, a boss cannot put himself in the place of a worker, and vice versa. They can have a very sympathetic understanding, but they cannot comprehend each other. Perhaps their chances of mutual comprehension would be greater if they knew the truth, that the relation of scientific knowledge is not a relation of practical knowledge.

The monstrous synthesis of the total novelist, simultaneously inside and outside, is a false solution to the antinomy of objectivism and subjectivism. It is a caricature of what I think should be the proper scientific posture: to return to my diagram, the thinking subject must be aware for example that they are in a situation where they can ask themselves questions. To think of the game as a game you have to move outside the game. To think of the habitus as a habitus you have to take a mental distance from the habitus. By definition, the thinking subject has to move outside the space in order to think of it, and in so doing comes to think of it as a problem, whereas one of the properties of the relation R2 (the relation of conditioning, incorporation) is precisely that the world is not a problem.

This relation will be the doxic relation, well analysed by the phenomenologists, especially Husserl; it will be the relation with the social world as self-evident, as spontaneously offering its meaning. Faced with a hammer, we don't act like an archaeologist and ask: 'What is that for?'; we pick it up and bang on a nail. The practical response to the existence of a hammer, if you have the appropriate habitus, is to hammer, without needing to formulate the question 'What is the hammer for?' or, *a fortiori*, 'What was the process that led to the presence of the hammer?' The argument that I have hardly touched on here – for the hammer to exist, there has to be a blacksmith; for the blacksmith to function, he needs hammers to forge the hammer; etc. – poses all the problems of the social origins of social objects; these problems are constitutive of a real social science but are excluded by definition from a practical relation with the social world. Consequently, if this schema is true, what is called for is a kind of knowledge able to transcend the subjectivism/objectivism opposition, but this must not be a purely fantastical transcendence, like a chimera.

Scholarly understanding and practical understanding

The first steps in scholarly knowledge – which I think will become the topic of the next lectures – should be to understand why this science of scholarly knowledge is in a sense still to be undertaken, since it has hardly started. It will be a knowledge of non-scholarly knowledge and yet also of scholarly knowledge, because I can understand what scholarly knowledge is by understanding in what ways it differs from practical knowledge, and vice versa. I have for instance revealed a lot about scholarly knowledge in saying that practical knowledge does not ask itself scholarly questions, and vice versa. I can therefore only further the knowledge of practical knowledge if at the same time I pursue the knowledge of scholarly knowledge and also, I have to say, the knowledge of the social conditions of scholarly knowledge.

So one of the first objects of study will be a science of practical knowledge, or a science of practice, and the second will be a science of this relation and what is implied for the sociologist's own knowledge by the fact that the habitus producing this knowledge is partly the product of the object that it is attempting to comprehend.

If, as I said just now, this science has virtually never been undertaken, it is largely because the whole philosophical tradition has always
considered that truth lies in scholarly knowledge, and that there is a
hierarchy between the two kinds of knowledge such that they could
think of no better way of considering the object than by lending it their
own subjectivity. Sartre's very fine description of the café waiter,[24]
which I shall read out to you, is a splendid illustration of what I have
just very briefly stated. The subject's habitus will produce acts of
knowledge, but not at all in the way that we usually understand them.
Hitting something with a hammer is an act of knowledge in the sense
that I understand it: the person using the hammer has understood
the hammer better than I understood just now how those wall charts
work . . . This relation of comprehension is characterised partly by the
fact that it is enacted by someone who is comprehended, in a different
sense, by what they comprehend. And it is also characterised by the
fact that the person comprehending employs in their comprehension
'things' that are the product of what they are comprehending. Briefly,
and anticipating what I shall be arguing throughout this year's lecture
course, if this relation of practical knowledge is doxic and seemingly
self-evident, it is largely because the structures of the knowing habitus
are a product of the structures of the social field.

The social world seems self-evident. And yet, in the 'disorientation'
that we feel on entering a foreign society, the gap between our incorporated structures and the new objectified structures provokes a feeling
of incomprehension, which, being intolerable, is immediately dissolved
by reinterpreting the objectified structures in terms of our incorporated
structures (which is where misunderstandings arise). In the case of the
scholars who do not understand practice – and fail to understand that
they do not understand it – it is because their scholarly ethnocentrism
consists in not understanding that not understanding practice is the
mark of the scholar. They have no chance of understanding practice
unless they understand that they cannot grasp it immediately.

I now wish to reflect on this relation of conditioning, but more from
the angle of how it affects the object. There is a major problem: what
I have called the 'field' that acts on the habitus (for example, the book
that, when read, affects and 'influences' – a deplorable word – the
habitus or the biological body that could become a habitus; or the
religious field, in so far as it acts on the biological body to create a
habitus) is obviously not the same field as the field perceived by a particular constituted habitus or the book read by one. I must therefore
subdivide the field. Reintroducing the habitus is not simply a 'spiritual
point d'honneur',[25] designed to display the humanist intentions of the

'human sciences'; it is more generally a way of escaping a 'physicalist' reading of the field in order to see the field as a field of action or a field of struggle. In other words, we should 'duplicate' the field, giving us a 'field no. 1', which is the field we know and invest in. It is a field perceived, a field of action, a field worth acting in – a book worth reading or needing to be read. For instance, with an educated habitus we are constantly solicited through the relation existing between the habitus and the object: when people speak of a film that we 'must see', this 'must see' does not work mechanically; it only affects someone who is disposed to be affected by this action. One of the paradoxes of the habitus–field relation is that the habitus helps to determine the determinations that affect it. I shall return to this paradox – and there are more to discuss – but when we read in a weekly review: 'This week's "must read"', 'This month's "must see"', etc., the 'must' is addressed only to a certain type of reader. Almost by definition, a daily newspaper or a weekly review has a profile of its intended reader's habitus, and it knows that these injunctions will by and large meet the conditions needed to be effective. This perceived field, this field of action, then, is different from the field as objectified structure exercising a structural conditioning. I call this latter field a 'field of forces', which gives me field no. 1 = field of action, and field no. 2 = field of forces.

I think that I have reached the limit of what I can expect you to tolerate in a first brief introduction, because all of this must seem quite arbitrary, and yet I shall go on to make you realise how necessary it is. I even feel sure that some of you have already felt this need because, in teasing out the different implications from among the habitus, the field and their relations, I have opened up the whole topic. I realise that you may feel that everything has been said in advance but that, at the same time, it is all rather vast: but this is the aim of my lecture course – to spend the year transforming this confused feeling of arbitrary necessity into a feeling of real necessity.

The examples of reading and the work of art

Now that I have made this schema more explicit, I would like to take another example in order to show you how we can use it to ask a certain number of questions. I shall, however, use only a small part of the schema, concerning the example of reading and what it means to read a book or a painting. I said just now that a social object in its objectified – that is, mutilated – form presents itself as something that calls out to be reactivated by the appropriate habitat. The letter can survive in material form beyond the habitus for which it was made as an institutional object. This is the case for example with all the scripts that we cannot decipher and, more generally, with most of the objects that we see in museums, which give rise to false readings. For although we are aware of the problem when faced with, say, the really dead letter of an unknown script, we tend to forget it in the case of objects from that kind of middle distance which is our dated history. Objects such as Quattrocento paintings, or *a fortiori* seventeenth-century paintings, are close enough to our subjective experience not to remind us that they are mutilated institutions; they are objects that we can experience even though we do not have the habitus that is written into the objective expectations of the object under consideration. Since they are not perceived as only partial institutions, these dead objects – it has often been said of *art nègre*, but we could just as well say it of a Quattrocento painting – now in a way acquire a habitus which is not the one that they lived with.[26] We project a scholarly habitus into the object. This is what Bakhtin, discussing reading in his book on linguistics, calls 'philologism'.[27] Philologism consists in injecting the simple experience of reading with a philological awareness, reading texts as if they had been written to be read by philologists, projecting into the reading the experience of a reader who for example comes to the text as if it is something to decipher: the fact of not questioning, as I said just now, this relation [R1] and the relation between this relation [R1] and the relation [R2], the fact of not questioning the relation between the two relations leads us to read works as if they had been written to be read in the way that we read books today.

I think that I can best explain this by pointing out that, since Baudelaire and, of course, Joyce, writers have started more or less unconsciously inscribing within their writing the expectation of a reading that is in fact a re-reading. These writers were born into a universe where there were professional readers for whom to read was to re-read several times, to write a critique, to look for hidden meanings and structures, such as echoes of Homer's *Iliad* in Joyce's *Ulysses*, and so on. They were people for whom writing was an institution that invoked tacit guidelines for the legitimate way of reading what they were writing. This is even more the case with a literary movement such as the Nouveau Roman.

There is then a pragmatics of reading: we tend to forget that the person who writes has something to say about the person who is going to read them. And the people born in this universe of professional readers have generated a whole literature which disqualifies a certain type of reading – skim reading or reading on the move – that fails to grasp the structures of the field. I have been discussing the writers, but the fact of living in a universe inhabited by professional readers, commentators, structuralists, semiologists and professors of literary history, where the institution of textual exegesis is everywhere to be found and even compulsory in school from an early age, affecting virtually the whole population living in a universe where reading is an institution, has social effects both on the unconscious pragmatics of writing and on the readings that the professional reader will make of any text: they will read texts as if they had been designed to be read, whereas a gymnastics manual is designed not to be read but to be performed and a Tibetan prayer book to be chanted, sung or danced. I have often said that one of the fundamental errors of a certain structural anthropology is precisely that it presents as texts designed to be read and analysed hermeneutically texts that were designed to be acted or danced, such as for example all the texts that describe rituals;[28] these texts are not designed for reading, especially not a structural re-reading looking for hidden correspondences. We can see proof of this in the fact that often these texts do not withstand the search for coherence beyond a certain point; they reach breaking point, because one of the properties of the logic of practice is precisely to be valid in practice – that is, only for the purposes of immediate need, and only up to a certain point. The fact of living in a social universe where reading is established as an institution drives us to adopt an unconscious relation to the book as object which will tend to spread to everything that we have to read, and will therefore produce a kind of 'philologism effect'.

Let us now return to painting, where things are perhaps even clearer, although perhaps more unexpected ... A very simple example: in Italian churches – I could give a long description, since I conducted a fairly detailed investigation,[29] but I will sketch the outline – nowadays we are likely to see a fifteenth- or sixteenth-century painting behind an automatic electric candle, unlit, then another a little further with two wax candles, both lit, and further on a very small sixteenth-century painting with a small Saint-Sulpice type of devotional medallion[30] surrounded by candles, inviting you to 'place your offerings here'. And what is really surprising is that you have the same painting somewhere else with no accompaniment, and a little further on another purely aesthetic one, but, between the two, a typical devotional scenario: St Anthony offering his rosary to the Virgin. And you will find everything sharing the same space: these subjects and their representations, the faithful at prayer before them alongside the tourists studying their *Guide bleu* [*laughter*]. It would take too long to analyse all of this, but I just wanted you to see what I had in mind. Observing all this struck me because I was thinking of what I have been saying to you: these objects can be treated as institutions. I mean that the first impulse of an educated citizen in our society will be to treat all of these objects as aesthetic objects – that is, objects soliciting an aesthetic habitus. For example, I imagine that if someone went down on their knees and prayed to a Fra Angelico in the Louvre they would be thought barking mad, unless they were suspected of staging an avant-garde happening [*laughter*].

In fact, we carry within us an unconscious representation of painting as an institution. The painting is dual: it is an object, and at the same time its other half is the habitus that it solicits, and it will only really become a living painting if it finds its appropriate habitus. We ourselves walk past these paintings with our all-purpose habitus – this is even the definition of the aesthetic habitus; it can apply to anything, it can constitute as aesthetic anything that makes us say 'That's beautiful', 'That's ugly', and so on. And in so doing we forget that these different objects are institutions that entail an implicit definition of the appropriate habitus expected: just as understanding the hammer is using it to hammer with, so understanding the painting is kneeling down, lighting a candle or making an offering. A fifteenth-century canvas, whether religious or humanist, called forth a certain kind of response or belief which is no longer ours, and which corresponded to the universe of Marsilio Ficino and others who mingled astrology and astronomy, myth and religion, alchemy and chemistry, who believed in Saturn and at the same time saw him in the form of a monk. A brilliant book by Seznec on the survival of the ancient gods reminds us of this.[31] He describes the sort of intermediate zone between antiquity and the modern period that we call the 'Renaissance', when ancient religions and Christianity mingled in a way that was not syncretism at all – syncretism is when different things are mingled – because the things themselves were really composite then: Saturn takes on the figure of a bearded little monk. In this case, the appropriate effect, what was needed to understand the picture, was to have the kind of complicated mind that tried to read into Plato a form of spiritualised Christianity. Let us imagine another picture: a picture in the international Gothic style invited its viewers to kneel before its gold, which was a different response.

You may feel that what I am saying here is relatively unimportant or even wonder why I bother to make this kind of commentary at all. Firstly, because it can act as a kind of paradigm of the error that I mentioned just now. The baggage we carry is a sort of automatic aesthetic response in the form of a credo: it is to stop, stand and linger in front of a work of art, to take time and trouble to contemplate and decipher it, to find in the catalogue what is represented by something like a serpent, which is in fact a banner inscribed with the words of the Annunciation.[32] Taking all this trouble suggests an ascetic attitude supposing a form of belief, a belief that endows the work of art with a certain status – considering our possible responses to a work of art, we could indulge in variations on a theme of Austin. Believing in the value of a picture is to adopt the aesthetic attitude solicited by the picture – which is neither to kneel down (which would be ridiculous or crazy) nor to pray. This analysis of the aesthetic disposition as institution obviously applies to a certain kind of work. When an educated person's habitus encounters an object that does not solicit their habitus, these are two mismatching halves which are not made to be stuck together as a whole. It is as if we had a red half and a blue half. Each half lacks its other half. A Siennese painter such as Simone Martini expecting the habitus of a believer wanting to pray finds itself confronted with a Parisian aesthete; the Parisian aesthete finds himself confronted with an object expecting him to kneel down before it. And yet they connect, without realising what is happening.

The epistemocentric perversion,[33] the archetypal scholarly error, can be destroyed only by a twofold analysis. To understand the aesthetic habitus, we have to study the field where this habitus is produced: for example, the habitus that I am likely to bring to Simone Martini is the product of museums. I recently read a very fine analysis by an art historian who showed how Goethe felt the shock of pure art in the Dresden gallery which was in fact the leading museum available to the educated man of his times. The existence of works of art uprooted from the social environment where they could function as ritual objects or exotic curios is what made possible and necessary the aesthetic response that consists in looking at a work in itself and for itself, without trying to attribute a function to it. On the one hand, the aesthetic habitus is the product of a whole nexus of things and institutions (the museum, the existence of a tradition of art criticism directed at reading the work in itself and for itself, and so on) and, on the other hand, the work to which this disposition is wrongly applied is itself connected with a whole set of conditions that produced the appropriate habitus in its time. I refer you to the work by Baxandall that completely revised the way we perceived Quattrocento painting, using an argument similar to mine.[34] Baxandall, for example, points out the detail that the two main colours used to enhance Quattrocentro painting are not the red and yellow we imagined, but blue and gold, because the blue was ultramarine, which was extremely expensive, and gold by definition was very costly. The artist who wanted to give his sponsor value for money would employ a lot of blue and gold, and he used a lot of blue when he wanted to draw attention to a gesture, such as that of St John the Baptist blessing someone. When we have lost touch with the sort of pragmatic knowledge that artists deploy in their work, our readings are quite inadequate.

On a deeper level, I was recently reading a classic text by Gernet on the use of precious metals, 'La notion mythique de la valeur en Grèce', in a collective work entitled *Anthropologie de la Grèce antique*. Gernet wrote: 'There is a quality of a religious order that attaches to the precious object in general', and, much more significantly: 'It is not only because an object has a religious function that it has value, it is because it is precious that it may become an object of consecration.'[35] In other words, we should not react with surprise when we look at a certain kind of painting enhanced with gold leaf, saying: 'How strange that painters continued to use gold to structure their backgrounds when Masaccio had already achieved a revolution in painting.' If there is a certain logic behind the use of certain materials, I believe that it is partly explicable as a search to produce an effect on the spectator, and this search implies anticipation of the encounter with a habitus that will enable the effect to materialise. The precious character of the objects has the effect of imposing value, which may be one dimension of the religious effect. Thus a certain number of works designed to house relics acquired the same form as the relic that they enclosed and enshrined; these works were encrusted with gemstones that were intended to be visibly as precious as the object that they contained. This effect becomes absolutely incomprehensible if we subject a complex reality to a purely aesthetic gaze.

To sum up. It is very difficult to undertake a concrete analysis in this sort of situation, but at least I will have tried ... If we are aware that a scholarly approach to the object is not the approach originally solicited by the object, we can find in the study of the material nature of the object clues to the habitus to which it did relate: for example, a reliquary encrusted with precious gemstones or a halo worked in gold and bearing the name of a saint are pragmatic indications where the craftsman has expressed consciously or unconsciously a definition of the appropriate habitus required. We can find the right habitus if we look for it within the work, but also in official documents or eye-witness accounts. In the case of reading for example, Roger Chartier has remarked that, when classical or picaresque novels moved from the learned world out into the world of the 'Bibliothèque bleue', thus involving a wider public, the paragraphs became shorter, being reduced from three pages to ten lines.[36] Here we have a minor indication of this pragmatics of writing which might pass unnoticed: the division into shorter paragraphs welcomes a reader with a shorter and less sustained span of attention. Conversely, there is a rhetoric of the use of the paragraph: writing very long paragraphs suggests the presence of a powerful current of thought; it expresses the breadth, width and magnitude of thought – in Sartre's *Being and Nothingness* there are hardly any paragraphs . . . You could analyse reading in the same way: if you keep in mind the fact that the object of the reading is itself designed to function in relation to a habitus, you can find in the object a quantity of signs indicating how it attempts to organise or satisfy the habitus in advance – for example, the use of underlining, italics, capitals, and the like.

I don't know whether this rather roundabout example will have had the effect that I intended: sadly, I feel certain that I have missed the target. In fact, one of the things that I have been trying to say today is that cultural objects in their material form, reduced to their physical dimensions, are mutilated objects that can be adequately understood only if we reconstitute them as they were intended: they are objects awaiting recovery and revival; they harbour expectations of fulfilment. Rather than leave this resuscitation to chance and allow an unfettered scholarly habitus to appropriate objects which invited a different habitus, it is important to maintain a self-conscious awareness of the natures of the scholarly habitus and the practical habitus, in order to make room for a social history of the various habitus of reading books, of perceiving works of art, of economic behaviour and so forth.

Programme of future lectures and questions from the audience

I shall leave it there for the time being. I simply wanted to use this little schema to show you how my lectures are going to develop. You see the main outlines of the plan, which may of course be subject to change. After a synoptic account of what seems to me to be the proper object of social science (one that exists as an institution in two forms, objectification and incorporation, as well as in the relation between these two forms), I shall first of all examine the theoretical functions of the notion of habitus: why we need to speak of the habitus in order to explain social practices, and how this enables us to avoid a certain number of scientific errors and difficulties. Then I shall go on to examine the notion of the field more systematically. I shall study it first as a field of forces, more precisely as a field of possible forces

– that is, as a physical state; it will function as a field as long as it functions without being constituted as a field perceived by a habitus. I shall describe the field as a space of positions exercising constraints on any agent entering this space, taking as examples a certain number of fields, such as the *grandes écoles*, journalism, labour relations and disputes. Then I shall proceed to examine the relations between the notion of field and the notion of capital, two relatively interchangeable notions that I shall attempt to elucidate, and then the problems posed by the homologies of structure between different fields. Later I shall go on to examine the field, no longer as a field of forces but as a field of action and a field of struggle. I shall conclude with the problems of the symbolic and symbolic struggles: when the field becomes an object of knowledge for a habitus, it becomes a stake in symbolic struggles. I shall return to a certain number of the themes that I broached last year, but perhaps in more detail.

During the interval[37] I was asked two questions. I have completely forgotten to reply – do forgive me. I shall not reply immediately, but I shall announce them so that you can think about them yourselves: 'Is an indigenous sociology possible?' This is a problem to which I shall return, and I hope that my arguments have already reformulated the question. It is a question that commonly relates to countries studied by ethnologists – that is, often post-colonial countries – but it also affects our own societies. Can we take as the object of our study a social universe of which we are members or a field of which we are part? Can a teacher study the field of education or an office worker the field of administrative relations? I believe that I have partly answered this question in what I have been saying, but the fact that the question has arisen means that the answer is not so obvious, and, as it is a very common question, I want to reply. The second question is this: 'If we need to understand scholarly knowledge first before we can understand practical knowledge, how can we avoid an infinite regression? We have to understand the mind that is trying to understand the scholarly mind trying to understand the practical mind that . . . and so on ad infinitum.' This is a very good question, one to which I shall return,[38] but I must say straight away that it is a kind of false logical aporia that has to be solved in practical terms. Raising this question commits us to setting up the scientific procedures that can resolve this question in practice. I think that what I have been saying today about our relation to paintings, for example, gives us the beginnings of a solution.

Lecture of 19 October 1982

Sense without consciousness – The mechanistic error and the intellectualist error – The temptation of the sociologist as king – Intellectual obstacles to the knowledge of the gnoseologia inferior – The habitus as orthè doxa

I would like now briefly to resume the main drift of what I was arguing last time and in so doing draw some first conclusions from the model represented by the diagram that I showed you. My reflections will be organised in three main phases: the first will be a consideration of the relation R1 of the schema – that is, the practical mode of knowledge and the logic of practice – as a preliminary to understanding how the social world works; the second phase will be a consideration of the field of forces and how it functions in terms of a physicalist logic; the third phase will consider the field as a field of action by reintroducing both the relation R1 and the relation with the habitus. First of all, then, I shall return to what I see as a precondition for an adequate knowledge of the logic specific to practice, and then, secondly, I shall review the theory of what I call the habitus as the basis of this practical knowledge.

Sense without consciousness

Without getting bogged down in methodological or epistemological preliminaries, I would like to draw your attention straight away to the theoretical function of introducing the notion of the habitus. If I have not indulged overmuch in this sort of meditation on the concepts that I have been using, it is partly from a reaction to the very common tendency to produce a theoretical and legalistic metadiscourse instead of genuine knowledge. In my opinion a theoretical discourse can be justified only in so far as it is able to produce scientific results. When it takes itself as its own end, I think that it has only a decorative effect, or a legalistic function, insofar as it claims to establish itself as a norm not so much for the speaker's discourse as for the discourse of others. The attraction of what we call epistemology lies very often no doubt in the fact that, applying a kind of metadiscourse to science and to the scientific practice of others, it sets us up as legislators of scientific practice. If the social sciences were to continue to spend their time looking at themselves in the mirror, as they have done so often, they would make very little progress, and this is what has often led me to avoid this kind of reflection. I am saying this because I am afraid that I may have excited that reaction among some of you. In the prehistory of the social sciences there was a kind of fascination with a certain number of problems inherited from philosophy, in the negative sense of the term, with depressing examination question-type topics 'on the sciences of man and nature', 'explain and understand . . .', or 'is there something specific to the human sciences?' All these discussions of the relation to the social world, which can have an important function in teaching – you have to teach something – and also in young people's discussion of the social world, should I think be shunned by scientific discourse. I don't think that this is some kind of positivist reaction. I am simply mentioning these debates in order to dismiss them. This is a particular case of the paradox of culture that I have already mentioned: the principal function of culture is to enable us to dismiss a certain number of problems bequeathed by cultural tradition. You need culture to be able to dismiss culture. If I return to the notion of the habitus, it is essentially to get our bearings in a navigational sense to try to situate this concept in a space of concepts where it functions *nolens volens*, and to try to define my theoretical position in a space of differences as accurately as possible.

Why is a science of practical knowledge necessary and why is it difficult? Why has it not been achieved earlier if it is as indispensable as I think it is? If I consider this knowledge to be indispensable, it is in order to avoid the very common error that I pointed out last week, which consists in projecting into the 'minds' of agents a representation of their practices which is that of the scholarly subject who is studying them (I shall give examples relating to economic theory, which is no doubt one of the most typical examples of the error of projecting into the action of the active agent the theory of the scientific subject).[1] This preliminary reflection is difficult and at the same time indispensable, because the theoretical alternatives that confront us are such that we always have the feeling that we cannot avoid one of the terms of the alternative without falling into the other. To take a simple example: if, for example, in a theory of power, or more generally a theory of the social world, we undertake to exclude the mechanistic vision according to which power relations would be pure relations of force, we find ourselves almost inevitably driven by unconscious mechanisms to adopt the logical alternative of a subjectivist theory, a theory of consciousness; having rejected a theory of power relations as relations of force, we fall almost inevitably into a theory of power relations as relations of complicity between the dominated subject and those who dominate, as if power supposed the conscious complicity of the dominated. I believe that this example of alternatives should oblige us to reflect on the nature of our knowledge of the social world.

The central idea that I would first like to develop is that there may be knowledge and meaning without consciousness. This is an extremely simple proposition, but I want to elaborate it at some length. Saying that the social world is a place of acts of knowledge, that social subjects know the social world and act in it knowing full well, so to speak, what they are doing, that they are orientated by their sense of practice and the social world in terms of which they devise their practices, that they are orientated by meanings that are not necessarily ends, does not imply at all that they are subjects conscious of such meanings and acts of cognition. I think that this apparent paradox stems from the fact that we live in a dualist tradition, more specifically the Cartesian tradition. I refer you for instance to what Husserl puts very clearly in *The Crisis of European Sciences*: we are so imbued with the dualism of consciousness and mechanism that we cannot think outside one or the other – that is, we expect human actions either to be determined by causes (an economic action will be determined by a certain number of economic or physical causes) or to be accomplished deliberately – that is, by a conscious act (by the rational calculation of an agent whose perfect knowledge of the space he is acting in matches that of the scholar claiming to know it).[2] I think that this is a fatal alternative, and if I draw your attention to it so forcefully it is because, firstly, it is important to keep our minds focused on what we need to transcend and, secondly, we need to understand that, if we do transcend it, as I believe I have done with the notion of the habitus, we will be subject to criticism by people who have remained within these alternatives and consider what I see as transcendence to be mere contradiction.

This is roughly what I intend to argue, and I shall now start to do so in greater detail.

The mechanistic error and the intellectualist error

We can always navigate between two positions that seem erroneous to me – I use the term 'error' because it seems useful: on the one hand, the mechanistic error, which consists in forgetting the existence of a mode of knowledge whereby human actions are guided by considerations of meaning, and therefore reducing actions to the product of mechanistic determinism, and, on the other hand, what we might call the intellectualist error, which consists in replacing the truth of the practical relations between social agents and the social world with the relation between the scholar and the social world – the error that I illustrated last time.

For an archetypal illustration of this error, I refer you to Sartre's portrait of the café waiter – I shall not comment on it but leave the commentary up to you – for I find it exemplary of this kind of amalgam or confusion of scholarly consciousness with everyday consciousness. I hesitate to read it because, as much as it is psychologically easy to criticise a text when one is sitting at one's desk and addressing a kind of theoretical adversary, so it is embarrassing to criticise them, especially if it is someone we admire, in a public monologue exploiting our position of authority. But I do so nonetheless because I find the example highly significant and because I often use Sartre. He is an admirable example, because he has a kind of logical force which leads him to push an error to its logical extreme. This is what Sartre writes:

> In vain do I fulfil the functions of a café waiter. I can be he only in the neutralized mode, as the actor is Hamlet, by mechanically making the *typical gestures* of my state and by aiming at myself as an imaginary café waiter through those gestures taken as an *analagon*. What I attempt to realize is a being-in-itself of a café waiter, as if it were not in my power to confer value and urgency upon my duties and the rights of my position, as if it were not my free choice to get up at five o'clock or to remain in bed, even though it meant getting fired and risk losing my job. As if from the very fact that I sustain this role in existence I did not transcend it on every side, as if I did not constitute myself as one *beyond* my condition. Yet there is no doubt that I *am* in a sense a café waiter – otherwise could I not just as well call myself a diplomat or a reporter?[3]

And so it continues. The absurdity of this speech may not strike you and did not always strike me – I first read it in another age. It lies in the fact that it amalgamates in the imaginary mind of the waiter the vision of a waiter engaged in action and asking no questions, who has the habitus of a waiter and can only think the thoughts of a waiter, who is not deliberately imitating anyone but is doing what he has always seen other waiters doing on the stage of the café, with the consciousness of the watchful subject constituting itself as a free subject of the meanings that he articulates and in so doing conjures up fantasies of liberation from the role of the café waiter, although he constantly relapses into bad faith and rejects this. It would be gratuitously cruel to continue with this, but I must insist on the paradoxical parallel between this demonstration and the subject of economic theory: *Homo economicus*, like Sartre's café waiter, is an active subject containing within his head the view of the scholar who is watching him act – or, rather, thinking his actions through as if he were being watched by someone else. Now that I have pointed out this error, you will find it everywhere: scientific discourse is full of it, largely because it is easier to write like that.

One of the difficulties with the argument that I am proposing is that it obliges us to call into question a certain number of automatisms of everyday discourse: we speak of the social world spontaneously in these terms. To avoid this kind of amalgam of the two relations to the social world that I distinguished last week in my schema – relation R0 and relation R1 – we have to conduct at one and the same time a science of practical knowledge and a science of scholarly knowledge that is not practical knowledge. In other words, scholarly knowledge must be aware that it is the knowledge of a knowledge that is not scholarly knowledge. This is something I want to emphasise: scientific theory supposes a theory of practice as non-theory, the expression 'theory of practice' seeming to be a contradiction in terms. In fact this is not easy, primarily for social reasons – which I shall mention briefly – but also for intellectual reasons, because of the contradiction that I have indicated.

When we are preparing the ground for an argument that seems sometimes almost too obvious and yet seems plagued with extreme difficulty, it is helpful to be able to draw support from the great authors who can help to authorise us and create belief in our authority. I want to read you some words by Husserl in *The Crisis of European Sciences* (the other function of the Husserl and the Sartre that I read out is to accustom you to accept a difficult language so that afterwards you will appreciate mine all the more [*laughter*], as long as you accept that my arguments merit as much effort as theirs, which is not a foregone conclusion). Husserl writes: 'What is actually first is the "merely subjective-relative" intuition of prescientific world-life. For us, to be sure' (the 'for us' is interesting; he doesn't say who 'we' are, but I

hope to explain) 'this "merely" has, as an old inheritance, the disdain-
ful colouring of the *doxa*.' (I was very pleased to read this judgement
of Husserl's: the *doxa* is an old tradition that goes back to Plato and
the Sophists; it is belief, opinion or representation, it is what is self-
evident.) 'In prescientific life itself, of course, it has nothing of this'
(which means that when you live within the *doxa* you do not despise
it); 'there it is a realm of good verification and, based on this, of well-
verified predicative cognitions and of truths which are just as secure as
is necessary for the practical projects of life that determine their sense.'[4]

This text forms a programme for what I shall be mapping out, by
giving as an object for phenomenology the analysis of the original
experience of the social world, the experience that is the foundation of
all scientific experimentation. This return to origins is made difficult
by the contempt in which it is held by tradition, which Husserl calls
the *doxa* and which is present both in philosophy – in the opposition
between *doxa* and *episteme*, which is noble and has to be wrested
from the *doxa* – and in the scientific tradition: science establishes itself
against primary error – you know Bachelard's arguments against
primary knowledge and primary error.[5] In fact, Husserl says throughout *The Crisis* that this science is itself extremely difficult, because it
supposes a break with all our habitual dispositions of thought, with
the Cartesian mode of thought, as I said just now. And nobody wants
to do it, because it is looked down on. It is despised because it entails
mobilising that kind of knowledge par excellence, the *episteme*, in
order to understand something that is its negation, the *doxa*: how can
we undertake an *episteme* of the *doxa*? What Husserl proposes is a kind
of paradox: you have to be quite mad and determined to transgress
social taboos – which is what is at stake – to set yourself the goal of
understanding the *doxa*, when the *episteme* was based on despising it
in the first place.

Writing on aesthetics, Baumgarten spoke of a *gnoseologia inferior*,[6]
and I find that this notion is a very good label for the schema that I am
going to try to expound. What I intend to establish is an inferior gnoseology, the gnoseology of a world of inferior knowledge, which goes
against the grain of the whole gnoseological tradition and the whole
tradition of the philosophy of knowledge. For example, we could take
Cassirer's arguments on the seventeenth and eighteenth centuries from
his *Philosophy of the Enlightenment*: the whole philosophical tradition,
which envisaged itself as a reflection on knowledge, especially that
knowledge par excellence that is scientific knowledge, and set its goal
as being able to think in the image of God. For in the last analysis
the proper thinker is the one who adopts a mode of knowledge which

has nothing to envy of divine understanding. I do no more than para-phrase Cassirer.[7] For Descartes, Spinoza or Leibniz, philosophy, in what I see as its essential aspect, epistemology, aims to provide human understanding with a method of access to a divine kind of thinking. There are more obvious examples in Spinoza, but the most significant example, and the one closest to the issues that I want to discuss today, is in Leibniz, who, in moving from analytical geometry – which already had the virtue, as he observed, of freeing the human mind from servi-tude to images and figures – to infinitesimal calculus, had the impres-sion that he was endowing human knowledge with a power absolutely analogous to that of divine knowledge which comprehends in practice the whole value of $\sqrt{2}$ and which, in so doing, can be seen to transcend the limits of human finitude. We might here relate all of Leibniz's remarks on the differential that encloses the whole curve and in a way allows human knowledge to transcend its temporal limits.[8] I shall obvi-ously not develop this point, but I mention it because one of the mys-teries of practical knowledge is precisely that it is completely embroiled in the temporal, and in order to know it you have to recognise its temporal nature through and through.

I shall now take a well-known example from the anthropological analysis of the gift. I shall merely indicate it here without developing it; I leave you to do that for yourselves. It seems to me that, if anthro-pological theory from Mauss to Lévi-Strauss has somehow missed something in the theory of the gift,[9] it is because the scholars, and Lévi-Strauss in particular, had the aim of reducing something sequen-tial to an instantaneous model, thus losing the specificity of the gift, which is that an interval must intervene; if you immediately return the same thing that you have received, or something different but equiva-lent, you destroy what constitutes the logic of the gift, the fact that it unfolds over time.[10] Here is an example that shows us the difference between the things of logic and the logic of things, as Marx said:[11] when the exchange of gifts is reduced to its logical formula, the model somehow destroys what it describes. Lévi-Strauss's model, which renders the gift and the counter-gift instantaneous, makes it clear that there is no gift without a counter-gift, which is very important, but we need to defend a theory of practical logic that is not the same as logical logic, for it introduces something that logical logic destroys – that is, the sequence of events. Lévi-Strauss's model is true on condition that we acknowledge that it is a theoretical model that confronts a model whose practice follows a different logic. Even if the gift does imply a counter-gift, it is experienced at the moment when it is given as being a one-way gesture, and, even if the counter-gift is a response to the gift, it is seen at the moment when it is made as a generous gesture and not as a response to the initial gift. What allows this kind of untruth or bad faith to exist is the interval of time introduced by agreement between the donor and the receiver, and there is a sort of complicity, an interplay of bad faith shared: for it to function, you have to pretend not to recognise the counter-gift as such.[12] My analysis is based on a very simple precept: the models designed to understand reality are in danger of destroying the reality that they describe unless we realise that a model is not the same thing as reality.

If I insist on this sort of theoretical hubris of the great Cartesians, on the pan-logical ambition of the great rationalist philosophers and their ambition to be masters of time – the example of infinitesimal calculus is typical – it is because this ambition seems to me to be present in the social sciences too, in particular in the structuralist tradition, and that it is in danger of producing in every domain effects analogous to the one I showed in the case of the gift. This mode of thinking after the manner of God, so to speak – that is, in terms of eternity, ignoring the existence of time – seems obviously linked to the philosophical venture, and it comes to fruition in . . . but here I hesitate, because you might find it odd to hear me launching into a rather cavalier history of philosophy to suit the issues that interest me. It would not be without interest, but the rather hasty nature of my comments on the philosophers might invite mockery and would in any case not add much to what I am trying to say. Anyway, you can develop my argument in your minds.

The temptation of the sociologist as king

Without wishing to enter into too much detail, I would like now to show how this kind of ambition to have a God-like view of the world and the social world finds its fulfilment in the Hegelian tradition. (You are bound to say that everyone knows this, it's obvious. But it is still important to take issue with these archetypal achievements: for me, one of the functions of the great philosophies is that they provide an extremely coherent development of tendencies of the human mind that are at work every day, and there is a Hegelian type of tendency at work all the time in the research of social scientists. If I linger over Hegel, it is not in order to make a philosophical speech in honour of a great writer; it is to find a historical document that contains the accomplished form of a tendency to err, the exemplary expression of a paradigmatic error in the social sciences. That may appear arrogant, but it is at the same

time very modest [*laughter*] ... No, it is true; if I didn't say that, I
would not be able to speak after saying what I have to say on someone
of that stature.)

It has been said, but without drawing all the conclusions – and sometimes we have to lay it on thick if we want to draw all the conclusions
– that the social sciences are still haunted by the temptation, to which
I briefly referred, to be the philosopher-as-God, who in the case of the
social sciences takes the form of the temptation to be the sociologist-
as-omnipotent-king acting through representation. This temptation
seems to me to be incarnated in Hegel's thought, as I shall summarise
it. (I offer my excuses to any committed Hegelians of strict allegiance:
since I shall certainly coin some barbarous phrases, let me say in my
defence that I am constructing a Hegel to suit the needs of my demonstration.) I think that Hegel gives systematic expression to a social
tendency that we might call technocratic. In fact, it's a sort of ... but
I struggle to express myself; I am trying to condense the argument
too much ... When for example in the *Philosophy of History* Hegel
describes history as the place of the development of the absolute
subject, different from ordinary human subjects, whether in the case
of ordinary individuals, historical heroes, or collective subjects such
as the State as nation or as world,[13] he is describing something that is
still at work in the social unconscious of those who claim to rule in the
name of science. I think that in any sociologist, and *a fortiori* in the
present state of the division of scientific labour, there is a dormant little
Hegel nourishing the ambition to confront the partial knowledge of
individuals with his absolute knowledge of all things. You can find all
this in Samuelson's manuals[14] or the works of Durkheim, who explains
brilliantly – as if he were transcribing Spinoza – how each individual
subject, driven by passion, struggles in the dark to follow his own
petty, personal interests, whereas the scholar – no doubt the sociologist
– in the name of science as universal, surveys these partial glimpses
of knowledge from on high and perceives them as perspectives which
he alone is able to unify totally.[15] The sociologist, as scholar who has
acceded to 'knowledge of the third kind',[16] attains the 'geometral', the
geometric point of convergence of all perspectives,[17] and from there
he can understand the limits of these individual parcels of knowledge.

We can find in Hegel this description of the limits that circumscribe
both the content and the consequences of the acts of any historical
subject. We can find in *Lessons in the Philosophy of History* a description of what I shall call the logic of practice, but it is strictly negative,
since practical logic is defined by its complete lack of this total unification, which remains the privilege or the monopoly of the scholar. The

total scholar is precisely the norm from whose viewpoint all individual sets of knowledge appear to be mutilated. The limits of an individual's knowledge, as he sees it, derive from the natural and economic frame of their activities – sociologists, and that includes me, think that the limits of the validity of the knowledge that individual social subjects may have of the social world depend on their position in the social world and on the determinisms linked to their specific condition – their cultural horizon, the mutual dependency of the individuals at a given moment, and the mutual dependency of the social agents over a period of time. These are by and large the factors cited by Hegel, and consequently what he calls the 'subjective liberty' of the individual agent is strictly limited both as regards their real possibilities for action and for self-consciousness or self-knowledge. But if the course of History is rational, given our increasing control over nature, this rationality cannot be attributed to any one particular subjectivity. There is then a point where the rational transcends the individual, and that is where the thinker is situated. You see now how the philosopher and the sociologist, who are so often seen as opposites, unconsciously play the same part; and if the young are so fascinated by the sociologist, it is because his role is that of God or the king, with an overview of all individual minds. This is the role that philosophy has always assumed, and sociology is merely its modern form.

To continue with the State – for the problem of the State and the State philosopher is a crucial one – Hegel sees the State as a realisation of the 'objective spirit' – that is, one of the results of that infinity of individual actions which do not possess their own truth and which find integration at a level superior to individual minds, where the philosopher will be able to grasp them. The State then is one of those realisations of the objective spirit that is the result of all those individualities. Rosanvallon has quite rightly compared Hegel's model to the invisible hand beloved of economists;[18] there is in the social world a kind of purpose that no one person can define and that it is the philosopher's duty to discover. It is astonishing to find Hegel opposed to economic liberalism, when a study of his reading has clearly shown that he borrowed one of his essential themes, the 'ruse of Reason', from the economic tradition. His model transcribes in another language this tradition, according to which the sum of all the individual actions acquires an objective significance irreducible to the individual intentions. For any of you who think that I have gone astray in discussing philosophy, I must repeat that all this is constantly present in the arguments of philosophers, sociologists and economists: what I am investigating with the help of the history of philosophy is the epistemological unconscious shared by the specialists in the human sciences, and more generally by all social subjects, because everyone today is more or less steeped in the human sciences, which have spread far beyond the specialists. The State, then, is the realisation of the objective spirit, and in it the unilateral and the abstract views of the historical situation combine and are integrated in a complex historical process that transcends the intentions, projects and minds of the agents – whether prince or bureaucrat, noble or bourgeois. This kind of objective significance transcending individual intentions endows the behaviour of the individual with an objective significance irreducible to any intentionally given meaning.

This is where we find the State bureaucracy and the technocracy that I mentioned in rather cavalier fashion at the start of this lecture: the State bureaucracy represents the incarnation of this universal vision and universal will. It is the site, within the social world itself, where the integration of personal interests, blind to each other and therefore to themselves, is realised. It provides the prince with the knowledge of the general principles and particular circumstances of each case, the range of reasonable choices and the comparison of the consequences of each action. There is an absolutely brilliant passage in *Outlines of the Philosophy of Right*: 'It is wrong . . . to demand objective qualities in a monarch; he has only to say "yes" and dot the "i".'[19] According to this very fine text, the prince ultimately does no more than sign: he ratifies and signs the dossiers prepared by the bureaucrats.

This is a most interesting analysis. We could find almost literally the same argument in Weber, who I think has laicised many of Hegel's arguments, which means that I may cite Weber's excellent 'Science as a vocation', which tends to be considered as the founding act of secular sociology, with its scholar who renounces politics. When Weber says that the scholar must offer clear knowledge of the compatibility of different ends, and of the means with the ends, and that the rest is up to the politician to decide,[20] I think that this is typically Hegelian. Hegel says that the State bureaucracy provides the prince with the knowledge of the general principles and the particular circumstances of each case, the range of reasonable choices and a comparison of the consequences of each action. But, when Weber formulates these ideas, we see the birth of a neutral and objective science, of scientific truth, and so on. As I have often said, subjects and fantasies, especially political and sexual, use euphemism in order to cheat the censor. The political fantasy of the philosopher-king is still alive today but is not expressed naïvely; it finds expression in euphemised and disguised form, and Weber was already subject to

stronger censorship than Hegel. Today you would find this euphemisation operating to an even higher degree.

This is why it is important to return to the sources with an exemplary
case, an equivalent to what that of Dora was for Freud,[21] where the
fantasy expresses itself pure and unalloyed. The bureaucracy, in this
logic, is the universal class – which in Marx will become the proletariat
– and this schema of the universal class is most important. At the other
extreme from the unhappy consciousness that feels alienated from its
activity and the world as a whole we find the satisfied consciousness
that an adequate knowledge of the world procures. This reminds us of
Spinoza: it is the satisfied consciousness of the bureaucrat who understands and accepts the world as his own. The bureaucrat is a kind of
Stoic sage who knows the State and the social world well enough to
accept them and appropriate them. The State, then, is the universal
aspect of civil society developed and made explicit – and for anyone
who thinks that I am inventing my own Hegel, I refer you to *The
Philosophy of Right*, §§182, 187 and 249. I have to point out, however,
since I have presented him as a unanimist and proposing a unanimist
vision of the State, that Hegel does insist on the duality of civil society
and the State. The State imposes two types of action: on the one
hand, to make explicit the latent universalism of civil society, riven by
antagonisms which are to be transcended in universal reconciliation,
and, on the other hand, to keep in check the particularism inherent in
the divisions of civil society.

To return to the pristine Hegelian model: the State is an object
that contains its own development, and the last stage of this development, which is the Concept constituted by the philosopher acting as
midwife for the State, includes the full materialisation of its potential
and the full appropriation by philosophical discourse – that is, by the
philosopher – of the inherent potential of the State. There is then an
essential relation between the State and the philosopher, between the
bureaucrat and the philosopher, the philosopher being, in a way, not
the prince's counsellor – that is quite a different role – but his assistant
in raising the consciousness – to use a currently fashionable term – of
the bureaucrat. If we reflect on how the labour of domination is divided
today, it is clear that this particular role is perfectly designed for the
sociologist, who is constantly invited to enter into contracts where he
is the one who provides the State administrator with his knowledge of
reality and his practical mastery of reality. The philosopher as midwife
to History is then the advisor of the bureaucrat, helping him to fulfil his
function as agent of the universal, transcending antagonistic individual
interests. He it is who reveals and raises to the level of Concept and

language the objective significance that the mere agent accomplishes unwittingly.

I am tempted to say that Marx is the same, *mutatis mutandis*; I had intended to develop this, but I have decided not to, because the transition to Marx is perfectly simple, even if it seems surprising. What I wanted to show with the paradigm of Hegel is the idea that the philosopher or the sociologist, when he acts the part of the philosopher-king, is as far as anyone could be from understanding individual actions and the logic of individual actions. In setting himself up as the thinker of the universal, he characterises these actions and their logic as deprived both of the knowledge of the universal and, what is worse, of the knowledge of that privation. Individual agents might believe that they could have universal knowledge if the philosophers were not there to tell them how individualistic and perspectival their vision of the social world was, and to remind them that their knowledge is purely and simply *doxa*, that they need to rethink completely what the nature of the social world is. The enquiry would not be easy, but I think that we could use certain types of interview technique to discover how much the sociologists' representation of their social function owes to this vision, to different degrees according to their position in the scientific field: the sociologist is someone who by profession feels that he has a right to define ordinary social subjects as deprived of knowledge of the social world and the knowledge of their privation. We might study the social usage of the word 'ideology' according to this logic, just as we might take Durkheim's use of the notion of spontaneous sociology or, to take a recent example, the uses in epistemology of the notion of a 'divide' – which is not the same thing as Bachelard's 'epistemological break'. The notion of the 'divide' – which is a divide between the sacred and the profane, between the holders of universal, therefore sacred, knowledge and the profane public of non-specialists – is a notion that has had an eminent social success, I believe, because it has incarnated that rather immature claim inherent in the scientific ambition, the claim to distance oneself from mere mortals and set oneself up as a sage.[22]

I have taken some time to elaborate this topic because it seems to me important to understand the difficulty of the mental gymnastics that constitute a conversion – you have to perform a somersault – and how far it is paradoxical to set social science the task of getting to know an inferior science that everything leads us to dismiss as epistemological obstacle, obscurity, *doxa*, spontaneous sociology, 'mistress of error and falsehood'.[23] It is the equivalent of the imagination for the philosophers of ancient Athens; it is hell and damnation. A young sociologist, encouraged by his master, feels immediately at ease with this kind of professional pride of a caste ('We are not naïve people who trust their intuition to understand the social world: we have questionnaires, techniques, concepts, classic authors, and so on'). If I labour this point so heavily, it is because, in a scientific exposition like this, there is the argument itself but also the force of persuasion, and, if I think that you have all followed and understood the argument, I am not sure that you have all been persuaded. So it is very consciously and intentionally that I say the same thing in several different ways, in the hope that one or other of these approaches will strike home and that everyone will feel implicated, because, in this matter, everyone, including myself, is implicated. This feeling of being king makes it very difficult to understand the knowledge of the social world that mere mortals may have.

Intellectual obstacles to the knowledge of the *gnoseologia inferior*

Having pointed out the social obstacles, I shall now attempt to indicate the specifically intellectual obstacles to practical knowledge. The intention of my argument is to say that there is room for this kind of common science to become a real science, although for conventional science it is nothing but a waste product. My objective is not exactly to say that all we need to do is retrieve and recycle the knowledge of the social world that the ordinary social subject has, but I do believe that it is a perfectly valid project to make a systematic trawl of spontaneous sociology, along with its instruments and concepts; in proverbs, sayings, and ready-made expressions there is a whole repertoire of social knowledge – actually very different according to social class – which functions as an instrument of knowledge for the purposes of practice. But that is not what I had in mind. Nor is it my intention to disqualify scholarly knowledge in favour of a populist rehabilitation of profane systems of knowledge. Perhaps I am mistaken, but my intention is to insert into the realm of scholarly knowledge both a knowledge of the limits of scholarly knowledge and a knowledge of the specific logic of non-scholarly knowledge. And that in order to be even more scholarly.

(I am putting these arguments in very simple terms because the communication of the results of sociological research is open to so many misunderstandings and encounters many extremely naïve objections. For example, you need to know that there are agents whose interest leads them spontaneously to seek the disqualification of scholarly knowledge: if for example from the heights of my authorised professorial chair I were to say 'There is no such thing as social science', there would be a lot of happy people, especially those who claim to be sociologists and who would thus be relieved of an arduous task [*laughter*]. The social investment that we make in truths and propositions concerning the social world is a constant obstacle to the communication of the results of research in the social sciences, and if it often happens that I mention, or avoid mentioning, certain things, it is because I try to control and anticipate the possible interpretations of what I have to say. But I can never think of everything, and just now I nearly forgot to point out something that seems very obvious to me, which is that I have no intention of rehabilitating ordinary kinds of knowledge, or even to constitute them as objects of scientific contemplation; to rehabilitate them ethically and politically does not mean rehabilitating them scientifically.)

My argument is that an adequate science of the social world must comprehend and include a science of the mode of knowledge that social subjects put into practice in their everyday activities. It is then a gnoseology rather than a sociology. I emphasise this because I am afraid of being misunderstood. There are many social psychologists working on these topics who go and ask people directly how they recognise whether someone belongs to this or that class, or create situations where people are obliged to display their reactions in practice, and thus reveal through their behaviour the tacit criteria for their distinction. This is not my project. I do not intend to go and stop people in the street; rather, I intend to make a scientific study of practical knowledge, what Baumgarten, whom I have already mentioned, called *gnoseologia inferior* – that is, a science of knowledge that is inferior in the hierarchy of gnoseologies, because its object is inferior – this is the contempt that Husserl mentions. This science is difficult because it is paradoxical – there is *doxa* in the word paradoxical – from the fact that it contravenes the scientific *doxa* (for scholars too, we must remember, have their *doxa*), and, among the doxical propositions that haunt their thinking, there are hierarchies and, in particular, a hierarchy of disciplines.

(A simple parenthesis in passing: one of the most powerful explanatory principles in the histories of art, science or intellectual activity is the role played in the practices and representations of agents, scholars and artists by the representation, or scheme of classification, that they make of the various disciplines and activities. The history and sociology of science have established that great scientific progress is often made by transgressing these hierarchies: for example by bringing high intellectual ambition to bear on a topic considered unworthy.

Ben-David and Collins show this in a celebrated article on the beginnings of psychology and the discovery of psychoanalysis.[24] A certain
number of great scientific revolutions have been triggered by people of
considerable intellectual and cultural capital who brought their talents
to bear on extremely unpromising topics, subjects of contempt that
nobody wanted to study in case they got their hands dirty. I think it
is very important in understanding the histories of science and sociology to know that in every period there are things that you don't do,
not because they are pointless but because they are too easy, and that
self-respecting people cannot let themselves down by taking them on
– that is what I wanted to say about *gnoseologia inferior*. These things
that are commonly despised are those that are in social terms easy, as
people say of a piece of music or a woman: you have to have nothing
to lose to go down the route of these socially lost causes, although they
are very fertile scientific causes.)

To return to the specifically scientific difficulty: Alexander
Baumgarten, a disciple of Wolff in the eighteenth century, forged this
concept of *gnoseologia inferior* when speaking of aesthetics, which
from the viewpoint of classical rationalist philosophy is the terrain of
feeling, sensibility and knowledge of the senses – that is, things that
from the perspective of God's thought have no existence. Baumgarten
says more or less that divine knowledge ignores the world of the senses
and knows only the universe of laws. Briefly, God has no time for
aesthetics. The divine thinker's perfectly clear and distinct knowledge
always operates at the level of the whole sum of universal relations. In
this perspective there is no aesthetic language or perception. Alexander
Gottlieb Baumgarten, a disciple of Wolff, who was himself a disciple of
Leibniz, and steeped in this ultra-rationalist logic, wanted to establish
the possibility of a science of the obscure and the confused that would
be neither obscure nor confused. There is the whole paradox. I was
very pleased to discover this, because it is a very clear demonstration of
what I had been trying to do and the contradiction that I found myself
facing: aesthetic perception is a *perceptio confusa*, as Baumgarten
says, in that it apprehends totalities that are entirely determined and
organised according to a system which is not that of the concept. This
aesthetic knowledge, whose logic is not one of knowing, does have its
own logic, its *logos*, and for this reason is entitled to a special theory of
knowledge that I shall call *gnoseologia inferior*. So now you see what I
am getting at.

Moving on, I shall not develop the analogy, but we might reflect on
Merleau-Ponty's criticism of the intellectualist tradition, on the subject
of perception, and all his efforts to undertake a kind of *gnoseologia*

inferior in order to establish perception as a form of knowledge that is not merely a degraded form of scientific knowledge. In order to break with the intellectualist tradition according to which perception is an incipient scientific knowledge, Merleau-Ponty wanted to establish perception as a knowledge endowed with its own logic.

As part of the work of reflection needed to try to understand the logic of practical knowledge, our main theoretical guide is obviously phenomenology, taken from the tradition of Hegel, Merleau-Ponty and Alfred Schütz, a German phenomenologist who became American and inaugurated the phenomenological school in the United States.[25] I am going to launch into a parallel history of philosophy as I did with Hegel; historians of philosophy will again shudder, but, for the rest of you, what I have to say will be better than nothing: sociology uses phenomenology to support the work that it needs to undertake in order to recover the practical knowledge of the social world. Merleau-Ponty, in the lectures that he entitled 'The human sciences and phenomenology', tried to show that an appropriate definition of phenomenology could reconcile the Hegelian and the Husserlian meanings of the word. He said more or less that, where for Hegel phenomenology is an effort to record the practical experiences (of knowledge, but also of life and culture, and so on) of humanity as they have occurred in history, and provide explanations for them, for Husserl phenomenology claims to 'plunge into experience to reflect on it and produce a theory of the hidden reason of History'[26] – in a phrase that Hegel could have written. In this way Merleau-Ponty attempted to reconcile the two intentions in a conception of phenomenology that bases the premise of any knowledge of the social world on acquiring knowledge of our primary knowledge. This conception of phenomenology, which I would willingly adopt for myself, is currently embodied in sociology by interactionism (Goffman) and ethnomethodology.

By taking the Husserlian tradition a little further, this sociological tradition can make use of the comparative method as an instrument allowing it to get to the root of the phenomenological *epochè*. There is a well-known letter from Husserl to Lévy-Brühl, which is historically interesting for the problem at hand, where he says that ethnology ultimately allows us to get to the root of the variations of the imaginary.[27] A systematic use of the comparative method, drawing on ethnology or comparative history, can then help us to operate a kind of sociological 'reduction' in order to produce a kind of sociological eidetic (my notes sound rather frightening, but I am using Husserl's terminology) – that is, a science of the transhistorical principles characteristic of the mode of practical knowledge in its differences from the mode of theoretical knowledge. It seems clear that reconciling the two phenomenologies in this way provides a technique and a mode of thinking, strategies of knowing, but also provides knowledge, and, without going so far as to say that phenomenology has completed the work of gaining knowledge of practical knowledge, we can now draw conclusions from the work published by Schütz or Husserl.

The habitus as *orthè doxa*

I shall now attempt briefly to set out a certain number of simple propositions concerning this practical knowledge. I shall start with an important question for me, which is the relation between the 'active subject' – whom I shall call the 'agent' – and the social world. Let me comment straight away on the word 'agent': it is obviously neither an elegant literary word nor a word that is pleasant to use in a scientific report, but the alternatives are so loaded with implicit philosophies that it has its negative virtue. The word 'agent' is preferable to the word 'actor', which implies role-playing; and I have always avoided the word 'role' because it implies the logic of a plan and its execution: there would be a script and the actor would perform a role that he had learned by heart. There is a whole philosophy of history and action implied by the use of the words 'actor' and 'role'. The word 'subject', in its turn, obviously reintroduces the whole philosophy of consciousness. It leads us to say that 'social subjects' are the subjects of their actions and of knowledge of the social world and to make knowledge of the social world depend on a thetic act of cognition. In the word 'agent', there is both the word for action and a certain impersonality: when we speak of an 'agent of the State', we get the idea of a relatively replaceable person. Even if it lacks charm, the word 'agent' corresponds to a philosophy of history and action that I find closer to reality.

But if I say that social agents are neither subjects nor actors performing roles, what are they? Does it mean that we have to return to those kinds of individuals deprived of universal knowledge who act without understanding the truth of their actions, as Hegel and the whole Hegelian–Marxist tradition describes them? In other words, are they producers of an objective meaning that transcends them and escapes them? In fact, the word 'habitus' is there to say that they are a locus of intentions of meaning, of meaningful intentions of which they are not strictly speaking the subjects, because that is not how they see the goals of their action. Basically, what I have been driving at is this: the principal function of the habitus is to register the simple fact that, being the product of the incorporation of objective structures – as I showed in my schema earlier – the incorporated structures of the habitus generate practices that can adapt to the objective structures of the social world without being the product of an explicit intention to adapt. The concept of habitus then allows us to account for the paradox of purposiveness without an end – I mean this not at all in the Kantian sense[28] but in the sense of the paradox of purposiveness not subject to the condition of an intention.

Social agents are constantly engaged in actions which – as with any human action, I think – claim to be defined in terms of a language of intention, either with reference to an individual intention ('He did that in order to earn more money', 'He resigned in order to save his honour', and so on) or with reference to intentions transcending singular individuals – that is, with reference to objective significance, which the Marxist tradition calls their 'objective meaning'. Since the habitus is a set of dispositions, or patterns of the perception, assimilation and acquisition of objective structures and objective repetition – for example, everything that occurs in the social world in the guise of something statistically regular, such as the division between possible and impossible, between impossible, probable, certain, doubtful, and so on – we can understand that, when it functions like a little generator to invent or engender something, what it produces appears to have been produced on purpose in order to adapt to whatever it has adapted to – since it is in its very logic to adapt as far as possible to the structures within which it operates.

The habitus then seems to me to be an important concept because it accounts for the illusion of purposiveness and for one of the principal illusions in the social sciences, as I shall show in a moment. I shall attempt to show that the notion of habitus allows us to avoid two illusions: the illusion of an individual teleology – the subjective illusion that is central to utilitarian economics and philosophy – and the illusion of a collective teleology that is at the heart of Hegelian–Marxist tradition. The notion of the habitus defines a principle that generates thoughts, perceptions, actions and words. It seems to obey external promptings and thus to be inspired by a desire to adapt to intentions, whereas it does in fact mostly adapt spontaneously. I shall take a very paradoxical example, which may cause considerable misunderstanding, particularly with people who, following the tradition of subjective teleology, are used to thinking in terms of the logic of *Homo economicus*. One of the most successful forms of adaptation to the social space is achieved by people who take to this space like ducks to water and who therefore do not need a pocket calculator to find their way. The prime example is that of people who succeed in a universe because they are made for that universe and have been completely fashioned by it: it is the inheritor who, having lived and breathed the same atmosphere since the day he was born, succeeds in his actions without needing to calculate them, which procures for him, in addition to the benefit of success, the supplementary benefit of being disinterested.[29] This is, I think, a universal proposition: excellence is always associated with disinterest – that is, the fact of attaining formal accomplishment without seeming to try, as if as a bonus. This is a definition that I often provide. In every tradition excellence consists in playing with the rules of the game – that is, in fulfilling the rules of the game in a playful manner; and, to show that you have understood the rules of the game, you play with the rules while playing – that is, you transgress them gently to show that you can both respect them and transgress them, but you have chosen to respect them. I think that, if someone were to make a comparative study of definitions of human excellence in very different societies, they would come up with some interesting results. I am thinking for instance of the ancient Greek *arete*[30] or, in our own educational system, the opposition between knowledge and a free attitude towards learning [*savoir*]. This is to be understood in terms of the logic that I have indicated: excellence sanctions such a perfect match between incorporated structures and objective structures that social agents find themselves constantly adapted to their universe without ever needing to try, without ever making a mistake or ever giving the impression of having to make an effort to adjust or compensate or find their footing. That is a paradoxical example.

We have clearly left behind any idea of calculation. Here we may introduce an expression that I often use: 'it all looks as if' – skilful, excellent behaviour, which could not be better if it had been calculated to perfection, is all the better if it has not been calculated to perfection. This 'it all looks as if' reminds us that we are dealing with a philosophy that is neither one of mechanism nor one of consciousness, and one of the propositions that follows from my analysis is that the theory of practical knowledge commends us to preface every proposition on human behaviour with the expression: 'it all looks as if' – which immediately changes our understanding, as you will see in a moment. Everything looks as if behaviour were motivated by the search for the maximisation of symbolic, economic, cultural or other kinds of profit in whatever game the people are playing, always remembering that, almost without exception, the players' behaviour is not consciously motivated by this search.

Seen in the light of this logic, what becomes of action? It is obvious that engaging in social science – whether history, sociology, psychology, or the like – is to undertake a philosophy of history and action, a philosophy able to explain or predict the principles that generate the function of social agents. What is it that makes social agents act rather than do nothing? This is a very important question because it is not self-evident. Why do social agents act in some spaces but not in others? Why does something that moves agents to act in a determined space leave other social agents indifferent? Why, for example, does what motivates a teacher leave a banker indifferent? It is here that the notion of habitus becomes crucial. In our everyday lives, as what I have been saying suggests, a very considerable proportion of actions are of the type that I have described: they seem to be guided by aims that they intend to accomplish, whereas in fact they attain these ends without the intentions ever being formulated.

To make myself clear I shall refer to a text by Plato, which seems to me to put it very well – once again, I don't think that I am citing a reference merely because it shows culture. Plato speaks of the *orthè doxa*, which may be translated simply as 'right opinion'. And he says more or less that the most successful actions are opinions rather than judgements – Husserl said that this is what philosophy has always despised; the *doxa* is an anti-*episteme*, a lack of *episteme* – an absence of truth that happens to work: 'It is well-aimed conjecture [*orthè doxa*] which statesmen employ in upholding their countries' welfare. Their position in relation to knowledge is no different from that of prophets and tellers of oracles, who under divine inspiration utter many truths but have no knowledge of what they are saying'.[31] In other words, how does it come about that you can stumble across the truth, find yourself instructed by chance, without the knowledge of the truth being your motivating force?

Perhaps you think that I am playing with metaphysics, but for me this is one of the fundamental problems for the social sciences. What I call the habitus – or we might say the 'practical sense' – is the practical knowledge and mastery of the patterns of the social world that, without even organising these patterns in conceptual terms, allows our behaviour to adapt to these patterns and to be ascribed to these patterns as if they had been produced by them. I shall repeat it again because I think it is vital for our comprehension: the action thus defined is then not a mechanical response to *stimuli*, not the product of a direct causal determination, nor a praxis inspired by a conscious project or rational plan. It is not orientated towards a composed and calculated end, in the sense of a 'maximisation of profit'; the activities of our practical sense are part of the ordinary order of our ordinary existence. As Leibniz more or less said, 'we are automats in three quarters of our actions':[32] in three-quarters of our actions there is a sort of coincidence between the agents and the *agenda* (the things to be done) or the *dicenda* (the things to be said), between our incorporated history or structures and the objective structures. In my opinion this is what *orthè doxa* implies: a sort of 'stumbling across' the truth.

We could show that what I am doing at the moment partakes of this order to a considerable extent: a considerable, indeed enormous, part of what I do – and, since I am in the process of analysing my procedures, we can argue *a fortiori* – would be nothing without the presence of everyone here, without the present location, and so on. A large part of what is being enacted here, of the events taking place here, is an encounter between a whole series of things, including institutions that are repositories of a long history: the history of the Collège de France and the histories of each one of us, the formation of a habitus that we have to trace back over several generations to understand. (That is one of the analyses that I shall censor, out of discretion; I wanted to show you that I never forget that I am myself involved in my narrative, and at the same time I am intimidated by the embarrassment of taking myself as object.) To understand what is taking place here today, we have to trace our steps back in time, and this would take until infinity, like the other day with the example of the hammer; you would have to understand the institution and, in order to understand all these communications both collective and individual, you would have to understand the circumstances in which the communication is made (the microphone, the room, the table, the glass, the tradition: there is a glass because the lecturer is supposed to drink, and so on). Finally, the few conscious intentions that function are circumscribed within an immense mass of acquired practice; if and when one or two rare conscious attempts at communication from subject to subject happen to take place, it is against this background of the multiple coincidence and random occurrence of everything objectively composing our Pascalian 'apparel', if not Althusser's 'apparatus'.[33]

I would just like to spend a moment more discussing this point, which may seem to you very far from sociological practice. In fact I think that one function among others of this kind of analysis is perhaps to provide the means of a sort of ethical control of one's own social practice and the social practices of others. From the point of view of scientific practice, it is an ancillary, secondary benefit, but I mention it in passing: without wishing to found a science of morals, as our ancestors of the Durkheim school did, I believe that we have the right to say that the kind of exercise that I have just led, if we could do it comprehensively in a real social situation, would have an absolutely capital ethical function (I say 'ethical' because 'political' would sound too grandiose) in so far as 'social subjects' would be much more of a subject if they knew that they are very rarely subjects and that in fact 'it speaks' through them – to add a Lacanian sense to Husserl's terms.[34] My voice is borne on a great cacophony of 'it speaks', and, if I am able to slip a little 'I speak' between the lines, you need to realise that the transaction taking place between us today is an institution. Obviously, these attempts to return to the *doxa* could be politically very useful if they taught spokespersons to know that they are spreading the word – in fact there are so many things here that I could develop and that I shall develop – of something that could be most important, fundamental even, for the social sciences, although obviously when it comes to writing of the social sciences this raises extremely difficult issues.

I would now like to respond to a question that someone asked me the other day: 'How can you escape from the infinite regression where, in order to understand practical knowledge you have first to understand scholarly knowledge? Then you have to understand the knowledge that is trying to understand the scholarly knowledge in order to understand the practical knowledge, and so on and so forth.' The person who asked me this question had understood me very well and had anticipated the difficulties that I would encounter. In this case, I do think that we can escape the circle in practice, for any work that makes explicit the principles of practical knowledge by integrating the scholarly subject's arsenal of different kinds of knowledge is, as it were, recycled in order to further increase the knowledge that the scholarly subject will have of the object. At every moment the knowledge acquired will enter the subject's fund of knowledge, obviously in a circular movement, but this is not a vicious circle at all: at every moment the knowledge that the scholar can acquire of his object and the modes of knowing reality that are part of the object accrues to his scholarly knowledge of the object and thus augments his means of knowing the object. I illustrate this point: is the scholarly subject an old-fashioned transcendental *ego*? The scholarly subject may become embodied in an individual scholar – that is, find a biological incarnation somewhere in the scientific field (for example, at this very moment I am as far as possible the expression of the sum of knowledge acquired by the social sciences) – but, the more advanced a science is, the more this individual subject transcends the individual *ego* that seems to be speaking. In other words, what is speaking at this moment in time is not an individual habitus, social trajectory or position in space; it is, I hope, the scientific field, with all its rivals, struggles, history, discoveries, historical conflicts and everything learned from these conflicts. The fact of knowing this may, I think, help to check certain errors linked to the distortions of egocentrism, but also to make progress in understanding the subject of this knowledge. In a way, getting to know practical knowledge is giving ourselves the means the better to know the scholarly subject in their attempt to break free from their condition: a social agent who lives their everyday life on the basis of practical knowledge but who, through the logic of the division of labour, finds themselves inserted in a space that tends to function as a collective subject transcending the habitus and interests of the individual. You may think that I am falling into line with Hegel and his view of the State. Might not my scientific field be a reincarnation of Hegel's State? This is a question that I shall have to face, but I must stop here.

Lecture of 2 November 1982

Positions and dispositions – The two states of history – A feel for the game – Practical knowledge – Investment in the game and illusio – Affective transference of the domestic libido and conformism – Critique of economic discourse – The economic conditions of economic practices

I had started by questioning the status of the sociologist and finished with another question, which you may have forgotten, and which I shall not answer directly today: Does establishing a science of the relation of the scholarly to the practical lead us into a new form of the Hegelian enterprise, as I have been describing it? Allow me to point out immediately two differences that I find important (and I believe that there are others). In the first instance, once it has been established as such, the distinction between the scholarly subject and the practical agent (in his everyday non-scholarly occupations), as I described it, reminds the scholar that he is still a practical agent necessarily situated in the social world that he studies, that there is therefore no absolute position, and that it is pointless even to look for an absolute position. I emphasise this because I think that it is a permanent temptation for the social sciences, no doubt initiated by Hegel. In every period sociologists have sought a privileged place from which the social world would reveal its truth to their thoughts – after the bureaucracy, there was the proletariat, then the new working classes, then the students, and so on.[1] This is a fundamental illusion which we can explain in sociological terms but which does not actually have a sociological foundation. The argument that I pursued last time therefore seems to me to show among other things that this never-ending search for a privileged place from which to contemplate the social world is pointless.

The second difference is that the scientific subject as briefly described at the end of my last lecture is neither an individual subject nor a collective subject, but a kind of strange encounter between a socially constituted habitus and the field of rivals claiming to produce the legitimate discourse on the social world; these scholars are then a kind of collective agent subject to such historical fluctuations that we cannot attribute to them the sort of fate that would lead them inevitably, if not immediately, at least in the long term, to absolute mastery of the social world. If the scientific subject is a scientific field, all the discoveries of sociology are at the mercy of a *coup d'état* or a revolution, from the left or the right, and, as I shall go on to argue today, we have to call into question any purposive philosophy of history.

Having briefly indicated what I found to be the essential difference between the scholarly relation and the practical relation to the social world, I would now like to analyse what seems to me to constitute the set of characteristics most typical both of the logic of practice and of practical relations to the practical world[2] in order to proceed to contrast my theory of the habitus with two purposive versions of the representation of action: the teleology of the individual and the teleology of the collective.

Positions and dispositions

I pointed out last time, while showing how the *orthè doxa* leads to stumbling across the 'right action' in an almost random encounter between a practical sense and a sense objectively inscribed in the objective structures, that a successful social action – that is, one sanctioned by the objective laws of a particular social field – was in a way the product of a coincidence between what we might call two incarnations of history, one in the body and the other in things or events. I took as my example our relation to a tool or an instrument, a familiar analysis that I mention here only to remind you: it is because the user of the instrument has adapted to the instrument that the instrument seems adapted to him, and the illusion of purposiveness that virtuoso behaviour, for example, produces – there is a very fine analysis by Hegel of the relation between the active subject and his body, where the virtuoso enjoys a magical rapport of immediate action with his body[3] – is dissolved as soon as this magical rapport appears as the product, not of some pre-existing harmony (say of a biological nature) but of an encounter between a socialised body and socially constituted objects. It is when a socialised body encounters objects structured by the same forces that structure him that this sort of immediate adaptation is established, lending behaviour the appearance of purposiveness.

In order to remove from this argument any suspicion of idle philosophising, in the negative sense of the term, I might take an example from various research projects in which I have recently been engaged. When we work on a social space such as that of management, the bishopric or the teaching profession, we note a very interesting phenomenon: there is a sort of correspondence between, on the one hand, the space of social agents characterised by properties pertaining to biological individuals – age, gender, social or geographical origins, academic qualifications, and so on, depending on the case – that is, the space constructed using properties pertaining to individual biological persons – and, on the other hand, the space constructed using properties pertaining to positions – in the case of management, firms categorised according to the size of their workforce or the amount of their capital, etc.; in the case of teaching positions, according to the discipline taught, the institution and its prestige, etc; in the case of the bishops, the characteristics of the bishopric, the number of nuns, the number of church schools located in a particular diocese, etc. When we construct these two spaces separately and then superpose them (I won't enter into the technical details of the manoeuvres involved in this), we observe a fairly exact correspondence between the space of positions and the space of dispositions. We might say that it all goes to show that the positions had chosen those individuals best suited to occupy them, or, *mutatis mutandis* – which is what we hear most as it echoes the language of vocation – it all goes to show that the individuals have chosen the positions most apt to enable them to express their dispositions, their vocation, their tastes and their talents. To sum up briefly, there is a kind of structural homology between the two spaces of properties, which, if you stop to think, are very different: for example, on the one hand, the characteristics of a firm such as its size, the size of its workforce or the structure of its capital and, on the other hand, the fact that the boss did or did not graduate from the École polytechnique, the École nationale d'administration or the Inspectorate of Finance.

These two spaces constructed with such different properties can be structurally homologous, with a few discrepancies that are themselves instructive: noting the homology makes the discrepancies or the contradictions particularly significant – I shall return to these problems when I come to analyse the notion of the field – and the discordant relation between the positions and the dispositions is often a source of innovation. In the case of such discord, there is a kind of struggle – here again this is a very anthropomorphic description, which is one of the great difficulties in making a scientific description of the social world – between the position and the dispositions of its incumbent where it is impossible to predict the winner: either the dispositions win and the post is restructured in function of the incumbent's dispositions, or the positions win and they transform the dispositions of the incumbent. Now that I have started I can't stop at that, so I must say that it is obvious that the outcome of the struggle depends in its turn on the positions and dispositions; a rigorous science is honour bound to identify the properties of the positions that have the best chance of overcoming the dispositions. Briefly, in a social space, for example, there are hard positions and soft positions, and a position of primary school teacher is a harder position than the position of a social worker. The people who import non-conformist positions into a hard position will therefore have a strong likelihood of being weaker than the position and being beaten by it, whereas people who import unorthodox and discordant dispositions into a soft position have a good chance of being able to mould the position to suit their dispositions. This explains, among other things, that people with certain dispositions are attracted more by a soft position than a hard position.[4]

I just wanted to mention this phenomenon, which is in general ignored by scientific discourse but which would merit several sessions all to itself. Let us imagine for instance a civil servant who enjoys acting aggressively from the safety of their desk. We may wonder whether this aggressive tendency is inherent in the position or whether it is inherent in the dispositions of the agent who occupies the position, but very often it is a false problem: we don't need to calculate the proportions that are due to the position and the disposition respectively, but we do need to understand how a certain disposition comes to end up in that position; we need therefore to explain the space of the positions, the space of the dispositions and the pathways that lead the various dispositions into the various positions. I hope that you do not think that I am playing with words: this does correspond to real life, and I hope that every one of you can draw on your personal experience and find empirical examples that will match my analyses. For me, this analysis draws our attention to an important characteristic of the social world. Crozier[5] gives a good description of the aggressive clerk who exploits the properties inherent in the position that he holds in order to give physical expression to dispositions that can only be expressed because they find the conditions for their expression in the position held. This behaviour challenges the view of a neat alternative between positional effect and dispositional effect. People very commonly impute the aggressive behaviour found in certain positions to the petty bourgeois dispositions of the people who fill these posts, who are aggressive because they are repressed; or else they will say that these dispositions are inherent to the logic of the lower echelons of the civil service. From my point of view, a rigorous description must take account of the match or discrepancy between dispositions and dispositions – that is, of the two systems and their encounter in a particular case. To pursue this a little further, let me take a different example: after May '68 we have all noticed the appearance of people who present a habitus clashing with what we were used to seeing in certain positions. For instance, where bus conductors and train ticket inspectors always used to be petit bourgeois, clean-shaven and neatly brushed and combed, suited to the function as defined in times gone by – that is, aggressive, disciplinarian and disciplined – we saw the emergence of people whose external signs betrayed a more lax and casual kind of habitus and a detachment from their function, as for example in the case of bearded bus conductors or train ticket inspectors, with a habitus that would have been more likely to be found until relatively recently among a certain category of intellectuals. This is a case of discordance where the kind of struggle between the dispositions and the positions – although obviously it is not a head-on struggle between the new bearded inspector and the position designed to be filled by a clean-shaven individual – involves the whole structure and space of the positions: reminders of propriety will arise from all around, because, if in the struggle with his position the individual concerned manages to impose his dispositions, the whole space will change, since a position is by definition a relational one (as we see in its etymology, 'situs'), so that the person who manages to displace the position shakes up the whole space. And in general there are people who do not want the space to move.

I think that by now you will have seen what I am getting at. This sort of coincidence – I think that is the least bad word – between the position and the disposition, which means that there is not much point in wondering whether it is the function that produces the organ or the organ that produces the function, gives rise to an action of the *orthè doxa* type. In a way the agents will slot into this action without its having been objectively and intentionally designed for this purpose, and this has material consequences concerning the subject – which is in fact the question that we always have in mind when we enquire into the meaning or the motives of an action. For instance, the action that consists in aggressively reprimanding adolescents who ride two to a motorbike is inherent to the role of a gendarme or a policeman, but at the same time it could be waived if the gendarme had a certain 'distance from his role'. I am borrowing this concept from Goffman,[6] who characterises certain positions as requiring a distance from the role. What is important is that the requirement of this distance from the role increases with social position: the higher we move up the hier-archy of positions – and it is true in nearly every field – the more the definition of the position implies that those who hold it have a certain distance and freedom from the position. I remind you that, last time, I mentioned the definition of excellence as the art of playing with the rules of the game. The higher up the system you are, whatever it is, the more keeping your distance from the position is one of the talents required. A gendarme is not able to distance himself much from his role, and it is important for him to have the dispositions that match his position; he needs to be aggressive if he has to reprimand. (I won't take this analysis further; I would say things that would either complicate the demonstration or oversimplify it.)

To a certain extent, when social agents take disciplinary action there is not much point in asking who is the subject of the action. The theory of action that I offer you suggests that the subject of this action is to be found neither in the named biological individual nor in their system of dispositions, nor even in the position concerned – as psychologists who draw up job profiles might suggest – but in this very complex rela-tion between the space of positions (because, by definition, I can define a position only by its position in the space of positions) and the space of the different habitus: the subject of the action is to be found in the relationship between the two spaces. One of the problems that I want to raise today has to be the extreme difficulty of describing this kind of action, because all our language is designed to express the logic of the subject: since our sentences have a subject, a verb and a predicate and it is so easy to say: 'It was the gendarme who meted out the punishment', whereas it would be terribly complicated and rather disappointing, as well as offensive to our need for simple explanations, to say that the punishment was produced by an encounter between the space of posi-tions and the space of dispositions.

The two states of history

The problem that I wish to approach today is one that has been raised repeatedly from the very beginnings of sociology, and every time that it arises anew it is, I think, glossed over by some over-hasty solution. For instance, in the days of Jakobson and Lévi-Strauss, the answer was the notion of the unconscious (not the Freudian unconscious, but the unconscious as derived from Lévi-Strauss's reading of Jakobson and Saussure).[7] I do not think that it is the unconscious: it is true that the majority of human actions are conducted without conscious scrutiny, even without the awareness of a so-called subject, but they take place nonetheless in a relation between subjective structures (a historical state) and incorporated structures (another historical state). In fact, all historical action is the product – although 'product' is not really quite the right word – of an encounter between two states of history: history in its objectified state, as accumulated in instruments, documents, rites, theories, customs, traditions, styles of language and clothing, and history in its incorporated state. In fact, the paradigm of the relation that I have described, which I shall not develop further here, is the relation between a habitus and a habitat, or between a habitus and its clothing.

We should now seek to exchange the Cartesian theory of subject and object that we have acquired, perhaps unconsciously, for a theory whose paradigm would be the relation between a habitus and a style of dress, mediated by taste. I refer you to the analyses that I developed at length in *Distinction*, concerning this kind of relation which may seem to express a deep-rooted harmony: the whole habitus is expressed in a style of clothing which exists only because the habitus has established it as its clothing. I shall not develop this further; it would take too long. I prefer to borrow a simpler and more striking example from Panofsky. This example is likely to strike you all the more because the problem with analyses that are satisfactorily rigorous is that we tend to understand them too quickly. This is why I am taking my time, creating suspense like a musician because what we have been waiting a while to discover becomes less facile, and we feel its difficulty a little more keenly: I am not trying to gild the lily, merely trying to let you feel the difficulty. In his *Essais d'iconologie*, Panofsky reminds us that the everyday gesture of doffing your cap – or one of its many typical social variants – goes back to a medieval tradition when knights wanting to display their peaceful intentions would raise their helmet slightly, as a way of showing that they did not intend to fight.[8] This is, I believe, a fairly striking example, whereas when I speak of dress in general you understand all too easily. The garment itself exists in a space of clothing, and if it is difficult to choose an item of clothing it is because it is marked out in this space as a phoneme is marked out in the space of phonemes; a garment is marked in the space of clothing, yet the garment itself is the product of a long history, as are all the other items of clothing, and ultimately we have to choose an item from a long and complex historical series.

In the case of the greeting, this apparently insignificant gesture that I perform at a moment in time *t* retrieves a whole history from the sediment of the ages and reactivates it. Of course I do not resuscitate the medieval action in Michelet's sense.[9] I am probably never further from reliving history than when I reactivate it, because I may not have the slightest idea that this tradition goes back to the Middle Ages. I am able to reactivate this history myself because I am myself socially composed – that is, a product of internalised history – and it is because I am history incarnate and am tuned in to this objectified history in the guise of the traditions to be found in manuals of polite behaviour that I presently perform this gesture, which in fact has nothing of the present about it. So there needs to be a rather extraordinary kind of encounter between two histories for me to accomplish a gesture in the present that is not perceived as historical, and I think that the majority of the actions that we perform are of this kind.[10]

To return to the first example that I took, the bishop acting 'in the name of' his diocese, who is 'his diocese in human form' (this recalls a formula used by Marx on one occasion, that 'the capitalist is merely capital personified'.[11] This is the only time that he uses the notion of habitus.) If the bishop, without even needing to desire to do so, fulfils the objective intentions of the diocese, if in the eyes of an observer familiar with his diocese he acts in such a way as to accomplish the objective intentions of his diocese, it is because through very complex and relatively independent mechanisms the conditions that produce the diocese and the conditions that produce the bishop lead to these correspondences. It is all too easy in this kind of analysis to lapse into a neo-Hegelian language and say that it is History reflecting itself. That sounds impressive, but in fact it is far from being true, and so I shall not say it.

A feel for the game

Before I come to the two cases that I have introduced, the subjective teleology that is at work in economic theory and the objective teleology of the Marxist tradition, I would like to reply to certain objections. Take the notion of role, for example, which is used almost automatically without a second thought by most of the people who practise sociology: I myself, instinctively, have always avoided writing the word 'role' – if anyone finds that I have, it was a lapse. It seems to be a received idea, and the notion is part of the basic vocabulary of sociology. When someone wants to pose as a fashionable sociologist, they talk of 'role' and 'status', which sound very scientific. But the notion of role, if you take it seriously, means that there is something written in advance (either a finished text or, as in the *commedia dell'arte*, a scenario, or even something like a computer programme) and people ready to play the part. This logic of playing a score or building a model is a precise echo of the Saussurian pattern, where 'langue' is opposed to 'parole', language to speech.[12] The agent is no more than an actor – that is, someone who performs a script written in advance. The style of thinking that I am suggesting restores to the agent a real responsibility: they are not someone who performs a programme established in advance, nor someone who draws up their own plan, but someone whose action might easily be described as if 'it seemed to go according to plan', which does not mean that there had to be a plan, but only a kind of bizarre harmony between a person's dispositions and their position, which resulted in someone who was thoroughly at home in their position somehow anticipating the expectations of their position: there is a kind of reciprocal solicitation.

To clarify this argument, the game and the feel for the game are the best metaphor: in every sport the players claim a special place for what they call a 'feel for the game', a specific form of the 'practical sense' which means that, say, a footballer making a pass directs the ball not at where his team-mate actually is at that moment but where he will be when the pass gets to him; this is the ABC of every sport. The feel for the game consists in placing yourself not at the spot where your opponent appears likely to send the ball but at the precise location that he is not signalling – to catch him wrong-footed. The feel for the game is that kind of sense of the history of the game which enables the game to take place at all, because at every moment there are players who have a feel for the game. This analysis gives agents a crucial role. They are not the *Träger* ('bearers') of Althusser's neo-Marxism,[13] where the agents are merely the instruments of the structure, performing the same task as the structure and don't even need to be there, since the structure by parthenogenesis engenders further structures and a new mode of production replacing the previous one. No, the agents are in fact extremely important: you have only to put a tennis or a baseball player on a hand-ball court (to use relatively familiar examples) to see that Althusser's model is wrong. And it is absurd to wonder whether it is the structures or the agents (or the dispositions) that are more important, because, in a game that functions properly, they are the same thing twice over. The logic is one where the agents, armed with their dispositions, are absolutely constitutive of the game: it is they who define it, who make it function, and the rule and even the constraints of the game are only effective for players who have a feel for the game, and this is crucial. In fact, having a feel for the game is to feel free with the game because you understand its needs: someone who has a feel for the game, for example, saves energy compared to someone who doesn't, because he goes to the right place straight away while the other starts off by going to the wrong place. In a sense, having a feel for the game is to be the person who meets the needs of the game and creates its reality. There is a whole series of paradoxes, and if after I have explained all these paradoxes you still want to insist on the opposition between 'determinism' and 'liberty' [*laughter*] . . . It is an extremely complex relation that customary antimonies confuse absolutely; so unfortunately (and I do mean *unfortunately*) I have to keep reiterating my analyses.

(In parenthesis, for those of you in the know: the critics who find in my research a 'worst-case finalism', despite my attacks on this in much earlier writings, are simply applying their 'subject–object' thoughts to analyses that have left this kind of thinking behind; they are using a finalist language in order to read analyses that have moved beyond this language.)

We could take the notion of a feel for the game further: the feel for the game is acquired in playing, which makes it a product of history. I am rather embarrassed at developing these arguments. Although when you are writing a book on phenomenology you can find a certain pleasure and even a sort of self-satisfaction in developing every aspect of a notion in the hope of exhausting it, when you are speaking in person to a very large audience you can feel embarrassed. I think that I would do better to let you develop these arguments for yourselves. That having been said, what is important in the 'feel for the game' is the fact that it is the product of a socially constructed experience and the product of a history that renders historical action possible. In fact, that sentence sums up rather well what I have been trying to say so far.

Practical knowledge

To continue with what I have just been saying, I would like briefly to describe the logic of practical knowledge. If you remember the inaugural schema that I sketched in my first lecture,[14] the relation between agent and field is a very special kind of cognitive relation. The feel for the game that I have described is a form of knowledge, but of an entirely non-theoretical kind: if you ask a rugby player who has just sold someone a dummy to explain the theory behind his move, he will probably not have much to say unless he is a professional commentator or teacher – like a coach, for instance. But that does not mean that performing his move did not involve an extremely sophisticated form of knowledge, a total, synoptic, immediate knowledge, translated instantaneously into action. This is the kind of knowledge that I now wish briefly to discuss.

I must insist that this relation of practical knowledge is not a subject–object relation where the subject conceives of itself as distinct from an object (*objectum*) clearly facing it directly from the outside – that is, constituted as an object and presenting a problem. I refer to the classic analysis made by some phenomenologists who are critical of the tradition of the philosophy of the subject, although I shall adapt it somewhat. The notion of the problem (*problema*) is that of something 'thrown before' you, and the world of practical knowledge, the world for someone who has a feel for the game, is precisely a world that does not seem problematic, a world where we have the answer before we consider the question, a world where we seem to have set out our goals before we have taken the decision to set ourselves any goals: we have responded by acting in accordance with these ends without the objective of the action being formulated as such and without our means being calculated towards these ends. You need to bear this in mind when you hear what I am going to say later, so that I don't have to repeat myself laboriously when I come to apply this argument to a critique of the theory of *Homo economicus*, the traditional calculating economist. The habitus does not see the world as an object or a representation (where the word 'representation' entails the idea of a global vision or spectacle). The agent is not a spectator – these are small points, but they are important; the subject lives within the social world and moves around inside it as in a familiar household. I refer you to Bachelard's analysis of 'inhabiting',[15] which we could apply directly, or Heidegger's analyses.[16] (The latter can still ring true, even if they have been twisted to take in the themes of blood and earth and other fascist tendencies, which I have discussed elsewhere).[17] Social subjects are inscribed inside the social world; they inhabit the social world – except in situations of crisis where it is precisely the instantaneous adaptation operated by the feel for the game, and the game itself, that are called into question. They do not stand up to confront the space as a spectator of the social field, they do not consider the social world to be a representation, they do not adopt an external and superior viewpoint. One very simple fact is that they do not draw up a schema, whereas all sociologists, for example, start their research project by designing models, schemas and genealogies. In fact, simply by substituting a house drawn on paper for the house that we actually live in, we activate a sort of objectification that supposes we are not lodged inside the house. To avoid misunderstanding me as singing the praises of participation – I have to say this each time, because different people come to different lectures, and the same errors keep recurring, and I have to exorcise them each time – let me repeat myself: I am not saying that inhabiting the house is the only legitimate mode of knowledge of the house. Phenomenologists often say this, but we can appropriate their arguments for our own purposes. I am simply saying that inhabiting a house is a mode of knowledge that the scholarly mode of knowledge must take into account.

The scholarly mode of knowledge must realise that it has to deal with people who know their house because they inhabit it, and we must realise that, as soon as we draw a plan of a house and study its zones of movement (as any architect here would know), we break with the experience of the resident who really inhabits the house and run the risk of projecting our experience as planners into the mind of the inhabitant who actually lives there. Similarly (and, again, I repeat myself, because I think that it is an important point), someone who inhabits a genealogy inhabits a family, which is not at all the same thing as drawing up a family tree. We inhabit relationships and spaces where we have cousins and pals, who are not to be confused with neighbours; we interact with people near and far, we know how to approach them, we have a feel for the game, we know how to behave, we know whom to invite, whom to lend to and whom to repay. When the sociologist or the ethnologist arrives with their schemas and says: 'He's a cousin, she's a first or a second cousin', and so on, everything changes. That does not mean, I must insist, that we should not draw up family trees, but when we practise genealogy we are using the objects 'family', 'kinship' and 'relative' to create a relationship that is not that of the native, who quite simply inhabits his family and is involved in a network of family relations.

Social agents, then, are engaged with the world; they are not spectators floating above it – whereas the plan is seen from above. They do not have a perspectival view of the world or see it as representation; they engage with reality and act and operate within it with no deliberate object of consciousness or reflection. In other words, the relation between the practical sense and the sense of the game (the 'feel for the game'), and even the sense of the history of the game, is not an external relation. In fact, what I am attacking here is the intellectualist tendency that leads people to describe social relations as relations of communication or knowledge.

Investment in the game and *illusio*

If we take this a little further, to 'play the game', to be 'caught up in the game' or 'carried away by the game' means that you are 'investing in the game'. I have used this expression several times. When someone has the right feel for the game, they respond in advance to the solicitations of the game – this is the essence of the relation between a habitus and a field – and, by the same token, they invest in the game, because any game with no individuals investing in it is not worth playing and is immediately abandoned. Investing in the game means taking *interest* in the game. The word 'interest', which I often use, is at the heart of my argument. I have introduced the notion of interest with polemical intent against what you might call the interactionist and culturalist vision that dominated the field of the social sciences during the structuralist period and gave the impression that social subjects were motivated entirely by the desire to exchange symbols. I want to remind you that even symbolic exchanges suppose the investment of interest, and the freest of games, like art or love, suppose a form of interest. But I am not taking the word 'interest' in Bentham's sense – I shall return to this: you must read 'interest' in the sense of 'being interested in something that matters to me'.

When you have a feel for the game, you don't enquire into the existence or the *raison d'être* of the game; you want to play, you have a *libido vivendi*. Each game imposes its own libido, and you could say that 'interest = libido'. But you could just as well say 'interest = *illusio*'. The illusion is the fact of desiring to take part in the game. In fact, the 'ludic' element is a false etymology (I think it was suggested by Huizinga in *Homo Ludens* – and, if not, it doesn't matter),[18] but it is still very useful. There are well-known jokes that are based on this model (the little Jewish boy going to mass, the rugby match described by someone who doesn't know the rules of the game, among others), and they show up the absurdity of a game when it is seen by someone who doesn't have a feel for the game, making its goals and interests, and in fact all of its activities, pointless. This deflation of the game is provoked by the external gaze of Husserl's 'disinterested onlooker'[19] that strips away the *illusio*, the immediate fusion with the game that is implied by the feel for the game. Then the game itself becomes an illusion. This would be interesting to analyse from a historical point of view, and I think that it is no accident that the analyses closest to those that I have to offer on symbolic capital, symbolic power, and the like were developed at the moment when the games of the court started to lose their significance: life at court, seen by the Puritan or Jansenist bourgeoisie, seemed to be a game of illusions, an illusory pursuit of goals that were not worth the trouble. All social games seen from the outside seem to be games of illusion, but the essence of a game is to produce the kind of habitus that does not call the game into question and to attract players so profoundly adapted to the game that they never ask questions of the game.

If we apply this to the intellectual field, we shall see straight away that things are not so simple; what we can say at the level of anthropology in general immediately becomes more painful if we apply it to something that is close to hand. The intellectual field is a game, and the people who play there invest in it an *illusio*, which is their very commitment to the principle of the game. It follows from this same property, which I shall discuss later, that it is very rare for people who play a game with a healthy *illusio* to question the existence or non-existence of the game. They may challenge different ways of playing the game, they can tell who is playing badly or using an unorthodox style, say if you should move to the left or the right, but they rarely ask if the game is worth playing at all. In fact, I think that these disputes themselves suggest a collusion (here the etymology comes in useful again: *illusio/collusio*) between the players, who all accept the validity of the game. For in any game the opponents are surely united by a fundamental complicity over the intrinsic value of the game. Does the fact of being inhabited by an appropriate *illusio* not entail a tacit recognition of the very validity of the game and, in so doing, the limits of the rivals' disagreement, which do not even have to be agreed, because they could not transgress them without calling into question their very existence as players? To put it simply, they would be sawing off the branch they are sitting on, which is something that groups very rarely do, or else they would be committing suicide, and it is possible to commit social suicide.

This analysis has nothing Platonic about it. We could study the problem of belief that I raised when discussing the religious field. In every field there is belief at stake: *illusio* implies believing it is worth the trouble to play the game. A game only functions in so far as it manages to convince all the players that it is worth taking the trouble to play it. This belief in the value of the game is so fundamental that it can take precedence over the belief that is the overt goal of the game. We could not understand the religious field if we did not understand that what matters is finding in the field of belief what is the right belief, the *orthè doxa*. The question of the right manner of believing (or of making people believe) is what is at stake in this field, but we would understand nothing about this field if we did not see that, in this field that encourages belief, the field only functions on condition that people believe that it is worthy of functioning as a field, that the struggle for the right definition of belief is itself an object of belief. I wanted to say that so that you don't think that I have wandered too far from social reality: with me we are never very far . . . at least, I hope so [*laughter*].

I will close this argument with the word *interest* – but I shall return to it at length later. The word *interest* must be taken in the widest sense; what interests me is what matters to me, what I find important, what motivates me to break free from tranquillity and indifference. As I said just now, what the feel for the game implies is the desire to play, rather than be neutral and remain outside in a state of indifference. We might well say that, in the scientific field, the *illusio* takes the form of the *libido sciendi*. In the case of the game it will take the form of the *libido vivendi*, which we might also call 'passion'. Here I would like to quote Hegel, who said that 'Nothing great has ever been accomplished without passion', which I think has always been misunderstood when set as a topic for a dissertation. In fact the question that I want to raise is this: What is it that makes people act? Why do people play a game when it is tiring and drains their energy? Why do people play rather than not play? Why do they work rather than not work? Of course we think we find the answers when we say that they have needs to fulfil, or that in the case of work we can't ignore the economic need. There are all sorts of ready-made answers. And yet even in the case of the economic field we must always ask why people play the game rather than do nothing. Because it is possible to let yourself die from hunger (there are anorexics, for instance). At the risk of shocking the materialist school, dialectical or other, I think that we must always ask why there is action, investment or interest rather than nothing. I shall read you the whole of Hegel's text:

> We assert then that nothing has been accomplished without interest on the part of the actors; and – if interest be called passion, inasmuch as the whole individuality, to the neglect of all other actual or possible interests and claims, is devoted to an object with every fibre of volition concentrating all its desires and powers upon it – we may affirm absolutely that *nothing great in the world* has been accomplished without passion.[20]

Here the word 'passion' describes not an emotional state but the logic of fetishism – that is, a belief that seems illusory to anyone outside the game, but one that is well founded – Durkheim said that religion is a well-founded illusion[21] – if we see it from the viewpoint of someone who knows the conditions of production of the game and the players. This passion then is well founded, even though it is illusory. The word 'passion' is interesting: it is something suffered because we cannot do anything but suffer this interest; someone who has the appropriate habitus cannot help playing, and there is no point in telling them that

they should 'stop playing the game'. Marx said of the Stoics who dis-
carded their golden goblets and drank out of wooden bowls or their
hands that this was a 'rich man's privilege'.[22] And there are in fact
forms of economic critique that are subject to economic conditions.
The logic of fetishism is such that it can always be described from the
outside as being illusory: there is nothing more illusory than a belief,
except that as soon as we understand its context we realise that it is
impossible to do without it and that nothing is more necessary than
this illusion: it is both a passion and a profound relation between a
habitus and a field. Someone who is caught up in a field is caught up in
the game. They can theoretically leave the game at any moment and,
from the viewpoint of the contemplative sage observing them, they
seem to be madmen investing in trivia. But they are so constituted that
they are ready to die for the game.

Affective transference of the domestic libido and conformism

Briefly, a remark that I shall not develop but which might interest
those of you who are interested in the relations between sociology and
psychoanalysis. Following the logic of what I was saying in my previous arguments, I would simply like to say that we must obviously bear
in mind that the primordial or originary investment takes the form
of an affective investment in the domestic group. In other words, the
social investment takes the form of an affect in the first instance. The
first form of the illusion then would be what Laing calls the family
fantasy,[23] that form of collective construction in which both the image
of the group and the image of each individual are constituted. This
would allow us to read the word 'passion' in Hegel differently and
reactivate another aspect of it: if investments in social games are so
deeply rooted, if the fantasies and fetishes are so real and necessary
despite being objectively illusory, it may be because these investments,
for example by academics in their Alma Mater, have something to do
with a transfer of primordial investments. It seems to me that we could
easily extend this argument to subject teachers' bonus payments to this
kind of sociological analysis.

   I have often denounced – in *Distinction*, for example[24] – the populist
illusion that consists in 'living' the experience of the people through a
bourgeois habitus or in any case a non-popular habitus, and thereby
destroying the relation that I have been describing all through these
analyses between a field and a habitus, experiencing the space of the
factory and the production line as lived by an intellectual with the

habitus of an intellectual. The most revolting social spaces – the shanty towns, the conveyor belt, and the like – are inhabited by people who have what you might call the appropriate habitus, which means that the experience that the observer may have of them is very likely to be false unless they make allowances for the difference. This, then, is a case where the distinction that I have made between the scholarly subject with a scholarly habitus and the agent engaged in the practical is extremely important. There is a form of projection of the self into the other, as the phenomenologists would say, a way of 'putting yourself in their place' which profoundly falsifies the issue, and there is a form of 'subjective generosity' which gives pleasure only to the generous donor. It is very important to understand this, because it explains why I am so shocked by a certain type of populist description of the working classes.

To take this a little further, we would have to analyse – and here I can give you only an outline – a case that is apparently the least favourable in the terms that I have described, the culture of working-class adolescents – the young delinquents, for instance – who show all the signs of rebelling against the social world that they inhabit and who seem to have internalised a kind of profound rejection of the world in which they live. I am drawing both on some recorded experiences and on a very important book by Willis that I shall note for you.[25] In this book, Willis studies two groups of marginal people, drop-outs or pariahs – call them what you will: on the one hand, the yobs who organise their lives around their motorbikes and, on the other hand, the hippies, very different in social origins and milieu. I shall look only at the first group, since the second is easier to analyse. These young delinquents, who strike us with the impression of rebellion that they project, are marginal. They challenge conventions of dress; their language is a permanent transgression of grammar and syntax, as well as flouting the censorship required by polite society. These rebellious tough guys are rebelling first and foremost against the old, who are more socialised and have already made concessions to their position and have dispositions better adapted to their position. They organise their vision of the world, as we can easily see if we analyse their language, around values of virility, roughness, brutality, violence, bravado, defiance and honour, which are simply an extreme form of the values inherent to the whole of the working class and in general all dominated classes, those – as Willis rightly emphasises – that foster a stable, solid, constant and, above all, collectively guaranteed world. It is most important that the *illusio* becomes absolutely necessary only when it is collective and shared, and one of the functions of the delinquent group, the gang, is precisely to provide a kind of meeting ground for the various *illusios*, and thereby to provide permanent reinforcement for each individual experience. This solid, stable world is also a very closed and defensive world, and Willis insists on its very restricted horizons: the people rebel within a relatively limited framework without calling into question the boundaries that hem them in. To a certain extent we might go so far as to say that their protest is so incomplete that it is conservative. They are rebelling within the limits of a universe whose structure they do not question. The provocations and insults and everything to do with their relations with women and their views of women could be analysed in the light of this logic.

This popular subculture seems to have broken with certain kinds of conformism, but in fact it is rather an extreme case of popular conformism and adherence to the virtues imposed by necessity, such as the virtues of toughness. The virtues of toughness are the virtues of people whose life is hard and who make a virtue of necessity; they become tough on themselves and on others; they don't give in and cry like a girlie, they rough each other up, pretend to fight, are always involved in violence because the world is violent; they practise karate moves all the time because you never know when it might happen, and it does happen anyway – after three o'clock in the morning they start looking for a fight. In other words, this universe, seemingly liberated and anti-everything, looks much more like an alternative, excluded, dominated universe. We could have a very long debate about this, but for the moment the best I can do is mention the topic and insist on the fact that it is a world of common sense and consensus, whose very logic, as you can see on a linguistic level, is to give a straight and narrow, solid and reassuring picture of the world: you call a spade a spade, you don't waste words, you know how to treat a bit of skirt, you don't mess about. We could make a long list of the formulae that express this almost pathetic desire to appropriate an unattainable world and to make a virtue out of necessity. I have been using the term 'conformism' (which is an objectivist word: 'conformism' supposes both that the possibility of transgression exists and that there are people who conform), but it is in fact a sort of primary adhesion below the level of conformism, and even below the possibility of calling the world into question: it is a doxic relation to the world. I shall differ from Willis when he talks of conformism, but I won't go into too much detail because I would have too much to say. I just wanted once more to show that these are not abstract analyses.

Critique of economic discourse

I need to speed up, because today I would like to tie up the notion of habitus so that I can start to discuss the notion of the field next week. So today I must rapidly try to confront the analyses of the habitus that I have been propounding with two rival theories: what I have been calling subjective teleology and objective teleology, or, if you prefer, utilitarian individualism – that is, an individual purposiveness with its theory of the rational choice, one of whose forms would be the theory of the game – and, on the other hand, an optimistic or a pessimistic functionalism – the tendency makes no difference – that is, a collective purposiveness finding an objective teleology at work in the social world, with the accomplishment of ends that transcend the individual agents, ends that nobody has willed and yet still come to pass. I am not repeating this for the pleasure of philosophising but because I think that scientific discourse constantly oscillates between these two poles. It is important to be able to distinguish between these two poles, since in writing you can pass from one to the other without even realising it – you can go away and look for examples in the texts – just as I showed just now that you can pass from an intellectualist determinism to a mechanical determinism almost in the same sentence.

The first point: I would like briefly to criticise what we may see as the anthropology inherent in economic theory, that sort of anthropological imaginary whose paradigm and privileged incarnation is *Homo economicus*. (I shall be peremptory and dogmatic, but not out of intellectual authoritarianism. In fact I do not judge the topic important enough to merit burdening you with a long demonstration with textual references when you can easily check for yourselves and verify or falsify what I am about to argue. If I am peremptory, it is quite honestly out of respect for you, in order not to waste your precious time.) The economy and economic theory seem to me to be compatible with both mechanism and intellectual purposiveness. We may indeed hypothesise either that economic agents act under the constraint of necessity and other causes established by economic science, or that they are fully aware of what they are doing. I took some time to grasp this distinction because the economic argument moves constantly between the two – that is, from a knowing subject to a known subject, *Homo economicus*, who is nothing but a projection of another knowing subject. Let us suppose that the housewife buying a piece of steak is buying it because she has read Samuelson:[26] she is fully aware of the implications of her purchase because she knows that she must buy her steak at this store and that it would not be economical to buy it at another, and so on; but in buying it she is also subject to various material constraints, and ultimately the distinction has little significance if we suppose that *Homo economicus* is a scholarly subject incarnated in the body of a (male) human individual.

In fact it seems to me that the utilitarian philosophy inherent in economic theory is based on two principles. The first principle is that agents go in search of what meets their interest, whether individual or collective. The interest of the individual is taken to be what increases the sum total of their pleasure and reduces the sum total of their pain. Here we might consider the interest of the community, which is resolved in some traditions by calling it the sum of the individual interests of its members. (As I speak, I hesitate, because it is always rather unfair to try to define the philosophy implicit in a scientific topic produced by so many and varied named individuals. I feel embarrassed because what I am describing seems to me to be the dominant paradigm in economics – and, given the dominance of the discipline, not only in economics – and I am using an alternative paradigm to describe it. In describing a paradigm as a single whole I am bound to be unfair, and at every moment I am tempted to say that there are exceptions. There are, for instance, economists who study the 'perverse effects' of import tariffs and export subsidies, called 'aggregation effects'. The perverse effects, which have been well known for some time, contradict what I said about reducing collective interest to the sum of individual interests. Everything that I have to say is liable to be judged wanting by this kind of criticism. I need to make this clear, since otherwise I could not continue, because, although you might not raise these objections yourselves, I am constantly thinking of them myself and suffering as I confront them.)

The second principle: the agents, conforming to their economic definition, calculate how to maximise their search for the greatest possible happiness, and the mathematics of pleasure provides the natural means to implement their rational practice, and also their ethics. In this case we have the right to undertake what Michel Foucault calls an archaeology and to detect, for instance, in the arithmetic of pleasures that Bentham calls a science of ethics or a deontology[27] an explicitly normative theory of rational economic practices that are at the same time well-grounded ethical practices, since virtue is what increases the possession of pleasure and avoidance of pain. This apparently positivist theory is still normative. It is clear in the founding texts, but it is also true of its apparently more rigorous forms. To explain why this theory is still normative, we can easily summarise the two points that I have tried to make: economic agents are guided by their own well-understood interest, and the notion of well-understood interest seems to me to sum up this philosophy perfectly, for the function of utility is strictly to serve the interest of an economic agent as seen by an impartial spectator. Along these lines, Adam Smith assimilated this viewpoint, which is both moral and economically rational, to that of an 'impartial' but 'sympathetic spectator'.[28]

To prove that I am not stuck in ancient history, I can quote a definition from a book published in 1977 by Harsanyi, a very good economist: 'Rational behaviour is simply behaviour that pursues well-defined goals in a coherent fashion, and pursues them according to a set of well-defined preferences or priorities.'[29] In other words, the rational calculator is the person who does what an economist would do to account for economic behaviour; his economic behaviour matches the explanation that the economic calculator would propose in order to give a rational account of it. On this subject I should have mentioned earlier Max Weber's classic analysis of rational behaviour in 'Some categories of interpretive sociology': rational behaviour is the behaviour that individuals would adopt if they understood their situation as fully as the observer does.[30] Rational behaviour, then, is the behaviour that agents would adopt if they were fully aware of the circumstances or, in other words, if they were in the position of the spectator who is not engaged in the action but who, seeing it from the outside, uses all the means at his disposal to know the circumstances and outcomes, the causes and effects, in order to understand the situation in all its complexity. Another reference, which obeys the same logic: 'The principle of utility must be based not on real preferences but on perfectly prudent preferences.'[31] It is of course the spectator who judges what is 'prudent', since he is able to use his knowledge to evaluate what is risky and what is not, and has an understanding of the different profits that an investment would yield according to where it is placed. Similarly, Harsanyi distinguishes between manifest preferences and true preferences, which are those that the agent would choose if, firstly, he possessed all the relevant information, secondly, if he always reasoned with the greatest possible care and, thirdly, if he was in the right state of mind to make a rational choice.[32] This third condition takes us back to the question of passion (the agent has to be perfectly calm and self-controlled, etc.), whereas the first two points refer to the sum of information available and the agent's ability to calculate. Thus there are always implicitly or explicitly two dimensions: the information (which should best be complete) and the process of reflection and calculation.

The hypothesis of well-understood interest is the foundation of this theory, which supposes a series of *petitio principii* that I shall list briefly. Firstly, agents are reduced to a utilitarian function. They are the locus of their utility – that is, the location where activities such as desiring, feeling desire or sorrow take place – and they are nothing else. In other words, individuals are known only by their utilitarian functions; there is no attempt to enquire into the social or historical genesis of this utilitarian function. This eliminates, for instance, all the individual properties that depend on their history in order to justify aggregating the individual preferences – and I assure you that if you look through this book you will find ample confirmation of what I am saying. A major problem for these economists is to pass from individual preferences to collective preferences: for is what is good for the individual good for the community as a whole? What gives us the right to aggregate individual properties? Are they not contradictory? Can we totalise things that are not totalisable? To justify the aggregation of individual preferences, which allows us to pass from individual preferences to collective preferences, from individual happiness to collective happiness – because that is what it is all about – Harsanyi introduces what he calls the postulate of similarity, which is interesting. (One of the virtues of economic theory is that it is obliged to make its own foundations explicit, which gives us a paradigm that is relatively easy to challenge: the axiomatisation, rigour and formalisation which are its strength are also its weak points because they also display its naïveties in a particularly striking way: if paradigms are softer, more flexible and less axiomatic, they are much more difficult to challenge.) The postulate of similarity is a brilliant idea: it allows us to reduce agents to a sort of universal humanity making abstraction of their tastes and education, and the like. The postulate that they can be aggregated depends on ignoring their tastes and education. But to end up eliminating tastes from a function of utility when we are talking about preferences is really astonishing (you can find this on pages 51–2 of the same book, if you wish to check). Here the postulate of common humanity is written in black and white. Another extraordinary formula: Harsanyi postulates that all individuals have the same fundamental capacity for satisfaction and dissatisfaction.

The economic conditions of economic practices

Another important thing is that this abstract universalisation or homogenisation, which eliminates taste in so doing, successively eliminates history, the origins of taste, the social conditions of the production of consumers – and, O paradox! – the economic conditions of the production of the economic agents. My first reaction as a sociologist during my enquiry into labour in Algeria was to be surprised at the situation of Algerian workmen who found themselves faced with a capitalist economy without having the habitus that this economy normally produces. My first task was to try to show that there were economic factors controlling access to economic calculations.[33]

To sum up this argument in a few words, with apologies to those of you who know them and have heard them a hundred times: there did exist, and there does still exist, an economic tradition studying undeveloped or pre-capitalist economies, enquiring into the sources of resistance to the capitalist economy in colonial or ex-colonial societies (it is the word 'resistance' that matters here). They invoked cultural and religious tradition. They debated whether Islam is compatible with capitalism, whether there might be an Islamic mindset that would prohibit interest being charged on loans, and they looked into medieval practices. These areas of research brought together ethnologists and economists, the latter asking the former to say what *curiosa ethnologica* might explain why those people did not act like rational economists, stopping working for instance when they had earned enough money (which is surely easy enough to understand), and the ethnologists would explain that there were taboos: the Saturday taboo, for instance. This brief summary is bound to be slightly caricatural, but it seems paradoxical that nobody asked a very simple question: What are the economic conditions that have to be fulfilled before someone can accede to economic calculation? Take a man, for instance, who is living in absolute economic uncertainty, like a sub-proletarian, an unemployed man or a part-time worker working two days a week and unemployed three days a week, who has an absolutely unstable habitus, spending three days here and three days there – does he have the objective conditions enabling him to adopt a calculating attitude? In other words, don't you have to have a minimal objective hold on the future to have the idea of taking a hold on the future by calculating? At the same time the high fashion, with Fanon, was to ask whether the Revolution would be started by the proletariat or the sub-proletariat.[34] This is a recurrent problem which is constantly posed in the same terms and can be rapidly summarised: What are the conditions needed for a revolutionary conscience to appear armed with a coherent plan, since a revolutionary has to confront the society in which they are immersed with an alternative representation of the future society in the name of which the whole of present society will be challenged? (This is rather a simple formulation, but it is as good as any other.) Surprisingly enough, people who have discussed revolutions have very rarely enquired into the economic conditions needed for the appearance of a revolutionary conscience, doubtless because, paradoxically, it is not the most dominated who are the most revolutionary.[35] This has been noted historically: the sub-proletariat is very ambivalent; it has a very ambivalent relationship to the future, it is a potential army for fascists to manipulate, it is often exploited by millenarian-type movements. It is rather in the proletariat, who, although they are exploited, have attained relatively stable living conditions in terms of employment and career, that the ambition emerges to take hold of the future and revolutionise the present in the name of the future.

These two analyses consist in asking a question about *Homo economicus* that the theoreticians of *Homo economicus* never put: Is *Homo economicus* a species of rational, universal man? The theory of *Homo economicus* is pure Descartes: to take the right course of action, it is enough to make the right choice; we are all capable of economic calculation, and *ratio* is universal. But there are economic circumstances conditioning our ability to make rational economic calculations, on savings and investment, for example, and these economic conditions are necessary but not necessarily sufficient. At this point we could raise the classic questions, such as the problem of Protestantism and the relation between Marx and Weber, but these questions are better formulated if we first put the question of the economic factors conditioning the possibilities of economic calculation. I mention this analysis only briefly because my main objective is to show what is at stake in the critique that I am engaged in here.

In the utilitarian-individualistic theory that I am describing here, the economic agent is a singular individual reduced to the ability to make well-informed calculations. What I think is that we should look into the genesis of this singular individual: Where does he come from? How has he been shaped? What is it in the social and economic world, where he has been shaped and where he acts, that makes him become what he is? And what should he be in this social world, since there must be more in the world than, for instance, a capitalist economy? The case of colonial societies, where a capitalist economy is parachuted into a non-capitalist society, represents a very interesting experimental situation. For Western Europe, Max Weber wonders whether the origins of capitalism are to be found in economics or in the Protestant ethic,[36] but these are two relatively indissociable things which developed during the same period, and so it is difficult to choose. On the other hand, in colonial countries, a fully-fledged capitalist economy was imported from the outside into societies whose agents had the pre-capitalist dispositions of the pre-capitalist economy in which they had been largely brought up: in this case there is a game, but there are people who do not have a feel for the game and are very unevenly prepared to acquire it. We can then, using statistical observation for example, try to verify whether the appearance of what we call rational economic calculation is linked to conditions such as level of income, stability of employment, level of education, and so on. It seemed to me in the study that I undertook at the time, on limited statistical bases (weak bases even, but there have been verifications since then), that economic behaviour of a rational type in terms of fertility (family planning, contraception), strictly economic matters (savings and investment) and education (investment in children's education) had a greater likelihood of appearing the more the economic agents were free from brutal economic necessity. The emergence of a revolutionary conscience of a rational rather than an emotional type varied according to the same laws. It seemed therefore that calculation and planning for the future varied according to the same pattern, and that the disposition to calculate and plan for the future, to have an active and rational disposition towards the future, to appropriate it through calculation, had to suppose at least some capacity to appropriate the present, as if people were all the more disposed and inclined to embrace the economics requiring them to appropriate the future the more they could count on an objective and predictable future in terms of career and future stability. In very simple terms, to be disposed to predict, you need things to be predictable for yourself. There are some important consequences: economic theory in the way that I am describing it requires predictable *homines economici* – that is, agents who are responsible and reliable.

To continue briefly to consider all the problems of insurance and modern forms of loans with interest,[37] such as the personal loans launched in the 1950s whereby banks grant credit, not against visible assets (as in the case of collateral security) but against guarantees that agents provide in so far as they have a career: the guarantee that you give a bank as a public-service employee in order to buy your house is neither land nor goods but your career. In the first instance they calculate how much you will earn over a lifetime. As the mortgage is an advance against your future life, they have to know if you are in good health but also if they can predict that your career is likely to be successful. Secondly (as bankers know in practical terms from their feel for the game), since you have a career, you are supposed to be a calculating being, and they can count on you not to break the bank. You could re-read in the light of this logic everything that is asked of you when you take out a loan, and you will see that you are being constructed as a social character, a *Homo economicus*, and that the bank is asking for information so that they can make rational calculations on your behalf enabling them to judge whether you are worthy of a loan. This is a very concrete scenario.

To return to the difference between this kind of analysis and the presuppositions of traditional economic theory: the theory of the habitus, using the habitus but also the notion of position (which I shall discuss later in the light of the notion of the field), reintroduces the whole history of the social conditions of the production of the person. If people's preferences are historical, I cannot understand a system of individual choices without knowing at least the individual history of the person concerned, and perhaps that of their whole family tree. Economic theory eliminates, along with the history of the historical agent, the question of the economic and social conditions that produce the economic agent.

The second abstraction, as I said just now, is the one that reduces economic agents to the state of pure calculators whose preferences are strictly adjusted to match their objective opportunities. Everything happens as if they were able to maximise their subjective efficiency and evaluate at every moment the potential yield of each of the different investments between which they have to choose. (I shall return to this point in a moment: ultimately, social agents are less removed than we might think from this rationalisation, but that does not mean that their rationalisation is based on calculation.) The agent then is posited as a calculator, choosing between different options and deciding in full awareness of all the issues – that is, after a fully informed scrutiny of the different options and their likelihood of success – as mentioned in one of the texts that I quoted just now. In conclusion, the utilitarian process posited by the economic analysis does not represent the interest of the agents as perceived by the agents; it is the representation of their interest as it appears to the impartial, well-informed spectator – that is, the economist. In fact, the *Homo economicus* is a fictitious construction and the agent is a sort of *fictio juris*, a kind of ideal being, born of the application of economic models to individual behaviour. This is the error whose principles I have described, which consists in reducing the logic of things to the logic of calculation, or rather in placing the things of logic – that is, economical calculation – in the minds of the agents. All these properties attributed to the economic agent are fictitious. If I insist more didactically than usual, it is because this is a truly dominant paradigm and, since everyone has it more or less at the back of their minds, I felt that it warranted a little pedestrian repetition.

All the properties attributed to the agent are fictitious. Firstly, usefulness and happiness are not the only possible ends of action – as the economists admit, for they do have occasional bouts of self-criticism. There are cases where people punish themselves or fail deliberately – and this failure-seeking behaviour disturbs the economists. Secondly, and more significantly, interest is not a kind of universal property possessed by a universal agent; it is socially defined. Interest is always defined with reference to a field. Interest is the *illusio* of a particular field. Interest is determined in the relation between a habitus disposed to perceive certain solicitations and a social space where these solicitations arise. Thirdly, as regards the principle of utility, it is most interesting to note that the economists themselves raise an objection to it: the principle must take account of the principle of asceticism. Bentham denounced the principle of asceticism as one of the obstacles to a science of happiness.[38] Yet from a sociological point of view, if we re-read *The Elementary Forms of Religious Life*, Durkheim insists precisely on the fact that culture is asceticism,[39] and, without wishing to rehearse Lévi-Strauss's argument, the opposition between nature and culture is an opposition between laisser-faire and asceticism. So Bentham is rather naïve when he says that we should establish the utility principle against the asceticism principle, which he sees as a clerical perversion. But he is interesting nonetheless, as the founding fathers always are, because they say naïvely what their epigones go on to repeat in more sophisticated terms. Fourthly, the logic of decision, choice and calculation is an anthropological myth. It is a sort of logicism, to use one of Husserl's terms, a logicism of the psychological. In our everyday lives, the most important decisions are non-decisions. I shall give you just one example. How many liaisons ('liaison' is a very interesting social word: we talk of liaisons between businesses, of amorous liaisons, and so on) are non-break-ups? We often don't know when a liaison started or how it will finish, and it often just carries on regardless. The social world is full of this kind of thing: critical situations where we have to take a decision are quite exceptional. The *krisis*, judgement or criticism that economists speak of occurs only in situations of catastrophe: buying a piece of steak is not a catastrophic situation . . . I must move on. That was slightly facile, because it is easy to make fun of this paradigm; it is so strong that it keeps coming back, with its formalisations and its affinity with mathematical calculation.

I wrote in my notes for this lecture: 'To speak of choice is often as absurd as speaking of choosing between phonemes.' In fact language leads us into saying such things. Thus linguists say that 'the speaker chooses between two phonemes', but obviously nobody ever did choose between two phonemes, by considering one phoneme as a phoneme and then considering a second as such. If at this very moment I had to choose between phonemes, I would have my work cut out! [*laughter*]. What we can say is that 'it all looks as if there was a choice'. I think that the greater part of economic behaviour is of the same order, and even perhaps that the most important and crucial economic behaviour is of the same order as the 'choice' between two phonemes. There would be room for a whole study of routine as opposed to critical situations. This critique of the depiction of decision might lead us to say – I think that it might even have been an economist who said it – that, in fact, the theory of *Homo economicus* gives us two economic theories: one valid for the economists and the other for the ordinary *Homo econimicus*. In other words, this theory, which defies all the evidence and places inside the mind of every agent a miniature economist, leads us to create a division between the modes of action valid for the ordinary man and the modes of action valid for *Homo economicus*.

To conclude, what is important in this paradigm is that it is based on the deductive ambition so often proposed as a model of science, whereas it seems to me that it implies a regression towards a state of science that we might call Cartesian. Here I am using the opposition that I find very pertinent, between the Cartesian and the Newtonian visions of the physical world. Ultimately, economic theory, as it functions today, expresses its deductive ambition through the construction of formal models based on a conclusive and normative definition of the agent concerned. It is a scientific definition that provides an initial axiomatic, starting from which we can deduce the real. It is no accident if this mode of thinking has affinities with importing mathematics into economics – Kant said of mathematicians that they were naturally inclined to a dogmatic style of thinking and an ontological type of argumentation:[40] with maths we pass from the things of logic to the logic of things, and we suppose that, once a thing has been *logically* established, it is *really* established. This type of dogmatic thinking tends to be associated with what the philosophers of the Cambridge school called the *morbus mathematicus*[41] – the formula seems to me very apt – which leads us into a kind of metaphysics which has all the appearances of physical thought.

Here, in opposition to these analyses, we might recall what Cassirer said of Descartes' thought – you can find this in *The Philosophy of the Enlightenment*, especially pages 53 and 63. Cassirer recalls (on page 44) that, in his *Regulae philosophandi*, Newton, contradicting Descartes, said that we should abandon pure deduction starting from principles posed *a priori* in favour of an analysis starting from phenomena, in order to propose principles that would install a dialectic between the phenomena and the principles, instead of sacrificing to deductive ambitions that produce many social effects but few scientific ones. In order to account fully for the efficiency and the social temptation of the *morbus mathematicus*, we would need to integrate what I often call the 'Gerschenkron effect'.[42] Gerschenkron is a historian of Russia. He wrote a classic study that shows how Russian capitalism did not follow the same logic and course of development as in England or France or other countries, for the simple reason that it started later. Simply because of this time lag, it took a different form in Russia. I think that there is also a Gerschenkron effect in the social sciences: they are victims of the fact that they started later. We can ignore the question 'why?' – that is, the reasons, especially the social ones, for their late start – and simply concentrate on trying to understand the social effects of the fact that they did so. Among these effects there is the possibility for the social sciences to import models that have functioned in the more advanced sciences in order to produce by deduction models that appear to function in the case of the social world. I shall not quote specific names, since social science is full of these often rather wild transfers of models which also happen to be accompanied by a transfer of the model-makers: very often when there is, for example, a surplus of mathematicians, there is a fallout of mathematicians into economics or sociology, and these model-makers, instead of constructing objects so that they can be conveniently modelled, look for objects that they can get their models to work on – and this is one of the most sinister factors.

If what I have said of economic theory and its philosophy is true – I may have caricatured it somewhat, but not excessively – we should find it difficult to understand why this theory has such social force and is so dominant. When a theory is theoretically weak but socially dominant, it is because it fulfils some eminent social functions, and because it has the social order and mental structures on its side. We cannot then be satisfied with a theoretical criticism that is bound to lose because it comes up against social forces. We must also try to understand the social forces that make the strength of very weak theories. When you work in and on the social world there is no scientific opponent more difficult than one who is theoretically weak and socially strong.

Lecture of 9 November 1982

Habituality in Husserl – Decision theory in economics – Escaping mechanism and purposiveness – The theory of the machine – The ontological power of language – Popular culture and popular language – Marxist teleology – The reification and personification of the collective – The solution of the habitus

I would like to go back for a moment to discuss Husserl's use of the notion of the habitus. Obviously I do not want to analyse the full history of its usage by Husserl or his predecessors. I just want to point out something very interesting for those of you who are aware of the tradition.

Habituality in Husserl

Looking through one of Husserl's works now, and others that I knew already, it occurs to me that we can see two poles in his use of the term habitus. At one pole, true to the idea that we traditionally have of him, Husserl explicitly places the habitus in what we might call the pure ego. The habitus then is a sort of principle of constancy, of self-coherence or, as he himself says, of consistency (in the sense that we say of someone that they are 'consistent'): the pure subject is capable of projecting constant and permanent intentions. In this light, the habitus would be a sort of principle of consistency of the transcendental subject. At the other extreme, in other texts with which I am more familiar, perhaps because they tend towards the direction that I wanted to develop, he says something quite different. This is a theory that Husserl calls 'habituality', and here he seems to align himself with a theory rather more of the empirical self than the transcendental self.

I want to read you an extract from *Experience and Judgment*, where he says:

> Our life-world in its originality, which can be brought to light only by the destruction of those layers of sense, is not only, as has already been mentioned, a world of logical operations, not only the realm of the pre-givenness of objects as possible judicative substrates, as possible themes of cognitive activity, but it is also the world of experience in the fully concrete sense which is commonly tied in with the word 'experience'.

For those of you who might still be confused by the ways in which I have been using the habitus, it seems to me that a useful, down-to-earth translation would be this notion of experience, in the sense that we speak of 'a man of experience': experience that is the result of an almost experimental confrontation with the world. This is what Husserl says: 'it is also the world of experience in the fully concrete sense which is commonly tied in with the word "experience". And this commonplace sense is in no way related purely and simply to cognitive behaviour.' This I take to match the sense of what I was trying to say last time: we can treat the habitus as a mode of knowledge as long as we realise that we need to understand this knowledge as obeying a different kind of logic.

> Taken in its greatest generality, it is related, rather, to a habituality [*Habitualität*] which lends to him who is provided with it, to him who is 'experienced', assurance in decision and action in the situations of life – whether these situations are definitely limited or are understood in general as comprising an attitude toward life on the whole – just as, on the other hand, by this expression we are also concerned with the individual steps of the experience by which this habituality is acquired.

I found this text very striking, because it basically expressed the essence of what I wanted to find in the notion – that is, both an experience in the sense of something 'acquired through experience', by confrontation with the patterns of the social world, with the emphasis on the mode of acquisition, and the experience that enables us to get by in life, to be experienced, which gives us, as Husserl says, 'assurance in decision and action in the situations of life'. 'Thus this commonplace, familiar and concrete sense of the word "experience" points much more to a mode of behaviour which is practically active and evaluative than specifically to one that is cognitive and judicative.'[1]

While reading and re-reading Husserl, I happened upon another, rather long, passage in the *Cartesian Meditations* whose theme is the self as substrate of habituality.[2] Husserl develops an analysis very close to the one that I am about to make. The most natural prolongation of his line of thought here would obviously be Merleau-Ponty's theme of our own body as bodily subject, as intentionality incarnate, and the whole theme of the habitual body that we would find for instance in the *Phenomenology of Perception*,[3] the habitus being that familiarity with the world of which Merleau-Ponty quite rightly said that it is an intermediate term between presence and absence. This expression seems to me to be very apt to describe what I wanted to say, which is that the habitus is neither an ever-present consciousness constantly on the alert nor an absent automatism. I shall not develop this theme further; I am simply continuing the analyses that I was referring to last time. I must repeat that I am not saying all this in order to draw attention to my originality. I had been using the notion of the habitus for my own personal ends, and in my own manner, when these sources appeared as a means helping me to take my thinking further. That may sound anecdotal, but I think that it is important for those who are engaged in the history of philosophy: it must often happen that you find sources which have become sources only in retrospect, thanks to the historians.

Decision theory in economics

A second recapitulation: last time, I was arguing that the theory of action or rationality, as presented in neo-marginalist and neo-classical economics, was different from my fashion of conceiving social science in that it proceeded by deduction, and on this topic I referred to Cassirer's well-known text contrasting the philosophy of science developed by Newton with that initiated by Descartes. This analysis is important in so far as economics, especially mathematical economics or decision theory (particularly Bayesian econometrics), is typically deductive; we find other examples in the social sciences, in Chomskyan linguistics, for example. These forms of science proceed by constructing concepts that encounter reality as something that can be deduced from the model. This manner of proceeding, which is not objectionable in itself, shows a particular kind of scientific bias which it is important to characterise in order to find our way about in contemporary styles of practising science. On this point, I was able, between last Tuesday and today, to acquaint myself with a book that is very typical of this kind of deductive thinking – I shall give you the reference. This work does not add anything essential to what I was saying last time, but I would just like to emphasise one point in pursuing my argument. I find very interesting from a sociological point of view the encounter that we observe today between philosophical decision theory and the economists' theory of rational calculation. It is made possible by the deductive tradition that characterises at least some currents of the two disciplines; sharing the same fundamental approach to science allows cross-fertilisation. These people ask in an extremely interesting way the very same questions that I have been asking myself and that I have tried to resolve with the notion of habitus: they keep asking whether the model that they are constructing to explain rational decision, showing what they call the 'subjective calculations of expected utility', is a normative or a descriptive model. One of their phrases seems to me to illustrate very well what I was saying last time on the subject of Bayesian decision theory which is described in this book: 'Both as a normative and as a descriptive theory, it is a model of human rationality.'[4] If we read the rest of the text, we note that the authors of the article are playing, consciously or unconsciously, with the word 'model', understood both as an abstract construction and as an ideal paradigm against which to compare reality. This theory then proposes to account for real behaviour and at the same time to be the model of behaviour as it ideally should be. This kind of double game, so to speak, which is quite explicit in this book, seems to me to be at the heart of the models of decision explicitly or implicitly at work in the economic theory. One of the questions that I want to ask is whether it is a real contradiction, and whether there is not a foundation to the fact that they can propose a formal model both as descriptive theoretical model and as normative theoretical model. How can a normative theoretical model retain a descriptive value? Is there not a paradox here, and is the theory at work in this model ultimately able to account for the principles of its efficiency? This is a question that I am asking, and I shall return to it in more detail.

   In fact, I find it difficult to discuss the details of this book without repeating things that I have already said, or without entering into very complex debates where I could not give you all the elements, but it is interesting to note that the authors constantly waver between two theories of action and thereby of science: one which consists in describing the theoretical model as a purely arbitrary artefact which happens to a certain extent to match reality, and which we may be surprised not to find even more absurd and meaningless than it is; the other which

constitutes a theory of action very close to the one that I have been suggesting and which argues that, in the end, it doesn't matter very much
whether the agents have the proposed model in mind when we want to
account for their practice, for in fact it all seems to look as if they did
have it in mind. I quote: 'The question is not whether people actually
consciously manipulate a particular formal decision-theoretic apparatus when making decisions. Just as an unconscious, intuitive grasp
of the laws of mechanics underlies the skill of a cyclist or a tight-rope
walker, so, in the same way, an unconscious, intuitive grasp of some
principles of decision theory may underlie human decision making.'[5]
Thus they construct a mathematical theory of decision, with subjective probabilities and subjective utility functions, which happen, up to
a certain point, to account for reality. In the same book, as I said last
time, the same authors can say at times that this is how it happens,
that this is what people do, and at other times that it happens unconsciously. In which case, anything goes, as in Chomsky, who evokes
sometimes a human brain that calculates and thinks mathematically
and at other times mysterious automatisms.[6] What is interesting,
nonetheless, in this theoretical uncertainty over the theoretical status
and value of this theory is that they ask very forthrightly how it is
possible for a theoretical discourse founded on the hypothesis that, by
and large, agents try to maximise their chances of success by taking
into account the probabilities of subjective success, to give a fairly
reasonable account of reality without assuming that everyone making
an economic calculation is a geometrician or a mathematician. That is
the question that I wanted to repeat so that you would keep it in mind.

Another interesting problem in this book: the wavering between
explanation through causes and explanation through reasons. Last
time, I told you, rather hurriedly, that ultimately the question could
be put in a single sentence: When they carry out a rational act, are the
social agents prisoners of circumstances or are they fully aware of the
circumstances? Are they prisoners of circumstances or are they following their reasoning? The economists also ask this question. They
broach it in passing, but in an interesting sentence: 'The common
cause can cause the act only directly: by causing the person to have
reasons for performing the act.'[7] I'll leave you to think about that, it
is very interesting . . . I hesitate rather to enter into this type of discussion because those of you who have a little philosophical culture must
have the feeling that you have been asked to go back to college to learn
about decision theory, and those of you who are at all aware of these
debates must think that I am oversimplifying and that I am avoiding
the in-depth debates where we do actually deal with decision theory

and the problems of economic calculation together. As I repeat on every occasion, I am raising these questions not for the sake of my epistemological reputation, but in the conviction that this type of reflection is absolutely indispensable today in order to practise sociological research, writing and thinking.

Escaping mechanism and purposiveness

Having recalled this problematic of decision as seen by philosophers and economists, I would like briefly to recall what I saw as the problem. I had pointed out, perhaps rather hastily, that in fact the notion of habitus appeared to me to be justified as a theoretical instrument, at least negatively, in so far as it enables us to escape the alternatives of mechanism and purposiveness. It allows us to escape both the mechanistic explanation in terms of causes and the subjective purposive explanation in terms of ends – the extreme form of subjective purposiveness that I mentioned last time. I also said very briefly last time that these two apparently antagonistic theories – explanation through causes and explanation through subjective ends – are in fact compatible, and I gave you the proof, as I have just seen in reading this book, that the same author can very easily pass from one to the other, and without even realising it can pass from writing about one to writing about the other. To understand this slippage from one theory to another that seems the absolute opposite, it suffices to think of the perfectly classical distinction in the grand philosophical tradition between what is called physical determinism and intellectual determinism. That will bring back memories of Spinoza for you, which may be useful on occasion.

Traditional philosophy distinguished an external determinism exerted by causes external to the agent, where physical, social or biological causes are imposed on the agent. The classical formulation of this is to be found in a well-known text by Spinoza: 'A particular thing (that is, a thing that is finite and has a limited existence) can't exist or be caused to produce an effect unless it is caused to exist and produce an effect by another cause that is also finite and has a limited existence.'[8] There is then no action without attributable external cause, without physical or biological determinism: liberty is only ignorance of the causes. Here we may find the philosophy of the *Ethics* helpful in deflating certain falsely modernist problematics. Then there is the intellectual type of determinism. Against Descartes, who argued that we are free to establish truth and values, Spinoza affirmed that it is impossible for a reasonable subject or a rational calculator to oppose logical necessity in any way: the apparently free act of saying that 2 plus 2 equals 5 is in fact an act of insanity. Spinoza denies the capacity of liberty as a faculty to allow us to assent or refuse to assent; we do not have the power to suspend our judgement in the face of logical necessity. If, after this somewhat antiquarian and didactic digression, we return to economic decision theory, we find ourselves faced with exactly the same kind of problem: some will say that the economic constraints are such that agents are bound to do what they do, while others will say that the agents are well informed. The theorists of subjective probabilities, for example, will demonstrate that rational calculation is practised within the limits of the information available, and we can call on Weber's theories of rational action to say that fully rational calculation supposes as full a knowledge as possible of all the circumstances of the game and, based on these data, an optimal calculation of the objective probabilities of the success of the action. You can see that the problem, if presented in this way, can be treated as a problem of socio-economic determinism or as a problem of intellectual determinism. Reading the economists between the lines, we see the difference. Some suppose that any economic agent whatever is subject to direct social and economic determinism, that they act in conformity with causes, while others will say that they are acting in full awareness, but it comes to the same thing. For if the models constructed by the scholar account for what agents do, it is simply because the agents are governed by causes, and the scholar, knowing these causes, knows what makes the agents act in the way that they do, the difference being simply in the degree of knowledge. The alternative between mechanism and purposiveness then is only superficial. Last time I analysed economic theories as an illustration of subjective purposiveness, but, as I have just shown, they can oscillate between subjective purposiveness and mechanism. There is another form of purposiveness, which I want to approach today: collective or objective purposiveness. In opposition to mechanism, we have two types of theory of action: one makes the singular individual the subject of rational action, the other seeks the subject of rational, historical action in a kind of collective subject, collective entities such as Class, Nation or State, and the like. Today I would like to show very briefly that the theory of the habitus, or, more exactly this time, the theory of the habitus plus the theory of the field, which I shall discuss later, seem to me to allow us to escape the illusions of economic purposiveness.

We all know what lies behind collective purposiveness. There are obvious examples in what we hear broadcast every day on the radio:

'The Nation tells us that . . .', 'The State has decided to increase indirect taxation . . .', 'The Church in France is resisting the tendency to . . .', or what we read in works by sociologists: 'The capitalist school system eliminates children from disadvantaged classes'[9] or 'The bourgeois State has decided to control the media'. We are so accustomed to these statements, which refer to abstract notions that claim to represent groups, communities or institutions, that they barely catch our attention. But what do they mean? Do they have a meaning? How should we investigate these statements to assess their social validity?

The theory of the machine

I think that the logic that consists in reifying the community, treating it either as a thing obeying mechanical laws or as an individual pursuing its own ends, finds its supreme form at a higher level of theory in the notion of the State apparatus.[10] The notion of apparatus is fantastical, because it is a finalised mechanism: the apparatus is something manufactured in such a way that it seems perfectly designed for its purpose. 'The educational apparatus eliminates the most disadvantaged' means that there is a kind of machine – although we don't know which *deus* has manufactured this *machina* – which, by its own fatalistic, mechanical logic (machines are always reputedly infernal), produces effects inscribed in its programme – it has been programmed, like a computer . . . This theory of society as a kind of machine can be compatible with two apparently contradictory philosophies: one which seems rather optimistic, the other pretty pessimistic. In one case, we have a *Deus in machina*, where the machine is serving a good cause. This is what social scientists call the functionalist theory: not only is society a machine that works, but it is a machine that works for the good, the better and the best; it is so tuned that in any event its effects are beneficial; it may seem to eliminate pupils, but in fact it is in their best interests. In the other case, we have a *diabolus in machina*, the infernal machine that is programmed to do everything possible to stop the social world doing what it wants to do. I could cite the texts. The machine theory seems to me to be the limit towards which all the mechanistic uses of reified or personalised concepts tend – statements that start with 'The working class . . .', 'The proletariat . . .', 'The workers . . .', 'The struggle . . .' or 'The social movement', and the like, are of this kind. There is a whole social verbiage projecting a naïvely purposive vision that does nothing more than translate into apparently noble language what are common-sense or café-conversation reactions of moral indignation, or reactions of the kind 'it was bound to happen'. The sociologist must be on guard, and warn others to be on guard, against these distortions of our everyday discussion of the social world, because this is our spontaneous way of thinking of the social world. Just as physics has had to discard our ordinary vision of the world, with all its enchantment and magic, and also what the child psychologists call 'infantile artificialism', so sociology must rid social science of social artificialism: there is an action, therefore there must be a subject [. . .] I think that all kinds of determining conditions converge to persuade both ordinary thinking and scientific thinking to think in terms of responsibility and a subject. The simple example of the terrible accident at Beaune involving two coaches[11] can be a parable to help explain what I am trying to say. This is a typical case of the kind of social phenomenon where our ordinary thinking makes us immediately want to find who is responsible. They have appointed committees of enquiry and judges, and the logic of the investigation will have run its course only when they have assigned a subject to the action. The report of the committee of enquiry, which is now available, is a lesson in scientific sociology on which all sociologists should meditate. I will spare you the details, but, as you may have read in the press, the committee of enquiry concludes that there were several relatively independent causes that were linked to the social characteristics of the agents concerned. We read that the driver was a 'temporary employee' and was 'tired'. We could take this further and say that there are types of habitus or people who seem to be responsible. At a still further remove, you would have to study more than just the 24-hour period preceding the accident. To understand whether or not he had been drinking, you would have to go back to his childhood, and even look at his grandparents ('grandpa' and 'grandma'). So you would have to trace a kind of historical genealogy of the agents. As for the material conditions, there is the condition of the road, the queues on the motorway (which depend on the timing of the holidays), the state of the vehicles (which depends on the company owning them, including the taxes they pay and their use of temporary labour, and so on). This does not mean that the notion of responsibility is not adequate: it can be, for it can be important in certain social games to find out 'who is responsible', but that has nothing to do with science. It is not scientifically adequate; in order to construct a system of scientific explanation, we need to study a system of complex relations between agents and situations.

Having looked at this example, we might now return to what people commonly say about the social world (discussing 'the crisis', for example), and we would see that the ordinary comments made every day by people paid to talk about the social world (journalists and politicians) are far more simplistic than the comments made by this committee of enquiry. Their statements regress towards propositions of the type: 'The State has . . .', or 'There are queues on the motorway because the tolls are not high enough.' They home in on a single cause and a logic of responsibility. What seems to me to be more important from a scientific but also an ethical point of view (this is a case where the two dimensions might coincide) is perhaps to submit the objective teleology haunting the world of ordinary thinking to a critique of the type that analytic philosophy imposes on language and on the paradoxes and paralogisms engendered by an irresponsible use of language.

The ontological power of language

Before I go on to discuss objective teleology – that is, Marxist teleology – I would like to say a few words about the analytic approach to the investigation of language, so that you will have it in mind. If it is important to give the right names to the elements of the social world, it is because, as common sense says it in a popular expression that I find perfectly adequate, 'you can say everything with language': everything can be said; you can even speak of things that don't exist.

Those who are steeped in philosophical culture will recognise here the tradition which, from the Sophists to Bertrand Russell, or in its present guise of analytical philosophy, consists in questioning the legitimacy of speaking of things that don't exist: Can you legitimately speak of something that doesn't exist, and, in speaking of something that doesn't exist, are you not granting existence to something that doesn't exist? This is what the Sophists after Plato called the problem of the 'goat-stag'[12] – that is, of the chimera – the kind of mongrel reality composed of two separate pieces that can exist because all things can be said, and, since all things can be said, all things can be thought and imagined. I think that, in sociology, when we say: 'The State has decided that . . .', it is rather as if we were to say: 'Non-being is' or 'the goat-stag is gambolling in the countryside'; we are making a statement that is grammatically correct and which has meaning, as Frege would have said,[13] but still has no referent. That it has meaning does not mean that it refers to something that exists. In different terms (I apologise to those who know this already for insisting on it . . .), when I say: 'The working classes are up in arms against paying taxes', I engage a whole set of presuppositions, exactly as when I say: 'The king of France is bald.' Bertrand Russell's famous example,[14] much loved of philosophers of language, implies as self-evident that there is a king of France. I seem to be saying: 'The king of France is bald', but, before I say that he is bald, I am saying that there is a king of France. Likewise, when I say: 'The working classes will not accept a rise in taxation', I seem to be talking of a rise in taxation, but I am saying firstly that there is a working class, which is in fact open to question. It is the same when I say: 'The State has decided that . . .'. In other words, I am drawing attention to the predicate, whereas I should be putting the question that is logically raised by the existential quantifier, which is: 'Can I say that the subject of my predicate exists? Does what I am talking about exist?'

I think that we have lost the habit of putting this kind of question largely because we are all steeped in the purposiveness of the collective, that soft form of Hegelianism which filters down through Marxism or journalism. We are so steeped in it that we lap up all these statements like mother's milk rather than cry out in protest. Logicians, on the other hand, raise the question of the ontological status of abstract realities: Do concepts exist, or do we conclude all is a question of nominalism? And, an old scholastic problem, should we settle for a radical nominalism or a kind of radical phenomenalism, according to which we would only ever speak of notions and never of reality, or should we take all propositions on the social world literally?

The critique of ordinary language, which is a phase in the history of science, ultimately assumes a particular importance and usefulness in the social sciences. But this critique of language which applies to all abstract concepts is particularly difficult in the case of the social sciences, because naming things with words in their case plays a part in creating reality: you cannot simply say that notions should be subject to logical critique; we also need to know that this logical critique inevitably opens up onto a sociological critique in so far as words play their part – as I have said here on several occasions – in creating reality. If, for example, somebody says with authority that the king of France is bald, it is no longer a logical question; it is a political question. If somebody says with authority that a 'crisis' is looming, they help to create that crisis. In other words, in the case of the social sciences, questioning the ontological status of the notions that we use to name the social world means questioning by the same token the political significance of the arbitrary use of notions which, when they are used with authority to imply and postulate existence, go towards bringing into existence what they designate. I think that the simplest and most striking example would be that of the existence of the social classes. If it is a problem which in a sense is both insoluble and already decided, it is precisely because it is central to the paradox that I have been describing: to say that there are two classes is an assertion, but when it is made by somebody who is authorised to speak on the social world this assertion helps to verify itself; it is self-validating. What I wanted to say – I have expressed it rather badly for a number of reasons, and especially because I fear that you might not see the need for this digression – is that social reality is partly created by social agents, in so far as they are speaking subjects. In this light, granting language an ontological status and power implies letting language play an eminently political role. In my notes preparing for these lectures I noted an example that will I think help explain what I intended to say and perhaps make it more tangible. Discussing the ordinary concepts that we use, logicians, and particularly Gilbert Ryle, remark that, since we rely on an unequivocal definition of what it is to exist, a definition based on the way in which physical things exist, we are led to ask inappropriate questions of things conceptual. For instance, on the concept of mind – I refer to Gilbert Ryle's book *The Concept of Mind*[15] – we will ask where the mind is situated: Is it in the body, in the head, in the organism, and so on? And we will end up with what Ryle calls the fallacy of the 'ghost in the machine', which for him sums up the philosophy of Descartes.[16] In other words, since we implicitly suppose that something that exists is something physical, tangible and locatable – to exist is to exist somewhere – as soon as we question the existence of a thing or a concept, the problem of its localisation arises. I could show you whole volumes or even whole libraries devoted to the problem of the locus or place of culture. A whole English-language anthropological tradition investigated the status of the thing called 'culture' and defined it as being what allowed two individuals to attribute the same meaning to the same behaviour and the same behaviour to the same signifying intentions. But where does culture exist? Similarly, we can ask where language exists, whether it is stored in the treasure house of our brains – you can refer to Saussure who gives a whole series of answers to the question.[17] Another example: in the same vein, we can ask where the generating principle of our actions lies. That is, where is the subject? Who is the cause? Where is the Archimedean point? In many cases you could say that the thing you are looking for is nowhere to be found. Often analytical philosophers say that the mind is nowhere, which simply means that the question is not pertinent, that you are asking a question that has no relevance to the object of your enquiry. In fact, replying 'nowhere' means 'question irrelevant'.

I think that, even without realising it, we are constantly asking the social world this kind of question. If we subjected the statement 'The

Church says that . . .' to Russell's type of critique, we find that there are in fact two propositions: one proposition affirming that 'there is something like the Church', which means that the thing called the Church exists, and another affirming that 'The Church says this or that'. Having placed in the universe something like a Church, we can then ask what it means for something like a Church to exist, and we will answer that the Church exists like a thing, in its canon law and its cathedrals, and so on. What I wanted to say is that we lead social science to make considerable progress when we refuse to make an ontological leap. Because ultimately when we say: 'The Church thinks that . . .', we are passing from one fact, that we can say the word 'Church', to another fact, that something like the Church exists and exists in the way that things do when they exist because we can touch them. This is the pattern of many of our debates.

Popular culture and popular language

I shall take another example and then you will see the point to this digression, which made me feel uncomfortable because I thought you were looking rather panic-stricken [*laughter*]. I shall now return to safer ground: I want to discuss the notion of 'popular culture' or 'popular language', which is a highly contentious issue. This is a debate that recurs whenever there is a crisis, and it is the same debate reinvented a hundred times over; the briefest historical overview will enable us to guess the whole sequence of debates to come. Why does a notion such as 'popular culture' exert such fascination? The answer could be found largely through a sociological study of intellectuals. It remains to ask why this notion is predisposed to obey the logic of the ontological argument that I have just mentioned. The demonstration would be very long and arduous because people are passionately committed to the issue – although I am not quite sure why. But if the debate is so obscure, it is, to put it crudely, because it is a proposition of the type 'non-being exists'. Culture, not in the sense used by ethnologists but in the sense that we usually understand it in a society divided into classes – for example, when we say that a man is 'cultivated' or that he has 'great culture' – contrasts with nature – that is, with the excluded, the dominated classes. Culture is what distinguishes the people in the dominant classes from the people in the dominated classes. On a linguistic level, for instance, we talk of 'crude words' and 'rough language', which correspond to the 'raw' as opposed to the 'cooked', in the traditional contrast between nature and culture.

Culture then is constituted in opposition to nature, against the uncouth – that is, those who live in a state of nature within the social order. To verify what I am saying, you have only to open a dictionary at any one of the adjectives of the type polite/impolite, rough, crude, etc.: you will find a system of adjectives organised around oppositions of the type nature/culture – that is, dominant/dominated, fine/crude, light/heavy, distinguished/vulgar. I must repeat the fact that culture is constituted in opposition to nature, in the sense that cultivated people are constituted in opposition to people with no social qualities, who live in society in the raw state of the brute – look up the adjectives 'raw' and 'brutal' and you will find an interesting cluster of attributes.[18] When people speak of popular culture they are creating a 'goat-stag': there is the cultivated being – and the uncultivated person is a non-being. They are speaking of a 'non-existent being'. They are saying that there are people whose culture is what culture is defined against. Some would say that the meaning of the word 'culture' has changed, that we are talking of culture as ethnologists define it, of culture in the sense of a life style, of a mode of living. But this is absolutely not true. The people who speak of 'popular culture' are claiming to do so as an exercise in rehabilitation, and they want to find in the thing thus defined as popular everything that seems to them to constitute the dominant culture: 'Think of slang, it's magnificent, it's worthy of Saint-John Perse!'[19] [*laughter*]. If we are able to create this kind of reality, it is because the producers and consumers of this notion have such strong social interests that they gloss over the difficulties, and also because contradictions in objective reality itself make this sort of projective text possible. I will give you another example – although I am not at all happy with it – and you can add to it yourselves: I have long thought that, if notions such as 'popular culture', 'popular language' and 'popular art' – and in fact all the symbolic phenomena that people label as 'popular' – are able to function, circulate and be understood, it is because people have a very powerful interest, perhaps a vital interest, in making a *coincidentia oppositorum* – which union of opposites is the very definition of magic – and in glossing over the difficulties. But I believe that it is also because we are accustomed to combining words and exploiting the capacity that symbolic systems have to detach themselves from their referents. When we apply systematically to sociology the distinction between meaning and reference, we see that the essence of the political discourse and symbolic struggles of everyday life is made possible by this capacity of language and of all symbolic systems in general to detach themselves from their referent – I forget who spoke of 'semantic detachment'[20] – and 'run in neutral' (Wittgenstein said of language that in many cases language is just 'idling').[21] Politics thrives on the abuse of symbolic power, this permanent semantic detachment that means that we can say anything. But the act of speaking them makes things exist. If I want to refute the notion of popular culture, I am obliged to speak of it, and in so doing I help to make it exist, which is one of the great problems in the political struggle: How can we fight against a notion without contributing to its existence? It is the paradox of the Sophists: as soon as something is thinkable and sayable, it has a form of being. As soon as I say, 'Non-being exists', non-being does exist. As soon as I speak of 'popular culture' to say that it does not exist, I help to make it exist.

I am not sure that I can do much better than that, but nonetheless I am going to try to repeat what I have just said so that you can at least see what my intention was. I wanted to say that it would be in the best interest of social science to import into the arena of scientific practice a form of the critique of language that a certain philosophical tradition has developed. This hardly ever happens, because the people who follow this tradition of analytical philosophy are no doubt those farthest removed from any interest in the social world, and the people who are interested in studying the social world are, often for social reasons (their training or dispositions, for instance), as far removed as possible from this tradition of analytical philosophy, whose examples such as: 'The king of France is bald' or the sophism of the Indian[22] seem to them to be quite gratuitous. I think that, beyond the subjective difficulty that I have felt today, there is also an objective difficulty, which is that it is always difficult enough even in our own minds to connect two things that we have learned at very different times and that obey very different logical patterns.

It is striking that the philosophers of this tradition very often invoke examples taken from the social world: for instance, they ask whether the University of Oxford is something other than the collection of its colleges or, another example, whether, when I have seen the three companies that compose the regiment march past, I should still expect to see the regiment.[23] They love this kind of humorous, arbitrary and very Oxford-style example, which they chuckle over without thinking of the social world for a moment. Which makes it difficult in this universe to think of anything real. I have attended meetings of philosophers of this persuasion, and I noted that it was sufficient to throw a real example into this world of thought to cause consternation. Having said that, I think that they are people who talk of the social world perhaps more than anyone. It took me a long time before I came to make use of this philosophical current and use it to reflect on my own practice and my own use of language. You should listen to what Durkheim, for example, says in *The Elementary Forms of Religious Life*, which is that logical concepts have been formed by the community, that logic is in fact the social world, that the theory of logic is a sociological theory.[24] We have all read that, but deep down we don't believe it any more, because it is part of the bedrock of sociological culture. I think that working on language in the light of this logic is to work on the social world – all the more since, as I have attempted to argue (but this was perhaps the point where I was least clear), it lies at the heart of the work of the political enterprise. The political enterprise is a labour of language, working through and on words, exploiting the inherent property of language – and not only of language – to be able to distance itself from what it is saying and to describe things that do not exist. This language has the property of being able to speak in a vacuum when there is nothing to say, but, even more strikingly, it has the property of being able to attack us with the ontological argument, and it constantly does so. In fact today I have drawn on the Kantian 'intention', which is to say: 'Take care, for when we say "the concept exists and therefore the thing exists" – or even, often enough, when we don't say it – we are mounting an ontological attack, and that is a political attack.'

Above all, I wanted to link two currents which belong to the same tradition of analytical philosophy but which are relatively independent: the current of the logic of abstract notions and the current, represented by Austin in particular, of those who enquire into the power of words. If we combine the two and ask what it is to speak of things that may not exist as if they existed, we should see that, when we are authorised to speak, we have the authority to make people believe that what we are talking about exists . . . that is what I really wanted to say. To say that social things exist, without questioning the truth of what we are saying, when we have the social authority to say it, is helping to bring people to believe that they exist, and in fact making them exist, all the time without questioning the difference between existence and non-existence. What does it mean for a social thing to exist? Does it have a specific mode of existence? What does this specific mode of existence consist of? If you remember, that is the first question that I put at the beginning of the year; those were the questions I asked at the start of the first lecture. Should we unpack this notion of existence? When we place the verb 'to be' in both of its senses [. . .] after a concept, what are we doing? Basically, to sum up, I simply wanted to say that we would have a better idea of what we are doing when we speak of the social world if we realised that we are constantly exposed to ontological slippage.

Marxist teleology

If I have placed this digression on the analytical philosophy of language here, it is because I believe that this ontological conjuring trick,
this metaphysical forgery – as used to be said of bogus ontological
arguments – and this pseudo-sociological writing, which leads us to
act as if things existed because we can speak of them, occurs most
frequently in the current of thought that we might call 'objective teleology'. I shall return to this point. I have explained how difficult it
is to describe the social world accurately; the very logic of language
encourages personification through the simple fact that we speak as the
subject of a sentence, meaning that we can not only assign predicates
to notions designating collectives but also simply treat these notions
as subjects of sentences designed to receive predicates, subjects of
verbs designating action; therein lies a whole teleology of apparently
self-evident history. In fact, objective teleology in its Marxist form is
inscribed within ordinary language. That is what I had in mind while I
was digressing: if we all have at the back of our minds a kind of 'soft'
Hegelianism, it is because it is in harmony with the deep structure of
language that I have described.

    That may seem rather crude and simplistic, especially at a time when
there is much discussion over the relation between Hegelian dialectic
and Marxist dialectic. (Here, again, I am embarrassed that I am going
to have to say things that are simple or even simplistic, but I think
that they are useful for the point of view that I want to develop.) It is
fashionable to say that the Marxist tradition broke with the Hegelian
tradition of objective teleology. As Marx declared (therefore it is true
– note the proposition 'Marx declared that he had broken with Hegel
. . .'), the end of history is not an ideal end fixed *a priori* but a material ending [. . .] 'inscribed in the process itself, of which its theory is
a reflection'. It appears in very clear terms in Engels's *Dialectics of
Nature* – I think that Engels is in fact a spontaneous sociologist and
that, when we speak of an epistemological obstacle, it is there that we
should seek it. I quote: 'Dialectics, so-called *objective* dialectics, pre-
vails throughout nature, and so-called subjective dialectics, dialectical
thought, is only the reflection of the motion through opposites which
asserts itself everywhere in nature, and which by the continual conflict
of the opposites and their final passage into one another, or into higher
forms, determines the life of nature.'[25] In other words, there is a kind of
harmony between the subjective and the objective, and this harmony
is the precise definition of purposiveness. The theoretical dialectician
as subject espouses in this way the theoretical movement of Nature,

which moves not towards an end but towards an ending – note the change of the wording. The end is not transcendence; it is discovered scientifically as the natural ending towards which the historical process is advancing – this ending is necessary (it presupposes an end). In brief, the philosophy of history is replaced by a science of history, by a materialist teleology – that is, by laws. As Marx said, there is no longer an ideal end fixed *a priori*; there are the objective laws of Nature. It happens that these objective laws of Nature proceed towards an absolutely necessary and inevitable end, socialism, and so there is an absolute meaning to history.

This kind of secularisation of Hegel's theological teleology is not in my opinion a radical change in philosophy but an *aggiornamento*. And this kind of covert purposive philosophy is in fact the *doxa* in which we are steeped; we can find it in all sorts of different people, in Weber or in Husserl. For instance, in one short text Husserl says: 'In our European humanity there is an innate entelechy that thoroughly controls the changes in the European image and gives to it the sense of a development in the direction of an ideal image of life and being, as moving toward an eternal pole.' [We have to remember that the text was delivered as a lecture in 1935 in Vienna.] And, a little further: 'The spiritual *telos* of European man . . . lies in infinity.'[26] For Weber, I refer you to a text on the process of rationalisation, which is a central element in his thought, and above all – it is the clearest text – to the Introduction to *The Protestant Ethic and the Spirit of Capitalism*, where he gives a sort of tableau of humanity from the Babylonians down to our own times in the following manner: a series of sketches – a term which recurs frequently: the Babylonians laid the foundations of calculation, the Chaldeans discovered trigonometry, and so on – has accumulated to give us a rational society, with rational law and music, and the like.[27] And in an extraordinary text on music, appended to *Economy and Society*, Weber describes the history of Western music from the Middle Ages down to our own times as a process of rationalisation and mathematicalisation.[28] In a very interesting book – which I have just thought of, I don't have the reference to hand[29] – the art historian Gombrich shows how the 'soft' Hegelian tradition, that kind of laicised Hegel, has haunted the whole social history of art through very different people, such as Panofsky. It is a kind of covert purposiveness, a scientific purposiveness; the end is not posited by a scholarly subject discovering the objective orientation of history; it is scientifically calculated, necessary and ideal (in the case of socialism). In a way, it is the same as Hegel, only worse. We have what seems to me to be the most pernicious form of ideology, ideology disguised as science – that is, the modern form of ideology concerning the social world, which takes on the appearance of science and in a way claims to be unanswerable. This end is no longer officially an ideal end, but it remains an end because we are necessarily advancing towards it. This purposiveness is even more mysterious than Hegel's and harbours all the mystique of the 'subjectless process'. There is a kind of movement towards an end. Nobody knows why we are going there, or how we are going there, but we are necessarily going there.

The reification and personification of the collective

The second objection that has been put to me is this: this end that continues to be posited, but on a scientific basis, is an end that has no agents proposing it and is completely independent of the practice of individuals. This is what seems to me to be most worrying from the point of view of a theory that takes praxis as its principle. The art of reifying the collective plays a major part here. Here I ought to rehearse – but I won't, because I don't have time – all the theories of the State apparatus and the functions attributed to the State to see how clearly they display what I call social anthropomorphism or social artificialism. When they say that 'the capitalist school eliminates', an end is posited, with no subject, but how can they posit an end in the absence of a subject? When they say that the State or the school is at the service of the dominant class, we imagine that someone has designated these ends and the instances that serve as their means. According to this sort of instrumentalist definition, the State is only the relay of an end whose proposer we do not know. We then have to refer to the 'dominant class', for instance, or a different collective subject, and we head off into an infinite regression. They ought to be brave enough to say that it is God in the end, but of course they won't, because their logic is supposed to be materialist . . . This sort of artificialism engenders many errors, as we see in the case of the State: since the State is described in a strictly instrumental logic, it transparently matches the ends that it is supposed to attain; this is why they can make statements of the kind: 'The capitalist State is dominant', 'The capitalist State eliminates', because there is a coincidence of the means and the ends, because it is entirely organised with a view to the end. Yet you need only to reflect on the kind of model that I am suggesting – I posit the habitus on one side and I shall go on to posit the field on the other – to see that the State is in fact composed of agents, each with their habitus. Remember the analysis of the public employee that I made the other day:[30] to understand the subway ticket inspector or the postman, you need time, you need to know the social conditions that produce the ticket puncher and the field in which he operates, etc. – you can't just make a statement such as: 'The State punches your ticket.' In fact this recalls the paradigm of the coach crash at Beaune – that is, a universe of extremely complex relations. To understand any 'output'[31] (whether a new law or an interview in the press) to which we allocate the State as subject, or of which we are tempted to assign the paternity or the initiative to the State, we need to refer to the whole space of what I call the field of power, which I shall say more about, including the internal relations between the dominant fractions of the dominant class, a formidably complicated universe of relations, that we must not abridge . . . You could at a pinch say that 'the State' is a kind of shorthand, but shorthand in such a case is fatal. I have now raised a number of objections to this kind of purposive philosophy or objective teleology. What I shall have to say, throughout the year to come, will be an account of what this misleading shorthand has to say.

As I said rather hurriedly just now, the reification of the collective leads on to two forms of functionalism: one optimistic and one pessimistic. But in both cases it is a formula of the type 'it was bound to happen' that emerges in the objective discourse. I am very reluctant to do this, but to make sure that you understand what I am trying to say I am going to read you some sentences which summarise the book that I have just finished writing on the problem of language:

A language is not formed spontaneously, as people often think; the enforced legitimation of the dominant usage corresponds to a political strategy. In France, the revolutionary school of the nineteenth century only devalued popular speech in order to better preserve the gains of the Revolution . . . This linguistic competence resembles a capital rewarded by distinction and power. Its holders manipulate it as one plays the market and take care to keep the linguistic capital unequally shared. It is important that there should be a restricted language to reign over ordinary speech . . ., etc.[32]

The sentence 'Its holders . . . take care to . . .' gives us an example of how difficult it is to speak of the social world without falling – no moral judgement intended – into purposiveness, without reintroducing purpose. There is in fact a universe of linguistic usage, where agents engaging in multiple and complex interactions produce discourse in conformity with general laws that become specific in each particular case: whenever there are two interlocutors, the structure of the market depends on the precise competence of the speakers, which depends in turn on their linguistic capital but also on their symbolic capital. All this is happening all the time, here, there and everywhere; there comes a time when we can say that there is a dominant, legitimate language, the one that is recorded in dictionaries, the one that you need to know in order to go in for politics or pass your exams.

And then there is a dominated language that you can also describe and assign social limits to. But as soon as we use shorthand, we will say: 'There are holders of capital who make sure that language remains distinctive', whereas linguistic phenomena escape our consciousness entirely. There is a splendid comment by Michelet on Frederick II of Prussia, who wanted to add a mute 'e' to the end of German words, thinking that this would make the German language more euphonious. It didn't last after Frederick's death: even he was not able to add a mute 'e' to the German language. In other words, these things entirely escape our control, which does not mean that they are not answerable to political action, or that the concentration of a language in the form of a standard, legitimate and official language that disqualifies local and popular speech has no connection with politics or the State. But there is no intention that we might locate somewhere in the social world so as to ask: Where? Who decided? Where is the decree? Who signed it? Who wanted it?, and so on. It does not even mean that a whole social class is involved: the greatest beneficiaries of linguistic capital are totally unconscious of the mechanism that procures this benefit for them, and it often happens that this ignorance benefits the dominated. It happens that the unconscious strategies of the habitus rise to the level of conscious and organised strategies, and especially collective strategies. [. . .]

It is interesting to trace the genealogy of this mode of personalised thinking on the social world because it is not certain that it is universal, and I was thinking how fertile the model of narrative fiction has been, although I shall not develop this theme, so I must ask you to look it up for yourselves. I think that, if the temptation to write of history or society in terms of personalities is so strong, it is on the one hand because of the very logic of language, but also because the models of writing that we are steeped in, notably the novel, are entirely organised around this fictional structure. An article by Michel Butor in *Repertoire II* seemed to me to shed interesting light on this question.[33] Butor, like most of the authors of the Nouveau Roman, reflects on the problem of writing and asks why this linear model of a story to be told has imposed itself so forcefully. It is no accident that the philosophy of history tells a story that proceeds towards an end, along the lines of what made a good story according to the definition of the novel that was dominant before Joyce. The writers of the Nouveau Roman are disconcerting because they interfere with the story and tell it the wrong way round. Although they are inspired by a literary project, I think that we need analogous work to be done in sociology for us to be able to speak rightly of the social world. I am building on this text by Butor that you can read for yourselves: he shows that the fictional model of the story is a succession of decisive decisions. The other day I referred to the philosophy of history according to decision theory, via *Homo economicus*. It all goes to make the life of *Homo economicus* look like a series of choices where he has to maximise the information and make calculations as a function of the subjective and objective probabilities. This is the typical model of the novel as described by Butor: a series of schemes of decisive individual actions which determine each other; if at any one moment the decision were different, the whole sequence would change, and, as a result, one energetic decision can change your life (see Balzac and Stendhal). He makes the very interesting point that Victor Hugo, in *Ninety-Three* more than *Les Misérables*, is an exception. What he says seems to me to be the right way of speaking of the social world: the novel is linear, 'the biographical form tends to establish in the work a "line" as continuous as possible [. . .]. However original the individual, he cannot therefore be considered as anything more than a remarkable point in a field of forces.' Whence the disappearance of the key character of the Romantic novel: the conqueror of Paris; for Butor, no more Rastignac. Real characters owe their historical stature to the 'circumstantial forces [. . .] that move them'. He then quotes the passages from *Ninety-Three* on Marat, who has become no more than a kind of medium – in the magical sense – through whom the forces of the field operate. Butor continues on the problem of fictional writing which seems to me to be the same problem as that of scientific writing: 'How can we grasp in words the seething flux of different textures, migrations and shifts caused or affected by such a plethora of elements?' And a little later he says: 'What is more, the forces that are suggested are known to us only through the intermediary of the individuals that they influence' (this is a major problem for sociology: most often we can gain access to the field of forces only by questioning the individuals who are affected by them and who express them refracted through the reactions of their habitus). 'We are obliged to conduct surveys, make statistical calculations, select samples, locate zones, poles and areas of tension.'[34] I have drawn on this example, rather reluctantly, because people often ask me: 'Why do you write like that?

Why do you write such complicated stuff, so badly and laboriously, etc.?' I think that the problem of writing is consubstantial with the problem of thinking adequately about the social world; changing the way that we use words can profoundly change our vision of the social world. That is what I wanted to add to my argument.

The solution of the habitus

The first conclusion that I want to draw now from these analyses of arguments concerning the habitus is as follows: in contrast to those different philosophies of action which are at the same time philosophies of history, the notion of the habitus enables us to propose a philosophy of action where the subject of the action is centred not directly on the apparent agent, the biological individual as such, but on that sort of biological incarnation of the social that I call the habitus (although I'm afraid that I shall not be able to develop this argument fully until I have explained the field). I am not sure whether I can do it in just a few words, but I would like to show how the notion of habitus in fact enables us to avoid raising the very naïve issues denounced by analytical philosophers – by Ryle, for example, when he noted that the Cartesian tradition asked things about the existence of the soul that were not pertinent, since the mind does not exist in the mode in question. I think that the notion of habitus is also an attempt to respond to the question of the mode in which the social exists. The social exists in the form of 'something' that we see manifest in two situations (although we should not ask where it actually exists). On the one hand, it is manifest through the process of acquisition and incorporation: social subjects are modified by social and economic conditions; as Husserl said, they are constantly transformed by experience – this is what the habitus is. On the other hand, we grasp the habitus as a process whereby the biological individual, who is reduced entirely to biological terms if we ignore the habitus, enters into a relationship with the social world, of which he is always partly a product, a relationship that is not reducible to a biological account. In fact the habitus designates a double relationship, comprising socialisation and a permanently lasting manner of entering into relation with the social world, a lasting modification of the biological given.

Here again, the danger of reification exists: I can already imagine statements such as: 'The petit-bourgeois habitus does this or that . . .' We feel compelled to reify and we forget that, logically, we cannot make the habitus the subject of a sentence. The petit-bourgeois habitus is thus a tendency to act against purposiveness. This is the theme of Terence's famous comedy *Heauton Timorumenos* (*The Self-Tormentor*),[35] and I think that it is one of the forms through which we can think of the *petit bourgeois*. If we have to characterise the *petit bourgeois*, it is someone who is disposed to enter into a relationship with the social world in such a way that their rebellion, resentment and moral indignation against society – which is one of the dispositions of the *petite bourgeoisie* – often has the effect of bringing on what they are protesting against. In other words, the *petit bourgeois* is someone who has the gift of making things happen that would not happen to them if they didn't object in advance to the fact that they were going to happen. This point is interesting for our theory.

This leads us to another point, with which I shall conclude: the paradox of the partial adequacy of the models constructed in the hypothesis of adjusting expectations to objective chances and real practices. How is it that the models which suppose that agents act in full knowledge – that is, on the basis of an evaluation of the probabilities of success, although we don't know how this evaluation is established – can have a predictive value? I think that one function of the notion of habitus (and even its principal function) is to explain this adjustment of the models to reality without having to resort either to the hypothesis of the rational economic calculator or to the hypothesis of crude causal determination.

To continue, briefly: this is what I call 'the causality of the probable', to borrow a term from Bachelard.[36] This process of socialisation, what Husserl calls experience, acquired through repeated confrontation with a social world structured according to a certain logic, a sort of disposition to anticipate and await what is going to happen, and moreover to help make it happen by expecting it to happen – in fact, this disposition to anticipate and await the probable – is acquired through the permanent confrontation with a structured world defined by a certain structure of objective probabilities. I shall return to this when I come to discuss the field, for one might say that the field is a space of objective probabilities (which is to say that, when you enter a space and go to a particular place, you have a 1 per cent, 20 per cent or 50 per cent chance of success). Experience – using Husserl's term again – in the sense of an acquired disposition is that kind of art of anticipating what is going to happen, and a part of social necessity only comes into being with the complicity of people so prepared for what is going to happen that they play a part in making it happen. This would be very relevant for understanding the phenomena of symbolic violence, and there are phenomena of domination that can only be understood in terms of the dominated collaborating in their own domination. [. . .] And there is no point in trying to look for the starting point of this process, which leads finally to my principle of non-decision: we are always caught up in the movement; it always started earlier; and so on. This analysis can lead us to adopt a very deterministic and fatalistic vision. I think that a certain number of you are going to say 'there is nothing to be done' and that ultimately the habitus has a transcendental character. That makes a lot of philosophical references for one day, but they are useful. I do not think that this analysis necessarily leads to fatalism.

The habitus is a product of history. Although we cannot meaning-fully say at what point the process starts, we can nonetheless grasp its logical development, and its deeper logic is well known: this involves problems of cognitive discord, along with a tendency to mitigate them; for example, it is difficult to imagine becoming prime minister, or simply an *agrégé*[37] or a banker, if you left school at the age of eleven, and there is a whole range of social warnings and sanctions . . . The social sanctions are very important, contrary to what we think if we universalise a bourgeois experience. One of the characteristics of the bourgeois experience is that the sanctions of the natural and social world are nearly always mediated by people you know, mum and dad and other family and friends, in so far as they form a protective screen. This is not universal at all. The experience of the popular milieu is quite different: the sanctions are much more rudely and directly imposed, as in Rousseau's style of education. Rousseau said: 'Don't tell him that he might get burnt, let him get burnt';[38] simply, this is the difference between a bourgeois and a popular upbringing. They give very differ-ent visions of the social world. Depending on whether you discover the social world physically, by having your nose rubbed in it, so to speak, or verbally, through dialogue: 'Now you know you must be careful not to . . .', 'Don't you think you ought to . . .', 'You should . . .', etc., your representation of the social world will be radically different.

That having been said, the fundamental law of the acquisition of the habitus will be the same: even the kind of habitus that I call a 'liberated habitus' – that is, one where you take your distance from the world and your role, and from what you say and do – is related to a form of social necessity, that may be characterised in terms of a relatively greater distance from necessity.[39] We might even say that the funda-mental principle of socialisation is the principle of 'making a virtue of necessity': by dint of discovering that we cannot attain certain possi-bilities, we finally give up trying. I always quote Hume here: 'We are no sooner acquainted with the impossibility of satisfying any desire, than the desire itself vanishes.'[40] This is a very surprising statement, but it is sociologically true: impossible aspirations are erased and forgotten and real expectations tend to adapt to objective opportunity. When you question people about the future – which is how I first got to know this law[41] – they have expectations that match their opportunities and they desire what they can attain, without this being mechanical. The principle of 'making a virtue of necessity' is linked, for example, with dispositions of submission to necessity in the dominated classes, who, if you come to think of it, are extraordinarily submitted to necessity.[42]

The habitus of necessity – that is, the habitus of the dominated – is a habitus of submission to order. It does not exclude forms of revolt but it is a habitus of necessity in the sense that the revolt is not primary. If people often find this idea shocking, it is because they misunderstand the experience of the dominated; as I suggested the other day, the problem arises when, in imagination or in reality, we occupy subordinate positions with our dominant attitudes: when they are inhabited by the habitus of the dominant, the positions of the dominated are experienced in a way that is different from the way they are experienced when they are inhabited by people who have the habitus of their habitat. In the light of this logic, you might ask me: 'But how can you explain the forms of habitus that appear exceptional, the liberated habitus or even the intellectual habitus and the transgressional habitus?' This is the very opposite of 'the grapes are too green';[43] and there is the proverb that says: 'The grass is always greener on the other side of the fence.' I don't have time to develop this argument further, but we could show that a transgressional habitus is the product of a certain kind of exceptional social conditions.

I would simply like to argue that, in order to account for the paradox that the models constructed according to this rationalist hypothesis are not even falser than they are, we need to posit a mechanism of causality by probability and something like the habitus as a lasting modification of the organism, which means that the social agents act as if they were determined by rational calculation of the likelihood of success. The important expression is 'it all seems to show': this reminds us that there is a gap between the model and the reality that the model claims to translate – a logical, mathematical proposition can account for reality without being the explanatory principle of that reality. The theory of the habitus enables us to account for this fundamental fact: when you suppose that social agents will act in a reasonable rather than a rational way – that is, that they will act as they ought to act in order to avoid conflict with the social world, given their capital and the objective likelihood of successfully challenging the objective laws – you can roughly predict what people are going to do. Formal models whose logic follows a highly eccentric philosophy of decision theory and subjective teleology are much truer than they should be because, in reality, social agents are lastingly shaped and transformed to adapt to the world in which they will act; this means that they anticipate necessity without having to calculate, which gives their behaviour an appearance of purposiveness ('He did what he had to do'). Think of the example of the feel for the game that I used last time; the fact that a player moves to the exact place where the ball is going to arrive while the player kicking it doesn't even know where he is sending it is the stuff of miracles or fantasies. The social world is full of similar things, of people anticipating ends that they have not posited. The habitus is the kind of feel for the social world and experience that enables people to adapt objectively, without calculating, at least within certain limits, more or less tidily depending on periods and conjunctures – it is not a universal law. And I believe that it is in the light of this law that we can understand the exceptions. I shall emphasise just one point, which I shall return to briefly next time: this necessity is largely and even essentially exercised through objective sanctions (ridicule or failure, for example) rather than through any deliberate intervention through education or verbal mediation. Having said that, there are actions, in particular the rites of passage that I call rites of institution, that use all the authority of the social world to increase and reinforce the objective sanctions of the world. In particular, the opposition between masculine and feminine reveals how rites of passage reinforce the objective sanctions of a real world that is itself divided according to the masculine/feminine opposition and offers a very unequal structure of objective opportunities [. . .].[44] The rites of passage mobilise the specific force of the social to increase this effect. And in the light of this logic, as I shall explain briefly next time, the educational system has a very special function in our societies: it is the leading institution of symbolic reinforcement of the sanctions that help to nourish experience, in the sense of an unconscious commitment to objective necessity.

Lecture of 16 November 1982

The adaptation of expectation to opportunity – Avoiding purposiveness – Interiorising the social – Incorporating necessity – Rites of institution – The call to order: the example of the relation of the family to the school – Social relations in the enquiry relationship – Surreptitious persuasion, symbolic violence – The paradox of continuity – Critique of the scholarly relation

I shall now attempt to resume what I have said in the previous lectures by returning to the schema that I set out in the second lecture.[1] I want to examine the difference between the relation R0 – that is, the scholarly relation to the social world – and the practical relation R1 to the same world. Last time I did briefly mention the relation R2, which is there to symbolise the relation between the field as field of forces and the biological organism in so far as it is liable to be socialised and thus constituted as a social habitus. This relation R2 – to which I shall return later – is a kind of genetic relation through which the incorporated social is constituted; in fact it describes the process of conditioning that is accomplished in a certain type of social condition. This process, which we usually call 'socialisation', could also be called 'incorporation of the social'.

The adaptation of expectation to opportunity

In my last lecture I argued that, in my opinion, one of the fundamental mechanisms affecting this process is the one that makes the aspirations of social subjects, or agents, tend to adapt to objective opportunity. This kind of very general law of predisposition seems to me fundamental in order to understand the social genesis of the habitus. It can be

expressed in the commonplace saying 'to make a virtue of necessity':
by and large we can say that social agents placed in a given social situation will tend to adapt their aspirations quite unconsciously to the
possibilities objectively written into these conditions. And I said that
one of the properties of the social fields would be precisely the structure of possibility – of 'objective potential' or objective probability, to
use Weber's terminology – that it offers either to an average subject
(which would make an interesting case to debate, to which I may well
return) or to a particular subject able to specify in their particular case
the value of these average probabilities. This relation between opportunity and expectation does not come out of the blue. It is constantly
at play in the social experience of the agent. I suggested an equivalence
between experience – borrowing the word from Husserl – and the
habitus. It is one of the meanings that we can give to the concept of the
habitus. Social experience as the incorporated form of objective patterns is the product of that sort of permanent adaptation of the biological agent to the world whereby objective patterns become immanent
rules for behaviour. As I pointed out, the incorporation of opportunity leads to dispositions that, being objectively adapted to objective
opportunity, give rise to action which can appear to be inspired by the
intention to adapt to those conditions. This analysis of the genesis of
the habitus accounts for the semblance of purposiveness that human
behaviour exhibits without having to resort to teleology as a principle
of explanation.

It is therefore because social agents are to a certain extent tenden-
tially adapted to the objective conditions that have helped produce
them that, other things being equal (that is, as long as the objective
conditions in which they have to act are not too different from the
objective conditions in which they were shaped), and without resorting
to any rational calculation, they quite spontaneously adopt behaviour
that tends to adapt to opportunity. The reservation made – 'as long as
the conditions in which they were shaped are not too different from the
conditions in which they have to act' – is important. In fact the habitus
tends in a way to reproduce the world that has produced it, but there
can be slippage along the lines of what we might call the 'Don Quixote
paradigm' – Marx uses Don Quixote as a metaphor on two or three
occasions, but does not do much with it.[2] For example, the process of
social ageing can be understood in the light of a slippage between the
social conditions that produced the agent producing the behaviour and
the social conditions in which this behaviour has to function.[3] When
the conditions of existence undergo a radical transformation in the
space of a generation, the social agents produced by these radically

transformed conditions can find themselves out of phase with the objective conditions that come to solicit their profoundly incorporated dispositions. Thus the agents can persist in generating behaviour that was adapted to a different state of affairs and now ends up acting against the grain – this gives us a state of counter-purposiveness.

In other words, if the notion of habitus enables us to understand one aspect of the relations between the conditions that produced the habitus and the conditions that govern the activity of this habitus, it also enables us to understand cases that do not match but give us a state of counter-purposiveness. The habitus shaped by conditions of penury, for example, can be ill-adapted to a situation of superfluity.[4] So these contradictions between the habitus and the conditions in which it has to act are written into the theory; and the people who understand the habitus as a kind of circular and mechanical reproduction of the conditions that have produced it have misinterpreted the notion – often deliberately, no doubt, because that makes it easier to criticise.

Avoiding purposiveness

It is therefore important not to make a purposive reading of this mechanism, nor *a fortiori* of the processes of socialisation itself. This leads me to another criticism that has been made of the notion, and which, like the previous one, addresses not the notion as I formulate it but the notion as formulated in order to criticise it. As you have no doubt understood from my insistence on denouncing all forms of teleologism, one of the functions of the concept of the habitus is to banish teleology while still accounting for its apparent presence. But critics can then reintroduce teleology – assuming that it has disappeared from the relation between the habitus and the field – on the plane of the relation between the conditions that produced the habitus and the conditions in which it then has to act. These critics will then quite wrongly describe the process of socialisation as a purposive, teleological process, saying: 'These people are produced in order to . . .', and they will ascribe to the powers that be, to the dominant, to the State or any other authority, the action of socialisation that leads people, for example, not to revolt. Now the notion of habitus is important for political sociology because an elementary error in the social sciences (and one all the more frequent because it is so elementary) is what our elders and betters called confusing law with custom – that is, confusing the consequences of wilful intention with the consequences of patterns of behaviour that are quite beyond the subject's control.

In the domain of political sociology – what I have to say may seem trivial, but not if you think of what people generally say about the political order – the error consists in believing that the maintenance of social order is necessarily purposive and deliberate – in other words, that there is no order without a subject: the political order becomes a product of political propaganda or action, whether physical or symbolic, a product of material or symbolic repression and oppression. One of the functions of the notion of habitus is to account for the elementary fact that, as I said the other day, a person can be shaped by revolting conditions without revolting against these conditions, in so far as the revolting conditions produce a habitus adapted to these conditions – that is, a form of acceptance of these revolting conditions. If we think in terms of Sartre's philosophy of the subject (there are some splendidly naïve and attractive examples to be found in *Being and Nothingness*), we could say that the world is revolting, not because it is revolting but because we are revolted, which is a variation on the theme of 'Is she pretty because I love her or do I love her because she is pretty?' – that is, the old debate between objectivism and subjectivism. This kind of consideration is only possible as long as we remain within a philosophy of consciousness and the subject, where there cannot be any effect that is not the product of purposive intention.

In the case of politics and the political order, the notion of habitus contributes something trivial but important, which is that a modicum of conformity to social order is immediately given as soon as there is any order; any social order, by the simple fact of existing, tends to produce among other things the conditions of its own perpetuation. In so far as this fundamental law of the tendency to adapt aspiration to opportunity is imposed in all social universes as soon as any social order exists, it always tends to become, if not recognised, at least accepted, because it produces people who have as their mindset something like an internalisation of the social order. Here we could analyse what we might call 'popular' realism – the adjective 'popular', as I said the other day, always needs to be placed between quotation marks and handled with care: the realism of the popular classes as a form of anticipatory adaptation does not necessarily imply resignation to given conditions and the given state of the world. The popular disposition to see the world as it is and in a way to accept it as such – calling a spade a spade, rejecting one of the fundamental dispositions of the bourgeois vision of the world, its relation of denial, self-mystification and spell-casting – is one of the cases of the relation between objective structures and incorporated structures. The objective structures impose themselves with particular violence and necessity on the most dominated, and they impose particularly rigid cognitive and evaluative structures that are strictly adapted to the rigid necessities that have produced them.

Here we might make what I consider to be an important analysis of the attitudes of the popular classes. In political matters, we could even compare this kind of realism, which is not scientific realism, despite resembling it in some respects, and which consists in accepting necessity as it is, with what Marx (in a very amusing text on Seneca and the Stoics in *The German Ideology*) called 'privileged self-denial', as when the rich denounce superfluous consumption.[5] Marx said basically that denouncing consumption is typically a consumer ideology. This made me think of what people have been saying in recent times about the 'consumer society':[6] there is an abyss between a certain contempt for necessity and this kind of popular realism, although the two may meet in a rejection of necessity, but with completely different motives. Briefly, we might contrast a certain kind of rejection with a more canonical kind of denunciation of the material living conditions of the dominant classes. This kind of experience of the world is linked to a particular form of experience, and in a way we could draw up a phenomenology differentiating between the social experiences of the world based on the idea that the law of adapting expectation to opportunity will produce different experiences of the world, in particular the degree of liberty available to human action, depending on the nature of these experiences. If we had to devise a questionnaire to study the spontaneous philosophies or theories of the different social classes, one of the crucial points would certainly be the opposition between necessity and liberty; the more determinist visions would most likely be approved by the more socially determined classes and the more libertarian or liberal (taking care not to confuse these two interesting variants) by the more privileged, who have enough distance from necessity to see themselves as able to negotiate with this necessity. That was a parenthesis, but I wanted to refute a certain number of false ideas that I might have provoked the other day in going too fast.

Interiorising the social

On the subject of this process of socialisation, I have drawn attention to the phenomenon of the adaptation of expectation to the field. I could have used a slightly different language, which I think may be particularly useful later when we come to study the relation between dispositions and positions in a social space – I often define the habitus as a series of dispositions (that is, lasting manners of being that are the product of the conditions of existence). I spoke of 'expectation adapted to opportunity', but I could have said that the incorporated mental structures tend to adapt to the social structures or, in other words, that the cognitive and evaluative structures invested by the social agents in their knowledge – in the R1 sense – of the social world are partly the product of objective structures or the incorporation of these objective structures.

I shall return to this point, which I have already approached more than once, but I wanted simply to raise this topic because it will become extremely important in helping us to understand certain phenomena within the specialised fields. For example, in the literary field, the scientific field or the university field, the taxonomies and systems of classification that the social agents very often use to think about each other or the social world or field where they find themselves are the product of the incorporation of the objective structures of the field. Thus oppositions such as young/old, which are very pertinent in certain states of the social fields when there are problems of succession or conflicts of generation – conflicts of generation being very often problems of succession – are rooted in the objectivity of the social structures and function in a slightly modified form in the minds of the agents who conceptualise these social structures.

The function of our major classifications, which are very often dualist and use contrasting pairs of adjectives (high and low, common and rare, heavy and light, for instance), is to put some order into the social world, to make us see it as ordered so as to make it understandable and find our place in it. They are a modified form of the objective oppositions to be found in this world and its order. The fact that they function in an incorporated state as a structuring principle, whereas they also exist in objective reality, is responsible for one of the fundamental effects of the adaptation of objective structures and incorporated structures – that is, our experience of what is self-evident and 'stands to reason'. The majority of the taxonomies, contrasts or words that serve in everyday usage to think of the opposition between the people and the non-people, or between the bourgeois and the people, are fantastically poor: you have only to open the dictionary at one of these entries (for example heavy/light) to see that this is an exemplary area where dictionaries are most circular: 'distinguished: see vulgar', 'vulgar: see distinguished'; 'heavy: see light', 'light: see heavy'; similarly with equivalents: 'light = facile', 'facile = useless', 'useless' leads you back to 'heavy'. These systems of opposition play a determining role, and a good deal of aesthetic discourse is nothing more than a system of adjectives or exclamations: Barthes said it[7] – and on this point I am one hundred per cent in agreement with him. These systems of adjectives, which are sufficient to give a decent reaction to a work of art, and often to a scientific study if we don't want to examine its logic, are very poor, and they obviously fall into a vicious circle; for them to function well, they need a much more powerful principle, which is none other than the correspondence between mental structures and objective structures. In fact these systems only work as long as we don't ask them to explain themselves: as soon as you ask them to explain themselves, even in a dissertation, they reveal their awful weakness.

The match between objective structures and incorporated structures is absolutely fundamental to a good social order: it is one of the deepest foundations of the political order – and here we return to what I was saying just now about the unintentional foundations of the political order. It is precisely what political protest does not call into question.[8] Political protest is rooted in this profound *doxa*. The circles of opinion that form the small universe of political debate where the orthodox will be opposed to the heterodox are bathed in the universe of the *doxa*. The universe of the *doxa* is precisely whatever there is no need to discuss, because it goes without saying, because of the fact that the mental structures are so in harmony with the objective structures that, as they say, there's no problem, there's no need to ask, that's how it is.

Incorporating necessity

I have started talking about something else, as I often do. So let me return now to the purposive interpretation of the notion of habitus. A first interpretation makes the notion of habitus purposive again, saying that the habitus is designed to adapt to objective opportunity: this interpretation cuts the habitus away from the social conditions that produce it, from the law of the tendency to adapt expectation to opportunity. A second interpretation, which refinalises the habitus, sees it produced not by a law but by the will, saying that, if there is an unconscious, automatic acceptance by social agents of principles and values that contradict their objective interest or their representation, it is because their dispositions have been produced by intentional and deliberately organised action. This interpretation is totally false; I reject it absolutely, and I must repeat what I have said more than once already, that the notion of the habitus is there precisely to account for the fact that there can be acceptance of an order without anyone having deliberately wanted to accept it. That is what I wanted to add.

To account for the habitus, and how its expectations tend to adapt to objective opportunity, I have referred only to objective processes. We could also appeal to psychological mechanisms, such as the tendency to suppress discord, which I mentioned last time. We can also call on the well-known 'theory of levels of aspiration'.[9] This is such elementary psychology that I hesitate to remind you of the process, so often observed, whereby in an experiment the social agent who sets himself a goal of 10 and attains 2 tends gradually to move the desired goal of the performance nearer to the level of actual attainment: he chooses 8 and manages 4; he chooses 6 and reaches 5; then he goes for 5 and gets 5. This kind of tendency to adjust aspiration to objective opportunity occurs quite unconsciously and without any need for the agent to intervene. A great proportion of what people acquire and incorporate as part of their habitus is not produced by any explicit human intervention.

I would like to emphasise this point a little more. Obviously, as a sociologist, as soon as I formulate a proposition concerning social agents 'in general', I immediately retract it, and if you pay attention you will notice that I often correct myself . . . So I must point out that it obviously happens differentially according to class: roughly speaking, we can say that, even in those classes where intervention and mediation by adult agents are at a maximum, the incorporation occurs to a great extent without this mediation, without explicit intention or reference to norms such as education.

The education that operates through the law of this tendency is therefore a subjectless education, with no subject as teacher and even no subject as pupil. In fact it achieves for the social order what Rousseau dreamed of for the natural order: an education where the agents engage in experiments and thereby gain experience. These experiments are overweening aspirations that meet with failure. They are unhappy experiences that force the agents to back down, and one of the fundamental social experiences – which sociology has strangely tended to ignore before I came to take it seriously (I am not saying that to vaunt my originality but, on the contrary, to wonder at the strangeness of sociologists) – is this experience of progressive disinvestment, which may just as well be satisfying as disappointing.

This could be another angle of approach that the sociologist might contribute to the theory of ageing that I mentioned just now: ageing, among other things (I say 'among other things' because what I was arguing just now was not exclusive), is that kind of process whereby we become realists and acquire the capacity to generate expectations that are adapted to opportunity: we no longer dream or let our hair down

– even if there are exceptions and some people do still insist on 'letting their hair down' [*laughter*]. Socialisation is a kind of permanent dialectic between what we would like and what we can have, between the reality principle and the pleasure principle, to use the Freudian poles,[10] or between utopianism and sociologism, as contrasted by Marx. We could say that the older we get the more we tend to adopt a sociological attitude. Sociologism is the tendency to see the world as if it were determined entirely by social laws. Marx contrasted sociologism with the utopianism that tends to place social power between brackets and act as if we could suspend the effect of social laws. I think that this kind of permanent struggle between the reality principle and the pleasure principle, between the *libido dominandi* (or *sciendi*, or whatever you prefer . . .) and the objective laws of the field, normally ends in the victory of the field and its objective structures, in so far as the struggle itself modifies the person who struggles. Here we could refer to the analysis of labour by Marx and Hegel: the work of the struggle transforms those who struggle (this is a commonplace, but it is important for an understanding of the workers' movement, for example), if only because they have to transform themselves in order to struggle, in order to struggle durably, and in order to struggle all the time instead of just from time to time. This kind of incorporation of necessity as part of the effort needed to overcome it is something absolutely fundamental. And that in fact is what is meant by the notion of habitus.

There is then this automatic but spontaneous effect of social necessity: the necessity principle imposes itself, and social conventions assert their existence when we want to transgress them. Another opposition that I could refer to here is the one that Alain established between the fairy tale and the fable: the fairy tale is a fiction where pumpkins become coaches – it's the pleasure principle – whereas the fable is the reality principle, where the wolf eats the lamb, etc.[11] In our everyday lives we move from the fairy tale to the fable; to gain experience is to understand that the social world has laws – shepherdesses rarely become princesses and princes rarely marry shepherdesses – and these social laws cannot be transgressed, they can only be transformed, and at the cost of much hard work. This kind of education with no agent as teacher and even with no agent as pupil is effected when our objective opportunity calls us to order: I would like to be a *polytechnicien*,[12] but unfortunately at the age of fifteen my school places me in an unsuitable class, and then at seventeen one that is even worse, and so on.

I shall return to this point, because the educational system in our societies is one of the great mediating forces through which the social order transmits its order and gets us to incorporate it. Sometimes it states explicitly – although often it does not need to: 'You are not talented enough to . . .', 'You do not have the right qualities to become a *polytechnicien*.' This is political philosophy, if you remember the example that I always like to use, Plato's dream in the *Republic*, which is that everyone would do what they are cut out for, what is in their essence:[13] this is what the social system obtains without needing a process as complicated as that imagined by Plato in the myth of Er[14] or deliberate political instructions consisting in saying to people: 'You are not cut out to be a managing director, but you would make a good street cleaner', which kind of explicit intervention would be indispensable if the social system disposed of no other techniques. However, things happen more imperceptibly; socialisation is a continuous, progressive process. This process often makes me think of the paradox of the heap of wheat: it is a drip feed; there are imperceptible inflexions that when you have ingested them all add up to a major change of direction. Thus the social world picks you up or knocks you down, makes you flexible or, contrariwise, asks you to stand firm, using a whole series of little interventions, which do not usually come from a particular agent. It is important to note that, in this way, necessity imposes itself as all the more natural and necessary for not needing the intervention of agents as instructors: we revolt much more easily against parental demands, for instance, than against those sanctions that appear to be the work of necessity. The interventions of apparently neutral and socially irreproachable mechanisms and mediations (such as the educational system) are extremely important in making us feel that these sanctions are almost natural.

One of the results or outcomes – I prefer not to use the word 'objectives', with its purposive overtones – of socialisation is the naturalisation of objective patterns: social patterns become natural, as I have said ten times today, by being incorporated in a marriage of objective and subjective patterns. This process of naturalisation is accomplished in a particularly successful manner when it is exerted through agencies whose action has the superficial appearance of Nature and therefore seems almost natural. These are social mechanisms (or rather quasi-mechanisms, for the word 'mechanism' tends to render the social world too physical) where society resembles nature the most. For example, the fundamental law of the transmission of cultural capital, which is that cultural capital generally goes to those who have cultural capital, basically operates, behind its natural façade, as a law of physics: 'You will have the academic success that is appropriate for the cultural capital of your family.' This mechanism goes entirely unnoticed (until the sociologists get their hands on it), and its effects are interpreted as obeying a logic of talent, choice and merit. These mechanisms produce a naturalisation effect. The objective sanctions appear to be the result of a kind of force over which men have no control and for which men are not responsible, and for which only nature, but now in human rather than physical form, is responsible. These mechanisms tend to impose a form of submission to necessity. I know that the realism of the popular classes, which I was discussing just now, is a shock to our naïve populism, but all of our enquiries show that belief in talent as a factor in academic success is greater the lower one descends the social scale. This is a paradoxical phenomenon – briefly, the common *doxa* is that, the more you belong to a social class where the chances of being eliminated by the educational system are greater, the more chance you have of seeing the educational sanctions as a just and purely natural sanction of naturally unequal talent. This social fact is a good illustration of what I was saying: social necessity takes on the guise of natural necessity and exerts its influence through certain mechanisms. A certain number of economic mechanisms are of the same kind, but they have been raised to the level of consciousness for many years now, and the tradition of political struggle over economic mechanisms has not yet affected the cultural mechanisms. Cultural oppression is much more unconscious, and cultural alienation tends to exclude any awareness of alienation, which is not necessarily the case with economic alienation.

I wanted to emphasise this point. We tend to forget it entirely, but I think that it has highly important political consequences for the way in which we envisage political sociology in particular.

Rites of institution

But what I wanted to emphasise is that the action of the social world is exercised not only through this kind of education without agents consciously teaching or taught. It is also exercised through deliberate educational interventions that I shall call 'rites of institution' or 'social acts of consecration'. I propose to illustrate this point very briefly to show how, in very different societies, social groups exert explicit action on the newly socialised young who need to be integrated into society and the social order. These explicit acts present the same invariant characteristics in very different social groups. To name this very general process, I use the notion of an act of consecration or rite of institution, taking the verb 'to institute' in the transitive sense that it has when we speak of naming an heir, appointing a successor, or installing a bishop. I shall not develop this theme at length, but you can read an exposé in the chapter entitled 'Rites of institution', in a book that I have just published called *Language and Symbolic Power*.[15] I would simply like to draw attention to the specificity of this deliberate action in comparison with the other mechanisms that I discussed just now.

Rites of institution reinforce in a way the effect of the law of the tendency to adapt expectation to opportunity or subjective structures to objective structures. It is in this sense that it has a function of consecration. As the word 'consecration' clearly suggests, consecration does not really add anything: you can only consecrate something that has already been done. But consecration does more than just sanction: it sanctifies. It says: 'This is how it is', but it does more, it implicitly says: 'It is fine like that.' It says, for example: 'You must be a teacher and be proud of it.' The real work of education, then, as opposed to the kind of education with no teacher that I have discussed at length, consists in reinforcing (not always, but in most cases) the action of the mechanisms of socialisation. This action of consecration, for example – if I take the risk of pushing it a little further – is exercised constantly within the family circle, whereas there again we normally tend to note, rather, the most striking moments of the process of socialisation. Arnold van Gennep, for instance, came up with the important notion of the 'rite of passage', which draws attention to acts that are carried out in all societies to mark various crucial moments – marriage, circumcision, confirmation, etc. – when people change their social status, pass from one social class or age group (youth, old age) to another.[16] In the text to which I am referring, I wanted to say that the interest of the passage has caused people to overlook a much more important effect, which is the consecration of people who pass the rite of passage as opposed to those who are not eligible. I take the example of circumcision because it seems very striking to me: as it is practised in many societies, circumcision is not simply the symbolic separation between the uncircumcised and the circumcised; it is the symbolic and real separation between the men as a whole, since they are potentially liable to be circumcised, and women as a whole, since they are not. The superficial opposition then hides a much more profound opposition between those who are consecrated, from the day of their birth, as being eligible to be circumcised, who will be recognised and treated as future circumcisees from the day of their birth, as opposed to those for whom this operation is irrelevant.

These remarkable acts amount to saying: 'This is what you are, and it is good that you are, as opposed to those who aren't, and it is good that they aren't' – it is important to note that these rites always involve complementary classes. They occur in the decisive, crucial moments of the life cycle, and the group mobilises more or less totally to take the operation in hand. For example, I have been able to show how, for the Kabyle, the group was more or less widely mobilised, depending on the importance of the occasion: the more important the passage, the more the presence of the whole group is important, because a consecration performed by everyone and in everyone's presence becomes unanimous, recognised and applauded by all; it is part of the public domain.[17] When you are baptised, it becomes public knowledge that you are a Christian. When the wedding banns are published, the news of your marriage becomes public property (unless there has been opposition). To give this operation of consecration its full force, you need the entire group to be involved, and, the more important the operation, the more members of the group need to be mobilised. This is the case with a tribe, but also I believe more generally. We see this operation of consecration on important occasions precisely when the whole group is mobilised.

I think that these big events are a kind of coronation and fulfilment, like a seal set on an infinity of little acts of consecration which take place every day from the day we are born, in the way for instance that in most societies we give boys and girls different clothing, we give people different food, some eat standing and some seated. These solemn acts of consecration – which are public, but also rare, because they happen only once a year or even every ten years – are in fact moments when we draw a line under a host of infinitesimal micro-acts of consecration to add up the total sum and integrate them into a whole. They have acted as the kind of drip feed that I mentioned just now to transform the habitus durably and make someone born a boy feel more and more a boy, proud of it and duty bound to be one (*noblesse oblige*), and someone born a girl feels more and more a girl. It is the same thing for those born white or black, rich or poor, etc.

I often say that van Gennep had a brilliant idea, but that at the same time he was very naïve: he let himself fall into the trap that society sets in drawing attention to the great disconnected moments – there I go, finalising again – as if he wanted to distract our attention away from these infinitesimal, continuous, banal, everyday acts. The essence of this consecration, I must insist, happens day after day, through quite insignificant acts, through the fact that, quite unconsciously, a mother talks differently to the elder and the younger child, through the fact that, quite unconsciously, she gives him a second helping of meat, and the younger quite unconsciously understands that the elder should be treated differently and starts treating him differently, and then, when it is time to marry, he happens to remain single, as is the case in many societies, and he works for the elder, he becomes an unpaid servant.[18] These quite astonishing things are possible because they start very early and take the form of almost imperceptible acts. This is society at work.

I would say that these acts of consecration, which are extraordinarily powerful because they influence our minds precisely because they are infinitesimal, are *acts of suggestion* – using the word 'suggestion' in the strong sense that it has in magic. I am taking a risk here, but I shall explain. With some hesitation, I take the liberty of referring to François Roustang's reading of Freud in his latest book, . . . *Elle ne le lâche plus*.[19] I don't feel qualified to discuss psychoanalysis, although God knows how many people do, which is a good enough reason not to do it . . . In this book Roustang asks whether psychoanalysis might not be placed in the category of the arts of suggestion. I would like to widen the scope of the question, to wonder whether the pedagogical activity at work in forming our inextricably social and sexual unconscious might not work through the kind of processes that we designate by the name of suggestion – that is, processes of imposition which obviously include relations of authority (albeit not in the sense of an explicit authority recognised and intimately accepted) and also more underground processes. I think that our education proceeds through insinuation, as in the example that I gave earlier, with the second helping of meat. These are things that ethnologists often fail to notice. To notice them, you need to belong to the society in question, but, when you do belong, you don't see them, because you are so used to them that they seem self-evident. It is this infinitely small aspect of social relations, which escapes both the insider and the outsider, that exerts a permanent action through which we gradually prepare to become what we are and do become what we are – that is, what the social world has said we were: we become a real man, a man of honour, an elder son, a younger brother, or a woman, for instance.

The call to order: the example of the relation of the family to the school

Among the acts that call to order, as I mentioned earlier, are vocal intonation and other manners of speaking. Someone should undertake a concrete study to show how the family exercises this call to order. I think that everyone here will know what I am talking about: if the educational system issues sanctions, the parents do too. Recently I had to interpret an enquiry which included the opinions of the teachers, the parents and the pupils, and it was interesting to see the contradictions that showed up in the opinions of the teachers depending on whether they were looking at the school system as parents or as teachers, and so on – you can imagine the different cases. The ordinary experience of the parents, especially in the social classes where access to the school system is traditional and natural, could be described *grosso modo* as a sort of conflict between the feeling of being able to lay down the law and yet coming up against external legislation. It is no accident that, as all the enquiries have shown, membership of a parents' association rises strongly in accordance with social class, which means (although things are actually more complicated) that the feeling of being able to lay down the law about the school system is greater the more educational qualifications you have, the more you participate in the school system, and the more you feel you belong.

This kind of conflict experienced by the parents who feel that they are entitled to challenge the school system when faced with sanctions that do not match their hopes and expectations must be negotiated in everyday life: it is your son who brings home a bad report and you don't know whether to encourage him to aim at a level of aspiration unrelated to his objective chances of success, given his level of attainment, or help him face up to lowering his sights by siding, as it were, with the reality principle. I shall not pursue this further, for fear of saying things that might be personal or cruel or both, but this kind of existential conflict seems to me to be the daily bread of our experience with the school system. Sometimes you can negotiate it with the tone of your voice, the words saying: 'Of course you are going to succeed', while the intonation adds: 'But I doubt it.' What will be heard is the 'But I doubt it', or perhaps both statements at once, which will then create a double bind[20] where the conflict with the school system will in fact be a conflict with the father who represents a certain relation with the school system. I shall leave it there.

I merely wanted to make you feel what would be the terrain par excellence of a real reconciliation of psychoanalysis and sociology, and I think that someone could make subtle and just analyses of the collective process of negotiation between the collective fantasy and the objective sanctions – I did not invent this; it is Laing who argues that every family conceals and maintains a collective fantasy.[21] For example, for bourgeois families, and especially those who had been able to pass on their position without passing through the school system, the school system has become the channel through which the reality principle intrudes on the family fantasy. (I am putting this very crudely, but even when I seem to say something casually I always have some statistics at the back of my mind, which doesn't mean that I am right . . . Let us say that I am more in the right than any of your spontaneous objections to what I am saying might lead you to suppose [*laughter*].) One of the most frequent questions asked during the survey was: 'What are the topics that you discuss most often in your family?' And what comes top in all the fractions of the dominant classes is the school system. It is the most common topic of conversation in the family.

You will see in one of the next issues of *Actes de la recherche en sciences sociales* a series of articles that emphasise the contribution that the linguistic unconscious can bring to the process of socialisation.[22] For example, one of the properties of spoken language is to have so many levels – syntax, lexicon, intention, etc. – that even the most careful speaker can never control everything, which is what makes a subtle sociolinguistics possible. At this very moment I am thinking of what I am saying, but a linguist might count how many liaisons I make, for depending on the number of liaisons that I do or do not make, compared with other makers and non-makers of liaisons, I reveal a property.

It is the same with every level of language, and if we had a kind of microscopic vision with a sociological dimension – that is what I am interested in, but it does not exclude a psychoanalytic dimension, for example – of the interactions between parents and children, we would no doubt see this sort of infra-language through which I think they communicate the most important things that I am discussing here, for example the anxiety of the father. One of the mysteries of sociology lies in the quite astonishing relation between the career of a writer and the position of their father, for example: the likelihood of becoming a novelist rather than a playwright (or popular novelist, or psychological novelist) is very strongly linked to social origins. We might wonder how this happens. We even find relations between subtler things: between the father's position at the moment in time t and the gradient of the position – that is, 'father on the way up' or 'father on the way down', etc. We may wonder how the rise or fall of the father is communicated. We don't imagine dad bringing home his payslips to discuss them round the family table. There are social classes where you know how much dad earns, and there are others where you can't find out, and it's none of your business. Having said that, the important thing is the way in which this 'Is dad doing alright?' is communicated, for this style of communication will go on to inform the whole relation of the children to the world, with all sorts of consequences (such as an enterprising spirit, for instance) that operate at the level of the habitus and will bear fruit forty years later. To return to my previous example, these infinitesimal things that function as calls to order, and that paternal or maternal realists are bound to reveal – even if avant-garde psychologists advise them not to – are I think conveyed through phenomena such as vocal inflexions – a falling intonation, an unfinished phrase, a tone of voice – so many things that in the current state of affairs escape our sociologists.

Social relations in the enquiry relationship

I shall take advantage of this foray into sociolinguistics to say that the enquiry relation itself is of this kind: in an enquiry relation, we are there body and soul; we are not just a questionnaire. Once again I am surprised to have been the first person to say this, but sociologists who believe in the first place that you can send absolutely anyone to interview anyone at all on any old subject, and then give it all to a computer to devise some statistics, show amazing optimism – the origins of which may owe something to their dad! [*laughter*]. The questionnaire has to operate in a social context: everyone knows that what is difficult is to prepare the questions, to bring them up, and to put them and phrase them in a natural and unobtrusive way. But this all takes place within a social relationship. A question can be radically transformed by the way in which it is put. It can take the form of an injunction in a symbolic trial of strength where we answer 'yes' if we don't want to look foolish. Or we might use a tendentious intonation to insinuate that we are 'putting the question because we are paid to do so by the Institut français d'opinion publique, but we know it's not really a question for you', and so on. A thousand things can be said through the tiniest nuances of intonation and tone of voice, or can be left unsaid and unmentioned simply through your manner of introducing yourself, walking in, knocking on the door, or saying hello. I always insist on this important precept for those who want to become professional sociologists: you must question the questionnaire; the sociologist must enquire into his enquiry; etc. But all that is only hot air if you don't realise that this engages the sort of issues that I have been discussing. The best you can do is to try to be aware of what you are doing, even in cases where you do things that are not programmed into the guidelines of the enquiry. You have to know what you are doing in order to be aware that what you are going to record will be partly the product of surreptitious persuasion.

For those of you who are not sociologists, I would like to repeat the paradigm formulated by Scholem,[23] one of the founders of Judaic scholarship, which is: 'I never say the same thing to the Jews of

Jerusalem, New York, Paris or Berlin.' It is more or less the same thing for sociology: I never say the same thing, which does not mean that I am lying, but the different potential listeners to a sociological discourse merit different arguments. For the practising sociologists among you who are only too deeply committed to questionnaires, what I have just said should suit you fine; for those of you who don't believe in them, and are (wrongly!) sceptical in advance, I say that the essence of a good questionnaire is to restrict these effects and then to control the conditions of the conduct of the enquiry. I am emphasising this because I do not want to encourage a scepticism which is unfortunately only too widespread.

Surreptitious persuasion, symbolic violence

I want to return to this effect of surreptitious persuasion that is permanently at work in the family. Obviously we should not psychologise it. In my example I was referring to a modern, bourgeois universe, which encourages a psychological vision. It's not that other societies don't have psychology, but the point is that it is not institutionalised: an elder brother is an elder brother, a wife loves her husband because her mother chose him for her – which was an answer given in one of my surveys. In fact, we have the feelings inspired by our social condition. This is never absolutely the case; there are conflicts between structures and feelings in all societies, but the margin left open to individual variations and individual expressions of the norms is narrower in many universes than in the bourgeois intellectual universe. These effects of injunction and insinuation are of the same order as those that are carried out publicly in solemn grand ceremonies – that is to say that each of the agents, dad or mum, brother or sister, is partly an agent of socialisation: an elder brother knows how he has to behave and how to treat his little sister. This means that the injunctions are much stricter and more systematic and methodical than I suggested in the example that I briefly mentioned.

To conclude on this point, what I wanted to say is this: the process of socialisation takes place through various objective social mechanisms, through sanctions for failure or rewards for success that the social order itself can grant, but these objective sanctions are complemented by socially manipulated sanctions coming from the whole group, in the most solemn cases, but also from the social agents acting continually in the most unconscious daily routine. From the viewpoint of educational efficiency, we should not underestimate these infinitesimal and invisible actions which work in two ways, through their action and through their invisibility. As I said just now of natural actions, invisible actions are the most difficult to fight against: it is easier to defend yourself or to revolt against an explicitly repressive education; the likelihood of interpreting objective sanctions as such is greater than that of identifying insidious persuasion. It is this kind of effect of misunderstanding and symbolic violence that led me to use the term 'suggestion'. The violence that I call symbolic – I like to repeat my definitions – operates with the complicity of its victim. The term 'complicity' is dangerous because, I have said before, it carries the risk of suggesting that the victim knowingly becomes their own executioner, whereas this complicity may be granted simply through misunderstanding, under the impression of not knowing who is doing what to us. The most absolute form of complicity with violence is that which we grant without realising that we are suffering it: violence unrecognised is symbolic violence – it is the very definition of symbolic violence.

The paradox of continuity

To help explain one of the effects of the act of consecration, I want to return briefly to the rites of passage. In *The Rites of Passage*, van Gennep draws attention to those moments when social groups inaugurate breaks, separating adults from children or the single from the married, for instance. In the example of circumcision, I emphasised the fact that the division or diacrisis enacted by the group is not the one that we think: the group is separating the circumcised not from those not yet circumcised but from all those who will never be circumcised. Briefly, what I want to show is that the majority of consecration rites have the effect of producing groups that are not necessarily those we would expect, groups that are only one of a potential number.

I shall now very briefly illustrate this with a rather wicked example: a pupil of the École normale supérieure will tend to feel himself a companion of the most important graduates of their times – Pompidou or Fabius,[24] for instance – rather than with his student colleagues. This phenomenon is perpetuated through the alumni newsletters. Another example: let us consider the performances of two groups of subjects, masculine and feminine, in the high jump (we could take something entirely different, like knitting or swimming). We might imagine a boy who wants to feel companionship with the girls' class at school: for example, watching the women's high jump on television, he might say that one girl can even clear 1 metre 80, while he can only manage

1 metre 40. This is an experience we may all have had personally. An individual B wants to feel companionship with an individual B', although from the point of view of objectively measurable achievement he may have nothing in common with him, but will not feel solidarity with an individual A, whose performances match his own, and he will feel even less companionship with an individual A', who is abomination personified, because he surpasses him in the very domains (speed or strength) that draw him to feel solidarity with B'. [. . .] A' is a formidable contradiction because it is in the name of what makes A' better than B that B feels solidarity with B' – he jumps very high. Obviously, if we set things out like this, the issues are clear, because we distinguish the boys from the girls straight away. But if we imagine a mixed class of children the phenomenon disappears: if you don't set it out as such, it disappears. For as soon as it is constituted in these terms, a whole process of manipulation is disguised. As soon as you posit some performance as a universal principle of classification (maybe your IQ, or your prowess in maths – or, rather, in whatever branch of maths is fashionable at the time), as soon as you establish a criterion as the decisive criterion (one particular definition of strength or intelligence among thousands), you find a justification for the division that made distribution according to this criterion possible.

One of the effects of the logic of consecration is then precisely to create groups that avoid the paradox of continuity. Every time that we measure a distribution – for example the distribution of wealth – we find a continuous distribution, but the social mind introduces divisions: Pareto, who can hardly be suspected of egalitarianism, said that nobody has ever found out where poverty ends and richness begins,[25] just as nobody has ever found out how to decide where short people end and tall people begin, and so on. Yet in our society everything is organised around the tall and the short, rich and poor, strong and weak, men and women, and so on, with that sort of dichotomisation that consists in producing discontinuity and incomparability out of continuity. Competitive examinations, which, as everyone knows, create essential differences that last a lifetime between candidates separated by a quarter of one per cent, are an exemplary case of this logic. Likewise, the difference in terms of performance between the most masculine man and the most feminine woman, as biologists know, is infinitely small, but the social world demands that we be classified clearly as male or female. We have dichotomised social identities, with considerable social consequences. One of the functions of the rites of institution, whether these be the solemn rites themselves or the infinitesimal acts of consecration that are the small change of these foundational acts, is to inculcate division and difference from every point of view in order to render the comparable incomparable and things identical definitively different. It is important to know this, because in the practice of sociology we constantly find ourselves in the presence of continuities, whereas the social world produces differences. The problem is to know how and why the social world produces these differences, and the rites of institution are one of the techniques that produce these differences. Through their symbolic sanctions they create differences that range from zero to infinity.

Critique of the scholarly relation

I would like to dwell on this point, which seems obvious to me but perhaps less obvious to some of you, and I would like to insist on it because a wrong interpretation of these notions of socialisation, conditioning, habitus, and so on, runs the risk of completely undermining the use we may make of the notion of habitus and introducing a philosophy that is the absolute negation of the thinking that this notion is intended to empower. I return to the schema that I showed you: I have studied the relation R1, I have studied the difference between the relation R1 and the relation R0, and I have just now studied the relation R2. What I would like to do now, as a transition towards the next lectures, which will focus on the notion of the field, is to study the relation to a field, whether field of force or field of struggles.

I would like to take a moment – which will not be very long – to recapitulate what I believe to have established concerning the relations between the scholarly habitus and the ordinary habitus engaged in action – that is, between the scientific subject and the social agent involved in a practical knowledge of the practical world. I would like to dwell on this, because I said at the start – in fact in answer to an objection raised by someone in the audience[26] – that it is possible to escape from this infinite regression, but I stated this in rather oratorical fashion. My answer, to the person here who asked whether we weren't starting the sequence all over again, was that this antinomy could be resolved in practice, in so far as the scientific knowledge of the social world could be used at every moment to study the subject of that science and in this way help the scientific subject to make progress. As my reply could seem to resort to sophistry, rather like a philosophy teacher answering an objection of the same type, I would like to treat the objection seriously and show that my reply had a practical justification.

How may we escape from this vicious circle and infinite regression? Can there be a scientific study of the subject of knowledge? Does the sociologist in his knowledge of the social world discover the elements of a scientific knowledge of himself as a knowing subject that would enable him to make progress in knowledge? Sociology is not an absolute knowledge – this kind of circle is indeed very worrying, and I am emphasising it for those of you who had already thought of it (and also for those of you who might not) – but this turning back onto the knowing subject what he himself has discovered in the known subject can basically be defined in terms of a very banal kind of logic that the tradition of philosophy from Kant to Husserl has always more or less attacked. It is something that philosophers do not very much like: it is logic as a practical discipline, like technology. Husserl discusses it at length at the start of his *Logical Investigations,* invoking the authority of Kant, who had already considered logic as a simple technology at the service of the scientific mind. Husserl quotes an author whom I have not come across elsewhere, Beneke, who had written a book on logic as a technology of thought.[27] I agree with Beneke, for I do believe that there is a technology of thought. I find his formula very good, and very humble – this is one of the reasons why philosophers dislike it: it is much less impressive than creating a transcendental logic [*laughter*].

Well, then, it is a technology: I look at the knowledge I may have of the social world to see if there are any techniques for examining the knowing subject. For this I shall bring together points that I have already argued to show that we have quite a bit of information on the question. I shall discuss these more or less briefly depending on how far I had developed them. Sociologists find in their own work the elements of a social critique of the knowing subject. Here I understand the word 'critique' in the sense of a definition of the limits of knowledge – that is, in the Kantian sense and not that of the Frankfurt School[28] – for sociology is a science that can criticise itself. I wish also to make clear that the critique I want to develop has nothing in common with the critique that is practised day by day in political struggles, and also in scientific struggles when they are reduced to political struggles. (For some time now people have been tending to reduce criticism of a position to criticism of the person who has formulated it – 'Where are you coming from?' – and they think that they have laid a body of thought to rest when they declare that it has been formulated by the son of X or the father of Y. I think that there is a sociological critique of sociological discourse which is completely different, and which considers the social position of the sociologist only very partially – it would be too good to be true if it was enough just to stop being a mandarin in order to be a good sociologist.)

A first point: criticism of sociology is directed first at the scientific subject as the upholder of a theoretical posture. I am starting with this because in fact this is what ordinary criticism tends most to neglect. I don't want to return to this point; I have dealt with it in depth in a book entitled *The Logic of Practice*, addressing the effects of the uncritical importation of theoretical postures into anthropological research.[29] Let me briefly remind you of the lines of this criticism: it is in fact everything that emerges from the analysis I made of the difference between the relation R0 and the relation R1. It is a critique in Kantian terms of the limits inherent in the fact of being a knowing subject, external to the action, contemplating action instead of acting it out, which does not imply that the inverse position, which consists in just acting, is justified: defining the limits of knowledge external to action – whose paradigm is the schema, the diagram or the genealogy, for instance – is intended to designate the limits of this exteriority and to acknowledge its impact on knowledge rather than let you think that you can negate that exteriority by immersing yourself in the object. The solution therefore is not participatory sociology. The theory of practical knowledge enables us to discover the limits of any knowledge that does not acknowledge itself as knowledge – that is, as not practical.

In the realm of economics, we have the whole critique that I made of the teleology associated with the notion of *Homo economicus*, that fact that we project *Homo sapiens economicus* onto *Homo economicus vulgaris*, gifting him with a scholarly knowledge of economic theory. In the case of ethnology, we have *Homo anthropologicus*, the ethnologist who, because he is the subject of the action, for example, mistakes family trees for the truth of family relations. The most striking case – I am only reminding you of these themes so that you can situate the whole set of what I believe to have established – is the analysis of myth or ritual: mapping unquestioned theoretical postures onto the analysis of ritual practice leads ethnologists to turn something that is a kind of gymnastics into a kind of algebra and to translate systems of family relations or rituals into the language of graphs or tables. Here we can find one of the things that I discussed in my first lecture on the subject of those perverse forms of ontology that we practise: to say baldly that 'the popular classes eat more beans than the privileged classes' is already ontology, because we are not questioning whether the popular classes really exist, or whether they exist only on paper or in statistics. Among the mistakes generated by failing to criticise the theoretical posture, there is that of giving real existence to what exists on paper, as schemas, diagrams and other kinds of algebra, which we construct in order to understand things, but which become the things understood. I could go on, but I think it is clear enough. Linguistics would be a prime example – Chomsky et al., – as would the deductivism that I denounced the other day. The first result of this critical reflection is in fact its discovery of a theoretical ethnocentrism.

If, in scientific, polemical, political or politicised struggles, theoreticism is one of the *ad hominem* insults that tend to replace analysis, what I find an even more dangerous fallacy in the social sciences is the sort of theoreticism inscribed in the fact of adopting a theoretical posture – that is, in the fact of being someone who asks: What is society? What are societies for? How do they work? And so on. These are questions, as I have often said, that someone acting normally does not ask and has no need to ask; everything is arranged so that they have no need to ask. Not noticing what is implied in the fact of being able to ponder these questions is to be ignorant of the question that you are asking, and thereby to produce a work of fiction. I could go on; everything that I have just said could be illustrated a thousand times over in the conception of a questionnaire. I refer again to the paradigm of the questionnaire on social classes where the sociologist who has never questioned what social classes are asks his respondent to tell him what a social class is. If you think about it for a moment, you will see that what I am describing should certainly be denounced.

Another, distinctly more subtle, effect that I want to mention briefly consists in neglecting to question everything that is inherent in the theoretical posture – that is, everything that is implied by the fact of adopting a theoretical posture. In 'theoretical' there is *theoria* – that is, 'contemplation', 'representation', 'spectacle'. This is a commonplace in philosophy teaching, but sometimes the old tunes do ring true: the vision enjoyed by *Homo theoreticus* is a bird's-eye view; it is the world as representation, in the sense of theatre and painting; it is a world that you camp outside and watch, preferably from above, with sweeping views and aerial perspectives (for geographers); you take photos, you sketch plans and draw diagrams, and you give the world a meaning that quite escapes the subjects involved. To know what people are doing – if I may give a concrete example of Saussure's famous critique: 'We need to know what the linguist is doing'[30] – I think that we need to know what the sociologist is doing. We need to know the sociologist's point of view, and we need to have a view on that point of view. We need to ask what makes this viewpoint possible both epistemologically and socially. It is very important to know what sort of social status you need to have to be able to afford the luxury of this viewpoint, which is not the exclusive property of the sociologist: technocrats, politicians, trade union leaders, all our representatives and spokespersons share with the sociologist a posture that belongs to people sufficiently removed from the social world to be able to wonder what it is, what it is made of and the way it works, and so on.

Among the things that we don't question, as I was saying just now, are all those things that are inherent in this theoretical posture – the overview, but also the instruments that we take on board in order to survey and to think: maps, diagrams and plans, as well as much simpler things such as systems of classification or basic oppositions. When for instance we sort income into brackets of ten, twenty or thirty thousand a year, why are we taking these round figures? Why do we divide people up into age groups? Why do we separate them by gender? There are all sorts of divisions that we fail to question. And in so doing, in not questioning our systems of classification, we fail to question what does not fit into these systems, which contain all sorts of ambiguities. I refer you to an exemplary article by Thévenot on this topic, which was published in *Actes de la recherche en sciences sociales* a few years ago. This is a strictly statistical critique[31] (rather than a naïve criticism of statistics of the kind that I warned you about when discussing the questionnaire).[32]

Lecture of 23 November 1982

A double-voiced discourse – Looking scholarly – Where is the sociologist coming from? – Sociology in the space of disciplines – The unconscious structures of the hierarchy of disciplines – Philosophy/sociology/history – Epistemological struggles, social struggles – Finding out what sociology does

The fact that sociology uses a language somewhat divorced from our everyday language is the source of a specific difficulty, especially when it comes to writing. Sociologists are faced with a choice; they can either use a completely arbitrary lexicon unrelated to ordinary linguistic usage, giving their concepts arbitrary denominations (such as X, Y or Z, for example), or they can make use of words that are already current in the social world. Most often, if only to establish a minimum of communication with their audience, sociologists choose to fall back on words from our everyday lexicon while subjecting the vocabulary to a radical revision. Notions such as 'group' and 'interaction' can thus be used in a scientific study, but with a position in a particular conceptual space and a different function from their ordinary usage. In the best case – that is, when the author of the study accomplishes this linguistic critique – he takes the risk of seeing his work demolished by ordinary readers who consciously or unconsciously infiltrate their own habits of thinking and styles of reading into his message.

I shall take the example of the concept of 'legitimacy': this notion comes with a whole political and juridical history, and Max Weber in particular gave it a decisively new orientation, associating it with the problem of violence and the definition of the State.[1] For a professional sociologist, the word 'legitimacy' then is loaded with a whole history; it has been subjected to a theoretical elaboration. In my own case, when I return to Weber's notion and try to take it further by investing it with concepts of mine such as 'recognition' and 'misrecognition', I am exploiting an acquired theory that I cannot suppose all my readers (or even, unfortunately, all my colleagues) to be familiar with. There is then a considerable danger of misunderstanding. And here I am considering only the best-case scenario, as I said, where the scholar producing the discourse aims for the greatest possible lexical clarity and rigour. But the difficulty increases with the fact that there is another genre of commentary on the social world, a kind of essay writing, which makes play with the polysemy of scholarly language.

A double-voiced discourse

Without lingering too long over this point (which merits further discussion, but it would take too long), I refer you, first, to a study of Heidegger where I show that a certain philosophical use of a sociological vocabulary gave rise to a double-voiced discourse, a discourse facing two ways at once.[2] There are kinds of discourse that are defined by this sort of divided intention: they appear to be using the language of the systematically coherent lexical system of professional specialists and, at the same time, are still using the language of the sub-systemic coherence of systems of myth that we use in thinking of the social world. I showed for example how a systematic play on words (such as *Sorge* and *Fürsorge*, etc.) to be found at the heart of Heidegger's theory implicitly reflects the ordinary theme of social welfare. In other words, we can hear Heidegger's official voice delivering a coherent theory of temporality, while continuing to hear a different music, like a *basso continuo*, which may be nearer to the truth, as the author unconsciously lets it float to the surface from time to time. I made a similar study of an even more sacred text, Kant's *Critique of Judgement*.[3] If anyone would like to follow my sacrilegious thoughts they may read the post-script to *Distinction*, where I try to show that we can make a double reading of the *Critique of Judgement*: the reading that Kant invites by drawing our attention to its overt coherence, and another reading, which I found also revealed its own coherence as I followed a kind of repressed but ever-present underground discourse.

I find this two-faced, double-voiced language very important because it is in fact the common parlance that is used to refer to the social world: in studying the social domain people rarely avoid using this kind of language – to such an extent that I think that all sociologists should ask themselves with every word that they write whether they are not doing precisely this. In putting this question I am of course laying myself open to my own argument being turned against my own discourse, and each and every sociological discourse: even when we undertake this work of elaboration in order to avoid these everyday connotations, are we not quite simply trying to rationalise an underlying discourse expressing our social fantasies? In other words, might the sociologist be to the scientist what the astrologer is to the astronomer?

The third example is what I called the 'Montesquieu effect', concerning the theory of climates.[4] This theory has been internalised by the educated unconscious and gives rise from time to time to learned debate: the question whether we should give credence to Montesquieu's theory still recently provoked serious discussion in *L'Homme*, a truly eminent anthropologic review.[5] Yet, when I looked through this text on the North and the South,[6] I was struck to discover a coherent pattern in it worthy of mythical thought as it exists in archaic societies: the North is coldness, frigidity and masculinity, while the South is warmth, sensuality and femininity, and so on. In a previous mode of thinking, I would have been satisfied with saying that this text, previously considered as an affirmation of geographic determinism, which could be revised and perfected, is actually a mythical system. But having recently re-read the text, after reading the double-voiced discourse by Heidegger that I have just mentioned, I discovered a second coherent pattern, an overt one that explained why people took this text seriously for so many years. My initial feeling of cleverness was naïve (this is one of the important experiences that we acquire when we practise sociology): if the text were really simply mythological, you would have to explain why such learned people had been taken in by it for so long. To understand why what was so obvious had gone unnoticed, the text must have had an effect, the effect that I have baptised the 'Montesquieu effect'. To persuade people to believe in his scientific character, Montesquieu had elaborated a whole rhetoric. He had conducted experiments; he had chilled a sheep's tongue and noted that its fibres shrank, which led him to conclusions about Northern people.[7] He quoted an English doctor . . . In short, he had mobilised a whole scientific apparatus, or apparel, as Pascal would call it,[8] to make people believe that he was able to prove what he was arguing.

As soon as there is a scientific field capable of producing science, we are exposed to the temptation of disguising mythical structures by cloaking them in scientificity. We are led consciously or unconsciously to reproduce the Montesquieu effect, if only to give a positive response to the expectations of the world in which we live. For the Montesquieu effect to function, the scientific apparatus/apparel is not sufficient: it also means that the deep structures of the scholar must match those of the reader and their unconscious minds must communicate – we often hear of the 'meeting of minds',[9] but what interests the sociologist is the meeting of unconscious minds. We do not ask much of a discourse that is structured like our own brain; and, if it is garbed in the raiment of science, we look no further. What constitutes the Montesquieu effect then is this combination, on the one hand, of an apparatus that is structured like a scientific discourse and, on the other hand, of the mental structures of the brains of the readers. To take this analysis a little further: I think that mythical thought these days no longer flourishes merely on the terrain of archaic societies. It seems to me that the 'savage mind' analysed by Lévi-Strauss,[10] which has been more or less eliminated from our thinking on the natural world, has taken refuge today in our thinking on the social world. There are two terrains where we spontaneously mythologise: the social world and our discussions of other people – especially their bodies.

Looking scholarly

The paradigm of the false science and scientistic mythology that I found in Montesquieu might be graphology or physiognomy. I have just been reading a book on Lavater,[11] who was the inventor of scientific physiognomy (not just 'physiognomy', for you can't invent something that everyone knows about already and for which, like Montesquieu's climates, there is an infinity of sources to hand, since these are very deep mental structures that are inextricably linked with our cultural tradition). Drawing on his practical experience, Lavater discovered a correspondence between facial features and internal dispositions. In order to manage the practical aspects of everyday living, we have a practical sense of decipherment of faces: we could say that a wide jaw betrays sensuality or that a high brow denotes intelligence, and so on. In fact it would be interesting to make a collection of the discourses that range from spontaneous physiognomy to would-be scientific treatises: you would find first what is unconscious and non-verbal, then what is verbalised in everyday language (upper/lower, closed/open, for instance), then what has been objectified in the language of popular science (in manuals such as 'How to become a leader', for instance) and, finally, what is objectified in a scientific science such as characterology or psychology for business. There is a continuum. The spontaneous kind of characterology exists first in the state of hardly verbalised practical schemas, then in formulae, proverbs or sayings – that is, in the form of partial verbalisations which are the equivalent of what customary law is to statutory law. Then there are rather higher levels of elaboration, such as political discourse.

What I have been saying about physiognomy is valid for many areas of knowledge. For example, there is a spontaneous sociolinguistics: someone who says, for instance, 'them things what I gave you', is immediately classified under 'popular class'. In the linguistic domain, we find the same continuum as for physiognomy. We apply the same type of unconscious schemas to language: people speak, for example, of 'raw language' or 'crude language', the opposition between raw and cooked being invoked to mark the division between legitimate and illegitimate language. The categories of myth (high and low, for instance) can apply to anything – language, feelings (there are noble feelings), character and physiognomy, etc. They have a vague coherence but are also partly interchangeable, linked by loose connections: there is not an obvious link between 'light/heavy' and 'high/low', but as soon as you look at two or three popular sayings you can see how easy it is to pass from one to the other. We find this system of loose, all-purpose oppositions structuring each particular domain. Popular language is likely to be called 'base', 'lax', 'sloppy', 'casual' or 'careless', for instance. What we find then is a dualist classification founded on hierarchical structures that are both cognitive and evaluative, for there is always a good side to every opposition, and this obviously comprises the terms that denote the dominant – that is, those who are manipulating the system of oppositions: 'high' is the head or the top, as opposed to the feet or the stomach or the genitals, etc. These dualist systems are always orientated. And for good reason: since the people who use these systems are judge and jury, they are at the right end of the taxonomy. In the case of language, these systems of opposition therefore initially reproduce, at the level of spontaneous sociolinguistics, systems of differences that are not entirely coherent, then develop into a semi-scientific sociolinguistics (there are for example two 'Que sais-je' volumes by Guiraud: one on slang and the other on 'popular French'):[12] this is the equivalent of Lavater in physiognomy – that is, a system of categories of mythical thinking (high/low, etc.) applied to a social object.

To return to Lavater: he was a man living in a time of crisis (roughly the French Revolution),[13] when the social universe was shaken to its foundations, who constructed a theoretical system enabling us to judge people according to the shape of their face. The system is very simple (high/low, large/small, and so on) and is based on cursory analogies: there are three parts to the human body, divided along the lines of Plato's tripartite classification,[14] and thus we recognise the leader from his brow and his head, the brow being to the head what the head is to the body and the body being to these upper parts what the people are to those who command them. The would-be scientific physiognomist, or scientific mythologist, endows this system of simple analogies with scientific airs. He may borrow from mathematics, for instance: Lavater draws graphs. One table that we have all seen shows a series of heads, ranging from the frog to the European *Homo sapiens*, via the Chinaman, and the Negro, who, obviously, represents the man of the people. Then the angles of the faces and noses, etc., are measured. So a whole apparatus of scientific rationalisation is constructed, because in the age of science you can't rely on some naïve mythology.

The success of this false science, in someone such as Balzac, for example,[15] relies on the conjunction of profound mythological thinking, which does not have to provide any scientific justification, with a scientific apparatus or apparel. This conjunction, which is that of the double-voiced discourse, produces the specific ideological effect characteristic of false sciences. Within the category of the false sciences, we obviously cannot lump together Lavater, Heidegger and Kant, although we could distinguish the differing degrees of rationalisation and kinds of mythology they use, and so on. But what I wanted to point out here is a set of discourses that, whatever their differences, speak of the social world, of the fears and social fantasies of their authors, while seeming to be speaking of something entirely different. The strength of scientific mythologies lies in the fact that they are 'as plain as the nose on your face'; they resemble those drawings where there are faces hidden in the shrubbery. If, before the publication of my study,[16] one had asked all the Heidegger specialists in France 'Where does Heidegger speak of social welfare?', nobody would have replied, because it is seamlessly integrated with his overt discourse. But, obviously, different authors use different strategies to produce this effect of camouflage (although, as I shall explain later, I should not really use the terms 'strategy' and 'camouflage', because they imply a completely intentional act).

I think that it is important to realise that sociology is constantly dogged by the dangerous temptation to use this two-faced discourse, with its dual aims and double benefits. If I insist so much on this it is because, as Bachelard often said, we are up against the most threatening and, at times, the most important opponent. We are justified in giving considerable importance to something that is important in a certain scientific struggle; and I think that the danger of this double-voiced discourse is one of the most threatening. That does not mean that there are not other dangers. For example, I would like to refer very briefly to the danger that consists, in its most general form, in speaking in the name of some title or function while imagining that we are speaking in the first person. I won't develop this point further; it goes together with the criticism that I shall go on to make (that is, Who is speaking when I speak?), but it is very important. Sociolinguistics then sets itself the task of understanding the social conditions of the production and the reception of discourse. A discourse, as I have said already, is an encounter between a product and a market. Sociolinguistics looks at the speaker, to understand how the discourse has been produced, and at the recipient, to investigate the structure of the linguistic market. This is why internal readings of a sociological nature, which consist in finding within the text, and nothing but the text, the whole truth of the text, are unreliable. It is true that the whole truth of the text is to be found in the text, but that is not where it is easiest to see it, because it is there only concealed, in disguised form. To understand the truth of the text, it is important to question what made it possible.

Although people often argue that sociologists are too tempted to go in for politics, I think that the divided discourse which addresses the deep mental structures of individuals – that is, their categories of perception – is a much greater danger. Beyond a certain point in the progress of the scientific field, the danger of a sudden outbreak of political discourse is increasingly unimportant. What is more threatening is a political discourse that adopts the external appearance of science. I am thinking for example of a whole section of the works of Marx that calls for an analysis in terms of the Montesquieu effect: there is in Marx a whole aspect of social philosophy (I mentioned this for example when speaking of a repressed teleological philosophy)[17] and social mythology dressed in scientific clothing. I think that, the more the scientific field becomes autonomous, the more the divided discourse will come to dominate, for, as scientific censorship increases, so primitive political drives and fantasies will be more repressed and discourse will take on a higher degree of euphemism: it will seem to speak of nothing, but in fact it will be speaking of nothing but the repressed, the social equivalent of the Freudian 'id', for I think that social subjects think of nothing but the social world.

Literary discourse is to a great extent crafted in order to avoid thinking of the social world, but it is absolutely haunted by it. It speaks brilliantly of the social world, but with such a degree of euphemisation that successive readers reproduce the denial that produced the text itself. I refer you to my analysis of Flaubert's *Sentimental Education*:[18] I show how *Sentimental Education* reproduces the structure of the dominant class as Flaubert saw it; at the same time, it is striking to note that, as with Montesquieu, the structure that hits you in the eyes, echoing Lacan's paradigm of 'The Purloined Letter',[19] had previously passed unnoticed by all its readers, including the most perceptive, such as Sartre.[20] The work of repressing the social that all authors impose on themselves – and it is because they impose it on themselves that they do it so well for others; it is because they are trying to deceive themselves that they are so deceptive – is reproduced in the interpretations made by its readers. Although I have insisted particularly on the advanced form of ideology that divided discourse represents (this is a common tendency in a scientific argument; we shift our bearings to target the most likely error at the moment of speaking), it does, however, obviously coexist with much more elementary forms, and there are still, even in the world of sociology, people who speak with a very limited degree of euphemism.

Where is the sociologist coming from?

I would like to remind you that what I am doing is showing how sociology can take the discoveries of sociology and redirect them back towards the practice of the sociologist. I examined the sociologist, firstly, as theoretician and, secondly, as the user of a socially marked language. Now my third phase will be to analyse the sociologist as the occupant of a social position.

In a historicist tradition that dates more or less from Max Weber and has developed in France since the war, there has been much talk of the social insertion of the sociologist and the historical insertion of the historian.[21] This has given rise to relativist arguments: Can you be inserted in history and have an objective vision of history? These problematics are persistent because they are recognised by the educational system. They encourage dissertations, but also passions. It was fashionable around 1945 to ask: 'Can I overcome the limits of my historical condition?' The question then had an existential implication, but it keeps returning in different guises ('Where are you coming from?'),[22] and people think that they have escaped the whole Kantian critique that I apply to sociology as soon as they have declared the professions of their mother and father. You will have understood from my way of speaking that I find this polemic a trifle naïve, in that it amounts to asking the person producing a scientific argument to reveal their social origins and reducing their discourse in a way to questions of class interest, as if there were a bourgeois, a reformist or a proletarian history. While the old debate about a 'proletarian science' or a 'bourgeois science' makes natural scientists laugh, it is still alive and kicking in the social sciences. It keeps recurring in more or less naïve forms: people still want to assess the scientific quality of a scientific study according to the social quality of its author, as if you had to come from the working-class world to be able to write about the working class. I am rather ashamed to have to formulate these naïve questions, in so far as I belong to the community that asks them, but they still have considerable social power: they are highly effective weapons in the practice of the denunciation, slander, anathema and practical Zhdanovism that form the (largely unconscious) logic of our everyday struggles: we can always get someone to shut up by reminding them 'where they are coming from'.

These questions, which I felt bound in all honesty to raise, mask others that are much more important and will seem obvious to some of you. A first question is how to know what it is to be what one is. In the case of a sociologist, for example, before we ask them about their family background and social connections, we should simply ask them about their professional discipline: What is it to be a sociologist? Might a part of the limitation of their scientific understanding be due to what it is to be a sociologist? Saussure says that we need to know what the linguist does (I often repeat this statement, because it seems to me to define epistemology): he says that we need to know not what Saussure does, but what 'the linguist' does.[23] Similarly, we need to know what 'the sociologist' does: the subject of a certain number of first-person discourses is not a specific, named French or German sociologist, it is 'the sociologist' – that is, the discipline of sociology. To know what I am as a subject of a sociological discourse, there is no need for introspection. I don't mean to say that ordinary questions of social origins, which I shall discuss further later in the day, are unimportant: they are important, but they cannot be investigated before we have looked into the position.

The subject of a sociological discourse, then, whether delivered in Berkeley, Paris or London, is *first and foremost* sociology, with its history, its accumulated capital and a certain number of obligatory problematics. A scientific discipline may be defined as a collective unconscious, which enables people to understand each other; they have a kind of unconscious consensus on a certain number of questions that they judge to be more or less important. But it is much more than that: what is likely to be the subject of the consensus is not even sociology as a historical discipline but the position of the discipline in the space of disciplines. To exercise strict control over a scientific practice such as sociology, you need to have an idea of the nature of the field in which sociology is located.

Sociology in the space of disciplines

I do not have enough information to hand to offer an absolutely rigorous analysis of how to situate the position of sociology in the space of disciplines in France, but I know enough to improvise a sort of student dissertation, which will have a double virtue: it will show how we may come to understand what a discipline is and how we can apply the discoveries of sociology to sociology itself; at the same time it will be an introduction to everything about the notion of the field that I shall go on to argue. The methodological and epistemological postulate that I intend to implement is that the subject, the 'I' that expresses the writings of all the sociologists in the world, will be the sociologist defined by the position that his discipline occupies in a space. This space of the disciplines will present some invariant features across the different societies but also variations: for example, it is not the same thing to be a sociologist in the 1960s in Paris, London, Harvard or Berlin, because, although there are invariants, the conditions will vary. I shall draw a diagram of my schema; it will serve as a useful exercise, but it is only provisional and is not designed to be memorable.[24]

To know where to place sociology, the first move is to ask yourself in what space it is located. I shall locate it in a university space, which requires a historical context: it is very important to understand how a science taking the social world as its object became feasible at a certain moment in history, how it emerged as a discipline in the university space. Since sociology is a university discipline, it is natural to place it in the university space. The first concept involved is the field of disciplines: this structure will impose itself on the agents, who will have to take it into account. The academic field is divided into disciplines that

+ Science faculty	−		
	−		Arts and social sciences faculty +
Mathematics, Physics Biology Applied Maths, Chemistry	Geo $\begin{cases} \text{graphy} \\ \text{logy} \end{cases}$	Economics Sociology Ethnology Linguistics	History, Philology, French (modern, ancient) Classics, Philosophy
	Practical, applied Empirical, impure		Theoretical Pure

have a hierarchical relationship with one another. How do we find the indicators of the hierarchy of disciplines? In any particular state of the field, ignoring any value judgement and just following the laws of the market, we can note as indicators the percentage of *normaliens* or *agrégés* in a discipline. This will reveal a rather simple, linear and one-dimensional hierarchy: from philosophy to geography (I am not locating sociology yet, for it is going to occupy a strange position, opposite both of these disciplines) the percentage of *normaliens* and *agrégés* diminishes, but so does the level of the students' social background. The nearer we get to geography, the lower the level of the students' social background. The social background of the professors diminishes too, but, as it is a more highly selected population in the first place, things are not so clear (which is an unsurprising feature). There is then a hierarchy of disciplines that corresponds to a hierarchy of agents, which is quite striking and can be seen in very different fields, to such an extent that you can reconstruct the fields using just two elements: the indications for the institutions and the indications for the agents that inhabit them. You can for example construct the field of literature by using the social background of the writers and at the same time the properties of the different institutions, such as the fact that the theatre can earn you a hundred times more profit than the novel and a thousand times more than poetry. Constructing a field, then, means taking into account information concerning both the positions and those who inhabit those positions. To construct the space of the Church, you use both the properties of the bishops and the properties of their diocese. In some cases, if you don't have enough information on the positions, you can construct a field just by using the properties of the agents. But when you have a reasonable amount of information on the positions and dispositions, you can look into the question of the ways in which dispositions adapt to positions. A law that I have already mentioned in these lectures is the existence of a global correspondence, apart from some occasional discord, between positions and dispositions. You can use any piece of information to help construct a field: the fact that historians say 'dumb as a geographer' reveals, for example, the social relation between disciplines; a historian can say it without having to justify himself and without fearing a riposte: if a geographer said 'dumb as a historian' it would be much less effective, because there is not a market for it.

Very close to philosophy, with some differences, we find French. But there is a second dimension (my vision is more complicated, which I shall explain). A field can enclose spaces that are themselves fields and which have as constants everything that they inherit from the fact of holding a certain position in the general field. A field will be organised according to oppositions reflecting those of the field in which it is enclosed, which will throw up all sorts of complications and paradoxes, especially concerning political positions. But I am running ahead of myself, and running late [*laughter*]. (I hesitated at length before discussing this matter, because it is very risky. At the same time I think that it can have an important communicative virtue because, if I thrust you headlong into the rigorous, demanding and rather tedious kind of formalism that I have been trying to construct to account for the notion of the field, you will grant me everything and nothing, which is what an academic discourse attracts; I would then be exercising my pedagogical authority to no real effect, which is not my aim in life.)

There is then this opposition between dominant disciplines and disciplines dominated. Within the dominant, you will find a mini opposition. I refer you to an article entitled 'L'Excellence scolaire et les valeurs du système d'enseignement français',[25] which analyses the performances of the successful candidates in the *concours général*.[26] The discipline concerned appeared to explain a lot, and we found a crucial opposition between the winning candidates in classics and those in philosophy or, to a lesser degree, French, since the winners in classics were more *petit bourgeois*, more obedient to the school system and more self-disciplined. In the organic state of the intellectual field, they had a stronger likelihood of becoming *normaliens*. As a general rule these people are oblates: institutions like people who like institutions, and the Communist Party, for example, adores people who owe everything to the party, who carve out a career in the party, who make it to the top owing everything to the institution and on whom the institution can rely because of this. They are inclined to be docile: they harbour a kind of visceral meekness that allows the institution to trust itself to their tender care.

The hierarchy would be simple if there were not the new disciplines of sociology, psychology and linguistics. In the case of linguistics, as its disciplines were not separated until recently – roughly in the 1960s – there would have been a single point for 'grammar-philology-linguistics'; but then there came a scission, partly for external reasons, which created a break between linguistics and philology. The case of sociology is different: it did not emerge from a traditional discipline. Or, rather, it did emerge a long time ago (with Durkheim) from philosophy. As the divide is older, we are less aware of this origin. History itself becomes a field: modern history comes very close to sociology, while ancient history remains much closer to philosophy. An interesting property of history is that it occupies a central position in the field of the arts, and, in certain conjunctures of the field, the central position can correspond to the dominant position – which means that the dominant position of history is not the same thing as the dominant position of philosophy.

This construction teaches us a first important lesson about sociology. Considered according to the criteria that I have used to construct the field, sociology is indeed a strange discipline. On the one hand, it has more agents possessing traditional indications of high rank than geography: it has more *normaliens*, more *agrégés* and more professors and students of bourgeois origins. On the other hand, it has more members of low academic achievement, as measured by the percentage of top grades in the baccalaureate, than the other disciplines. It is, then, a bimodal discipline. It is dual precisely in terms of the criteria that we used to construct the space of the disciplines, and we may wonder what position it does in fact occupy.

This space of the disciplines is itself situated within the space of the faculties. So we should now introduce the science faculties, since we are discussing the 'social sciences'. Within the space of the scientific disciplines, we will find a hierarchy running from mathematics and geology to physics and chemistry. This hierarchy corresponds to a hierarchy of the social background of the students and professors and to a hierarchy of prestige, reflecting different levels of academic nobility. I once attended a debate between representatives of all the different scientific disciplines, and, to speak of these disciplines, the people constantly used the vocabulary and schemata of the pure and the impure, the beautiful and the ugly, the theoretical and the empirical, the material and the ethereal. If the systems of mythical oppositions that I have been describing are so effective, it is because social reality is often objectively constructed in this way: geology contrasts with geography like heaven and earth, like high and low, and mathematics is to geology what philosophy is to geography.

Sociology earns a double minus [*laughter*]; it is 'neither . . . nor . . .'. It is less literary than the other arts disciplines and the least scientific of the scientific disciplines. We could spend hours deriving all sorts of properties and comments from my schema; however, we would not draw any ultimate conclusions, we would have a host of questions requiring empirical answers. I am offering it not as a body of validated propositions but as a system of hypotheses, only partly checked and validated, that form a model which gives rise to a whole set of questions, investigations and verifications that need to be dealt with. Formulating it with this aim in mind, I am simply going to extract what seems pertinent to the problem that I have set myself: What does sociology have to offer when we seek both to understand what might happen to the sociologist without his knowledge and to verify the workings of the sociologist's unconscious?

Sociology is in fact a discipline situated between two spaces, the space of the arts and humanities and the space of the sciences, which are engaged in a struggle to dominate the university space. I should indicate this on my diagram with a sign showing this dynamic. Here, again, I am going to say things that may seem peremptory to you but which I think can easily be verified (with indicators such as the hierarchy of streaming in secondary-school classes): in a different state of the field, I think that there would have been a global '+' for the arts field as opposed to the science field, but we live in times where the '+' is tending to pass over into the scientific field – although this is not conclusive, for there is a struggle for domination, which is one of the properties of the field. Fields are in fact spaces of potential forces, and in this they are comparable to physical fields; but the social agents engaged in these fields are endowed with a habitus struggling to transform the structure of the space of potential forces, using forces that depend on their position in this space of potential forces. There is then a struggle for pre-eminence between these two fields. In his famous *Conflict of the Faculties*, Kant constructs the field of struggle of the five faculties of his age – the faculties of art, literature and science, medicine, theology and law – and he describes the logic of the power struggles between these different faculties.[27] To make my model complete we should introduce the faculty of law, which played an important part in setting the syllabus for economics;[28] the law faculty also harbours a form of normative sociology and competes for the monopoly of discourse on the social world. The schema is simplistic, but its very simplicity says something important: sociology is a strange discipline in relation to this space marked by the opposition between the arts and the sciences. This means that it is liable to be especially tempted by the structure of the divided discourse, and that independently of its object – sociologists are likely to cite the inherent difficulty of the object of their study to justify their predilection for divided discourse, with its Montesquieu effect of disguising social reactions with scientific reasoning. (I hadn't intended to argue that: it was only during the interval that I thought of this link between the two parts of my lecture, between the passage on the dangers of divided discourse and the passage on the schema.)

Another point: the style. A German sociologist, Lepenies, has written a very fine study of Buffon, who said 'Le style, c'est l'homme'.[29] Lepenies shows that, in Buffon's times, a strategic problem in the natural sciences was to know whether you should write well or not.

Writing well or badly both had benefits: what fine writing earned you in fame, reputation for elegance and academic titles risked being lost in the area of scientificity. I think that sociology shares this tension. A strategy employed by philosophy at a time when it was not the dominant discipline, but was striving to become it, was to write with a certain lack of style, to set oneself up as rigorous and non-literary. If you question the teachers in the *khâgnes* (preparatory classes for the *grandes écoles*), you find systematic differences between teachers of French and philosophy, who find each other's works 'obscure but profound' or 'brilliant but superficial', etc.[30] Sociologists also have a problem with writing: if they write too well, they will be called unscientific; if they write too badly, they will be called illiterate. They are therefore caught in a 'neither . . . nor . . .' structure, and they are always in danger of being told this [*laughter*]. You see: sociology, when you apply it to yourself, can be a lot of fun! In general, sociology is used above all to behave aggressively towards other people, to reduce them to their social characteristics, whereas it can be very useful and have a liberating effect in enabling us to understand why we suffer [*laughter*]. Sociology doesn't stop us suffering; it enables us to understand why we suffer.[31]

The unconscious structures of the hierarchy of disciplines

One of the effects that have a very strong impact on sociologists is what I call the 'Gerschenkron' effect. I have already told you about this.[32] Gerschenkron is a historian of Russia who shows that, having started later in Russia, capitalism developed differently there. Sociology is a latecomer. The degree in sociology is the most recent in our faculties.[33] Sociology lacks seniority; and, in any space, seniority means nobility. As a new discipline, sociology flourishes in the new faculties and institutions and is still always rather 'neo', compromising, disturbing, under surveillance. At the same time, like all upstarts, it is combative and aggressive. It will obviously strive to undermine the hierarchy. The hierarchy drawn up by Auguste Comte[34] was a sociologist's strategy: he was establishing the hierarchy of disciplines as a sociologist. This is interesting because I would not have placed sociology where Auguste Comte placed it. I would have placed it very modestly where it is now [*laughter*]. That having been said, I shall in a sense be going further than Auguste Comte, since I am arguing that sociology can conceptualise the space of the disciplines. I could say that it is at the apex of this space, which is a manner of taking a dominant position. Philosophy founded its domination of the other scientific disciplines in this way, basing itself on the sort of normative discourse we call 'epistemology' and aspiring to found the other disciplines (supposedly unaware of what they are doing). I think that we can understand many epistemological struggles in the light of this logic. It is possible to make a sociological study of Kant. Sociology then distinguishes itself from other disciplines by its claim to conceptualise them. In other words, it refuses to stay in its place. It says that its place is the starting point for rethinking the whole social universe. That is one of the properties of sociology.

I think that this ambition to dominate can also explain a very striking difference. I have forgotten to mention psychology. We find it in the same sector as sociology, but with a big difference from the point of view of its personnel: sociology is masculine and psychology feminine, which is very important, because the masculine is the party of politics, power and domination, whereas psychology espouses the private, the intimate, the feminine and the fictional. These unconscious structures, as I describe them, which govern the division of labour between the sexes, obviously have something to do with the division between disciplines. If these structures of opposition function so easily as mythical structures, and if so many quarrels between disciplines are in fact disguised class struggles, it is because the structures of opposition that we find in the fields express the structures of the division of labour between the sexes and the structures of the division of labour in general. Based on the oppositions between the theoretical and the empirical, between pure and impure, between heaven and earth, many debates on the hierarchy of disciplines have an affinity, without people realising it, with political debates, but completely disguised: to support theoretical physics against applied physics, to say that applied maths are pigswill or geography is mindless, is to formulate judgements that are in some mysterious way motivated by class, although people have no idea that they are. In fact, depending on their class habitus, people are not distributed by accident in the space of disciplines, and the mental structures that they import into the space are in harmony with the structures that govern the space. You can find dozens of texts where, on the pretext of discussing epistemology, theory and the reorganisation of the faculties, there is a whole social unconscious at work.

Philosophy/sociology/history

To get this schema to speak, we could continue to analyse the global structure and refine the model. But we can also look at the disciplines

in pairs. I have already started to contrast philosophy and sociology.
This opposition is still important for understanding many current
theoretical debates and intellectual options – for example, the fact that
at a certain moment in time many philosophers reorientate themselves,
albeit in a particular way, in a sociological direction. I think that this
opposition helps us to understand different ways of practising sociology: we can make reference both to philosophers and to sociologists,
or just to sociologists, or perhaps to philosophers recycled as sociologists, or even to sociologists who philosophise, and so on. The movement of philosophers towards the social sciences was very noticeable
in the 1960s, when the economy was expanding, which reminds us
that fields enjoy a degree of autonomy from the overall economic and
social space: what happens in any particular field is a retranslation of
external phenomena, but in terms of the specific logic of each field. In
the 1960s there was a technocratic-scientistic phase, when scientific
norms prevailed. It was no accident that a great number of studies
of the time ended in '-ology' – grammatology, archaeology, etc.[35] –
whereas fifteen years earlier they would have been presented as 'foundations of', 'origins of' or 'structure and genesis of', etc. In this space,
philosophy dominates sociology, in terms of canonical, traditional
norms, from the point of view of the division between the theoretical
and the empirical: since philosophy has no material object, it is pure;
its hands are clean.[36] Here I am plumbing the unconscious depths of
the gaze that philosophers turn on sociology: the implicit definition
that people have of 'theory' is that of a pure reflection lacking material substance, lacking statistical tables or data. The further one moves
from philosophy, the more one becomes bogged down in material and
the less one is burdened with theory. Consequently, a historian situated
at a neutral point in the space of historians will be subject to a social
demand for theory much less pressing than would a philosopher, or
even a sociologist.

For the sociologist is more empirical than the philosopher but
more theoretical than the historian. These are quite basic social facts:
whatever his status in the specific division of labour of his discipline,
a sociologist cannot make a move without a minimum of concepts: it
is part of the social definition of his role to have concepts, however
crude, whereas the social definition of a discipline such as history, at
a time when it occupies a central, neutral position, allows a sort of
compromise between scientific, theoretical and stylistic approaches.
A statistical analysis of the styles of historians, philosophers and
sociologists would greatly benefit from reference to this schema. Fine
writing is tacitly required in some disciplines, whereas there are others

where fine writing is suspect. There are also disciplines where you need to show that you are able to write well but without indulging in it exaggeratedly.

Each of the relations in the schema teaches us something about the discipline in question. History for example is in the centre of the field. It is a canonical discipline, with a very high percentage of *agrégés* and a very strong degree of integration within the educational system. There is a basic consensus, a general agreement to say that X is, or is not, a historian, whereas sociology, which is a dual discipline in its position and its definition, is very divided and very controversial; there is very little agreement on the definition of the sociologist. In its social image, history is one of the humanities. It speaks of man, but in humanist terms. Thus it is linked with culture, whereas sociology is linked with politics, since culture has historically been defined as the non-political (although the detailed demonstration of this would take too long). This is not the case for sociology, which explains the differential diffusion of history and sociology. There are dozens of historical broadcasts for the general public on television, historical collections sell widely, and historians have a considerable status: history is linked with culture – that is, with what is socially and politically neutral. If we explored this relation further, we would find more properties: sociology would be less reliable and less well validated; it would have no models, or very few.

Another comparison, which would be very useful for a social history of the cultural unconscious of a whole generation, would be the comparison between ethnology and sociology. From a strictly theoretical point of view – I may seem to be making dogmatic statements, but I think that you are able to see the arguments behind them – there is no particular reason for the distinction to exist. And yet it is a very powerful social distinction, and ethnology came to be called anthropology – which was a classic philosophical label, as in Kant's anthropology – at a time when it dominated the field and was presented as the fundamental science studying the universal nature of man.[37] Anthropology has a completely different position from sociology in so far as, like history, it is perceived in the wider social context as belonging to culture and not calling into question the structure of the social world.

Epistemological struggles, social struggles

This kind of analysis enables us to understand not only the whole range of choices that different people have to take but also an array of alternatives that will face anyone needing to write a sociological study. I have tried to show it in relation to the problem of style, but we could also look at it, for example, in relation to attitudes towards the use of statistics and the recognition (or not) of the division between qualitative and quantitative sociology – treatises on sociology divide along this line. When we find such primitive divisions at a certain level of theoretical ambition, it means that there is something social behind them. Briefly: the division between quantitative and qualitative sociology is unimportant, but behind it there lies the opposition between quality and quantity, between the elite and the masses. Another opposition of the same type is the division between the macro and the micro that results from the Gerschenkron effect, allied to the structures of mythology: the broad thinker is opposed to the narrow thinker. This opposition is a variant of the masculine/feminine opposition: in Kabylia, the man knocks the olives down off the trees and the woman gathers them up; the man chops the wood and the woman collects the branches. This is one of the fundamental structures of the division of labour between the great and the small (or petty), between the general (social philosophy, universal thinking,[38] general philosophy, general theory, etc.) and the specific. This opposition is one of the channels which mediate the division of labour.

A parenthesis: I have been discussing the correspondence between these structures and the social properties of the agents holding these positions – but how is this correspondence mediated? How is it that more girls are attracted to psychology than to sociology without anyone persuading them? Why should there be more male than female theoreticians? Why should the masculine be associated with the general? The word 'general' should make us stop and think, and it was a woman, Virginia Woolf, who said: 'General ideas are generals' ideas.'[39] What are the channels of mediation that lead women, at every crossroads, to travel towards the particular? The mechanism that I am now describing – that is, the existence of objective structures and a space of possibilities – affects the social agent not in a mechanical way but through subtle mediations, through the intermediary of the perception that they have of the structures, since the agents' very perception is structured along principles homologous to those that structure the space itself. So the geographer will say: 'I am only a geographer.' As soon as people from different disciplines meet up together, these issues surface, and some of the epistemological struggles that are experienced as purely theoretical conflict – Bachelard's commentaries can often be very easily translated into sociological language – are in fact, without people realising it, social struggles.

This is also the case with epistemological struggles over 'positivism'. The word itself does not mean much: it is usually an insult. To treat your enemies or rivals as 'positivists' is to strike a dominant pose; the 'positivists' are often the dominated – women, upstarts, geographers, and the like. 'Positivism' is thus passed off as a Mickey Mouse science, and the theoretician, who does not deign to calculate or deal in figures, thinks he is above the mêlée. In this struggle, everyone is generally at fault, the theoretician as much as the positivist. The word 'historicism' is the classiest form of the insult: it means: 'I myself think on a global scale, and I have to say that your study of the French bourgeoisie of the 1980s is narrowly historicist. You go to so much trouble for something simply stupid . . . although obviously it sells to the masses' [*laughter*]. For his part, the positivist will defend himself, saying: 'I'm a geographer; I know that I'm as dumb as a geographer' [*laughter*]. If Marx was right to say that the dominant are dominated by their domination,[40] the dominated are also dominated by their domination, and among the factors that dominate them is their acknowledgement of the qualities in whose name the dominant dominate. So the geographer will say: 'I'm no genius, I'm not a theoretician.' And he will criticise those who have 'no figures and no data', according to what I call an epistemology of resentment: as Nietzsche said: 'I am weak, therefore all should be weak.'[41] In the case of the geographer, social reasoning is transformed into academic reasoning: 'I changed course, I took option B in the baccalaureate,[42] I only just passed, I had good marks in history and geography, but not in philosophy. I said to myself "I don't like philosophy" and at the same time "I don't have any philosophical talent." So I internalised the techniques, and that's come to be my habitus and now I *love* geography' [*laughter*]; which means: 'I must accept what I am, so I must like figures and data, and nothing else; not only is there no problem with not having ideas, but it's better not to have any; ideas are suspect.'

I shall take just one example, the only one I have to hand: if you go to ask historians how you should practise history, all the judgements that you will hear will boil down to this: 'I must not try to do anything I'm not able to do.' It's the same all over. In psychology or geography you find this kind of structure, with the high-minded who don't want to lose status: 'I won't touch empiricism, I wouldn't know how to, and I would get my hands dirty' – here we have the dominant dominated by his domination. It is true that there are people who step down from an elevated position, such as philosophy, towards a very low discipline, such as psychology. There is a very fine article by Collins and Ben-David on the great scientific discoveries where they describe this very trajectory,[43] which is all the more improbable because this move would normally entail an enormous loss of capital. When you are able to be a philosopher and you put on a sociological hard hat, you really lose capital and you lay yourself open to attack from all the professors of philosophy, who are going to say: 'He's only a sociologist.' To engage in this kind of improbable venture, you have to have special properties. You have to be slightly weird and be dominated from another angle – say, your social background. I was wondering, for example, why sociology was founded by Jews, why philosophers were silly enough to engage in sociology and write for *L'Humanité*,[44] when the choice of a spiritualist philosophy would have been so much more profitable. Normally when you are at the dominant pole you are attracted to the pole that is in your interest. You need a really peculiar disposition to go uphill against your own interest; you need a *conatus*[45] coming from somewhere else. That having been said, once they have arrived in this downgraded position, the great concern of these atypical agents is to retrieve their starting position, and they accomplish great scientific innovations: for example, they transform a verbose psychology, which was quite rightly dominated by philosophy, into a scientific psychology; they subvert the space, and in fact they do it by following the logic of the space. That is another property of these spaces: to accomplish this kind of subversion, you need to import both a great capital of authority and legitimacy and an incorporated capital in order to redefine the position. Fields are spaces where a shift of place that entails a loss of capital meets a considerable force of resistance. They will tell you, for example: 'You are crazy, you will destroy your career.' A biography of Goblot by Viviane Isambert-Jamati illustrates this very well.[46] If you bear in mind the model that I am describing, you will understand the emotions and passions that the biographies describe: you have to be crazy to do things like that. Along the same lines, you can read the biography of Bourgin published a few years ago. Bourgin was a follower of Durkheim.[47] The people who shift position like this come up against forces, but these forces are not ineluctable, and when your position in the field is subject to the play of a certain number of forces you can, to a certain extent, transform that position and the forces that play on it, and thus shift that position.

Obviously, the different properties that I have identified cannot claim to be based on an exhaustive analysis of sociological practice: what I have in mind is French sociology at a certain moment in time. To understand better, you would need to project a series of mental snapshots of the image of this field in different periods. The field is not the same in 1960 as it was in 1880. The comparison of these different structures would enable us to discover the constants, which are partly nominal: it is possible that philosophy remains constant, but a position that is nominally constant may change simply because things around it have changed. Even supposing that philosophy in itself has not changed since Victor Cousin, it must have changed enormously, given the changes happening around it. That is the argument in terms of the field.

Finding out what sociology does

I could proceed in two directions: I could reflect on the historical development of the field or reflect on methodology. I would merely point out that, if I know now rather better what sociology does, I am speaking only of French sociology at a certain moment in time. Another possibility would be to make comparisons across time or space. I could, for instance, look at the American model and wonder whether it corresponds to a field of the same type, whether there are any invariants. History would be in a fairly analogous position. For example, about fifteen years ago there was a debate in the United States over whether history belongs to the humanities or the sciences.[48] This is a recurrent debate, which basically asks whether history should tell stories or describe structures. So you can see that it is another mistake to believe that sociology historicises every problem. In fact it provides keys to understanding the historical form taken by a debate that is nonetheless a real debate. There are indeed great debates that recur in history, as recorded by the history of philosophy: since the same causes produce the same effects, the same problem remains open and the same debate occurs all over again.

We can now understand that a vast proportion of the properties of sociology are not located in sociology itself, as a naïve sociologist wanting to start out by questioning sociologists might suppose. What my schema shows is that 90 per cent of what happens is the product of the position of sociology in the space. In other words, I want to substitute a completely fragmented and relational sociology for the minor, substantialist sociology that you can explain by means of a simple monograph. The truth of sociology lies in this space of relations that is outside of sociology. This does not mean that there is nothing within sociology to understand: I can in fact ask myself how and with what properties people come to take up the position of sociologist. I could then see if there is a correspondence between the positions and the dispositions.

Basically, sociology occupies one position in reality and one in its pretence. It would be interesting from this point of view to interview the historians by asking them, as do social psychologists, to choose from a list of adjectives to characterise sociologists and other disciplines: pretentious, pompous, noble, nice, modest, etc. I think that the sociologists then would see themselves very likely designated as 'pretentious', quite rightly, given the structure of the position that they inhabit. Is this pretence in their dispositions or their position? It is a false problem. The question that we should ask is the following: What dispositions do you need to be a sociologist, given the position that it implies. It is the same question that I put when I ask what Flaubert had to be to occupy the position that he did.[49] This represents a complete inversion of the problematic of Sartre's enormous undertaking: we need to understand the position and the function held in terms of a structure of objective possibilities and things to do, as an ensemble of probabilities that are just waiting for people to accomplish them. The question to be put then becomes 'Given the structure of probabilities, what did the people who occupied it need to be?' There are different ways, ranging from the more pretentious to the more modest, of occupying a position, and, in the struggle between the pretentious and the modest, we shall find a field.

I shall not continue, for I would be obliged to speak of myself.[50] It's not that I would be ashamed; I would be prepared to do it for my own benefit, but there is no point in my making a public display of it. This is another problem with sociological discourse: the most positively intended discourse is always heard as a normative discourse, because in general we speak only in order to say 'it's good' or 'it's bad'. Whereas I have been making the effort to avoid normative propositions, and, when this was not the case, I have accompanied them with a laugh or a smile to show that I knew that I was being normative. If sociology is difficult and improbable, it is precisely because people are so involved in the game that they are not at all disposed to objectify it. But the fact of objectifying it in the sort of tone that I have been using gives an absolutely extraordinary liberty: avoiding the theatrical as much as the will to power ('I shall dominate you' or 'you will dominate me'), avoiding interdisciplinary romanticism as much as naïvety, you can discuss this very dramatic thing that profoundly motivates the sociologists' choice of topics for research, the works that they publish and how they view them, their intellectual commitment or, again, their answer to the question: 'What are you working on at the moment?', their self-image, and their intellectual pretensions. If there is a manner of becoming at least partly the subject of your own sociological practice, it is in knowing this. You can go further and say what I have not said, for I have censored and hidden a lot, always observing the Scholem paradigm: you cannot say whatever you like, wherever you like.[51] It is not that what I censored instead of saying is particularly awkward but, rather, that you would find it too easy to understand, and therefore not really understand it. That having been said, I hope that you will be able to extract from my schema everything that I have not said: you can, for example, ask yourselves why you are sitting here at all.

Lecture of 30 November 1982

Sociology as taking liberty/liberties – Positions, dispositions and stances – Sociological bodies and academic styles – Positions attained and positions in the making – Mental structures and objective structures – Transformations of the field: the case of the university system – The refraction of external constraints – Strategies of struggle – The boundaries of the field – The intellectual field

As I announced at the outset, my analysis claimed to have a dual function: on the one hand it was to show what sociology applied to the scientific field could contribute to sociological knowledge; on the other hand it was to serve as an introduction to the notion of the field. I would like first briefly to indicate what this type of analysis supposes. Several people here have put questions to me on different occasions asking me both what the implications of a scientific study of one's own milieu and world are and whether something like a sociology of one's own universe was possible for the sociologist. Rather than reply *in abstracto*, I have tried to answer concretely by attempting to show that we could subject our own social position to analysis, and I would simply like to indicate briefly what at least the most important aspects of this analysis imply for me.

Sociology as taking liberty/liberties

It seems to me that this kind of analysis is only difficult because it implies taking what we normally call liberties – that is, adopting towards the universe that encloses us an attitude normally excluded in practice by belonging to that universe. If sociology, in particular the sociology of select and closed milieux, is often very difficult, it is because, when we are excluded from these milieux, we do not have access to them and, when we do belong, we feel at home and have no desire to sociologise them. The sociology of these universes is therefore possible only if we take liberties with the implicit norms of the universe, which are in general tacit rules of politeness, etiquette, good manners and behaviour that function as a censorship so deeply incorporated that we don't even experience them as such, and therefore the idea of taking liberties with things that are so evident and sacred does not even cross our minds. In any analysis of the world to which we belong, a sort of violence towards this world is needed to destroy and call into question what Sartre called the 'inertia-violence of the institution'.[1] This violence tends to be forgotten because it is written into the order of things. In general it becomes apparent only when it is challenged, even on marginal and apparently unimportant issues. I often quote the word *obsequium* (obedience) by which Spinoza designated the relation that links the citizen to the State; he said that this relation of *obsequium* is what profoundly and unconsciously unites citizens with the social order in which they participate.[2] This kind of fundamental reverence is manifested, for example, in forms of politeness, in the respect for forms and in forms of respect. This fundamental adherence to the social order is displayed precisely in trivial formalities; when someone transgresses what any social universe demands of its members, they are reproached with not honouring a ritual that would cost them nothing. But it is precisely these trivial formalities that the social order demands respect for; they are of prime importance; they are the gift in exchange for which the social order grants recognition through membership. If very often sociology shocks by touching on absolutely essential aspects of social experience, I believe it is because, in order to exist, it must commit improprieties much more serious than people outside the world being analysed would realise.

To take this analysis a little further: I finished one of my lectures by referring to Karl Kraus, an astonishing figure from fin-de-siècle Vienna who had practised a kind of sociology of intellectuals:[3] for example, throughout his life he edited a review in which he wrote three quarters of the articles himself, criticising the misuse of language characteristic of the journalistic and political environment that he inhabited. This person seemed to me to exemplify a form of liberty needed to overcome the primary form of violence that I see encountered by those who try to understand the social world, which is the violence at work in the intellectual field. This is why I find that all the forms of subversive denunciation that are initiated from beyond the intellectual field are always somewhat hypocritical and at the same time rather gratuitous and useless. The sociology of intellectuals – as I keep repeating – is not at all just one chapter of sociology among others; it is the preface to all sociology; it is the basis for establishing scientific liberty. It has to take liberties with the secret, hidden, unwritten laws of the intellectual world in order to engage in a real intellectual study, since the defenders of common sense and decorum are nearly always supporters of the moral and social order and very rarely of the scientific order. The struggle against this particular domination starts with a fight against the magic of the word, against the everyday manipulators of language: Kraus spent his life fighting against a weekly review – one not so different from many of our own – which he criticised not so much for its political stand (or failure to make a stand) as simply for its negligence and carelessness in the realm of language, which is the only area where intellectuals have an account to render, because it is the only area where they wield any power. (I don't much like playing the prophet, but I wanted to make the underlying implications of my argument more explicit so as to avoid appearing to persuade you by stealth.)

If we need to practise a kind of methodological anarchy and take liberties in our scientific dealings, it is in a way in order to grasp liberty itself. As I have already said more than once, I think that the question of liberty with which people always challenge sociologists, simply because they tend to uncover determinisms, does not take the same form as it normally does when put to others. Liberty is not given in advance but is something that has to be taken and constructed. By this token, the work that involves taking liberties, in order to detect determinisms, is part of the means of acquiring a real liberty in the face of these determinisms. This being so, what I am saying raises the question of the privilege of liberty. (I am only raising these questions because a certain number of people here have put them to me orally or in writing. Otherwise I would probably have glossed over them, not at all because I would not have had to face them myself, but because in general I dislike those who use this language: they are abusing their power and moralising, as if morals belonged to them. I am answering these questions because they have been put to me, and I would not want to appear to find them insignificant or ridiculous, or not to have an answer.)

One of the issues that I have encountered in the studies that I have undertaken, where I try to make determinisms visible – starting with those that impinge on the person who is working to make the determinisms visible – is the nature of that liberty which, whether perceived as an unjustified pretension or as a sort of privilege, is rather disagreeable for those who do not share in it. The liberty that is in fact implied by sociology as I practise it in your company – and I could pursue my analysis further, but I have taken it as far as I could without offending your sensibilities – is absolutely not a monopoly. If sociology may be taught and published, but also if many people fight it and try to limit its diffusion as much as possible, it is also because it aims to share a privilege, to universalise liberty. (All that seems so pompous and oracular that I frighten myself, but it had to be said, and I am only saying it because people oblige me to say it.) Since sociology provides us with a knowledge of determinisms and therefore the possibility of breaking free from determinisms, so writing or broadcasting sociology to the world at large in such a way as to make it intelligible without distorting it means working to disseminate and universalise the possibility of such liberty. For example, I was quite deliberate when I said last week: 'I shall not take this analysis further; you have seen enough of my method to develop it for yourselves.' My project in fact is to offer neither theses nor even hypotheses, but a manner of thinking that people can practise, even using it against my arguments; the possibility of criticising my arguments is constantly not merely implied but actually solicited in what I am arguing. It seems to me that at any moment (oh dear, now that I have started, I shall follow my oracular muse all the way and then, afterwards, we shall return to the substance of the debate) there are scientific agents or literary and artistic agents – for it is not always science that brings this promise of liberty – who achieve better than others some human potential that previously had not seemed possible or even thinkable.

It may seem strange to you, but I am thinking of one of those anecdotes that we often find in the history of literature and art. We usually read them in the hagiographical vein in which they are presented, whereas I think that we should read them differently. For example, we read that when Michelangelo went to visit Pope Julius II, who was paying for his work and supporting him, Julius immediately asked Michelangelo to sit down, to make sure that he could not sit down without permission. I think that this was a historic act: the liberty that Michelangelo took as an artist – not to wait for any temporal power, even with spiritual dimensions, to exercise the slightest authority over him – was not a personal liberty: he was taking this liberty on behalf of all artists, and also potentially for all the men who, through him, can understand that they may sit down before the prince invites them to, whereas there are crowds of intellectuals and artists who remain seated when they should stand, and stand when they should remain seated. These virtues, which are celebrated by hagiography as singular virtues, only remain singular because they are celebrated as such.

I could also take the example of Aretino,[4] that strange fellow whose epigrams were so famous that princes and noblemen paid him not to write them: his very silence was sometimes sufficient to inspire fear. This is one of the possible structures of the relations between intellectuals and power. It is important to know that such a character existed and to perceive him, not as an exception, but as a representative of one of the forms of human nature. Hagiography leads us astray because it composes characters in a transcendental mode where they cease to be accessible, where they are so exemplary that nobody can emulate them. Sociology, on the contrary, is a profoundly democratic science: unlike the other sciences, it questions the man in the street and records what he has to say; it is a science that has learned that there is something new to learn. The sociologist must be the only intellectual who is never bored: he listens; he always finds something new to learn and understand, wherever he is, in whatever situation.

This science with its democratic method is also democratic in intention. People reproach the sociologist with this kind of lucidity; they accuse him of being either too stupid or too intelligent. This is the sense of many of the questions that I am asked, notably by philosophers: 'What right have you to place yourself on high over the social world, at that kind of absolute point of view that until now was reserved for us?' In fact the sociologist does not place himself at all at that absolute viewpoint, or up in the clouds with Socrates.[5] He puts himself there to say that anyone can put himself or herself there if they accept a certain kind of training. This is more or less what I was arguing last week: I wanted to show in practice that in fact it is possible to submit one's own social universe and social position to an analysis without complacency or narcissism, and that this is not a unique exploit reserved for the chosen few but something accessible to anyone prepared to acquire a certain intellectual training and technical expertise, and also – both of these conditions are equally important – to acquire an attitude towards their own position, which is in fact much more rare, for certain types of apparently aggressive self-analysis are in fact a supreme form of complacency.

Intellectuals for example have sheltered themselves from sociological analysis by practising it on themselves in an excessively hyperbolic and hypertrophied way, which very excess enables them to spare themselves. You could see the whole of Sartre's work in this light: this kind of masochistic self-analysis is in fact complacent, not least because you always put yourself in the position of being the person whose analysis of yourself is unsurpassable – 'nobody can analyse me better than I can'. The analysis that I am proposing here does, on the contrary, ask to be superseded: as long as it is committed to a collective and progressive enterprise, as I suggest, it is clear that it will be superseded time and again. For this to happen it simply needs to be undertaken with an approach that is one neither of heart-searching nor of a guilty conscience – the types of analysis that were much practised in the Sartre years. I think that, if the sociology of intellectuals is one of the most underdeveloped sectors of sociology, it is largely because this kind of uncompromising habitus is sorely lacking there. We are in fact a social thing like any other, with the difference that we claim to be thinkers of ourselves. If you look up 'intellectual' in the index of *Distinction*, you will find a better formulation of what I have been trying to say: the truth about intellectuals escapes intellectuals, because they think they are able to grasp their own truth through the ordinary techniques of reflection and self-analysis; this illusion of liberty is what determines intellectuals.

That was my preamble. I doubt if I surprised anyone: I have only said out loud what was so obvious from my tone of voice and my approach that you had all understood it in advance. But once things have been said implicitly and displayed in practice it is better to state them explicitly, because that changes everything.

Positions, dispositions and stances

Having considered the conditions that this method implies, we should see what aspects of the notion of the field my argument has so far revealed. I am not going to set forth a systematic presentation of the notion of field – this I shall develop in due course; rather, I shall give a sort of practical demonstration of the presuppositions implied in my argument so far. The first proposition is that there is a general correspondence between positions (for example, the position of a discipline), dispositions (the habitus, the stable and lasting kind of life style that the agent brings to this position) and the explicit stances that they adopt (in the form of practice, discourse or representation). We can postulate and note a certain degree of correspondence between a post as geographer and the dispositions imported into this post along with a certain social origin. We could say too that geographers are to historians what geography is to history: fewer geographers have studied Latin, there are fewer of them, they are humbler, and they are of humbler, provincial origins. We will find then a correspondence between the positions objectively lived in a space – that is, defined in a space by their relation to other positions in terms of '+/–', 'above/ below', 'left/right', 'beside/between/on the margin', etc. – and the dispositions that the social agents import into this space.

This leads us to enquire into the nature of the subtle mediations that empower this correspondence. In the case of women, I started in my last lecture to suggest that we should look for the explanation of this correspondence in the match between, on the one hand, the incorporated dispositions and structures through which men and women conceive of the social world and the division between men and women and, on the other hand, the objective structures. By and large, although not inevitably, social agents choose their own destiny, and they like the positions that destiny allots them. Put like this, it seems blatantly simplistic and almost revolting, so I shall state it in a much more nuanced form: social agents are much more disposed to accept the positions in which they find themselves than we generally believe, or even than they say or think. There is a kind of *amor fati*,[6] a love of their social fate, that guides the choice of a vocation, for instance, with people saying that they want to do whatever it is that they are destined to do, or that they cannot do anything other than what they are cut out for, or that they have the talent to do whatever it is that they happen to be bound to do in any case. The most typical example of this *amor fati* is to be seen precisely in the area of love and relations between the sexes, where we find that social agents, even in societies where the regulations controlling matrimonial exchanges are strictest, adapt to their social fate, with all its constraints, much more than we tend to believe – which does not mean that everything is perfect and that all is for the best in the best of all worlds. But in fact they do embrace their social fate much more willingly than we might believe. Since I shall return to this point, I shall not take it further now.

There is then a correspondence between positions and dispositions, and also, via the dispositions, between the positions and the stances adopted. From the philosopher to the geographer and from the mathematician to the geologist, social agents can be situated at different points in the space that I have already indicated, and the holders of the different positions will adopt stances: they will sign petitions, choose political parties, take stands during periods of crisis like May 1968, write pamphlets, books and newspapers; they will also express opinions, answer surveys, buy one book and not another, criticise one newspaper and subscribe to another, etc. All these stances, mediated through dispositions, correspond to positions much more closely than they would if we posited a random relationship. If we know the

positions of the agents in a space and the dispositions that these positions normally entail, we then have a good chance of predicting the
stances that the agents will adopt.

Sociological bodies and academic styles

I took two examples. The first was the pretentiousness of sociologists,
which is less a stance properly speaking than a disposition – that is,
a matrix of stances. I refer to an analysis by Canguilhem taken from
Idéologie et rationalité dans l'histoire des sciences de la vie (Vrin, 1977,
pp. 33–45): sociology more than biology is tempted to be pretentious,
biology more than physics, and physics more than mathematics, and
this pretentiousness is manifest in their scientistic ideologies – what I
called the Montesquieu effect[7] – that is, in their ambition to resolve
social problems of practical and juridical importance, without considering the positions involved. Canguilhem continues: this pretentiousness of the social sciences leads to 'discourses with scientific pretension
held by men who are in fact only putative and presumptuous scientists'.[8] If you remember, I drew attention to this bimodal, fragmented
and split position of sociology. It has a very low position in reality and
a very high position in its aspirations, a status that we could describe
in Lenski's terms as a major 'decrystallisation'.[9] Lenski speaks of
decrystallisation in the case of individuals who possess very disparate
properties, like certain cinema actresses whose work has made them
rich and famous but who are illiterate, or like a tennis champion who
is very rich but black. These properties belong to the same person, but
at least one of them is very weakly correlated with the others, whereas
most often people's properties correlate with each other (when prestige
increases, income and social status increase).

The sociological corps is characterised by this kind of decrystallised
status. The split position of sociology is expressed in the coexistence
of very disparate people, some socially and academically over-selected
and others selected socially but academically under-selected. I said
last time that sociology is 'neither . . . nor . . .' but that it claims to be
'both . . . and . . .' (it claims to be scientific as well as theoretical). This
dual position of sociology is found in the definition of the post, in the
description of the properties of the corps, but also in its very productions, in the style and behaviour of sociologists, obviously to differing
degrees depending on their position in the sub-field of sociologists. I
should in fact continue this analysis – I had deliberately finished at that
point: the analysis that I had made of the position of the sociologist in

the space of disciplines was only partial in any case, and it should be continued by an analysis of the position of each individual sociologist in the space of sociology.

To illustrate this correspondence between people's positions and the stances they adopt, the second example was that of style. There, too, it would take a long study. I mentioned an article by Lepenies which has not yet been published – I received a proof copy.[10] Inspired by Lepenies's arguments, I tried to show that the different sciences faced the choice, as early as the eighteenth century, between either a rather scientific style, indifferent to qualities of literary form (which does not mean indifferent to form altogether), or a literary style attentive to form. It would be interesting to use this perspective to review the analysis that I sketched of the structure of the division of labour between the different scientific disciplines. In fact, to verify the hypothesis of a distinct division of labour between them, we could look for objective indices of the attention paid to style: firstly, those relating to the use of language (whether French or other), which, if they also measure other things, cannot be entirely independent; then, having checked the linguistic variants, there are indices that measure the degree of attention paid to language. Without drawing final conclusions, I had made a systematic study of the *agrégation* reports for all the literary and scientific disciplines.[11] I did not think of this last week, but I can say now that what I gathered from this matched my analysis perfectly: in the scientific disciplines, the specifically literary concerns (which does not mean formal concerns) increased, the lower one descended in the hierarchy of disciplines; the attention paid to style became increasingly greater as one approached geology; in the literary disciplines, the attention paid to literary form was obviously at its maximum in classical studies, but diminished regularly the lower one descended in the hierarchy of disciplines. There were no boards of examiners for the human sciences, but when we enquired of people in a position to judge, we noticed a singular characteristic: in these sciences there was a greater indifference to formal issues. We could take the analysis further by comparing the reviews published in the various disciplines and their norms for accepting and presenting manuscripts. I think that even today these contrasts could serve to found a diacritical distribution of the different disciplines. For example, if we compared historians and sociologists in this light, we would find a whole set of systematic differences – the claims of the sociologists to conceptualise being correlated with a sometimes ostentatious indifference towards anything concerned with writing. Sometimes, from wanting to imitate the natural sciences, there is a kind of ostentatious refusal of fine writing which often tends to serve as an outward sign of scientificity: negative attitudes are always the easiest to acquire – ostentatiously writing badly is one of the most economical ways of adopting the appearance of science. Briefly, we could compare and contrast philosophy, history and sociology and measure the different types of stylistic difficulty or obscurity that the three disciplines produce.

I think that using metaphors rather than concepts would be an interesting factor in distinguishing between historians and sociologists today. The massive reliance on metaphor by historians, which is both a means of avoiding the concept by default and a way of appearing elegant, is opposed to the absence of metaphor in the sociologists. This is linked to phenomena of dispositions: historians are more likely to have studied Latin and are more likely to have taken the classic academic route, such as the *grandes écoles*. But although resorting to metaphor is an effect of education, it is also an effect of position. History is a relatively untheorised discipline: the only indigenous theory produced by historians is Braudel's theory of the 'long time',[12] which is in fact a negative theory. In its present state, history is colonised by its neighbouring disciplines. It is a catch-all discipline, a discipline that borrows something from ethnology, something from economics, and even something from econometrics. This discipline, which is dominated in terms of theory, affirms its specificity essentially through writing, and this metaphorical writing is both a sign of distinction and membership of the humanities and a manner of avoiding the issue of conceptualisation. (I am sorry to have to put it like that: if there are historians and sociologists in the audience, I must be shocking all of you by letting slip surreptitious value judgements, which I try not to do.)

To take the analysis of style further and show how styles of expression are linked to position, we should also contrast the position held by sociology with that of economics and the styles that sociology hesitates between and sometimes makes coexist. For example we could, as one American sociologist has done, distinguish the social sciences according to a relation between model-making, which is represented chiefly by economics, and the refined, almost novelistic descriptions used in ethnology, which is the least 'model-making' of the social sciences. Obviously, as each of these disciplines is itself a field, people will be distributed according to these poles within each discipline: the structures will not be linear and cut and dried but more complex, including inversions, for instance.

I wanted simply to give these two examples because they help us to grasp the phenomenon of correspondence between positions held and stances adopted.

Positions attained and positions in the making

The second property that became apparent from my analyses was this: in a field, in a structured and hierarchical social space, the positions exist independently of the agents, which leads us to distinguish in a field positions in different states: there are positions that are given, stable and structured, sometimes legally registered and guaranteed, and positions still in the making; we might in general terms contrast positions attained with positions in the making.

I have been discussing two issues that now need separating. Firstly, the positions exist independently of the agents. For example, the position of geographer involves certain constraints that are incumbent on the geographer. If it happens that someone who 'ought' to have been a philosopher turns up in a position of geographer, the constraints of the position will weigh heavily upon him. There will be a kind of struggle between the requirements of the position and the requirements of his dispositions, and you cannot tell which will win. I gave an example of these struggles, referring to an article by Ben-David and Collins:[13] sometimes people bring to an inferior, dominated position a capital considerable enough to transform the position into something corresponding to the dispositions that they are importing.

Secondly, this work of restructuring positions according to one's dispositions is more likely to succeed the less the position is regulated, objectified and structurally and legally guaranteed. For example, in the field of social positions that we normally call the field of social classes, as we describe the positions after the people who hold them, there are ambiguous points in the social structure, places as yet to be determined or which are ill-determined, which we shall call new professions or developing sectors.[14] In recent times, the positions of social workers represent a sector where the posts are still not clearly defined: the diplomas that give access to these posts are themselves not clearly defined, which means that people holding the same post may be widely dispersed. The flexibility of the post and the dispersal of its holders create unstable zones of conflict where relatively unpredictable opportunities for change and innovation exist. In any social space, in any field, there are oppositions of this kind.

In the field of literary disciplines, for example, the positions that echo those of the social sciences are themselves much more open, much less regulated and less crystallised than traditional positions. This means that, according to the postulate – which is proven in practice – of the correspondence between positions and dispositions, there will be a greater likelihood of finding in these open positions agents of disparate dispositions or dispositions inclined and disposed to benefit from opening up of these positions. If you compared the journalists of a newspaper such as *Le Monde* with those of a newspaper such as *Libération*, or if you compared the professions of primary-school teacher and special-needs teacher,[15] you would find very specific cases that would fit my analysis. Likewise, if, in the world of the arts, you took an established and well-regulated literary genre such as the theatre in the nineteenth century and contrasted it with the novel in the phase where it was starting to establish itself, you would find the same kind of opposition.

To repeat: firstly, the positions exist independently from the dispositions; secondly, the positions are distinguished not only by their position in the space, by their topological properties (above, below, between, etc.), but also, other things being equal, according to their degree of closure and rigidity. This is an important property that helps us understand quite a few problems. For example, in the little model that I presented, the disciplines are contrasted according to their relative flexibility: sociology is much more flexible than geography.

In the public mind this might seem to be partly a question of strategic choice. For example, to return to the question that I put just now, asking what are the mediating forces that bring the dispositions and positions to adapt to each other, we might wonder whether there is some kind of miraculously given Leibnizian harmony. This is often supposed to be what I am trying to say, whereas in fact that is not at all what I have to say. In the public mind there seem to be safe positions with predictable careers (you know when you enter how you will finish up) and, on the contrary, risky positions with high but uncertain benefits to match. This is the alternative that I indicated between the route that leads to the profession of art teacher and the route that leads to the artistic professions, or that between the journalist and the secondary-school teacher. There are always crossroads, in every age. In the public mind these alternatives are experienced as choices and are often thought of in terms of a logic of greater or lesser risk and the likelihood and importance of the ensuing benefit. I think that this kind of everyday intuition corresponds to something objective, and here we find something that I have been saying all through these first lectures: every social agent could choose a more or less adequate practical alternative. We must not make of the practical knowledge that I have referred to on several occasions a science of the herbivore that would never eat poisonous grass: people do very often get their social sense wrong, but this danger is very unequally shared. As I have already stated, the significance of an investment in an academic (or artistic) qualification varies considerably according to inherited capital.

That having been said, some kind of practical knowledge of the social space allows us to predict the degrees of rigidity associated with the different positions. For example, we can see statistically that the more people are deprived of capital, the more they tend to choose investments that are safe but yield low profits, as opposed to risky investments with a potentially higher yield: they will choose to become art teachers rather than artists, and, as there is a whole series of crossroads of this kind in a school career, we tend to find adaptations ultimately leading to this kind of equation: 'son of a farmer = geographer'. This, then, is one of the forces of mediation that empowers these correspondences.

In a social space, or field, there are then positions independent of the people who hold them, and the structures of these positions are unequally rigid or flexible: the potentials and futures objectively written into the positions on offer are closed and mapped out in advance to different degrees, not only for the agents trying to predict them but also in objective reality. These positions will be sites of struggle for the imposition of a definition of the position. They are places of refuge. Sociology for example is partly a refuge discipline. It assembles different people and will be the site of a struggle to define the future of the discipline, which will mark the success of one or other of the camps. A new position still not clearly defined will from the very fact of its availability and openness attract agents with markedly diverse dispositions, and this diversity will favour a particularly intense struggle.

Every discipline is the site of a struggle for the dominant definition of the discipline – this is another property that I shall deal with later – just as the scientific field as a whole is the site of a struggle for the imposition of a dominant definition of science, and each discipline will be the site of a struggle for the imposition of the dominant definition of science, since it is in everyone's interest to impose the definition of their discipline that best enhances their own capital and to say that science must be what they themselves practise. That may sound reductive, but it is easy to verify: people who undertake statistical physics will say that statistical physics is at the forefront of research. It is perfectly normal, part of everyone's moral code and their morale: to practise science, you have to believe in it, and believe that what you are doing is the future of science. This struggle to impose one's own definition of science is at the same time a struggle to obtain the greatest profits from one's scientific investments. If it is the definition of science as I practise it that is imposed, I will reap the maximum rewards. If on the contrary a different definition of science is imposed, all my investments will be structurally disqualified and nullified, unless another scientific revolution comes to rehabilitate me. This last point is interesting for those of you who are historians of philosophy, art or science: there are posthumous struggles where it happens that, for the needs of the present cause, someone needs to rehabilitate one of the past losers; there can then be a sudden rise in their share values. If for example a partisan of the 'nouvelle critique' says that Taine invented everything, Taine or anyone else who had destroyed positivism can suddenly move ahead of Lemaître.[16] In a sub-field, then, there will be a struggle to impose the definition of the future most favourable to each category of holders of capital. The future of the discipline will depend on the outcome of this struggle. It is likely that thirty years from now sociology will be quite different from what it is today. And the same will no doubt apply to the professions of social workers: a dominant definition will have been imposed and codified, and candidates will be selected with reference to this clear and codified definition written into the educational syllabus and the criteria for selection and reproduction. In this case, the bimodal kind of structure that we tend to find in the disciplines that are still flexible will disappear. Here is another indicator in passing: to describe a position, we can observe the properties of the people who hold it. As I said right at the start, this is one of the circles that we cannot escape when we work within this logic: although we can know a position independently of the people who hold it, the best information on the position is provided by a statistical analysis of the holders of the position, and the property of dispersion for example is a useful aid to understanding the position. This does not mean that the analysis of the positions does not afterwards provide confirmation of the properties that we have found by analysing the dispositions. We could for example try to see the degree to which the profession is codified, the existence of a code of deontology, what the American tradition of the Chicago School calls 'indices of professionalisation':[17] a highly professionalised profession (with a common code, common criteria for selection, and common diplomas) will have properties shared by the agents but also properties in the law and in its professional conduct. These go to make up a second set of properties arising from what I have been saying. I was insisting on the fact that the positions exist independently of the individuals, and I gave a second property: these positions are unequally objectified and codified.

Mental structures and objective structures

A third property is this: the systems of classification that social agents put into practice in order to conceptualise the space that they inhabit are related to the structure of this space and seem homologous with the structure of this space, so that we may suppose that they are partly the product of an internalisation of the space. A very good example is this: if you study the space of sports activities, which functions to some extent as a field, it is interesting to study the terms in which the adepts of one sport discuss rival sportsmen – for instance, in the space of the martial arts, what the wrestlers say about those who practise aikido or judo; or, in a wider context, what these martial athletes say about those who play rugby or football. Rugby players call football players 'armless' and say they don't know what to do with their hands, with whatever that may imply, whereas the footballers accuse the rugby men of 'having a finger in the pie', with all sorts of social and sexual overtones. The way that the agents spontaneously discuss the practices concerned and the taxonomies that they use to think of these practices are related to the very structure of the space where these discourses and systems of classification apply.

I believe that it is extremely important to note that there is a correspondence, precisely in order to separate the level of discourse from the level of analysis. For example, my approach allows us, if not to avoid an error, at least to be aware of it. At the time when I was working on the teaching corps, I had collected a dozen or so analyses where sociologists were suggesting classifications to distinguish between the different categories of teachers in higher education.[18] What was very striking was that all these taxonomies were using indigenous categories, such as *jet sociologist* – the international sociological researcher, spending all his time on the plane – which might be used verbatim or, on the contrary – which is even worse – be rebaptised in a scholarly language and become, for example, an opposition between the universal sociologist who flies a lot and the specialised sociologist who does not travel much and does not speak a foreign language. The taxonomies used are very often a mixture of indigenous taxonomies, refocused and relabelled, and scholarly categories deriving from research. This error, which I find very serious, is only possible because people fail to make the distinction, and fail to look into the correspondence between the structures themselves and the representations or categories through which we represent the social world. In most universes, insults, nicknames and all the various hostile classifications that social agents use to typecast other agents are extremely interesting. I keep repeating this, because it is important: the word 'category' comes from *kategoreisthai*, which means 'to accuse publicly'.[19] We see it all the time in art history: most of the names of schools of painting are insults coined by critics or rival schools, which were then adopted by the objects of the classification, sometimes as an act of defiance, sometimes as an acceptance of their destiny. In the everyday social world, people spend their time classifying themselves and each other, and one of the first tasks for any researcher is to collect all the categorems as ingenuously as possible, to record them, trying always to know who it was that produced them, who uses them, and what is their effective field of application. It is worth looking for the origins of these categorems in order to learn about their structure. For they are in fact not as arbitrary as they may seem, and the more or less amateur typologies that sociologists often reproduce under the name of science are less false than you might think: in spite of everything, even the least talented sociologists record some part of the social truth, precisely in the form of the words that they use. In so far as these words themselves express the structures that have produced them, some part of social reality passes into even the most vacuous typologies.

In conducting such scientific research, an inventory assembling the categorems with a view to constructing the space of categorems – what each person says about the others, etc. – can provide indications, for example, on the opposition between dominant and dominated. For instance the dominated are often obliged to accept and use the definitions that others give of them – there are countless examples: there are social identities that are nothing but an insult accepted, and they are not the most pleasant. We should not analyse the categorems one by one: if you take the categorem *jet sociologist* without contrasting it with those who stay put, you don't understand it at all. These categorems are stances adopted which will lead us to suppose that they constitute a field in themselves, like a space of phonemes, which will function according to a system of complex oppositions. If we reconstitute this space of categorems bearing in mind, firstly, that they may express the structure of the positions, and then that the uses that people may make of this space of possible designations will depend on their dispositions, we will have made good progress. For example, if tomorrow I had to study the cinema, I would start by asking myself what the technicians call the cameramen and what the cameramen call the . . . My first task then would be to record this kind of lexicon, which is itself often pregnant with a whole sociology, for obviously the insults are only effective if they touch a raw nerve, and in order to do this they must contain a grain of truth.

Transformations of the field: the case of the university system

I want to discuss another feature that seems to me interesting and important, and which you might not have noticed because I have not drawn attention to it. The little model that I drew up for you is rather dated. It was valid for the period from 1970 to 1975, and it seems to me that it already needs adjusting. That does not mean that it was not valid for the date at issue; this link of the model to a specific historical moment does not invalidate it. One of the advantages of thinking in terms of fields is precisely that this allows us to construct reality in its historical detail while at the same time allowing us to discover its invariants and derive its transhistorical laws of operation. One of the questions raised by the field is the question of change: How does it change? (I am obviously not going to give a full answer to this question, for, I must repeat, what I am trying to do here is merely to explain my intention: I first proposed a description of the field to try to show that the sociologist could analyse his own sociological practice and also to give you, by way of transition, an example of an analysis using the logic of the field; now I am engaged in an attempt to clarify some of the properties characteristic of thinking in terms of fields, before moving on to a rather more systematic exposé of the reasons that make me think that we should think in terms of fields. My argument may seem disjointed, but it is closely focused on a particular example, which is I think an educationally valuable procedure – forgive me if I am wrong.)

In the case in point, as in many other fields, I believe, the mediation through which change occurs is often a morphological change – that is, a change in the number of agents associated with the different positions. For example, to understand the transformations of the university field, we should take into account – I won't say 'in the last analysis'[20] – the mediation through the increase in the proportion of children attending school, which itself depends on a transformation of the relations between the different social classes and the school system. These are things that have been studied in 'La Défense du corps'.[21] The transformation of the social use of the school system made by the different social classes is manifested in a considerable increase in the number of children attending school and in increasing competition for access to the educational system and the rare goods (diplomas) that it dispenses, with side effects such as the devaluation of these diplomas, and so on. These changes produce specific effects in the field of teachers in higher education: the influx of students generates effects liable to change the structure of the balance of power within the field of university disciplines. This influx of students differs from one discipline to another, and, if you were asked why, you would encounter a problem similar to the one I faced when questioning the relation of women to different types of intellectual activity: for a given educational or social capital, what is it that leads a person of a given gender to choose one discipline rather than another?

The differential influx of students into the different disciplines produces differential effects: the growth in numbers of the professorial body will be unequal in quantity as well as in quality, depending on the discipline. For, in fact, depending on their position in the space of the disciplines, the different disciplines will respond differently to the need to house a greater number of students. Here we see another property of the field emerge: the disciplines that are placed highest in the traditional hierarchy will treat the influx of students differently from the disciplines placed lower. They will develop their professorial body – or let it develop – differently, in quantity and in academic quality, judged for instance in terms of the proportion of *agrégés*. (I am rather embarrassed here: since this is a very complicated analysis, which is very difficult to present in a few sentences, I keep telling myself that I probably shouldn't be telling you all this, for my argument does not really require so much detail. But I am going to explain more fully, anyway . . .)

The canonical disciplines such as classics can respond to the influx of students by digging into their solid reserves of *normaliens* and *agrégés*, which means that their professorial body can increase in volume without much change in its academic social quality. In these disciplines it looks as if, with a few exceptions, they try first of all to use up all the male *normaliens agrégés*, then the male *agrégés* who are not *normaliens*, then the female *agrégées*, and then, when there are no *agrégés* left, the *capésiens* [holders of the CAPES teaching certificate]. This is the kind of logic we see at work in the aristocracy, and it is classic for a dominant corps that does not want to lose status: they try to defend the purity of the corps – that is, the norms that regulate recruitment to the corps and constitute the value of the position held by this corps – by striving to introduce as few foreign bodies as possible who might devalue the position by devaluing the inhabitants of the position. The corps, for example, will be feminised, but with *agrégées*, and there will be choices to make: whether to prefer a female *agrégée* or a *non-agrégé* man? Of course nobody actually puts it like that. They ask around: 'Do you know someone who would fit this post?' It is statistics, when all the figures are added up, that show us the cumulative result of a mass of individual decisions, which are not even decisions but the product of a series of random compromises that result in the process that I have been describing.

In the new disciplines, lacking structure and history, there is no reserve of *normaliens agrégés*. There are not even any *agrégés* (this is not at all a value judgement but an institutional judgement: as a sociologist, I shall understand nothing of an institution if I fail to rehearse the values that the institution uses to identify itself. If criticism is due, this is the wrong target to aim at, the basic sociological error of those who are too clever by half). Having no reserves, the institution looks to the outside and introduces into a body that is already bimodal, dispersed, and divided into an over-selected fraction and an under-selected fraction, people who import into their position dispositions that are totally alien not only to the dominant definition of the position but also to what defined the legitimate occupation of the position ten years earlier. Things are different in the dominant disciplines, where the tenured staff and their assistants are the same, apart from a thirty-year age gap, with the contrast between them being only one of seniority. In the completely organic state of the educational system, each master reproduced himself in a chosen successor and saw himself reflected in him; there was no problem, no conflict. This is rather like the cyclical, eternal time of archaic societies. By contrast, the corps wanting to reproduce itself in times of crisis is obliged to recruit people of quite another species (this is a problem that occurs in other situations), people who have none of the properties that characterised the legitimate holder of the position and who, moreover, do not always have the properties socially required by the position as defined: for example, in many disciplines around the 1960s, the assistant lecturer[22] played a role very similar to that of the professor. It was almost the same role; there was no difference in their tasks.

Obviously the appearance of people recruited from outside the traditional reserves creates a considerable tension between the two corps, whereas, in the organic state, the tension that existed took the familiar form of the traditions of succession. As Leibniz said, time is an order of succession.[23] In society, too, time is an order of succession: there is no measure of social time other than knowing who comes before and who comes after, who is the predecessor and who the successor. Morphological pressures have for example the effect of throwing up contradictions between the predecessor and the successor, whether because the successors are not at all what successors should have been in the times when successors were called upon to succeed, or whether they import into the position dispositions that make the time separating the successor from the predecessor seem intolerable – there is

a tacit, hidden criterion, but a very important one: every successor
is chosen in respect of their aptitude to wait until the time is fit and
proper for them to succeed; nobody wants their successor to hustle
them into an early grave [*laughter*]! The contradiction will above all
be one of numbers: where once the professor had one assistant, now
there may be one professor and, say, forty assistants. This means that
the structure of expectation of the assistant will not be the same at all.
Whereas the single assistant had an absolute probability (equal to 1)
of becoming the successor, the assistant who is one among forty can
no longer think of himself as a successor. Unconsciously he thinks
differently of the position of professor, and in this new structure,
dating from just before 1968, he tends to mock and subvert it. That is
one of the effects of morphological pressure.

As I have already said more than once, because of the internal equilibrium of the corps and the division of labour, this space is a space of
positions that can equally well be described as a structure of the division of the labour of cultural production. But the internal hierarchies
of each discipline, and the relation between the disciplines, will change
significantly. The disciplines in which the contradictions in the mode
of succession will be greatest can, for example, play a leading part
in expressing the contradictions felt by all the disciplines in varying
degrees. This refers us back to the eternal problem of finding out why
certain groups harbour revolutionary intentions: there are places in
this space where the contradictions in succession will be maximal, and,
in the event of a revolution, that is partly an in-house conflict, a palace
war of succession; it is obvious that these people will be the bearers of
the early-warning message. I have chosen the example of the arts faculties only because it was easier for me; it would be easy to show that
there are very similar phenomena in the science faculties.

The refraction of external constraints

I normally picture the fields as shaped like ellipses, and I posit external forces acting on them – one of the properties of all fields being
their capacity to react to and retranslate these external actions. An
economic crisis, even if it takes the form of a restriction of credit, can
affect the field of nuclear physics, say, only through the mediation
of the structure of this field. Fields have an autonomy from external
constraints, which is translated into a capacity to restructure these constraints in conformity with their own internal logic. It is not the educational system that engenders a demographic explosion. This comes

from outside, in the form of an influx of students: the numbers rise, first in the sciences, then in the arts and then in the law. This becomes reflected at the level of the professorial body in the need to increase the number of professors providing the instruction and in the problem of deciding best practice: How can the quality of education be maintained at the same level? These individual strategies are a sort of collective policy. Statistics enable us to perceive these strategies of the defence of the corps that no single person wills but which gradually take shape and bring about a relative revolution in the professorial body, as well as in the sometimes conflictual relations between professors and assistant lecturers, and even a redefinition of their posts. When people recruited to fill a post are too far removed from the specifications of the post, the post itself becomes absurd or even untenable. It then has to be redefined through all sorts of negotiations. They say, for instance, that they can't teach in the old way any more, that they should no longer give formal lectures, and they redefine the structure of the position in order to import their dispositions. Of course they never make purposive, cynical or naïve declarations such as: 'I say that we should no longer give formal lectures because I don't want to give any more.' There are varying degrees of manipulation of the relation between dispositions and positions. The whole structure of the field, including the hierarchy of the positions linked to the reserve of *agrégés*, is involved in the retranslation of the morphological effect, and it is through such mediations that the external impact will be refracted and give rise to a different equilibrium: new disciplines and a new hierarchy of disciplines will emerge. The balance of power between the disciplines will become transformed by the fact that each field is the site of a struggle for the definition of the legitimate mode of belonging to a field – that is, for domination and for the legitimate principle of domination: I struggle inside a field not only in order to dominate but also, more subtly, to lay down the legitimate principle of domination; within the dominant class, for example, is it more legitimate to dominate through intelligence or through money – that is, through cultural capital or economic capital? In the struggle within the field of academic disciplines, certain disciplines can find comfort in the situation. In fact, the different disciplines are unequally threatened by the influx of students and by the problems that the numbers pose in terms of professorial recruitment or new teaching methods. There can be dissent. The transformations of the balance of power in these relatively autonomous fields are often linked to external circumstances, and it is in response to an external crisis that dissent within a relatively autonomous field arises.

By the way: if the periods created by literary historians, who use the dates of 1830, 1848 and 1870, for instance, to separate them, are not all that wrong, even though they have hardly been thought through and result from a simple transfer of classroom dates, with their historical breaks, it is because these historical breaks do enable a transformation of the balance of power within a sub-space. In the case of the university field, the growth of the professorial body had as its first effect a transformation of the internal equilibrium of the division of labour. There was also another effect with important implications for the sociology of knowledge: there was a considerable increase in the number of agents placed in the position of teacher of higher education, whose status in the previous state of the field required its holder to write books and articles. *Agrégés* who would have been teachers in a *lycée* were appointed to university positions: the fact that they moved from a position which does not require you to write books to a position that does would have an effect on their production; people who were not contractually obliged to write books were going to feel that they were now obliged to do so. There are a lot of factors to study here, such as the increase in numbers of books written, the appearance of new publishing houses, and so on. There is more to be studied here, but in any case there is this effect.

An external phenomenon is retranslated into the logic of the field. It stimulates the appearance of new disciplines and new reviews. It transforms the space of production and also the structure of the space of consumption. In fact, another very important phenomenon is that the increase in the number of students means an increase in the number of people with the status of student. I have often investigated this: what I call the acts or rites of institution that appoint an individual to a social position have the effect of imposing obligations, according to the logic of *noblesse oblige* – to tell someone 'You are a student' is to tell them 'You will read *Le Monde*, you will go to the cinema, etc.' It is also to tell them: 'You will read books', so that, for the professorial body, the considerable increase in the number of students has the effect not only of increasing the size of the teaching body but also of considerably increasing the potential readership of their publications. We could extend the analysis to examine what is happening in today's intellectual world, but I shall not do that now.

Strategies of struggle

On the other hand, I would like to insist on the fact that the struggles within the field are designed not merely to gain victory but also to define the aims that are at stake in such a way that they offer the best chance of winning the battle. There are then in the struggle two strategies: a naïve, first-degree strategy that amounts to saying 'I am the strongest', or simply overcoming the opposition, but also the other strategy that amounts to saying: 'We are going to compete in the game that I play best.' This is one of the major factors for change in fields in general and fields of scholarly production in particular: the struggle often takes the form of a struggle to define the aims of the struggle, and thereby to define the legitimate manner of fighting. For example, if you are a featherweight and you manage to ban all-comers' contests and allow only featherweight contests, you are the winner. In the same way, if there is a general geography, you can go for a more specialised form of geography. The division of disciplines has worked like that since the Middle Ages, and there is a very fine article by Kantorowicz on the birth of one of the specialisations in the juridical professions:[24] we prefer to be first in our village rather than the second in Rome. The scissiparity subdividing the fields is a strategy enabling us to redefine the aims and the norms of the struggle. Another way to wage the struggle is to overthrow the definition of the legitimate manner of winning. This is a common heretical strategy designed to hoist the dominant by their own petard, by opposing them with the ideal in the name of which they dominated but which they have ceased to honour. This is the return to origins, the return to the straight and narrow; it is the reformist strategy.

Of course these subversive strategies are always present in a virtual state in any field. In an organic period, when the neighbouring social environment is calm, they are non-starters and can even be 'recuperated' – this seemingly naïve expression is in fact dangerously purposive; it supposes a desire by the dominant to pay attention to the strategies of the dominated and have the conscious intention to misappropriate them. I am often accused of pessimism when I show that subversive strategies in an organic period may to a certain extent play into the hands of the dominant. An example of this logic would be Marx's analysis of partial revolutions,[25] which, like that of 1848,[26] are in a way conservative, because they help to reinforce the systems of defence and do not damage anything decisive. In most of the fields of scholarly production, such as the literary field – the scientific field is different, and I will tell you later how I see this specificity – the attempts at radical subversion have some chance of succeeding only if they can import the effects of external social change, such as morphological changes or economic constraints, and exploit them by retranslating them into the internal logic of the field.

The boundaries of the field

The last remark I would like to make about the schema that I showed you concerns the problem of the boundaries of the fields. One of the most difficult points raised by this manner of thinking is the problem of boundaries; on the one hand, the boundaries of the field itself – which I draw as a clearly defined ellipse – and, on the other hand, the boundaries between the sub-fields. These boundaries are important for research, but at the same time we need to avoid turning them into lines of division, like national frontiers. What are these boundaries? If for example we think back to the foundation of sociology, we find that a good half of Durkheim's methodological and theoretical reflections were inspired by the need to struggle on the borderlines: he was always out in the Wild West; he was fighting on the fringes of psychology with his opposition between individual and collective representations; he was fighting on the margins of philosophy when he said that you had to rephrase in positive and scientific terminology the traditional problems of the philosophy of knowledge.

Some of the energy spent on struggles within a field may have as its aim to defend the boundaries of the field, or those of a sub-field, to fight against encroachment and annexation. I spoke just now of the strategy of scissiparity that consists in subdividing a field in order to be absolute master of a small sector if you can't be master of a whole empire. The inverse strategy consists in laying hands on a whole sector, to conquer and annex it by showing for example that boundaries don't exist. If you show that individual representations are only phenomenal, that they are only an incorporated form of collective representations, you can swallow up psychology.[27] One part of the struggle between disciplines consists of boundary disputes or wars of annexation. These wars are obviously not waged by just anybody: it is no accident if it is the dominant in each field who wage these wars and who are their eponymous heroes, like the noblemen in the feudal wars. There is a very fine analysis by Butor of the noun 'noble': the nobleman is the person who fights in the name of a whole county or a whole region, with his name enlisting the whole community alongside him in the fight.[28] When Durkheim fought against psychology, it was every sociologist who was fighting through him and with him in the battle for domination. These border struggles are extremely important, but an ordinary field does not usually have precise legal boundaries. One of the major problems faced by any study of fields is to know what belongs and what does not. One way of finding out is to note whether the effects of the structure of the field affect one or other position. The problem then is to find indices to determine how far the effects of the field are effective: for instance, are the struggles engaged in by the holders of a position in geographical sociology the same as those that divide the sociologists or, rather, those that divide the geographers?

To repeat myself – in the hope of explaining it better each time: the notion of the field is constructed against the temptations of realist thinking, against the temptation to take seriously what seems obvious in the social world: biological individuals, socially fabricated objects, physical interactions between biological individuals as manifested in exchanges of words or objects, etc. The notion of the field is constructed against spontaneous realism, the spontaneous substantialism that grants reality only to what can be seen or sensed through our everyday modes of perception. The notion of the boundary is born in this way of a realist manner of thinking, requiring a field to exist in some place, have a certain height, length and breadth, and therefore end in a boundary somewhere.

The intellectual field

The issue of the limits of a field is present in every field. To take an example that I have used many times before (because I think that repeating things can be useful): if we think of the intellectual world in terms of a field, we immediately realise that one of the fundamental problems of this field will be the struggle to know who is part of it. I might even say that one of the properties by which we might best characterise the position occupied by an intellectual in the intellectual field will be the stance they adopt over the criteria for inclusion in the intellectual field. The proper object of a sociology of the intellectual field is to study the struggles for intellectual supremacy in imposing the dominant principle of definition of the intellectual field, and thereby to help dominate it. When I impose a dominant principle of definition, I impose a principle of limitation and therefore of exclusion – there are those who are 'in' and those who are 'out'. But my boundary will be a closed frontier only during certain states of the intellectual field, when I shall be sufficiently dominant to be able to set the conditions of access.

This property of the boundary, which we tend to think of in terms of a reality – Is there or isn't there a boundary? – is a historical property that we need to feed into the model: I see it not as a singular property but as something that is an issue for every field. When we think in terms of fields we imply that every field is concerned with the question of its boundaries. But the historical form that the boundary takes in each field will vary, depending for instance on how strictly the field is coded. Here we find something of the same opposition that we saw just now between strong professions and weak professions. A strong profession will have very strong deontological and professional codes and a very high standard of entry into the field, with very clear procedures for inclusion and exclusion. But such a strong boundary supposes a certain state of the field: it needs those who dominate the field to be dominant enough to have complete control over entry into the field, because in this way they also neutralise the dangerous effects that are produced when you let in everyone who asks to enter; this protocol has a name, it is the *numerus clausus*.

Something that probably nobody realised – which is why sociology is nonetheless rather extraordinary – is that there is a very interesting consequence of this struggle to prevent all and sundry from entering. There is a simple form of the struggle for a *numerus clausus*: where university entrance is concerned, the *numerus clausus* seems to have the aim of limiting the number of students who obtain a degree. But in fact it is much more subtle. The *numerus clausus* is an unconscious means (because it could not be made entirely explicit) of trying to control in advance the unpredictable consequences (although the specifics cannot be anticipated, you can tell more or less how the situation will evolve) that would result from entry into the field of a mass or even just a large number of people who threaten not to have the same properties as the people who previously entered the field, and who will have fewer and fewer of the properties that used to grant access to the field. This enormous influx is then accompanied by a transformation of the entrance requirements, which are not necessarily an entrance fee; there are all sorts of conditions of membership for a club (for example, you may need two sponsors and have to come from a milieu where you can find a sponsor). Being able to control the entrance requirements means being able to shelter yourself from the relatively unpredictable effects on the structure of the field and its internal balance of power that would be caused by the influx of a collection of people who could, as I explained just now, give support to the positions of the dominated in the field and their subversive strategies.

To resume, we could say that, if the boundaries are well drawn, clearly defined and well defended, there is not a cloud in the sky. I often use this image of boundaries that gradually lose definition as they merge into the clouds or the edge of a forest;[29] fields are often like that. These misty boundaries sometimes take the shape of clearly marked legal borders, as between France and Switzerland. Just as you can be in France and a moment later find yourself in Switzerland, so you may be an intellectual or a priest, then suddenly change clothing or vestments and encounter rites of passage that make you pass a frontier, cross a threshold. This supposes that those who dominate the field are able to impose the boundary. It is not the boundary that interests them but the state of order in the field: to maintain it, they need to impose boundaries. I have taken the risk of causing confusion, but next time I shall proceed differently. I shall try to set out the theoretical principles that have led me to think in these terms and to derive the general principles of my methodology.

Lecture of 7 December 1982

The structural mode of thinking – From symbolic systems to social relations – Parenthesis on the genesis of a corpus of knowledge – The field of forces and the field of struggles – Thinking a social position – How do we construct a relational space? – The distribution of capital and the different structures – The inter-fields – Return to the structure of the distribution of capital – The interdependence of field and capital – The major kinds of capital – Conversion of the kinds of capital

I want to bear in mind the comments that you have made, which have made me realise that, contrary to what I had thought, I was still moving rather too fast, since there were things that I found self-evident which need more discussion. I pointed out last time that the notion of the field was constructed in terms of a reaction to a certain number of modes of thinking, or, more precisely, in terms of the application to the social sciences of a mode of thinking, that we can call *grosso modo* structuralist, and in so doing I am afraid that I may have incited some of you to understand what I had to say through the idea that they have of structuralism. This is why I want to go back over some of the argument.

The structural mode of thinking

The notion of structure, as introduced into France by structuralism, has a very wide range of application. You could well say that it is coextensive with modern science. (These are things that I would not have said because they seemed too obvious to me, but I think that I should say them to avoid a potentially dangerous misunderstanding.) In my view, what is important in structuralism, much more than the notion of structure, which we could haggle over, is what we might call the structural or, more precisely, relational mode of thinking. In his book *Substance and Function*, Cassirer tries to show how this mode of thinking has progressively imposed itself in mathematics and physics.[1] In an article for the review *Word*, which happened to be the last article that he wrote, he tries to show how linguistics itself, especially Saussurian linguistics, which I think he came to know rather late and imperfectly, is just one case among others of the application of this structural mode of thinking that was first elaborated in the natural sciences – mathematics and physics – and which has gradually come to apply to all branches of science.[2] I find this article, which appeared at a moment when everyone spoke of structuralism, particularly important. Using his own particular logic, Cassirer – who had an absolutely fantastic historical and theoretical culture – tries to relocate the genesis of the structural mode of thinking in the different sciences.

So here I take a step backwards in time – this is one of the reasons why I had cheerfully missed out this stage in my historical retrospective of the genealogy of the notion of field. In or around 1968 I had written a paper where I tried to show that the structural mode of thinking was basically little more than an application to the field of the sciences of a much more general mode of thinking, which does not mean that it was not extremely original to extend it to the social sciences.[3] Referring to Cassirer and Bachelard, who seemed, at least for my purposes, to say more or less the same thing in their two different languages, I tried to show that the application of this structural mode of thinking to the social sciences introduced a radical break with the mode of thinking that Cassirer and Lewin – an important author for the study of the notion of the field[4] – call the substantialist or Aristotelian mode of thinking (Lewis tends to say 'Aristotelian', Cassirer 'substantialist') that tends to consider things in themselves rather than in their relations with each other. What is important in Cassirer's work is that he shows that this style of thinking is not congenital, so to speak, but that it has been a very recent and difficult conquest in the natural sciences. In mathematics, for example, it was only by resorting to a very high degree of abstraction that they managed to overcome the tendency to consider geometrical realities as self-contained entities and proceed to think of geometrical realities as a pure system of relations and grasp geometrical figures in their mutual relations, instead of grasping their particular existences. I quoted Bachelard, for example, where he says that

The greater the variety of surfaces to which a line belongs, the more real it is. . . . The 'reality' of a mathematical idea is a func-

tion of its extension and not of its intension. . . . Mathematical
thought comes into its own with the appearance of such ideas as
transformation, correspondence, and varied application . . . it is
through such a process that mind may measure its grasp of mathematical reality.[5]

Consequently, what is important – and here I agree with Cassirer – is
that, in modern mathematics, points, lines and planes can be replaced
by an infinity of entirely different objects without requiring us to
change the propositions that we can formulate about them. Discussing
physics and the work of Hermann Weyl, Cassirer shows in quite analogous fashion that physical science has managed to construct its object
only at the price of a sort of derealisation, desubtantialisation and
destruction – those Bachelardian terms that we all have at the back of
our minds – of intuitive and tangible notions such as that of force, for
instance. I continued by trying to show how this effort to desubstan-
tialise, which is not easy in the natural sciences, was especially difficult
in the human sciences, whether considering symbolic objects such as
myth, ritual and religion or, *a fortiori*, ordinary social objects such as
groups or institutions. In fact, in both cases the 'realities' that we need
to derealise and dissolve in favour of relations – which is a theme that
I have been developing at length during my last lectures – are particularly resistant to desubstantialisation, given that these realities may
consist of, for example, the individual person, whom the scholastics
liked to designate as the *ens realissimum*, the most real reality.

So if I do occasionally denounce with mildly polemical humour the
personalism that haunts the social sciences, it is obviously because I
do not find the personalist type of ideology very appealing, but it is
also because I think that a personalist mode of thinking is profoundly
incompatible with a scientific mode of thinking in the social sciences,
since it sets up the individual, one of our most intimate concerns, as
something that may not dissolve, that may not be reduced to a sort
of product of the field. I particularly liked to quote Hermann Weyl,
who said that a physical element is only a product of the field.[6] When
we are discussing individuals, it is obviously difficult for us to think
that historical characters, or even we ourselves, are simply a product
of the forces at work in the field.[7] In order to accomplish something
that came to seem self-evident after a whole series of revolutions in the
natural sciences, social science then had a particularly difficult task to
accomplish, and that on two different levels.

Structuralism, in the historical sense that we now habitually understand it (the structuralism of Jakobson, Lévi-Strauss, and the like), has

accomplished this break at the level of symbolic systems. It has undertaken to think of symbolic systems, such as norms, myths and rituals,
in terms of relations. We should remember how symbolic systems were
thought of before they became subject to the structural mode of thinking. One of the obstacles to thinking of myth or ritual in structural
terms is the fact that our ordinary intuition, which thinks of the elements independently of their relations, makes partial interpretations,
following a logic rather like that of Freud's interpretation of dreams.
People were rather too eager to say, for example, that 'Ploughing is
the sexual act', based on a sort of intuition that was the intuition of
a system but constructing it on the basis of one single element of the
system. The structural discovery that consists in thinking of symbolic
systems as systems of relations where the individual element has no
significance outside of the system is not obvious. It offended that
spontaneous tendency, illustrated by the notion of 'the interpretation
of dreams', to consider the symbolic elements in direct relation to their
referents without referring them to the system. It is true that this reference implies a long and painful detour: if, in order to understand what
the plough has to tell us, we have to look at the ploughshare, then
at the wheel, and then at the whole universe, it is long and arduous,
whereas practical logic tempts us to take a short cut. The structural
mode of thinking was not self-evident, and in fact the tree of the isolated symbol hid the wood of symbols; you could not see the system
for the trees.

From symbolic systems to social relations

But, and this is what I have been driving at, there was a second stage,
where I tried to move on to a structural mode of thinking. It consisted
in using a relational logic to think not only of symbolic systems but
also of systems of social relations. On the symbolic level, the transposition was easy enough, sometimes too easy, because – although
this would require considerable debate – I think that people failed to
respect the core of the structuralist endeavour – that is, the structural
mode of thinking – and indulged quite mechanically in all sorts of
games and transpositions. Rather than consider that what was at stake
was a relational manner or method of thinking, they went looking for
equivalences. You had on the one hand Jakobson and on the other a
ritual or a symbolic system, and people went for a system of almost
literal one-for-one translation, looking for paradigms and syntagms,
and so on. This fashion lasted for some time. That having been said,

it was even more difficult to move over to the system of social relations in which the symbolic systems operated. There were countless obstacles that prevented people from applying the structural system of relations, as I have been describing it, not only to the system of stances adopted but also to the system of the field of positions: one obstacle was a certain type of rigid, ossified Marxist thought, which was past its sell-by date but had the appearance of relational thought, but there were also specific obstacles, such as the fact that the social world lends itself much more to realist thinking than to symbolic systematisation. In a way, as soon as you start to think of a system as a symbolic system, it forces you to think in those terms. But to keep in mind, when you are discussing the relation between the boss and the workman, the secretary and the director, and the like, the fact that you should not think of any of these relations – which are all too easy to understand in isolation – without referring them to the totality of the system, is very difficult for all the reasons that I have given, and also from the very fact that the division of scholarly labour offers positive rewards (as shown in a very fine article published in an English-language review). If you describe the relation between master and servant, you are immediately published in the major international reviews: yet it is as if you were publishing an article on some phoneme, without reference to the language system. Thus a whole set of social obstacles came to be set up in opposition to the mode of thinking that I thought should be imposed. The difficulty of thinking in the structural mode was aggravated by the fact that it was very easy to pass from the synchronic level of symbols in a state of *opus operatum* to the level of the field of the production of symbols. And many studies confused the two.

I now come to another reference that I wanted to make and which inspired me to offer you these reflections today: in the wake of the work of the Russian formalists that was reinterpreted in terms of a structural logic in France,[8] there developed a school that we might call literary-structuralist, especially in Israel.[9] It seems interesting to me precisely because it marks the difference between what I am suggesting and what you might get from a rather mechanical transfer of the linguistic notions that are currently dominant. This school starts out from the idea that, to understand the works of a period, you have to make them into a system, which is already an important and interesting break with traditional literary history – 'the man and his works' or its variants – because it is not difficult to create a false methodological revolution that keeps the essential intact. Thinking of works in terms of their relations, these critics discover the properties of the spaces of literary products; for example, they generally note the opposition between a centre

and a periphery of the literary space, changes that consist in bring to
the centre things that were on the periphery, for instance.

But, although they had started out from the system as defined in
linguistics, they somehow managed to keep their heads in the clouds
of ideas: what happens in literature is a history of relations between
literary things. Basically, this is what I would have arrived at if I had
started out from the notion of the semantic field as proposed by Peirce,
whose variant of structuralism argued that you cannot think of a
concept or a notion independently of the differences within which it
functions.[10] If for example I had taken this as my point of departure for
a study of literary history – or the history of philosophy, which would
present the same sort of problems – I would have been led to say that
the space of the works, as a symbolic system, includes the explanation
of the meaning of each of the elements that go to make up the space.

In saying, as I did just now, that we should apply the relational
mode of thinking not only to the space of the works but also to the
space of the producers of the works, I was introducing a clear distinction between the two levels of analysis and thereby raising the question
of the relations between the field of stances adopted and the field of
positions. In fact, at the time when I was writing these articles, I had in
mind a schema of the following kind: the idea that there was a space of
stances; for example, over here, orthodoxy – which we can place in the
right-hand part of the ellipse by virtue of the Greek language[11] – in the
left-hand part, heterodoxy and heresy, and in the centre a neutral zone,
where we would place the followers of the Russian formalists, such as
Tynianov and Schklovski. We could also indicate what is dominant
and dominated, central and peripheral, at the level of the cultural
products.

But my hypothesis was that I ought to construct a second space, the
space of the producers; I would have called the previous schema 'the
space of stances adopted' and this second one 'the space of positions'
where the producers are located. And my hypothesis was that this
space of stances was a projection of the space of positions. I postulated
the existence of a homology between, on the one hand, the positions
held (by writers, musicians, ethnologists, etc.) in the real space of social
positions and the division of labour in, say, literary production and,
on the other hand, the positions taken by the corresponding stances in
the space of stances. To develop this hypothesis, we could say that it is
very improbable that someone who is over here, on the left of the space
of positions, could even think of holding a position located over there,
on the right of the space of stances. In another article that I wrote
around the same time, I quoted a joke by an eccentric fellow called

Arthur Cravan, who thought of Paul Bourget, a Catholic member of the Académie française, as a ballet dancer dressed in a tutu.[12] This kind of extravagant imaginary variant, this polemical exercise of the imagination, is most interesting because it is a structural exercise. (If you have trouble getting to sleep at night, you could amuse yourselves by imagining the people over on the left here doing things that are typical of the right; it is usually very funny. In the other direction, it is not so good, it seems too parodic.)

In other words, constituting the space of social relations of production as such leads us to distinguish clearly the two spaces and raise the question of their correspondence: Do the transformations that are situated here, on the plane of positions, correspond to changes over there, on the plane of stances? This is a question that immediately arises. Can we imagine that the orthodox will be replaced by the peripheral unless something has happened over here to reinforce that position? At the same time we face the question of what is happening outside this relatively autonomous field, which is a question that I raised last time. This distinction, which seems to me in retrospect so obvious that I forgot to discuss it with you, was very difficult to establish. (The proof that it was not so easy is that what I have been saying was inspired by objections that were put to me by people thinking that my arguments were based on unspoken assumptions, whereas in fact these were merely things that I considered way beyond their scope, and therefore forgot to mention – this often happens to me, or perhaps I am imagining it, but in any case that's how it seems to me, and so it is important for me to mention it.)

To recapitulate simply what I have been saying: there is a very common danger in the use of the notion of the field, and there was a time, during the 1960s, when the word 'field' was used in a rather vague way by a certain number of people, including myself at the start (as I have admitted in all honesty), under the influence of the mode of structural thinking that was in the air at the time. In these rather muddled usages the word 'field' designated something that confused cultural products with the space in which they are produced. It seems to me that the notion of *episteme* as then understood also mixed up these two planes.[13] The notion of culture was also deployed indiscriminately on both planes. I am emphasising this in order to show that we should distinguish clearly between the field of stances and the field of positions and accept that, in accordance with my logic, a stance adopted does not contain its own motive force within it. The field of stances may live in a state of contradiction; we cannot imagine a sort of parthenogenesis, a change deriving only from the plane of stances itself. It is on the

plane of struggles within the field of positions – for monopoly, domination and subversion – that we find the movement that then proceeds to
reveal itself on the plane of the field of stances. That, then, is more or
less what I wanted to tell you. I would be very pleased if I thought I had
managed to say everything that I had intended.

Parenthesis on the genesis of a corpus of knowledge

Just one thing that I have not said but which seems important to me (as
these are things that I have found useful professionally, I suppose that
they can be for others) is that one of the difficulties in intellectual work
lies in relocating things which appeared historically in your individual
biography at different moments and in different contexts: some were
learned academically, others rather from personal reading, outside of
study. What we have learned remains attached to the method of its
acquisition, and intellectual work, which is a work of unification and
integration, must eliminate the adhesions left by these modes of acquisition. For this undertaking, one of the things that I found extremely
useful – and I hope that others may too – is to have at least a minimum
of historical or social information on the corpus of knowledge to be
acquired. I would like to take this opportunity to say something that I
find important: one of the traditions of the French educational system
is to divorce bodies of knowledge from their historical origins – and we
could make a sociological study of the reasons why, as did Durkheim
in *L'Évolution pédagogique en France*.[14] We act as if *Morales du Grand
Siècle*[15] had been born from the thigh of Jupiter, without discussing
Paul Bénichou, his writings or his masters, which means that this
system creates ahistorical brains and sets them up as isolated individuals hardly able to communicate. Among the manners of making
the lonely communicate, there are indeed historical genealogies –
'So-and-so was the pupil of So-and-so', etc. This may come down to
the fact that in France there are very few pupils and very few masters
[*laughter*] – that was cruel, but not without reason.

One thing that we should say about the Russian formalists, which
is also a way of warning you that the rest of my argument is likely
to seem polemical, is that they were imported into France during the
structural period chiefly by Tzvetan Todorov. In fact I was debating
recently with someone who spoke of 'Todorovism' to designate the
structuralist reading of the Russian formalists, who could, however,
be read differently. People read the Russian formalists (essentially
Propp[16] and a few others), but they forget that the word 'formalism'

was an insult addressed to the formalists by their opponents. The formalists were not formalist at all, in the sense that it was understood in France – that is, they were not semiologists at all. They did not consider literature as an autonomous space enclosing its own internal references, although I have to stress that they did not entirely escape what I would call a formalist temptation, since they had started out from an analogy with linguistics and had treated literary systems as if they were symbolic systems independent of the field of their production. I don't know whether you follow my argument, but I think that it is important, because, as far as I can see, French intellectual life has been fixated on this kind of debate for the last twenty years. This is one of the reasons why I thought that I should return to this point: I feel that I have moved beyond the structuralism/poststructuralism debate, but I fear that I may be seen as ignorant, which would not matter much if it did not threaten to lead to misunderstandings or incomprehension.

Another of the numerous obstacles to understanding is the permanent temptation to reduce the new to the familiar, which is one means that the cultivated use to defend their culture. (I feel free to say these things out loud, but it would be indecent to write them down [*laughter*]: one of the roles of the teacher is perhaps to say out loud things that may be important but that we don't feel able to commit to writing.) Reducing things to the familiar, as a means of reinforcing your defence system, leads you to miss out on different kinds of information and understanding, and I think that a form of critical humility or circumspect modesty is very important in scientific practice – but, there again, it is not something that the French system particularly encourages. (That was something I wrote in my lecture notes, but forgot to say before.)

The field of forces and the field of struggles

Having said that thinking in terms of fields is an application of the structural mode of thinking to the space of social relations, and thereby to cultural relations in so far as they express social relations, I would now like to present a brief synopsis, without developing them individually, of a certain number of the properties of the fields. I shall start with the opposition that I set out last time between the field of forces and the field of struggles. Here again, this is an area where I feel that I have achieved some clarity after spending a period of time in a state of confusion: I think that for quite a long time I used the notion of field rather indiscriminately, now as a field of forces, now as a field of struggles, depending on what food for thought the particular object that I wanted to study in this way had to offer. There again, this is something important that we learn from working in empirical research: things offer themselves up for reflection in certain specific ways; some beg you to respond as a physicalist, while others tempt you to react as a representationalist. The connection that you have with the particular object of study plays its part. Thus you are much more likely to be physicalist if you are faced with a totally unfamiliar object, and I also think, as I shall try to show, that the physicalist vision comes quite naturally to those who hold a dominant position in the social space, in so far as judicialisation is a form of physicalisation. So we should question at every turn the epistemological propensities inherent in any particular object of scientific study.

The distinction between the field of forces and the field of struggles is important in terms of methodology. It obliges us to choose between different procedures in the practical conduct of research. If you set up a field such as the academic disciplines or literature as a field of forces, it means that you are more or less deciding to construct a field containing a permanent interplay of potential forces that may remain invisible as long as nothing intrudes into their space, but will affect anything that does encroach on this space. How can we recognise these potential forces? What yardstick should measure them? How can we define the structure of a field of forces? These are the first questions to ask when we think in terms of fields of forces. How do we name the positions held in this field of forces? How do we characterise each one in relation to the others?

The logic of the field of struggles is a mode of thinking that comes much more naturally to us, if only because we are accustomed to the word 'struggle', which is all too frequently pronounced in the political universe. If we use the language of the field of struggles, we can say that the literary space is a field of struggles in the sense that there are agents who use the weapons at their disposal to try to win the prizes that are at stake in this space. If we speak of a field of struggles, we place ourselves in a universe that is meaningful for the agents who inhabit it, and within which actions motivated by conservative or subversive intentions are set in motion with the intention of preserving or transforming the balance of power.

I do not propose to do it here, but it would be useful to demonstrate that the Marxist tradition has never really distinguished clearly between the two senses (field of forces, field of struggles). Marxists move constantly from one to the other, and, although this confusion may be beneficial for economists, it poses all sorts of problems for scientists. For the purposes of this demonstration, I am distinguishing between the two types of definition of the notion of the field, but I must point out that it is really only by the operation of reason, by conscious abstraction, that we can make this distinction: in the real world we cannot think of a position for one moment without thinking of it as a place from which the people inhabiting it will launch their struggle to hold on to it or transform it. In other words, at any moment positions may engender stances aimed at transforming their position. The field of forces constantly serves as a place within which struggles to transform the field of forces unfold. We need therefore to distinguish between these two phases of construction of the object of study while knowing that this is an abstract creation.

Thinking a social position

So, I have set out this distinction, while admitting that it is impossible to see it as anything other than a theoretical abstraction. Firstly, then: the field as a physical field or field of forces designates the field as a sort of theory of the state of the positions held by the agents, groups of agents or institutions in the field of forces. The social world, seen in these terms, is a space of potential forces, an order of coexistence in which each agent, singular or collective, is defined by their position within the space – that is, by all the properties written into the point in the space where they are located, properties that are inseparable from the global structure of the space. When we speak of a position, this does then constantly remind us that the only properties in this space are relational ones. In fact it is impossible to define a position in any way other than in relation to the global space of the positions. To speak of the middle classes independently of the upper or lower classes is meaningless, and the lower classes themselves, which we very often assume to be a kind of ground zero in relation to which we can study the other classes, become meaningful only in relation to the other classes as the point below which there is nothing, or (to avoid a common error) the point above which we might find something. When people attempt to understand the emergence over the last twenty years of what people naïvely term 'a call for education' in the popular classes, they forget for example that one of the properties of the position of the working class, in a society where there are manual labourers of immigrant origin, is that maintaining their position – which is not ground zero, despite their populist image as the lowest of the low – can imply strategies aiming to keep their distance from those who have nothing and are nobody. This position of potential decline can help explain strange and unexpected forms of behaviour, which may for instance seem conservative, simply because they do not fit in with the idea that we had of their position when we were thinking of it in substantialist terms.[17] Thus this position and its holders owe a considerable part of their properties to the fact that the position exists in a space and takes on meaning only when seen in relation to others. One of the properties of a position is that you cannot be where you are and be somewhere else at the same time, which gives us another fundamental and axiomatic property, which follows from the fact of thinking of the space of a position as such: I cannot be where I am and somewhere else at the same time. I cannot 'put myself in your place . . .'. This very simple proposition ruins a whole phenomenology of communication, of the meeting of minds, and a whole lot of things that were inherent to the 1960s. It is sociologically impossible to 'put yourself in someone's place . . .'. This 'putting yourself in their place' is most likely to be a game, like the exercise imagined by Arthur Cravan, where you import into a position something that is impossible and unthinkable in that place. This should cause us to reflect critically on the notion of populism . . .

I am sorry to be so hesitant: I am not certain enough of my views to express myself more confidently, especially because I am led to say things that seem excessively trivial. But even if this is a retrospective justification, I do quite simply constantly find it necessary in my work to reflect on things that seem trivial in order to make progress, which is particularly difficult in the social world, because, as I often say, we already know everything in advance in practical terms (so that making things explicit smacks of the obvious), but at the same time we are prevented by our half-digested theories from taking these trivia seriously. For example, I prefer not to talk of the 'working class/proletariat' or the 'lumpenproletariat/proletariat': these are formidable obstacles to thinking in relational terms because they substantialise and even personify the working class. I say these polemical things only to point out the specific difficulty of the social sciences, where it is difficult to think seriously on things that are trivial but fundamental.

It requires a mixture of humility and theoretical audacity to remind ourselves that to be in one position is not to be in another position (Leibniz had interesting things to say about this), which is bound to sound trivial because everyone knows what it means to have a position somewhere. I constantly face this difficulty, and I prefer to admit it because I know that I am going to suffer. Knowing that being in one place is not being in another place is not being utopian. The considerable debate over Mannheim's theory of the 'rootless, unattached intelligentsia' – which I invite you to re-read – as opposed to Gramsci's 'organic intellectual'[18] illustrates what I have just said: Can you be somewhere and elsewhere at the same time? Sociologically speaking, to inhabit a position is to be somewhere and not elsewhere, except perhaps in your thoughts. But what does being 'elsewhere in your thoughts' mean? Since your thoughts depend on your position, it means that you would inhabit one position but that you would have the thoughts of another position.

If you have taken in what I have been saying, you will have realised that you have to be able to think of your position as a position if your idea of the thoughts of others is not to be too imaginary. You need to draw all the conclusions from the fact that, if you inhabit a position, you cannot be elsewhere. We often need to start out from something quasi-tautologous if we want to unravel the threads that will lead us out of the labyrinth of half-knowledge, received ideas, old-fashioned Marxism, and the like. If you can say that to be somewhere is not to be elsewhere, you can ask yourself what it means 'not to be elsewhere'. It might help to phrase it differently and say, 'Being something means not being something else', or 'Being a boss is not being a worker'. That's not a bad start [*laughter*]. To use a classical distinction, the negation can be either contrary or contradictory: Is it simply being other (the boss is an other) or is it antagonistic? Yet we may wonder whether there is a global response valid for every position. For example, within a class, are there different positions? Will the kinds of difference within a class be different from the kinds of difference between classes?

These are the sorts of reflections that thinking in terms of relations generates. You might also say: 'Does being what I am mean being in another mode from how I would be if I were elsewhere?' But, then, is existing socially always the same, whatever the position you hold in the social world? Can we postulate a sort of anthropological universal that transcends all positions? Are some types of alienation generic (for example, our relation to fashion), or would even such generic alienation have a specific nature according to the position where it is experienced? This is another very important problem. It is very easy to think of relations in terms of dominant and dominated, and it is better for pedagogical and heuristic purposes to speak of 'dominant' and 'dominated' classes than of 'bourgeois' and 'working' classes, because it is difficult of think 'dominant' without thinking 'dominated', as they are relational concepts. Finally, even the opposition between 'upper' and 'lower' is better than those ragbags of the 'bourgeoisie' and the 'proletariat', which start to take on a life of their own and tempt you to envisage the possibility of a bourgeoisie with no proletariat or a

proletariat with no bourgeoisie. To think in relational terms is therefore to try to keep in mind that, finally, you cannot talk about anything
that happens in the social world without referring it to the whole of the
pertinent space: 'Any determination is a negation', as Spinoza said,[19]
and this is particularly true for the social world.

I will give you another example, concerning culture and the whole
debate over culture/counter-culture/anti-culture/popular culture. Is
'popular culture' (note the quotation marks) just different or is it
antagonistic? People argue about this distinction without wondering
whether the question has not been created largely by the fact that the
same word is applied to two different positions in the space, where the
same word cannot coexist. In fact, for a simple reason that I discussed
last time, since the notion of culture has been constructed in opposition to the vulgar, it is difficult to see what a vulgar culture could be.
The notion of 'popular culture' is yet another product of the 'putting
yourself in their place' manner of thinking. We think we can do good
for other people by putting ourselves in their place. The populist errors
of intellectuals are often the result of the idea that they can do nothing
better for the people than put themselves in their place. They mentally
put themselves in their place and think what the people would think
if they were intellectuals, or what they ought to think if they thought
normally – no escaping the normative [*laughter*]. All of this derives
quite simply from the trivial propositions that I hesitated to discuss. I
should continue, but that is a first point.

How do we construct a relational space?

These positions obviously exist independently of the agents that
inhabit them – this is very important. They are determined by their
relations with the other positions much more than by their relation to
the agents that inhabit them; which does not mean – I keep repeating
this, but I shall say it once more – that investigating the agents does
not teach us something about their positions; obviously we frequently
have no other means of getting to know them. As I was saying just now
when discussing the symbolic system, just as, in order to understand
the act of ploughing, you have to make a detour through harvesting
and agricultural ritual, in fact through the whole mythical space, so
in the same way, in order to understand a position such as that of a
domestic servant, you have to understand the whole structure and
development of the space. Another typical example: the peasantry is
studied by rural sociology, but everything I have been saying implies

the destruction of rural sociology. This follows from my opening tautology: 'A position is a position.' There is no urban sociology either, and there are not many different sociologies or reviews or even people [*laughter*]. You see, tautologies are important; you should always start with tautologies. For those who undertake scientific work it is important – although I do not usually underline it, given my habitual discretion in feeling that there is no point in making people suffer – to ask yourself why we have come to study young people in the western suburbs of Paris, or write a monograph on a village in Provence, or study the fourteenth-century English manor. I think that it is because there are a whole lot of real social obstacles to constructing the world in terms of fields. To recapitulate: if I proceed as I should and I study the boss/the servant, I am referred back to the whole space, but as I move from one thing to another I shall be led to think that I must study everything that happens in the educational system and the social world, which is impossible. The problem of the right construction of the space is knowing where to make reasonable divides. The choice of a subject and a research strategy is not the simple hypothesis referred to in manuals of epistemology, it is the allocation of scarce resources; knowing that the time I have available is limited, that I can normally work only three days a week, and with various given constraints, how should I invest my efforts in such a way as to derive the maximum benefit? I mentioned last time the monograph studying one school as opposed to something more extensive on the whole group of *grandes écoles*: this is the kind of concrete problem with which many researchers are faced. The problem then is to find how far I have to go to find a space intelligible enough for me to understand as much as possible of what I wanted to understand and the threshold beyond which I lose as little as possible in terms of understanding.

To return to the rural monograph: Can we study a village as an empire within an empire, and forget that the educational and the economic systems transcend the village and that the matrimonial system is starting to follow? The sociologist turns up and, since his statistics relate to the village, he draws a bold line around the *commune* and declares: 'I decide that this is what interests me, and that the principle of explication lies within.' Why does he proceed in this way? First of all, and most essentially, given the social demands on him, it is something highly regarded: it has a name (the 'monograph'); there are reviews that publish this kind of article; and so on. And then there is the fact that the material is constructed in that way: the statistics are constructed at the level of the *commune*; at the level of the *canton*, things are more difficult, and, at the level of the *département*,[20] everything is amalgamated and mixed up together. Different documents are created and recorded in particular ways.[21] There are then many obstacles that render the simple precept of 'thinking relationally' formidably difficult to put into practice, and when by chance you do happen to put it into practice, you are constantly warned to revert to a positivist vision – epistemology intervenes: 'It is better to study a very small object well than a large one badly', 'If you aim too high . . .', etc. It is moralising, but translated into epistemology. This often happens with epistemology: the advice of directors of research is often inspired by 'folk wisdom'. All of this, I repeat, is not polemical at all, but Bachelard described science in terms of polemics,[22] and we forget that science is polemics in the long term: it is fighting against problems, opponents and badly constructed objects of study; it is breaking down preconstructed topics and reconstructing badly constructed ones.

This research encounters difficulties which are essentially social, but, having said that, I feel bound to say that one of the problems is to construct the space and the principles that structure the space. If I study a field and the positions in the field in relation to one another, how do I establish the units of measurement that will enable me to say: 'This one is far from that one, this one is close to that one, these two are adjacent, this one is up here and that one is down there, this one is on the left and that one on the right'? 'What force does an agent need to move from here to there? Do they need ancestors or money, qualifications or cheek?' These are questions which arise when we face a field: we need to define the structuring principles. What is this structure? What is the structure of the balance of power? What are the forces at work? We cannot speak of the structure of power relations without discussing the distribution of capital. In other words, I introduce at a stroke several words: 'structure', 'distribution', 'capital', 'specific capital' (which I think will suffice). We need to gloss all these words, but I am honestly reticent because I feel uncertain about each one of them, and I am using them rather in the hope that I shall gradually learn what they mean. You may think: 'If he really finds them so poor, why does he use this situation of scientific authority to debate them?' In my defence, I would say that, for me, it is a lesser evil, and that these words are a set of tools that work, that enable us to deconstruct poor systems and construct better ones. But my system does not have the refinement of an elegant scientific doctrine, and I do regret this.

The distribution of capital and the different structures

For the field of the academic disciplines, I gave you indices of capital and indicators that were more or less universal standards. To measure what matters in a field, you need to ask what is effective and efficient – that is, what you need to have in order to act and succeed in achieving the specific goals. This is no minor matter: the specific goals are, according to the field, academic prestige, religious authority or literary prestige. What do you have to have in the field concerned in order to succeed? What you need is a specific form of capital, whose distribution will be structured in a certain pattern. We can imagine certain broad classes of structure by drawing on the obvious analogy with economics. You may have a structure of perfect competition: if the agents and institutions engaged in the field have the same capital, all the competitors are equal. For example, if the goal is to be the tallest, they are all of equal height; if it is to be the swiftest, they all have the same pace; if it is to be the best capitalist in the economic sense, they all have the same capital; if it is to succeed in the educational system, they all have the same cultural capital; and so on. The opposite pole is a totally unequal distribution, as in the case of the absolute monopoly, where a single agent or set of agents concentrates all the capital in their field. A question inevitably arises in this case: Is it still a field, not in the sense of a physical field but in the sense of a field of struggle?

(Here I am obliged to introduce something that I had announced for later: I think that a field where the integral monopoly is achieved, if indeed that is possible – rather than an imaginary extreme – a field where for example the religious capital or legitimacy would be entirely concentrated in the hands of a single person or group of persons, would no longer be a field but, rather, what I would call an apparatus. I shall return to this point. I think that we should reserve the notion of the apparatus for a situation corresponding to a completely mechanical space answering to an almost physicalist analysis, where it would be sufficient to know what the monopoly holder wanted in order to know what would come to pass: there would be absolutely no possibility of subversion in the field, which would therefore be a field with no history; in fact there would be no more history. I close the parenthesis, I shall return to this point.)[23]

Between these two imaginary structures which are never realised in practice, there are the real structures in which there is an unequal distribution of the specific capital considered: some people have a lot, some rather less, some even less, some very little, and some almost none. It is this distribution that we can measure. The notion of 'distribution' is extremely useful. In the case of the construction of the university field, I was looking for a universal standard – that is, a unit of measurement of the educational capital that would be common to different people (geographers, historians, and the like). The title of *normalien* is one measure. I could also have taken the top grades in the baccalaureate, the percentage of prize-winners in the *concours général*, for instance – that is, a specific index of capital – using the hypothesis that, in the case of the educational universe, the principle underlying the hierarchisation – other things being equal – is educational capital. It may happen that when we analyse it we find that the educational capital itself is diversified, that we need to distinguish between various sub-species of capital, such as a canonical educational capital that leads to the Sorbonne or a more heterodox educational capital that leads to other educational establishments. The space would turn out to have a more complicated structure, with not just one dimension but two or sometimes even three, which obviously implies a constant state of struggle within this structure: the more complicated the space, the more complicated will be the struggle over the principles of hierarchisation.

Here I am anticipating the second stage of my argument: as a researcher, I place myself outside the field and I look for something that will enable me to constitute the space in such a way that the space thus constituted will give me both intellectual insight and powers of prediction. The best distribution will be the one that enables me to understand the maximum of what people say and what they do. Concerning the structure of the social space or field, the underlying hypothesis in *Distinction* – and here I am anticipating again – is that the social space, or, if you prefer, the field of class relations, can be constructed using two major principles of hierarchisation: economic capital and educational capital. But in fact, in order to grasp the space in all its complexity and recognise all the relatively autonomous fields, you would have to introduce a considerable number of dimensions corresponding to the different principles of hierarchisation, which, importantly, are themselves hierarchised and relatively autonomous one from the other, as are the axes in a correspondence analysis. This structure of the principles of hierarchisation is designed to enable me to understand why it is that people find themselves in the place they are in, and, being where they are, why it is they do what they do. In keeping with my definition of the field, it is then an explicative description. It is a space of positions that explains how the people who inhabit their positions act, all things being equal, and always depending on the relative autonomy of the habitus – but let us leave it there for the moment. The space then is constructed on the basis of the hypothesis that there is a dominant principle of hierarchisation, which is the unequal possession of the specific capital at stake in the field. Obviously we have to explain what this specific capital is: Why is it specific? How is it generated? Why does it function within the limits of the field and not elsewhere? How is it converted when we move from one field to another? Is it engendered within the field? Is it a product of the field, and, if so, how can it be the organising force of the field?

The inter-fields

Obviously there does exist a structure within each field, but – if we reflect in comparative terms – there are places of intersection between fields. One example would be places such as national planning committees, where people situated in different fields come to meet.[24] One problem in these sub-spaces is the management of the hierarchies between the fields. Another place of the same kind would be the literary salon: even if it is not the only question raised by the salon, we might wonder how this hierarchy is managed within this rather superficial sub-space whose capital is linked to different fields. One hypothesis would be that the hostess responsible for the salon uses diplomatic strategies to manage the relations, knowing that she is dealing with people who are all leaders in their domain and whose sudden cohabitation in the same sub-space creates problems. One question to ask might be whether the salon is going to be constituted as a field of fields – that is, a terrain where the different fields will confront each other by the intermediary of their representatives – or if, on the contrary, the people will, so to speak, leave their fields 'in the dressing room' and enjoy neutralised relations. We could think about this with reference to very precise social places, since the mode of thinking that I am presenting in its abstract and axiomatic form functions best when applied to particular objects. It is likely to inspire us to put questions and, at the same time, to tear away the realist mask donned by these concrete spaces.

I imagine for example that you were not thinking of the salon in the way that I am suggesting: a salon is Madame de . . ., who extends a formal invitation to guests who are well situated in the hierarchy of the aristocracy, for instance. Like a structuralist thinker, Proust placed the salons in the space of the salons and knew very well by the same token that the people who frequented the salons were themselves situated by the salon that they frequented at the same time as they situated the salon.[25] To think of Madame A's salon in structural terms, we have to understand the structure of the ruling class. To understand its position in the space of the salons, to understand who belongs and who does not, to understand even how things transpire in the salon when Madame A receives both X and Y at the same time, we also have to understand the division of labour between the sexes. A very important fact during the whole of the nineteenth century is that the women of the dominant fractions served as go-betweens (in all senses of the word) between the dominant and the dominated fractions – that is, in Flaubert's terms, between the bourgeois and the artists. In my opinion, this role can only be understood by using an analysis of the structure of the division of labour between the sexes and the forms that it takes in the different fractions of the dominant class.

(To be entirely convincing here, I would need to go into too many detailed arguments. So I prefer to leave it there rather than say things that might seem superficial to you, although in fact they are not.)[26]

Return to the structure of the distribution of capital

The structure of the distribution of capital is the structuring principle of a field. To construct the structure of a field, we shall find ourselves, as always in any relational analysis, in a hermeneutic circle: to formulate the slightest hypothesis on what might be the structuring principle, you have to know already things about the field concerned, and you can only know things if you have already used a hypothesis to investigate it. For the university field, for example, we proceed in fits and starts: we hypothesise that the educational hierarchy is the common standard, then we perceive that this structuring principle does not completely account for the structure of the space, that people considered in terms of this principle of hierarchisation are identical, yet in reality they are nonetheless different, which implies that we have to take into consideration a secondary principle of hierarchisation that is independent of the first and perpendicular to it. Little by little, in fact, we see the space take on the form of a vicious circle, which is in fact dialectical: in so far as we understand that the structuring principle is better constructed from a better knowledge of the practices that it brings into being, so this structuring principle enables a better understanding of the practices that enable us to construct it. (What I have just been saying is in fact a summary of research that, in the case of our recent study of the Church, took two years.[27] We say: 'Right, if we construct it like that, there is this principal opposition, then there is a secondary opposition, and then there is another one over here.' Research is like that. Unfortunately, when we speak in general terms, as I am here, we are obliged to present general propositions that may seem almost vacuous but are in fact very difficult to construct.)

The construction of the distribution of capital is then fundamentally a hypothesis about the nature of the capital at stake. To say what this capital is, I shall take an analogy: this capital is the specific energy that is at work in the field in question.[28] This physical analogy, with all the risks that it implies – although it conforms to the logic used by physicists at least in their popular writings – seems to me legitimate in that it enables us to understand and account for reality. If you think back to the questions that I was asking just now, this specific energy is what allows us to account for the relations – relations of domination, for instance – as well as their transformations and movements within the space. As I said last time, a field can be pictured mentally as a geographical relief map: movements in one direction are more difficult than movements in another and demand a particular form of energy, one of the problems being to know, for example, how energy accumulates here rather than there. How does the initial accumulation and capitalisation occur, given that we enter a field entirely devoid of content and capital? Is it by conquest or theft? Is it by importing an external capital transformed into internal capital? This second possibility corresponds to one relatively frequent scenario that happens in the passage from one discipline to another, as we can see in the case of Freud, where the capital of a doctor was converted into the capital of a psychoanalyst (or, in the case of Fechner, the capital of a physicist was converted into the capital of a psychologist).[29] Very often, in the scientific field, academic capital is converted into scientific capital: most of the research conducted in the sociology of science reveals how the initial capital is constituted by the titles of the most prestigious academic institutes and professional careers.

Capital is that kind of social energy that operates in a determined space and can be concentrated in the hands of a few. It will be distributed among people, it can be manipulated – and here I am anticipating again – it can be appropriated and guaranteed. The role of the law will be to guarantee the monopolistic appropriation of a kind of capital or a part of the capital at stake. The effects of what the Americans call 'certification', through the 'entitlement effect'[30] exercised by an academic qualification, legal entitlement or property deed, are to guarantee appropriation of the social energy accumulated and effective in a given field. There is then a sort of reification: the title somehow puts the capital out of harm's way; it becomes untouchable, it belongs once and for all time to its owner. I shall return to this (I already alluded to it just now), but this judicial sanction or objectification in terms of the law is a form of physicalisation: if everything existed in a juridically guaranteed field, nothing would change and there would be nothing more to play for in the field, because all the prizes would be allocated in advance. The dream of the dominant is to freeze the field in the state it was in at the moment of their domination. Weber said that the dominant always have a theodicy of their own privileges,[31] underlining the fact that, for him, the great religions were theodicies of the privileges of the dominant. The notion of the field implies that, since it depends on the principle of domination, the theodicy will change because it will need to justify the different kinds of capital: those whose domination is based on cultural capital will have an ideology of cultural meritocracy and the gift; those whose capital is their land and heritage, such as the aristocrats, will have a theodicy of land and blood.[32] To put this neutrally, without implying intention, we could say that the dominant tend to reify and physicalise a state of the field that suits their desires, through the elementary form of objectification offered by the religious discourse as theodicy of privileges or, in a more advanced form of legitimation, through the legislation that says that what is must be, and that all transgression will be met with sanctions, thanks to the monopoly of the legitimate violence specific to the field in question.

Thinking of Weber's theory of the State being defined by its monopoly of legitimate violence,[33] we could say that one of the goals at stake within each field will be to gain the monopoly of legitimate symbolic violence within the field – for example, the monopoly of consecration or excommunication. Capital, then, is the social energy accumulated in the space, and, as I said just now, it is distributed more or less unequally. Basically, the major principle of variation – if we exclude the two extremes of absolute monopoly and perfect equality – will be the degree of dispersion or inequality. The form of this structure will be one of the factors that explain what occurs in the field. But what is the capital that is at stake? How does it function, how is it accumulated and how does it make itself manifest?

The theory of the field leads ineluctably to a theory of capital or, more precisely, kinds of capital, which constitutes a new point: the balance of power that I described just now, which may appear in the guise of a distribution of the forces specifically engaged in the field, will materialise in the structure of the distribution of a particular form of capitalism, what I call a 'kind of capital'. The problem of the relation of the kinds of capital to the notion of the field would require a vast exploration, which I shall undertake another year. Here I simply want to sketch the major themes, for to speak of the field is automatically to speak of capital, and capital is both what is engendered in the field and what is at stake in the field: it is both something that drives the field, motivating people's actions, and something that only has value in the field. It is a contribution (in the end, there has to be one . . .) that structuralist readings of Marx have contributed: capital only functions in relation to a field.

This is true of any form of capital: it is within the field that the social energy that functions in the field is born, and this energy is effective within the limits of the field within which it is generated. Let us take the simple example of the religious field: the specific energy, which we might call roughly 'the energy of consecration' or the 'capital of specifically religious authority', that consists in the power to 'consecrate' is both the product of the functioning of the religious field and the goal of the struggle within the religious field. This capital of consecration will be unequally distributed between different religious agents, who are either going to preserve and augment the capital acquired, by concentrating it further or by reinforcing the orthodoxy (which will be the strategy of the dominant), or discredit the capital accumulated by others, by disqualifying the religious agents who temporarily hold the monopoly of the specific authority, and by casting doubt on the belief that founds the monopoly. This struggle will engender the very belief that motivates its efforts: it is precisely the religious struggle for the monopoly of religious authority that gives birth to the belief in the need for the struggle and the value of the goals that justify the struggle, and so on.

The interdependence of field and capital

Once again, I have moved from the field of forces to the field of struggles, from the physicalist plane to the plane of representations. It is very difficult to do otherwise. When we grasp a field at a given point in time through objective indicators, we can try to grasp the structure of the distribution of capital without reference to the actions that transform this structure, but we cannot avoid referring to the very history of the field of forces, in so far as the capital accumulated is the objectified product of this history. If the physicalist metaphor cannot ultimately be sustained, it is because at every moment the agents engaged in the struggle characteristic of a particular field invest in their struggle for the monopoly of the capital concerned the capital that they have acquired in previous struggles, which they possess either in the objectified form of material goods, such as sceptres, crowns, symbols, crosses, books, and the like, or in incorporated form. That said, my objective is simply to insist on this kind of total independence of the field and its capital. This is the reason why I have spilled over into the notion of the field of actions, no doubt because it is impossible to found this inter-dependence entirely on the physicalist plane: we have to move on to the plane of the field of struggles and introduce the notions of habitus and belief, and so on, especially for fields of symbolic production. On this plane I should say that there are as many different kinds of capital as there are fields: there is interdependence between the definition of the field and the definition of the capital involved. When I speak of a cultural field, I am automatically speaking of cultural capital; when I speak of a religious field, I am automatically speaking of the religious capital that is not only at stake but is also a product of the very strug-gles to appropriate this prize.

A simple way to recognise this interdependence is to observe what happens in a field using a viewpoint from another field. You can quite easily produce an effect of ethnological disturbance by describ-ing what happens in a field with the innocent eyes of someone who inhabits another field, with the naïve view of Montesquieu who, having nothing invested in a field, considers the field without having any stake in it or any belief in what is at stake there.[34] If, for example, you study the senior civil service through the eyes of an intellectual, one of the big problems will be to manage to detect what 'motivates' a senior civil servant, and then, having discovered it ('my office has two windows', etc.), to understand how that manages to 'motivate' him. In the opposite direction it will be the same thing, and people will not understand why you publish in the *American Journal of Sociology* rather than another journal. And yet in both cases it may be a case of life or death; the leading American journals for physics, for instance, have 24-hour switchboard operators taking calls from scientists reporting their discoveries, so that the opportunity to sign a discovery with one's name after twenty years of research may be decided in a few minutes.

When we discuss a field we are obliged to include its struggles. I wanted to give you some insight into this. The metaphor of gambling is useful on the simple plane of the 'field of actions' but is inadequate on the level of the 'field of forces'. The reason why I keep insisting on treating the plane of the field of actions independently, when it would be easy to treat it in terms of the field of forces, is because this enables me to give tangible form to the priority of the positions over the strate-gies engendered by the dispositions. It is in order to make it clear that at every moment history arises from the structure (which arises from the history), but that at every moment it is the space of positions as physical space that explains what is going to arise, including things arising that are going to change the structure. I believe that it is important to bear in mind that this structure of distribution implies strategies within the field concerned: imagine a big pile of chips here and a very small pile there, and then there will be people with a medium-sized pile . . . When we start off by thinking of the space of positions, we remind ourselves that the strategies that are going to arise here or there to transform the space have their origins in the structure of the space, even if we must not forget that the structure of the space is itself at every moment the product of strategies of the moment *t-1* whose aim was to transform the space (within limits determined by the structure of the space in the state *t-1*). This is the reason why I keep insisting so much on the priority of the physical structure of the space and its interplay of forces, as opposed to the field of struggles.

This interplay of forces is then a relation between the positions, defined as positions held within the structure of the capital. Just now I referred to positions that could be defined in terms of left or right, and so on. Now, looking at the positions in a distribution, I would say: 'This one is at the top or the bottom or in the middle of the graph, say, and it is this position that can be defined by properties: in this place we find 30 per cent of *normaliens*, 60 per cent of *agrégés*, and whatever percentage of sons of professors, and so on. These are basic indicators, but we can reconstruct things differently and say: 'There is educational capital of scientific or literary kinds, of a consecrated or unconsecrated nature, and so on.' The people who are in this position have properties, but these properties define them only so far as they situate them in a space of properties, and what is going to explain their practices will not be their properties directly – the fact of being an *agrégé*, a bishop, a theologian or a hairdresser, for instance – for these properties do so only in so far as they define a position in the space of the properties that are active within the space in question.

The major kinds of capital

Even if in fact there are as many kinds of capital as there are fields, I have suggested distinguishing a certain number of the major kinds of capital in order to construct what we normally call the social space – that is, the more general space within which agents may be classified overall without distinguishing between specific kinds of capital or field. It seemed to me, on both empirical and theoretical grounds, that to construct this space we had to make a very basic choice, taking a small number of kinds of capital that can themselves be specified and subdivided[35] – particularly economic capital and cultural capital (each of which can be further specified; I shall return to this point). All the different kinds of capital can be distinguished from one another according to whether they are more or less institutionalised and juridically guaranteed, but they can also be specified according to secondary variables in different sub-fields. To give you a simple example in the case of cultural capital: to understand the space of the academic disciplines, I had tacitly introduced the distinction between literary capital and scientific capital, and in so doing I implicitly raised the question of the relations between these two kinds of capital, of their convertibility, of the evolution of the exchange rate at different times, a dominant capital having a more favourable exchange rate than a dominated capital, and when we say that 'the sciences are rising faster than the humanities', it means that you will need much more literary capital than in the previous generation to reach the same level. These are very basic matters. Obviously the units of measurement and the calculations of the exchange rate are relatively simple in the case of economic capital, because there is a quantifier, money itself. For cultural capital, we need to find relatively subtle indicators to measure, for example, the relative devaluation of the capital of the humanities in relation to scientific capital.

The third kind of capital to distinguish is what I call social capital, but this would be much more complicated to analyse. You can say, as I have done, that it corresponds to what we normally call 'connections', but this is a dangerous, because institutionalist, definition, since 'connections' constitute a reconstructed object that seemed imperative but must be deconstructed in order to grasp social capital as being the capital associated with membership of networks of connections. Social capital designates everything that affects an individual, an agent or a group through the intermediary of their 'connections', whether institutionalised or not, with other agents or groups. It can have a multiplying effect on other kinds of capital: having a social capital can easily double your economic capital, and, although economic capital is attracted to economic capital, it is because a kind of social capital, embodied in the form of connections, can give you 'credit' (in the strong sense of confidence and credibility, of being reliable in the future as well as the present). In credit there are a great many things that depend on the effect of social capital. So, in general terms, those are the three kinds of capital that I distinguish. They seem to me to be the three kinds that are universally effective, since they can accommodate and subsume all the subdivisions that are linked to particular fields.

Conversion of the kinds of capital

One of the problems posed by the distinction between different kinds of capital is that of their exchange rates. This problem can be posed in physicalist terms: what is the loss incurred when economic capital is exchanged for cultural capital? What is the expense of energy, and what kind of energy is involved when economic capital is transformed into cultural capital? You would need to spend time, for instance: one difficulty with exchanging economic capital for cultural capital is that you cannot buy cultural capital instantaneously. You cannot buy incorporated cultural capital, just as, until recently, you could not acquire an instant suntan; you had to spend time on it [*laughter*]. The analogy is interesting because it is absolutely of the same order: there are things that you can get straight away at their published price, as soon as you pay cash on the nail for them. The exchange of economic capital for cultural capital takes time, which is why social judgements need to stigmatise the late arrival, the outsider. If time plays such a large part in social perception – time means tradition: antique furniture, time-honoured titles, the old aristocracy, the historical dimension[36] – it is because antiquity or maturity measure the time taken to exchange, and therefore the rate of exchange. The passage from economic capital to cultural capital has a price. You do not retrieve all the energy that you have invested, because you had to spend energy on the exchange itself.

Similarly, in transforming economic capital into social capital, you cannot buy connections: on the contrary, acquiring connections supposes a whole process of work. These remarks are inspired by my reflections on what we have called traditional, archaic or pre-capitalist societies, where social capital is one of the essential forms of capital:[37] one of the only things that you can accumulate in these societies is a capital of relationships, connections and debts, real or moral obligations, sometimes legally sanctioned. In these societies economic capital can achieve very little on its own, and in fact most of the things that can be bought in our own societies are not officially for sale. Benveniste entitles one of the chapters of his *Dictionary of Indo-European Concepts and Society* 'An occupation without a name: commerce':[38] in ancient societies, commerce as a self-avowed economic activity was so shameful and dishonourable that it did not have a name. In these societies, when economic capital is at work it can never work in personal terms: it must always be disguised; you cannot pay cash, you cannot buy a smile, whereas in our societies all things, smiles included, can be bought, some more easily than others. Pre-capitalist societies are the site of an enormous process of socialisation, which is a process of transformation of economic capital into social capital, through gifts and the maintenance of relationships, and such like. You could find the equivalent in our societies in the work spent on fostering connections among the nobility: Monique de Saint Martin shows in her work on the des Brissac family that, in order to be a duke it is not enough to be born a duke (although it does help); you also have to work continually in specific ways to preserve that capital. This is another example of the effect of the field: viewed from a petit-bourgeois position, you would say: 'These society gents do sod all' . . . without realising that inaugurating festivals, opening charitable foundations and dispensing goodwill is very hard work [*laughter*].[39] This work is very important to preserve the inherited capital of nobility and make it bear fruit and earn profitable returns.

Another example is family relationships: in a study of the Béarn and Kabylia, I showed that, whereas an objectivist vision of a genealogical kind considers these relationships as given – the family tree shows all the cousins – in reality, you have only the cousins that you cultivate.[40] There is an old French word, the verb 'to cousin': you only have cousins if you 'cousin', if you frequent and cultivate your cousins; you cannot ask a cousin for help if you have seen them on numerous previous occasions without ever asking them for help [*laughter*].[41] Everyone knows this, but they do not draw conclusions from it to use in their theories. We need in the first place to note that the word 'cousin' exists, whereas it does not necessarily have to exist: in many societies you would immediately distinguish between, say, a 'first cousin' and a 'cousin twice removed', which would fragment the class of cousins or the generic concept of 'cousin'. The fact that there is not only a word but also a collection of representations, duties, obligations and obligatory sentiments, and so on, is very important and effective: it shows the effect of institutionalisation, objectification, nomination and legalisation. Nomination is a first step towards judicialisation and legalisation. But ensuring that the cousin does not remain merely a nominal cousin but becomes a real cousin requires a work of 'cousining', which in practice we do without seeing it as a task – on the contrary, it is work in denial, work that we do without wanting to admit it, which adds to the difficulty of taking account of it in our theories.

That is one example of what is implied in passing from one kind of capital to another. I could take other examples. Within the space of cultural capital, for example, what are the conditions of the transformation of the capital of a physicist or a historian into the capital of a sociologist? The laws of transformation will be of the same kind:

paying the entrance fee and gaining rights of passage into neighbouring fields will imply a work of conversion and exchange, which will obviously depend largely on the relative positions of the fields in question; the work of conversion and exchange will take quite different forms and will be longer or shorter, harder or easier, depending for example on whether you are trying to exchange economic capital for cultural capital or the capital of connections. If you have been feeling unconvinced by my argument, I think that you could really feel the effects of the field by reflecting for instance on the example of crossing boundaries, for that is where we see the majority of the effects of the field and the effects of conversion.

Next time, although I shall still be using a physicalist viewpoint, I intend to insist on the effects of the notion of the field that result from the fact that, although fields each have their own specific logic linked to the specific game that is played there, they all tend to have relatively invariant forms of operation. There are phenomena of homothety[42] and homology between fields – the fact, for example, of being dominated in a dominant field – which give rise to entirely paradoxical social effects, especially in politics. To give you pause for reflection, I shall take an example that is close to you, but not too close; I wrote a paper a few years ago on the field of *haute couture*, which is a space like any other: I have not kept up to date with recent developments, but at the time Dior held the dominant positions, and there were people like Ungaro and Paco Rabanne, for instance, who were dominant and dominated, then in the middle there was Courrèges.[43] The people who were in the dominated position when the enquiry took place, just after 1968, spoke of their relations with the dominant and said, in the language of contemporary leftist students: 'We must get fashion out into the street' [*laughter*]. We should consider the fact that such relatively autonomous fields are situated very high up in the social space and share a homologous relation with the field of social classes, with all its consequences. (You can make mental experiments yourselves, trying to place for instance the Centre national de la recherche scientifique, the scientific field or even the political field.) Since they have a homological relation with the field of the social classes (or with the overall space within which they are situated), these fields give rise to ambiguous or duplicitous behaviour; being on the left-hand side of the relatively autonomous field may lead you to feel that you are on the left of the surrounding field as a whole. I shall return to this point, because expressing it like that will no doubt have left you feeling that you understand everything – and nothing [*laughter*].

The field of haute couture

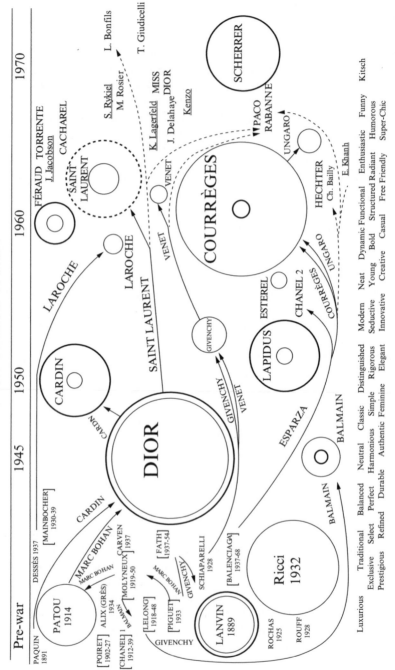

Lecture of 14 December 1982

A manner of thinking – The field and the statistical aggregate – The concept of the field 1): theoretical itinerary – The concept of the field 2): practical itinerary – Field and milieu – Field and interaction – Field and network – Field and positions – Field and representation of the situation – The space of objective relations and the space of interactions – Field, group, population, individual – Representations and practical sense – Homologies between fields

I have referred several times to the notion of the field but without ever offering a rigorous definition. Today I would like to move on from the sort of intuition that I have stayed with so far in my examples and make a first attempt at a systematisation. Since the number of sessions that I can devote to this theme is limited, I shall hope to give you a kind of synopsis and save the detailed developments for another year.

As I did for the notion of habitus, I would like therefore to try to highlight the theoretical context within which the notion of the field has been constituted and, at the same time, give a somewhat simplified synoptic view of the properties of the field. I shall go about this rather like an American journalist: starting with a few sentences saying what the whole article will say, so that there is time to develop the argument and there is hope that even the reader who stops after the first paragraph will still have an overview. I shall try to break out of the vicious pedagogical circle that we all know, where it is as difficult to use a concept without having defined it as it is to define it before your audience have become used to seeing it function. In fact I have already been showing you the concept of field at work in the case of the university system, which everyone here has experienced. Bearing in mind these analyses and the properties that they have revealed, I would now like to show you what underlies this notion for me.

A manner of thinking

The first principle is this: the notion of the field is not a thesis, nor what we normally call a theory. I pointed out when I first used the notion that it was a manner of thinking, a sort of mnemotechnic term that, when faced with a problem, provides the techniques for the construction of that object. On that occasion, using the example of the space of the *grandes écoles*, I showed that thinking in terms of field immediately excluded the possibility of studying one *grande école* as such, dissociating it from the space of the *grandes écoles*. This methodological preoccupation often confronts the researcher with a very painful alternative: whether to study extensively everything that has to be studied in order to construct the object correctly or, rather, to make an in-depth study, with all apparent rigour, of as small an object as possible, but constructed in defiance of the real functional logic of the social world. Should they for example study the École des arts et métiers, a relatively circumscribed object that can be approached at once synchronically and diachronically and on which you can accumulate all the information you need, or the whole set of *grandes écoles*, knowing full well that this would then reduce the amount of data you can use, that your relation to the object cannot be so well developed and that you will then be exposed to the usual positivist criticism 'Some things have been overlooked', for instance?

Social science, as a science dominated and constantly threatened in its scientific identity, because it does not follow the regulations of the day, finds it very difficult to resist the temptations of the punctilious and even pointillist ideograph[1] that provides all the appearances of scientific rigour, seemingly hard-won, but attained in fact with minimal effort. One of the functions of the notion of the field is to recall to the ranks of theory those people who would prefer to wallow in the satisfactions of the monograph or the ideograph. The example of the *grandes écoles* is quite typical: if, as the notion of the field suggests, the truth lies not in each *grande école* but essentially in the relation that it entertains with the other *grandes écoles*, we will exhaust ourselves trying to exhaust the singular object of 'one particular *grande école*' without finding what should have been our object, unless we do so by mistake or as an extra (because in spite of everything there are effects: even if you put the most stupid questions to them, the *polytechniciens* will be obliged to talk of the other schools and say, for example, that they were led to choose between the École normale supérieure and the École polytechnique, for instance). The same would be true of the literary field. You can exhaust Vigny without understanding half of what you would understand if you knew that the truth lay in the relation that he entertained with a space. It is striking to note that the inexhaustible monographs on Vigny's love affairs or Musset's political opinions seem riddled with holes as soon as we investigate them structurally, by which I mean from the angle of the space of relations in which the people who are the object of these monographs operated.

The notion of the field, then, is a manner of taking seriously this primacy of relations that is so often mentioned in the social sciences without much idea of what it means. As I have said for the notion of the habitus, it helps designate a vision of the social world that contradicts our spontaneous vision. Indeed, what we spontaneously see of the social world is individuals or groups of individuals; thus it is very common for people who are not sociologists – for example, scientists from the material sciences – to believe that they are doing sociology simply by making analogies with the theory of gases or stochastic phenomena, and such like. A traffic jam on the Place de la Concorde is of course an interesting social fact,[2] but I think that sociology must go beyond two kinds of immediate image: those of the individual and the sum of individuals – and even that of the interactions between individuals. The notion of the field aims permanently to abolish these three images. It is only in certain configurations that the social world approximates to a sort of Brownian motion of elementary particles colliding with each other, producing something that you could grasp statistically. We need to realise that crowd phenomena have been the focus of a whole series of fantasies, since the crowd, together with the popular masses, is one of the most difficult objects to study, because the other classes have projected all their fantasies on to them (they are the same fantasies in both cases).

The field and the statistical aggregate

It is true, then, that the social world does not always function as a field (it takes certain social conditions for a social world to function as a field). It is only under certain conditions that the social world escapes the state of an aggregate: for example, the collection of people who are on the main concourse of the Gare du Nord at a given moment in time do not form a field; they are only a collection of people who happen to be interacting episodically. The movements of the crowd or the masses are, however, only one particular case of the state of the social world, which cannot be reduced to the forms of Brownian motion – that is, the physical interactions of people contacting, jostling and colliding with each other. Nor is it a sum of individuals engaged in states of symbolic interaction. The social world is sometimes thought of as an ensemble of countless interactions whose aggregate produces something that is irreducible to the sum of its elements: economists have long used this insight to study the logic of perverse effects and the paradox that sees individual actions in many cases change their significance as they are aggregated with others. The aggregate of individual actions is also a particular state of the social world. There is, then, the Brownian state, the aggregate state and the field state.

The field state is a state where the relations between social agents are not reducible to physical or symbolic interactions. In fact the agents' interactions include something whose source is not to be found in the interaction. If agent X speaks out and agent Y remains silent, the principle behind their different behaviour does not lie in the properties of the interaction. We cannot account for it by saying that the person who speaks is the person who 'takes the initiative'. So why does he speak out? What was the property he possessed that led him to speak?[3] In many cases – at any rate in the cases that the notion of the field seeks to establish as the privileged object of social action – the properties of the agents can only be understood if we introduce relations that transcend the coincidental moment and the episodic nature of the interaction. To take this analysis further, we need to distinguish between the structure of the relations that constitute a field and the interactions that take place there. The interactions are one of the points where the structure of the field materialises, and in invoking the notion of the field we are saying that, to understand what happens in a social space, we need to postulate invisible structures. What happens at the École des arts et metiers, for example, has its origins in the objective hierarchy of the schools, whose index may be constructed using complex indications referring to the founding date of the school, the social origins of the pupils, the value of the diploma on the different educational or other markets, and so on. In other words, in the practice of each of the individual agents of this space we may find, as long as we know how to look for it, the trace of this invisible structure, which disappears if you do not construct the complete space.

We cannot think in terms of the field without asking ourselves how to construct the field. This is why I said at the outset that the notion of the field is essentially a method of constructing the object. It is a way of reminding ourselves that doing sociology is not studying any old thing: 'adolescent girls aged fifteen to seventeen in the southern suburbs of Paris', 'the condition of women in France since 1980' or 'the Roudy Act'.[4] If sociology wants to avoid studying nothing at all (however dressed in scientific clothing), it must construct a space in such a way that what happens there finds in the space thus constructed its explicative principle, or, more precisely, the essential part of its explanation. It is the notion of relative autonomy that leads me to make this qualification: the fields are relatively autonomous from the space surrounding them, and we find in the space of the *grandes écoles* the essential part of the explanation of what happens in this space, with the qualification that I mentioned last time, that this space is itself the site of forces that are the retranslation of external forces expressing themselves according to the specific logic effective inside this space. This, then, is a first indication of what is implied by the vision of the social world that is involved when thinking in terms of the field.

The concept of the field, 1: theoretical itinerary

Before developing this point, I would like to return to the reasons why I started talking about the field and showing it at work. My aim in so doing is not to give you a potted history of my own thought but, on the contrary, to give you a means of checking what I am going to say by pointing out its limitations, and perhaps to help those who would like to master this manner of thinking. In this way I intend to demonstrate an important pedagogical principle: it is much easier to understand structures of thought when we know their origins; we understand the discoveries of the scientists of the past when we understand the problems that they set out to resolve. The history of science should have its place in our scientific education. For my part, I am offering you a retrospective construction, which will inevitably be biased. I shall strive, with the utmost honesty, not to rearrange it, but unconsciously I am bound to structure it towards its known conclusion.

The first and perhaps the most essential thing that I want to say is this: the notion of the field, like most of the notions I use (habitus, cultural capital, symbolic capital, etc.), is one that I have employed because I could not do otherwise. My concern was neither to affirm my theoretical distinction nor to import a noble concept like those of theoretical physics or Lewin's psychology.[5] It is a concept that I have used because I needed this word to designate something whose identity was rather elusive, and the word pointed to it rather than designated it clearly. In fact I started to talk of the field without being too sure what I meant. I admit this now, at the risk of increasing the vulnerability of concepts that I am going to say are extremely vulnerable in any case. (In my defence, I should say that this is a common occurrence, but scholars do not admit it because it is not usually in their interest, and epistemologists are even less likely to admit it because they do not know it, and they always consider science in the state of an *opus operatum* – that is, a science already acquired. We should make an exception for the Bachelardian tradition, for Bachelard emphasised the importance for science of trial and error, or guesswork.[6] Yet, despite that, people still tend to forget it.

So I did at first use the notion of the field without being too sure what I meant. I first used it in an article entitled 'Champ intellectuel et projet créateur', written towards 1964–5 and published in *Les Temps modernes*, giving it a sense that I soon realised was wrong, but I think that, if I had not used the notion in that way, I would not have been able to discover my mistake (which shows why we need to make mistakes in order to make progress in science). In this article, I explicitly identified the notion of the field with the notion of a space of interaction.[7] I tried to break with the tradition of literary history that looks for the explanatory principle of the work within the work itself, or at best in a biography constructed in relation to the work. To tear myself away from this traditional conception, I tried to find the explanatory principle of the literary production or intention in the space of relations between the literary producers – the writers. But I still had in my mind a definition that I would now call 'interactionist': I thought that what transpired between writers was reducible to their interactions. So my progress was only apparent. By drawing attention to the contacts between the writer and other writers, the writer and the critic, the writer and the publisher, among others, I remained within the ultimately banal logic of the literary historian's notion of 'influence': this is the sort of archetypal notion that a scientific approach needs to deconstruct and demolish completely. 'Influence' is a kind of long-distance magical transaction accomplished through the real interaction between agents.

If I had used this logic to work on empirical material, I would have questioned the agents about their real relations, and I would have ended up with a kind of analysis that does exist – interactionism – which I have mentioned several times in connection with the Chicago School. The 'network analysis' currently used by certain American sociologists (for instance, to account for the power structure of a small town or systems of influence in a university) consists in trying to construct the network of relations of all the people concerned.[8] The technique of the enquiry might consist in asking people for their diaries, taking down the names, and noting the correspondences. People record in their diary the people that they meet, and thinking in terms of a field leads you to formulate the hypothesis that these meetings are only superficially circumstantial; for ultimately what these specific meetings or interactions project is a space of possible encounters and the logic of a field.

However, a network of interactions is not a field, and the notion of the space or field of interactions presents risks (here again I am speaking sincerely and openly, to help you to understand what I am doing, and not at all to define the absolute using the traditional Hegelian logic of the course of lectures that reveals the genealogy of your thought as a royal road leading ever upwards towards the heights). There is an equivalent concept in rural sociology, the notion of a universe of inter-acquaintance. It is useful in defining a village community in a non-realist and non-empirical manner, and it is a concept that I found very helpful at one point. But, in my experience, these tangential versions of the correct notion are the most dangerous, precisely because they stick close enough to the right version to obscure it for the duration. This space of interactions, then, is not the field, although sometimes there is no other way of grasping the field than apprehending it as a space of interactions and trying to establish a sociogram[9] ('Who did you go on holiday with?' and the like). A sociogram can be useful, as long as you have access to the pertinent variables, of course (because, if you forget to ask the child to tell you their parents' professions, you can look for hidden structures as hard as you like, they will not reveal themselves all by themselves – or they may be there, but you will not notice them). The space of interactions, then, is one of the possible manifestations of the space that I call the field, but this manifestation has the property of revealing what it reveals only in disguise.

The notion of the field as I was using it was very close to the notion of interaction, but at the time I had tried to derive its content from the useful but purely verbal theme of relative autonomy. My use of relative autonomy goes back even further: in the 1960s, in the lectures that I gave at the École normale supérieure on the literary field, I obviously could not avoid coming across the notion of relative autonomy. But this notion had only a negative value: it amounted to saying that the social bodies that depend in the last analysis on the economy have their own particular logic. To speak of a field, then, was to try to render operational something that was, as is so often the case with Marxist concepts,[10] a concept with considerable academic effect but little scientific import, one of those notions that are fairly useless outside the lecture hall or the examination room. The notion of the field thus consisted in saying that this effect of relative autonomy might depend on the possible existence within the social universe of sub-universes where different games are played, which have their own rules and structures that reconfigure the external influences. At the time, I often used the metaphor of refraction, saying for example that, given the relative autonomy of the fields, the political oppositions between conservatives and progressives would be transformed through a logic that would retranslate the opposition between the right and the left into the terms of the laws of each particular field. The notion of field thereby becomes a way of defining the notion of relative autonomy by trying to establish the mechanisms that are triggered by this autonomy, which they in their turn empower.

From there I moved on to a properly structuralist notion: I quite lucidly admitted to myself the opposition between interaction and structure, and I became absolutely convinced that the field was not reducible to a space of interactions, that there was a structure transcending the interactions, although it did become manifest in these interactions. Re-reading these articles in this logic, they acquire a pedagogical virtue, because we can see the errors. (I do not like practising self-criticism, because it is a way of trying to benefit from the errors as well as the correction of those errors.) I can refer you to the texts if you want to read them for yourselves.

Constructing the notion of the field as a structured space led me to wonder what the principle of this structure was, how the structure was organised, how I could grasp it empirically, and what would be the meaning of the 'structure of the literary field' or the 'structure of the religious field'. This was one of the rare times that I have made what I would call a 'little discovery' in the process of giving a lecture: I was expounding Max Weber's famous analysis of religion from the section entitled 'Sociology of religion' in *Economy and Society*, and his description of the key agents of the religious world (the priest, the prophet, the sorcerer). I had been very struck when faced with Talcott Parsons's translation[11] – since Parsons very unfairly dominated the field of the social sciences in those days, I was obviously keen to show that his reading was not right[12] – by the fact that he completely omitted to translate what he thought were simple transitions between the different chapters devoted to the sorcerer, the priest and the prophet. Noting this absence, and delighted to discover the mistake (you can see how social motives – the young sociologist's desire to undermine the senior sociologist – can have scientific virtues; this illustrates the fact that, in the scientific field, unhealthy motives can produce effects that are not unhealthy),[13] I thought a lot about those passages, which were half way between simple transitions and a kind of indication of the relations between the different agents and seemed to show signs of thinking in terms of a field. As I was myself minded to think in terms of the field, I said to myself that, basically, Parsons had suppressed all the indications that Weber gave of the relations between the religious agents. In other words, where people had previously seen portraits (seeing them as 'types', an odious word) of the key religious agents who were present transhistorically in every religious universe (the priest, the prophet and the sorcerer), by accentuating the transitions between the transhistorical and therefore invariant figures, we could now see religious fields. But, in that case, you would have to see that the prophet could be defined only in contrast to the sorcerer, who himself had to be defined in relation to the priest, and you had to construct the space – which Weber had not done at all – within which these agents were to be defined. I

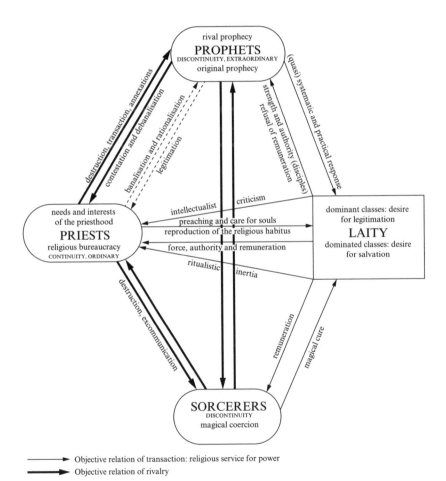

shall not prolong this analysis but, for those of you who might find it amusing, I can recommend two articles that I wrote at the time: one was a re-reading of Max Weber's text published in the *Archives européennes de sociologie*, and the other a reconstruction of the religious field, now unencumbered by the debt to Weber.[14] In these two texts I tried to show how what had always been seen as portraits of religious agents should be understood as the description of three invariant positions that could be found in the different forms of the religious field.

I don't know if you can see the change, but where Max Weber, like everyone who creates typologies, was caught up in the typological logic of the realist definition (because, although there are priests, sorcerers and prophets, there are also slightly sorcerous priests or somewhat priestly prophets), the fact of constructing the space and simply sketching this ellipse showing contrasting positions led us to question not only the interactive relations but also the structure of those relations, given the fact that what one agent does to another varies according to whether he is dominant or dominated. The priest burns or excommunicates the sorcerer when he can, but, when he cannot, he comes to terms with him or canonises him. This insight changes everything, and we see immediately that this line linking two agents in my schema can designate real interactions (what they do to each other: they criticise, insult and excommunicate each other, they issue bulls, and so on). We cannot describe these interactions without considering the conditions that make them possible, which I did do later. In other words, I am obliged to think both of the relations and of the structure of the interplay of forces that is expressed in an interaction. At the same time, I can think of the variations of this space in such a way as to understand what Weber had described as invariants. These exemplary positions are very likely to be realised in every religious field. Even their absence is interesting: in a situation of priestly monopoly, the other poles will be 'squeezed', but the fact of using the model of the field then obliges us to wonder where the prophet has gone (in a monopoly situation, the prophet has been annexed and his prophecies integrated into the official dogma). I am only summarising very briefly what was a much longer study, two long texts of about fifty pages each.

Through applying my notion to the religious field and this sort of reinterpretation, I think that I have made progress, on the one hand, in marking more clearly the opposition between interaction and structure and, on the other hand, in importing into my manner of conceiving the notion of the field the analogy that Weber had introduced between the religious field and the economic field. In fact I was, and still am, fascinated by the way that Weber was able to think of the fields of symbolic

production by analogy with the economic field. Weber's analogy contributed to the notion of the field while obliging us to consider what
had made it possible: if Weber was able to think of the religious field
using the mode of thinking characteristic of economic thought, it is
perhaps because economic thought was also thinking in terms of fields
and because, behind the notion of a religious field or an economic
field, there was a more general theory of fields giving rise to all these
analogies. I could expand on this theme if it was interesting enough,
but you can see already that my itinerary towards the transposition
of economic concepts is very different from the one usually imputed
to me. Starting out from what I still see as a brilliant transposition
of economic concepts onto the symbolic field, we are led to rethink
not only the fields of symbolic production *but also* the economic field,
thinking of it as a field. Of course I shall take care for the time being
not to address this last topic here, for, given the relation of domination
between disciplines, sociology cannot approach economics, especially
the very foundations of economic thought, without fear and trembling.
Having said that . . . I am thinking of looking into it [*laughter*], and I
might as well admit it, since you are bound to find out sooner or later!

The concept of the field, 2: practical itinerary

That, then, is more or less my track record. But retrospective reconstructions are always slightly false, and they may lead us to believe
that in the end this concept of the field took root through a reflection
on texts and concepts, which is not at all the case. In parallel, from the
very beginning, I was involved in personal and collective work on the
real problems of the field. I have mentioned the collective enterprise
at the École normale supérieure, where we studied the literary field in
the nineteenth century,[15] and we came across absolutely real problems
at every turn. For example, when we started to study a population of
writers in terms of a field, we discovered the antinomy between population and field. Briefly, the field of nineteenth-century writers can only
be grasped through indications that are nearly all attached to individuals (biographies, books, and the like), which means that the elementary
temptation is to do what literary sociologists such as Escarpit have
done[16] – that is, use statistics – and set out, for example, to compare the
social origins of the symbolist poets and the Parnassian poets, or study
the evolution of the proportion of graduates in law, medicine and the
arts, and others, among writers during the nineteenth century. In other
words, they take as their object populations treated statistically. But

the empirical work on the populations gives rise to the following question: Might it not happen, in certain fields, that some positions have only one place, in which case, might statistics, which work on groupings (for example, a category of fewer than fifty individuals would not be meaningful), destroy the very object that we are looking for?

There was then in practice a kind of permanent conflict between the notion of the field and its consequences (the idea that you had to find pertinent positions, or *situs*, that were meaningful through their opposition), not only in the way of constraints but also in terms of the tempting facility of statistics, which entail a mode of thinking in terms of populations that are aggregates, like the people on the station concourse. Working in terms of the field implies, for example, studying the position of the agencies of consecration. In a literary field there will be agencies of consecration, which are agencies of reproduction of the producers and consumers. Where the literary fields are concerned, the education system will become – and it is not just a change of name – an 'agency of production of the producers and reproducers', for instance. A constructed position that is capable of being grasped through the properties of its inhabitants is characterised by its impact on others, even if the others are not in direct contact with it. (Something I have not yet said, because I think it is obvious, is that the effects of structure operate even in the absence of interactions – although in fact they may also operate through interactions.)

One way of characterising these positions in relation to each other – that is, according to how they really are – is to describe the statistical properties of the people who hold the positions. But in practice these studies are beset by conflicts: for example, if I am studying the state of the field in France in the 1950s, how do I handle the dominant position held by a single man, Sartre, the one-man band who dominates both literature and theatre at the same time? Yet I am not forced to write a monograph on Sartre because, given that Sartre is defined as dominant, I can only understand him by understanding everything that he dominates: Sartre is the field; the field is Sartre. This is the kind of problem that I refer to only in passing, but which was accompanied by, or more precisely preceded by, reflections of a theoretical or abstract nature that I have recounted separately elsewhere.

Field and milieu

Now, how can we define the notion of the field in the space of notions that are neighbouring but contrasting? Firstly, for the sake of convenience, and at the risk of disappointing, we might say that the notion of the field is to a certain extent synonymous with the notion of the 'milieu'. I believe that this notion was introduced into social science by Claude Bernard. In *La Connaissance de la vie*, Canguilhem tries to establish a kind of genealogy of the concept of the milieu, showing how it passed from Newton to the life sciences and from the life sciences to the social sciences, until its use became so common and banal that it ceased to convey any meaning at all.[17] This is why the concept of the field, which gives more force to the meaning that we want to convey, seems preferable to me. That said, studying the genealogy of the notion of the milieu does have its uses, if only to understand the everyday social uses of the notion and to draw attention to the gap between the worn-out vocabulary used by scientists and the rather more rigorous terminology of the social sciences, as well as the attention that the latter pay to work on language, as I do systematically in my own writing. So, the notion of the milieu as used by Newton ultimately indicated a sort of vehicle for action at a distance, which Newton also designated as the notion of ether. (You will see in a moment the use of this foray into genealogy.)

The milieu, then, is what enables us to describe this action at a distance and thereby break away from the Cartesian physics which decrees that action exists only in the form of interaction and collision. This notion of the milieu seems important to me in so far as it enables us to see that thinking in terms of the field compares to thinking in terms of interaction (take Goffman, for example), as Newtonian thought does to Cartesian thought. (These analogies are always rather wild and dangerous, and I suggest them only in the hope that they may help some of you to make some use of the notion.) The notion of the milieu then is constructed in opposition to the notion of contact, just as the notion of the field is constructed in opposition to the notion of interaction. Here I would like to quote a passage from Marx, to whom I might attribute the paternity of the scientific use of the notion of the field (in certain times in history, that would bring in a lot of symbolic profit!): 'In all forms of society there is one specific kind of production which predominates over the rest, whose relations thus assign rank and influence to the others. It is a particular ether which determines the specific gravity of every being which has materialised within it.'[18] This is really the notion of the field ('a particular ether which determines the specific gravity of every being which has materialised within it'). Obviously I came across this text after a prolonged use of the notion of the field. (And I am surely the only person to have noticed it, although heaven knows how many people have read Marx, or pretend to have read him!)

The genealogical reference to Newton then was useful in connecting Newton, Marx and the ether. What is in question in the notion of the field is, I think, the idea that Marx had grasped in practice, according to which the social world is a space of objective relations irreducible to interactions. If there is one thing with which we can certainly credit Marx, it is to have seen more than the other 'founding fathers' of sociology that the social world is not reducible to interaction between agents. There is the famous passage from *The German Ideology* where he says: 'Sancho thinks that the boss and the workers need to meet if the boss is to influence the workers';[19] but in fact it is the whole economic structure that intervenes between them. The worker and the boss may never have met, and yet there is no doubt that it is the boss who dominates. This idea that there are objective connections, independent of individual consciousness and will, as Marx said, is what constitutes the notion of the field. The notion of the field is more than that, but the idea is important in helping to tear the notion of the field away from interactionist interpretations.

Field and interaction

I would like to expand on this absolutely central distinction between field and interaction. As the interactionist outlook is the one closest to the outlook of the notion of field, there is a major epistemological danger, and in practice as soon as we lower our guard we start indulging in interactionism while believing that we are still thinking in terms of the field. The clearest example is to be found in Weber's thought, as I have described it: in *The Sociology of Religion*, Weber starts out from the individual agents (the prophet, the sorcerer and the priest) and in so doing reduces the effect of the religious agents' actions on others to their actual interactions, ignoring the structural constraints linked to a position in a field, limiting these effects to those of attraction and repulsion – to use a physical metaphor, to be explained in a moment – that accompany membership of a field and govern the form of subjective interactions. The subjective interactions, then, do not contain their own truth; they are governed by the structure within which they take place. This definition of the notion of the field might, if you like, be called structuralist (I am deliberately upsetting the boundaries between different theoretical traditions). I say: 'if you like', but in fact I myself am not so keen. I must repeat that this is not because I am claiming to be original, but because the term is fraught, given what structuralism has come to mean in everyday usage. This structuralist conception

– but I had better not call it structuralist – describes the social universe as a universe of objective relations that do not have to be directly and immediately realised in interactions, but which do orientate practice, including direct interactions in particular. In so doing it rejects the interactionist vision, which is ultimately a psycho-sociological one, according to which the truth of relations, as indicated by the ordinary meaning of the term (as when we say: 'they are related to' or 'they share a relationship with'), would be found in the experience that people have of them. It is true for example that it is one of the properties of certain positions in the social field to have relationships.

Another example that helps us to grasp the difference between interaction and the structural effect is the notion of social distance. I have several times analysed the condescension strategies that are used in the process of interaction[20] in order to deny a distance that is not actually visible in the interaction. In a sense, the realist observer cannot understand these strategies; he can have an intuition of them but he cannot give an account of them. In fact they occur between people who are close in physical space but far apart in the invisible space that is social space. They confront two people (the aristocrat and his groom, the modern professor and his student) separated by an objective distance that exists in the guise of a system of social distances and sanctions measurable with indicators (differences in salary, seniority, age, career, background and present circumstances, and so on).

The structures of domination must exist somewhere, however invisible, for the strategies that waive them to be meaningful. The strategies of condescension whereby the dominant symbolically deny their distance and make a sacrificial offering of their domination to the dominated prove the existence of this social distance in the very act of denying it. Another example is in the relations between the sexes: paradoxically, letting the women go first is a strategy of condescension. Or, again, the strategy of condescension whereby a philosopher gives an interview to the inaugural issue of a geographical review[21] can be understood only if we bear in mind the space that I described in my last lecture. In our practical experience we encounter so many social situations that we could set as questions for an eighteenth-century style of academic competition, asking candidates to 'Explain what is happening in this social situation'. Only a structuralist, in the sense that I have argued, can account for what part of an interaction depends on a strategy of condescension.

Another, more sophisticated, example: the strategies through which someone dominated seeks to become familiar with someone dominant: he behaves casually, and doesn't keep his distance. These strategies too – although much more complicated in this case – can be understood only with reference to an objective distance that both the subject and object of the intended familiarity know and recognise, the latter seeking to deny the distance, which he recognises in the very effort to deny it, through actions intended to bring the person whose familiarity he seeks to his own level. It is the Groucho syndrome: 'Why should I want to join a club that would accept me as a member?'[22] [*laughter*]. They are very complex strategies that we practise publicly and know how to recognise, but which are formidably difficult to analyse as long as we are restricted to a psycho-sociological approach. We need to factor in this gap between different objective structures that nobody sees but which act powerfully, including and above all through actions that are intended to deny them. I will leave you to consider the problem of popular culture, and you will see that it is analogous with the familiarity-seeking model. I shall not develop it here because it would be a distraction and take me too far afield.

Field and network

It is never easy to transmit a message in the social sciences, and we constantly have to adjust our line of fire. The interactionist contribution is remarkable enough, and I would not like to give the impression that I am sweeping aside, as is common practice in French ideological struggles, the enormous scientific contribution of the Chicago School. In fact it is this very same sociology that now enables us to refine our analysis of condescension. This is how the dialectic of science works: we are obliged to criticise what we respect the most. I say this quite sincerely: I have great respect for this manner of thinking, but I think that we must criticise its limitations, precisely because it is so close to the truth. Basically, it is a form of realism, and even naïve realism, which considers that what exists for the scientist is only what can be touched. You can film an interaction. Contrariwise, you cannot film the structure that governs the interaction, and thinking in terms of a field means exposing yourself to criticism, just as when you use the notion of the habitus. You can never exhibit a habitus or a field, and I don't think that you could ever put one under the microscope. And yet that does not mean that they do not exist. They exist through manifestations that we could not understand otherwise, and which in fact do not exist otherwise.

The same would be true for the 'network'. This is an example of a scientific effect produced by an analysis in terms of field or structure:

it may happen, as I said just now, that certain phenomena of field or structure can only be grasped through analyses of networks. Thus Pinto devoted a major study to the 'friends of the *Nouvel Observateur*', analysing the network of people connected with the review in different ways (those who write articles, who are themselves celebrated, or who celebrate others).[23] This analysis was bound to be interactionist, because there was no other way of grasping a certain type of objective truth, and it immediately lent itself to ordinary readings, shall we say in the manner of Régis Debray (here I really have to cite him), which resort to ordinary ways of thinking and reduce the effects of structure to effects of conspiracy. One of the reasons why thinking in terms of the field is so difficult is because we are looking for something invisible that can only be traced through things visible – that is, through people. But we know what networks of people are: they are conspiracies, secret societies, networks of people sharing common projects, dangers and ambitions – and we find ourselves immersed in the teleology and everything else that I have already been criticising. And so it ends up being thought of in terms of who is responsible (and it is all 'Bernard Pivot's fault').[24]

I should add – I always mention this, because it makes social science difficult – that all these tempting errors are cumulative: an intellectual who discusses the intellectual field is walking through a minefield where there is much at stake; he has enormous, if concealed, vested interests which multiply every temptation to err. The inquisitorial style of thinking that has been identified with political thinking for generations, and which consists in conferring the status of concepts on what are basically insults ('You are nothing but a . . .', 'You are the son of a . . .', 'You are only a mandarin', and the like), then comes to aggravate all the tendencies that I have mentioned, and it leads to committing scientific errors that are increasingly political errors. This is an example that I don't want to take much further, because it is too contemporary and close to the bone; it would cause reactions of the kind that I am attacking, but it does give an idea of how difficult it is to practise sociology. The sociologists that I find most efficient are those who constantly call into question their own modes of thinking, and I think that this is vital in a science where we are constantly threatened with relapse into the state of our ordinary – that is, biased – vision.

The interactionist vision, in so far as it situates the principle of action and interaction on the plane of interaction, leads naturally to a Machiavellian type of philosophy of history, a conspiracy theory where there is someone responsible, whether an individual, a network or a group of conspirators. Thinking in terms of fields has the effect not of dissolving responsibilities but of excluding thinking in terms of responsibilities, of excluding for instance the question of who is responsible for what is written in *Le Nouvel Observateur*. It also avoids the temptation of moral indignation. A Swedish sociologist has written a very fine study of the role of moral indignation, claiming to show that this disposition was particularly rife among the petite bourgeoisie.[25] This propensity for moral indignation, which leads them to hunt for someone responsible on every occasion and organise witch hunts (something that we all know), can also reflect the social origins of the people who practise sociology, and it may in a particular case come to reinforce and crown something already prepared by a series of theoretical and empirical errors.

Field and positions

The notion of the field leads us then to think not of interactions but of positions: instead of seeing a space of visible individuals and interactions (contacts, exchanges of gifts, backhanders, rewards and mutual congratulation, and the like), we now see only positions analysed in terms of an abstract space that we have to construct, with the vicious circle created by the fact that it is by constructing the positions that we establish the space, and it is by constructing the space that the positions are established. For example, instead of thinking of the middle classes in terms of a median income, we shall consider them simply as being 'in between': they are the people who are neither above nor below, those who are not yet above but are no longer below, or those who are no longer above but not yet below.

As soon as we start thinking like this, we are led to put some very simple questions: What are the properties that people owe to their present position and positions they have not yet held, or to their dispositions? We define the position of the petite bourgeoisie as neutral – neither one thing nor another: yet the *petit bourgeois* position is the most 'positional' position, the one where we see most clearly that it owes the greater part of its properties to the fact that it is 'in between'.[26] When we are looking above or below, things are not so clear, but Marx's statement that the dominant are dominated by their domination[27] reminds us that those who are apparently easiest to think of in terms of the absolute are in fact thinkable only in relational terms: you cannot think of the superior without positing an inferior. This is very simple, but if we follow this train of thought all the way and draw all the conclusions, we shall see that we have a topology in which no element, position, site or point has any meaning outside of its relation to the other points. It is what it is only in so far as it is not what the others are.

The essence of a position, then, is essentially that it is different from the others. For example, a playwright cannot write both light entertainment and socially relevant art-house drama. You cannot be everywhere at once in the social space, although this is what the intellectual dreams of.[28] This means that Mannheim's statement that 'the intellectual is defined by his absence of position'[29] appears as the archetypal ideology of those who, taking the notion of space literally, think of themselves as situated not within it but vertically above it. Ultimately, we cannot think of this space otherwise than as a network of objective relations (and no longer as a network of interactions) between positions that will impose their constraints on the holders of the different positions. To take this a little further, we might say that the field is a space of possible forces that will affect all those who enter the space, at first in the form of forces of exclusion that render entry difficult and then, once they have entered, in the form of forces that impel them in one direction or another.

If I had to sum up everything that I have to say in a single sentence, I would use an image (it is because it was used by Marx that I draw attention to it): ultimately, the social world is constituted by spaces containing forces that may lie dormant or that may operate as soon as something enters; newcomers will encounter these forces, and their capacity for resistance to them will be proportional to their capital – that is, their habitus – their incorporated capital and their objectified capital. To use another metaphor, we could say that the field is a space in relief, which means that, in the space of the academic disciplines for example, if you want to move from geography to mathematics, you have to climb. This image also implies that, if you come from far below, you will be tense and nervous, and it will show. Just as, when we were discussing strategies of condescension earlier, we had to suppose something transcendental, so we do when we wish to account for a phenomenon we may observe, which is that the people known as 'intruders' – a pejorative word that expresses the viewpoint of the dominant (towards the 'latecomers', the last to arrive) – often bear the traces of the effect of having to resist the forces of the field, whereas those who are born in the position that they inhabit are able to float in a state of weightlessness. This metaphor, like all metaphors, is false, dangerous, provisional and disposable, but it is pedagogically useful because it enables us to tolerate the more pedestrian aspects of the argument.

Field and representation of the situation

To return to the distinction between structure and interaction. The structure of the positions in which the agents find themselves engaged inflects their interaction, and its activity may be mediated through the representation that people have of this structure – it is here that interactionism becomes interesting. I shall return to this point in more detail. One of the questions raised by thinking in terms of fields, and which has deeply concerned me, is that of the mode of action of these possible forces. Do they operate as in a physical field? Should we take the analogy with physics all the way and say that the field as I have described it is a field of forces that would act in a determined way on people who enter it, or do these forces work only under certain conditions – that is, on agents predisposed to let them act, in so far as they know and recognise them? Interactionism, which by its genealogy is the product – loosely speaking – of crossing Schütz's phenomenology[30] with Mead's social psychology,[31] is very attentive to phenomena of meaning and interpretation, and it tends to find the explanatory principle of behaviour in interactions – that is, in the representation that the subjects have of their interactions. Anselm Strauss, one of the leading representatives of the interactionist current, has thus tried to formalise the notion of a space of interactions, which is tangential to the notion of the field, via the concept of the 'awareness context':[32] Strauss argues that what is decisive in a practice is the awareness that the agents have of the awareness that the other agents have of their awareness; there is a kind of infinite play of mirrors (the interactionists have been heavily influenced by phenomenologists such as Schütz, Husserl, and the like, but not by the early Sartre). For Strauss, the source of interaction would be what he calls the 'situation' – the word 'situation' is often prominent in social psychology – which is in fact the representation that the agents have of their situation, understood as the representation that the other agents have of them (the infinite play of mirrors again).

In Goffman, there is an attempt that is very reminiscent of marginalism: the social world is supposed to be the aggregate of all the actions inspired by the representation that agents have of the representation that the other agents have of their actions; and the aggregate of all these acts, referring successively to the others and the values that these others give to other agents' actions, leads to a social transcendence.[33] This is interesting because, if we follow this logic through, we end up with a philosophy of the social world where each of our acts, say of respect, contributes to the structures of respect that are only the aggregate of all respectful acts; whereas, from a structuralist point of view, the acts of respect will be one of the manifestations (in the same way in fact as many acts of disrespect which, as a pure product of the logic of inversion, recognise the structures through the very act of rejecting them) of the structures of respect that transcend the individual acts of respect through which these transcendental structures are expressed. I don't know whether that is clear, but I am doing my best! The stakes, both theoretical and political, are enormous, since the interactionist viewpoint leads ultimately to a vision of a liberal, marginalist or spontaneous order, depending on where you place the accent. In this logic, each individual would be basing the principles of his action on the perceptions that he has of others and the perceptions that the others have of him. Which is fair enough. We cannot then charge interactionism with pure physicalism, where social agents would be like iron filings on the loose in a magnetic field. In fact I think that social agents are determined in their behaviour by their representation of self and others, it being understood that this representation of others is a function of the position that the person representing and the person represented hold in the objective space.

It is true then that representation intervenes, but it is structured by the structures of the representer and the represented. Depending on my position in the space, I will see different things: depending on whether I am dominant or dominated, I will see the world from on high or from down below, and this means that I will see something different. My representation of the world then can motivate my action, but it will not be a visible motive, because the representation itself will be the product of the structures that structure this representation. In other words, if there is a space of different *situs* or positions, the sociological analysis of the *situs*, which is a topological analysis of this space, must entail both the analysis of the positions and the analysis of the representations that the agents have of their own and others' positions. This also means analysing the stances that agents, depending on their positions and dispositions, will adopt in and towards this space, whether in the form of acts, declarations of opinion, or the like.

The space of objective relations and the space of interactions

I think that I have persuaded you, but I still need to take the argument a little further. Personally, I could give it a miss ... [*laughter*] but I must insist, because I know – as you can see from the genealogy that I referred to just now – that these are things that take time to understand

and have to be digested slowly. We understand them straight away, but on an abstract level. Take the statement 'epistemological breaks are social breaks': we understand it in a couple of seconds, but it takes a whole lifetime for it to become a real source of practice; there is in sociology an aspect of 'initiation to Zen' where you are made to spread your work over a long period of time because things can be understood in so many different ways. In my own teaching I always experience a conflict between communicating an argument that is very easy to understand and communicating something that should be transmitted in discursive argument but rarely is: a profound conversion of dispositions, modes of thinking, and the like.

I would like to add an example here to illustrate things better. Interactionism points out that any exchange of a message communicates an informative content (a message that says something) and, simultaneously, something about the sender of the message and the structure through which the communication is channelled (for example, it communicates an order). This is a tendency that the interactionists share with Austin's classic analyses:[34] saying something is always saying something about the conditions in which we are saying it. It is a simple but extremely important principle, from a sociolinguistic point of view, for example. What the interactionists do is fine, but they forget to ask where the force of this meta-message, communicating the conditions of the reception of the message itself, comes from. In fact we should say that all messages tend or claim to communicate a message concerning the sender of the message and thereby intimating the conditions appropriate for its reception. All messages contain at least the request to be listened to and believed: to speak implies: 'I ask you at least to listen to me!' Yet this is obviously not something that is automatically granted. Since it is not part of their way of thinking, the interactionists do not even consider what conditions would be required for the meta-message enclosed in every message to be heard and take effect, what is the problem of authority, and what are the social conditions in which the message is not only acknowledged but recognised as legitimate, worthy of being not only listened to but believed and even obeyed.

One last example of this gap. In the Palo Alto School there are interactionist readings of the family as a space of interactions[35] (this has become the fashion in Paris now, fifteen years late), and they reproach orthodox psychoanalysis with forgetting that the space in which our original experiences are lived is a social space (this is both true and untrue, but they feel they need to say it). They think that they introduce the social aspect by speaking not of individual experiences but of interactions. So they replace the individuals and their individual history with a network of interactions in which they participate, as if the family were nothing other than the aggregate of all these interactions that affect or traverse the individual subject. In fact it is very easy to show that, from the structural viewpoint as I present it, the interactions within the family take on meaning only as the materialisation of a structure (for example, the division of labour between the sexes) retranslated in the family space in the guise of economic inequality between, for example, the father and the mother. In many societies, the division between the sexes is retranslated into an economic divide. In a society where inheritance is transmitted through both lines, masculine domination can also coincide in certain cases with female domination, with the woman being economically richer than the man, which creates a chiasmatic structure. And we might ask what effect the fact of being (or not) the product of a chiasmatic structure has on the structuring of a personality.

I shall not prolong this analysis, for, since I have given you four or five examples, you can do it for yourselves, but you can see that, if considering the family as a 'space of interactions' constitutes progress, it is a kind of progress that occludes another. Understanding the family as a structure of interactions is not making a sociological study of it. It is not even interpreting its social psychology (I think that social psychology can only exist as an adjunct to a structural type of analysis). This is not at all a question of the hierarchy of disciplines: I believe that an analysis of interactions that ignores the interactions as places of the actualisation of structures is ideological. This is why social psychology is so successful (in business, for instance): it enables us to believe that we are manipulating structures whereas in fact we are manipulating things structured by the structures, which enables us to adjust the structures without altering them. It is no doubt true that studying the interactions of the family is the only way of grasping their structures. It is through a continuous in-depth observation of the time that the mother and father spend talking at the dinner table, and on what topics and occasions, that we may grasp the structure. But it is by studying their family trees, the professions of their parents and grandparents, the social, cultural and economic capital contributed by the two partners or their families, that we can find the keys to understanding and explaining the different interactions observed. The structure of the two spaces, the space of interactions and the space of the objective interplay of forces, must then always be considered together.

Field, group, population, individual

After this distinction between the space of objective relations and the space of interactions, I shall look more briefly at a second distinction that I have already mentioned in passing: the field as opposed to the group or the population. I shall be brief, but I think that it is useful because nowadays any educated person has been exposed to some degree or other to Durkheim's ideas on collective representations and on the fact that the whole is not equal to the sum of its parts.[36] I think in fact that the notion of field enables us to understand both what Durkheim spent his whole life trying to define and why his intention turned into a kind of holistic metaphysics (with its extremely dangerous political dimension) that has often been denounced. The notion of the field enables us to escape another opposition that ordinarily takes hold of sociology, the opposition between the individual and the group. Since he failed to establish the effect of the milieu or the effect of the field, Durkheim constantly thought in terms of an alternative between the individual and the collective (this opposition recurs persistently). In my humble opinion, he lacked the notions of 'field' and 'habitus', and by the same token he spent his whole life caught up in the opposition between the group and the individual.

As for the habitus, I have already explained my position. I shall say a little more on the notion of the field. Durkheim had a powerful insight into one effect of the field that manifests itself in this way: when the couplings between two phenomena change, the results change, even if the elements have not changed; when you change the relation between two elements that remain physically identical, you obtain different effects. This relational effect led Durkheim to believe in the existence of an efficacity of the whole, of the collective or the group as a totality transcending the sum of its parts. In fact, I think that when we speak of the field we seek to designate a simple effect: the space of the *grandes écoles*, for example, produces something that is not reducible to what would emerge from each *grande école* studied separately. To mention just one of the effects – which would take too long to explain, so I will merely state the principle – in general the *grandes écoles* help to reproduce the elite or the dominant class, and the like, but the space that they form produces a much more subtle effect that is irreducible to the individual effects of each *école*, by reproducing a structure of differences that is largely the very structure of the dominant class and the division of the labour of domination. I shall return to this analysis,[37] but I cannot think of a better example to show how fields can produce effects as such. In this case, in fact, the field reproduces a system of differences (that is, a system of relations). Since I referred to it just now, I shall not insist further on the fact that to think in terms of fields we need to avoid the temptation, inherent in the ordinary notion of the group, of thinking in terms of a population.

Representations and practical sense

The third distinction that I would like to make, and which I have already sketched by reintroducing representations into interaction-ism, is this: Should we consider the fields in a physical manner, as fields of forces, struggle or action into which the agents introduce their representations of the field? Now that you have in mind the schema that I drew at the beginning, you will obviously immediately see that we can think of the field in its own right as a space of positions acting as a space of potential forces affecting all those who enter it. But if we know that these fields are apprehended by social agents endowed with a habitus – that is, schemas of perception and appreciation that enable them to structure this space and apprehend it as organised not inherently but through its manifestations – we can see that the field of forces also functions as a space that is enacted and to some extent represented.

If now we reintroduce everything that I was saying about the notion of the habitus, the social space may then be activated by our practical sense as a space endowed with meaning, without being the explicit object of even a partial representation. That having been said, it is obvious that it may accommodate representations. I will explain further, but this is something that you should have understood already after everything that I have said on the notion of habitus. I have said this time and again all through the term: one of the dangers of ordinary thinking is to think that there is only meaning where there is represen-tation, whereas there can be meaning for our practical sense without there being any representation in the sense of a 'mental image' drawing a visible, perceptible or objectifiable configuration in pictorial or lin-guistic form. We can then act in the social space as if it had meaning without representing it as such, which does not mean that there are no partial representations. I do not think that we could live in a social space with no representations.

Even if we feel perfectly at home in a social space, there is always a minimum of representations: for practical purposes, we make partial objectifications. For example, to live comfortably in the space of the universities you need a practical mastery of this space. (The fact that, very often, when I objectified certain words rather playfully, people laughed straight away, showed that they immediately mastered the subject – laughter is a sign of immediate understanding.) Agents have a mastery of their space and of the beginnings of objectification. The insult, for example, that I have mentioned more than once ('dumb as a geographer') is the source of one such objectification and materialisation of the space. Social agents then are both structured and activated by the structures of the space that affects them through the mediation of the practical intuition they have of it, which is itself partly the product of the structures of this space and other, homologous, ones. (This is very important: if an academic had to make his way in the university with a practical sense completely produced by the university, or if a bishop had to establish himself in his see with a practical sense entirely structured by the religious field, I do not think that they would manage very well.)

Homologies between fields

I said 'the product of this space or other, homologous, ones': I think that one of the most original effects of the notion of the field is that it enables us to understand the effects of homologies between fields. Thus a geographer will invest in his contacts with a philosopher things that he may have learned from right outside of the field, things that the field will constantly remind him of and reinforce – as in the case of a habitus adapted to the field but acquired in the homologous social space. If, roughly speaking, all spaces tend to be organised according to +/− oppositions (dominant/dominated, where the space of the social classes is concerned), people may invest in their practical sense of orientation (the practical sense is more or less a sense of orientation, I think that is the right metaphor), in the space of the university disciplines, say, something that they have learned in the space of the social classes on the basis of the transposition enabled by homologies: dominant/dominated, masculine/feminine, inferior/superior, theoretical/ empirical, pure/impure, disinterested/interested, and so on.

If the field of forces works, it is because the forces at work there operate through the mediation of the habitus, which is partly the product of the field of the forces that affect it. The habitus is a product of conditioning by these structures, but this product structures the space within which it acts. When there is a perfect match between the structuring structures of the habitus and the structured structures of the field, everything seems natural, the world is self-evident, you feel entirely at home. This perfect match is never achieved, but the mechanism is there. The structures of the habitus are then determined by the structures of the field or a homologous field, and in this way they solicit an effective match with the effects that the structures of the field exert on people's habitus in the form of the practical sense 'that's what I need to do', 'that's right for me', or 'I like that' – that is, in the form of propensity, agreement, *libido dominandi* or *libido sciendi*, and the like.

I shall finish here and leave until next time the opposition between field of forces and field of struggles, which is useful and which I need for my synoptic exposition of the properties of the notion of the field. For the purposes of my analysis I shall be obliged to distinguish between two aspects: 1) the properties of the field as field of forces – that is, as a space of positions determining behaviour; and 2) the properties of the field as field of struggles destined to transform or preserve the field of forces, it being understood that the force in the struggles to transform or preserve the field of forces always depends partly on the position held in the field of forces. I shall therefore distinguish between the two definitions of the notion of the field for pedagogical reasons. But it is important for you to keep in mind that this is only an academic distinction, which is indispensable for understanding certain properties that must nonetheless be superseded.

Lecture of 11 January 1983

Physicalism and semiologism – Structure as crystallised history – Roulette and poker – The alternatives of income or trade – Amor fati – The fertile terrain of the literary field – Art versus method: charismatic ideology and the 'sociology of literature' – The field as mediation – Literary field and intertextuality – A chiasmatic structure – Automation, hierarchisation, institutionalisation – The intellectual in the field of cultural production

As I do not have much more time at my disposal, I propose to shift the focus of the theoretical analysis of the notion of the field. I shall try to conclude by discussing the main theoretical points of my argument on the notion of the field and offering a systematic analysis in these terms, applying it to the terrain of the literary field, which is the archetypal terrain where the notion of the field has established and imposed itself as an instrument of knowledge. It is the terrain where the notion has functioned for longest and where the most important research has been conducted, either from within or from outside the field itself. It seems to me therefore to be the one that best allows the possibility of showing the fertility of the notion, as well as the difficulties that we find there, and the problems that it poses.[1]

Physicalism and semiologism

I would like briefly to prolong the reflection that I left you with last time, on the subject of the necessity of treating two aspects of the notion of the field together, the field as field of forces and the field as field of struggles or actions. In a way, the distinction between field of forces and field of actions is artificial: it is imposed only by the requirements of an expository argument. At the same time, it is relatively unavoidable in so far as it indicates a methodological priority. This is the point that I would like briefly to emphasise: the definition of the field as field of forces or space of possible positions is an epistemological priority in the sense that the struggles, strategies and actions of a field depend at all times on the state of the interplay of forces. For any scientific procedure, then, it is indispensable to start by constructing this space and its objective structures to provide an explanation of what takes place in the space being studied; with this priority we are asserting a materialist postulate.

This field is a field of forces, but it is also a field of struggles destined to transform or preserve the field, since these struggles are themselves determined in their form and their orientation by the structure of the field of forces. Although this argument may seem circular, it seems necessary to me in order to avoid the alternatives and dichotomies that social thinking tends to find imperative, and not by chance. Someone has written an article on the frequency of these dichotomies in social thinking, which is constructed around oppositions such as community versus society. These oppositions between two terms almost always have a considerable social impact but very little scientific authority. Their social impact is great because in general they correspond to real social oppositions and conflicts, since conflicts are constituted in terms of a dualism, even when there is a third position or option. It is very easy to transpose this dualist thinking from the objectivity of the social world onto a kind of social thinking that claims to be objective. Thus raw social facts are imported into social thinking. Very often in my experience of research I have been led, not by a petition of principle but by the logic of my work, to supersede these alternatives that prevent us from considering reality in all its complexity. In this particular case, the double definition that I propose is not only useful but also designed to be superseded. It allows us to conceptualise a difference in a very real manner through the fact of having clearly posited it as such.

In saying that the field is a field of forces but also a field of struggles destined to transform or preserve the field of forces, I am attacking two positions that sociology and social science in general have constantly to confront, because the essence of these twin opponents is to be eternal, constantly to recur in barely disguised form, which fosters a *philosophia perennis* [universalism][2] that seems to me to prevent any progressive scientific movement, not to mention the backing that these dualist options receive because of their usefulness in teaching and in writing three-point essays. These oppositions then have an extraordinary social force, and if you try to supersede them you find yourself in an awkward situation, all the more so because these positions of supersession, unless presented as Hegelian transcendence with all its metaphysical overtones, are often perceived as eclectic by people whose sole categories of perception are dualist. This is a law of perception: you see only according to your structures of perception, and, since most people's minds are socially constituted to think in these categories, any attempt to supersede, unless it passes unnoticed, is dismissed as a fault or condemned as eclectic (eclecticism, as you know, is the hell of thought: all parties agree to condemn it). These matters are relatively important in helping explain what I am going to argue, even if they are peripheral to the argument itself.

My definition then attempts to overcome the bipolar opposition that constantly orientates scientific thinking in the social sciences. On the one hand, generally speaking, there is physicalism, whose formula 'to consider social facts as things'[3] is the clearest and most precise definition. According to this epistemological position, which uses the physical world as a model for the social world, the field is a field of forces, a space of positions and a space of forces that will affect any object entering the field. There is no obvious word to designate the other position. Of course we could contrast physicalism with a form of personalism, spiritualism or subjectivism. In our own times we could call it the 'sociological pole', although nobody has yet claimed the name. This would correspond to what is known in France as 'structuralism', which is a manner of defining the social world as a place of communication, as a system of signs, where actions in the social world are understood as acts of communication, exchanges in the sense of symbolic exchanges (matrimonial exchanges, for instance, are seen as exchanges of women seen as symbols). This kind of semiological vision is opposed to the physicalist vision. It treats social facts as signs, whereas the latter treats social facts as things. It leads us to reduce social matters to sign systems. By saying that the field is a field of forces but also a field of struggles, I supersede this opposition. I say that the field is a quasi-physical space in which agents are subjected to forces that drive them and orientate their actions, but that, since these agents have socially constituted dispositions, namely their habitus, through which they perceive this field of forces, they are not manipulated by the field of forces like so many iron filings. They 'think'; they take a practical stance towards the space, either in the mode of the sense of practice or, more rarely, in the mode of representation. In so doing they constitute the space. They activate it, while at the same time being activated by it: they activate the space according to a logic that is to a great extent imposed by the space itself.

Structure as crystallised history

To take the example of the writer: if any of you wanted to become writers, you would enter a given space where certain forces would affect you. There are ambitions, established writers, the Académie française, places of consecration, a capital whose structure is already objectified, people known or unknown, and so on. Entering as an unknown, you will have to make a name for yourself and will be subjected to forces that will affect you differently according to whether you have some other kind of capital. And yet you will not be blown about like a straw in the wind. You will act. For instance, you may through an error of judgement offer your manuscript to a publisher who does not correspond to your position, and, if I am right, he will redirect you to your natural place, the place that you would have naturally sought if you had had a sense of orientation. You would offer a manuscript to Robert Laffont and be redirected to Éditions de Minuit (although in general it will happen the other way round).[4] The law of the field will then operate, not in a mechanical fashion but through the more or less accurate perception that you have of the field. If you are well born, if your habitus is fashioned by laws homologous to those that regulate the field you are entering, and *a fortiori* if you are a product of the field itself, your perception will lead you straight to your natural place.

The theatre, for example, is one of the domains where there is a strong professional heritage and where to succeed you must be more or less born in theatrical circles. Without connections in theatrical circles, in the first place you don't feel the desire to write for the theatre, and, if you do, you have no chance of finding a producer. The forces that affect the new entrant, this new particle entering the field, take effect then through actions that suppose acts of perception: they will read or not read your manuscripts, they will base their judgements on their practical feel for propriety ('it's allowed' or 'it's not allowed'; 'that fits' or 'that doesn't fit'; 'that will be a success' or 'that won't'). These actions affect a subject who already assesses and navigates the space with an independent *impetus*, who is not entirely a creature of external forces. For example, if you want at all costs to be published at the most symbolically gratifying and the least economically rewarding pole, you can choose to remain unpublished rather than publish in a place that does not suit the image you have of yourself.

It is then this kind of dialectic between the position – that is, the field as field of forces – and the dispositions through which the field of forces constitutes itself as field of struggles, which underlies both structure and change in the field. This is another widely rampant opposition; the dichotomy in academic dissertations between 'structure and change' or 'structure and history'. In the definition that I am proposing, it is obvious that structure is history and history is structure. Structure is crystallised history, and at every moment history will be, if not governed, at least strongly orientated by the structure: what the agents will do (or try to do) in a space in order to transform the structure, which is the distribution of capital at a given moment in time, will depend on their position in the structure – that is, on the capital that they have acquired.

Roulette and poker

This is the analogy of the poker player that I have used on several occasions. We can imagine a social world whose model would be a game played completely from scratch, such as roulette. This world where we start again *ab initio* after every round does not correspond at all to the model of poker. I think that, if gambling exerts an almost metaphysical fascination,[5] it is because it is one of the only places where you can radically change your social position in a second. It is a place that gives an experience of the Cartesian God, of continuous creation; if my number comes up, I become richer and more powerful, and so on. It is one of the only places where social rules may be suddenly suspended or abolished. In most games, however, the very strategies of the players depend on the previous moves. And the social world is of this kind: at any moment the player may either bluff or pass, and his audacity will depend on the size of his pile of chips.

One of the properties of the social space that I am describing depends on the fact that the social world offers chips of different natures.[6] There are cultural, social and economic chips. Depending on the overall importance of the number of chips and their structure – the player may have only economic chips, or both social and economic chips, or a few chips of all three kinds – the strategies will be different. We should not forget that this structure will also owe a part of its properties to its relations with other structures: I can find myself faced with someone who has nothing left or someone who has more than me. These structures of capital are also structurally related to each other, which may or may not be understood by other people, and this is an interesting point. In a game it is very important to have information on what the others possess. Yet if in the social world we may know what others possess, we never know this completely. The social game would no doubt be entirely different if at every moment we were aware of our own structure and the other structures – for example, if people's incomes were publicly displayed. One part of the specific originality of the social fact is the fact that people do have information about the volume and the structure of the capital of the other players, but at the same time their information is never complete.

The moves of the different players will then depend at every moment on the structure of the distribution of capital – that is, not only on the structure and the volume of the capital possessed by the player but also on the relative structural and relational value of the structure of this capital in the structure of all the capitals of all possible agents. A very simple but very important property, for example in the literary field, is audacity. It is true moreover in most universes. There are social positions that we cannot occupy, and cannot even think of occupying, towards which we cannot move, unless we have a high idea of ourselves. These positions, which are generally rare and difficult to hold, are appropriated by people who have the particular property of having resources to fall back on. It is quite simple: the less you risk, the bolder you can be. When people take apparently considerable risks, it is because in fact, despite appearances, they risk less than others. In the literary field for example, avant-garde positions run the risk of having to hold out for a long time without a market. The charismatic ideology at work in the milieu explains this law of the avant-garde as the need to work for posterity and create your own market, which is true, even if it is so transfigured ideologically that we need to be on our guard. These positions suppose that you are working for a market that does not yet exist, but meanwhile you have to live and enable the producer to keep on producing. There are all sorts of ways of solving this problem. Sometimes the writers have wives who work to make ends meet. There are also menial jobs: school assistant in the nineteenth century, jobs in publishing, and so on. And there is one solution without which a large proportion of nineteenth-century painting would not exist, which is unearned income.

The alternatives of income or trade

There is in fact the alternative between income and trade: there are those who choose to make a living from their literature, who are treated as 'mercenaries', there are 'tradesmen', and then there are those such as Flaubert, of whom Goncourt said: 'Flaubert has all the luck, he has an income.'[7] Without this income, we might not have had Flaubert. The structure of the distribution of objectified or incorporated capital is at every moment the principle driving people's strategies, although we should bear in mind that the dispositions enjoy a relative autonomy from the positions – this point is important to avoid relapsing into a mechanistic and determinist vision. In a given space, any position whatever (whether dominant or dominated, for instance) is largely responsible for governing the greater part of the strategies of its holders, in so far as it is through a position that the forces of the field operate. That said, and it is in this sense that the field of forces is more than just a field of forces, the effect of the position will depend on the dispositions of the person who holds the position. It will also depend on the nature of the positions, which, as I have already indicated, may be more or less clear-cut and restrictive.

Many career choices for example turn on the alternative between income or trade: it is the choice between becoming a writer or an academic – or a critic, in the nineteenth century; it is the choice between, on the one hand, audacity, risky wagers, and large but unpredictable profits and, on the other hand, less audacity, safe bets, but of much less value. That generates two very different types of personality. The profession of writer has the particularity of being quite strongly indeterminate without, however, being completely open: there are moments when it is not open at all, and sometimes, because there has been a writer before, one inherits a position, defined at least by the fact that the great man was Hugo or Gautier; then you have to take this fait accompli into account. That having been said, this definition will apply only within the limits of the dispositions of the person who confronts the position in question, and the outcome will depend on the confrontation between this position and the dispositions: either the dispositions will come to transform the position, or there will be a sort of permanent struggle, with compromises and changes.

Amor fati

To sum up this first point, the field is defined as a field of possible forces, a space where forces appear whenever an agent enters. You might even speak of a space where you cannot do whatever you like, a space within which you are pulled, pushed or orientated, even if the forces are not experienced as forces, even – and here my second point intervenes – if they are apprehended for example as vocation. One of the ruses of social reason is that the social world sends you cheerfully where it wants you to go, makes you want to go to the only place that it wants you to go, and you wouldn't for anything in the world want to go anywhere other than the place where it wants to send you. This is the *amor fati* that I have already described in the past.[8] To explain, I would say that the majority of biographical experiences are of this kind. Most often we go where the social world would have sent us in any event, but we go there willingly. This is what is called a vocation. There are obviously exceptions, and they are very important: it needs only one, and that changes everything – it is called freedom.

The field, then, is a field of potential forces that affect people who enter the space, but – as I have often said during the first part of my lecture course – since the social world is present in two forms, both objectively in the structures and in incorporated form in the agents' unconscious, it is also a field of potential actions. And the opposition between structure and change, which you know I find quite artificial, corresponds to two ways of viewing the same thing: when you consider this field of forces, which is also a field of struggles, in a state of equilibrium (as you contemplate the pile of chips between two rounds of poker), you see a structure, for, in Hegel's words, 'essence is past being';[9] this field is an objectified and reified past, it is made of resources acquired and accumulated; but seen from a different angle it is not reducible to this, since actions designed to transform that past will emerge from the past itself. For example, it is in reaction to their dispossession in the structure and distribution of capital at a given moment in time that the dominated can be led to try to transform the structure, on certain conditions and in certain contexts, when the usual match between objectified structures and incorporated structures has been suspended. In fact the Marxist model that we have rather vaguely at the back of our minds is a particular case of a much more general model, which is that of the relations between a structure founded on the opposition between positions defined by the unequal possession of some capital or other and a change that is somehow written into the structure. It is in fact the structure itself that creates the opposition and engenders the actions designed to affect the structure, to preserve or transform it, depending on where you stand. I am saying this briefly because I don't want to spend too long on this point, but I didn't want to leave it up in the air.

The fertile terrain of the literary field

Having exposed the main points of the problems that I wish to raise, I now propose to look at the example of the literary field, because it is a terrain where there is a considerable accumulation of research and because it shows very clearly the efficiency of a system of thought that is above all a method, a way of thinking rather than a doctrine. It is not something that you just talk about but something with which you do things and produce effects. This is the reason why the solution that consists in using a specific case to display the method at work suits me better than the formalism of the general exposition illustrated by rather disconnected examples. One of the reasons why the terrain of the literary or artistic field is particularly favourable to the application of this method is that these terrains lead us to think against the grain. This universe offers itself up to our thoughts, even thinks itself, in a way that is absolutely antithetical to the logic that I am proposing with this notion of the field; there are few terrains where spontaneous, home-grown sociology is as profoundly opposed to what I see as scientifically correct sociology. It is no accident if it is one of the terrains where sociological enquiry is most difficult, since writers and artists define themselves as irreducible singularities and absolutely refuse to be investigated or questioned. But at the same time, once we overcome these difficulties, I think that it is one of the terrains where my method can produce the most fantastic effects and where a bold intellectual investment may yield the greatest benefit. It is a terrain where, once you start working on it, it seems unthinkable that you didn't think of it earlier and where the material seems somehow to offer itself up as if it were made to be thought of in this manner.

This is complicated, and you must be thinking that I am contradicting myself. There is an indigenous discourse on the literary world that excludes the scientific approach. It is a charismatic type of discourse according to which the creator – an interesting word – is the son of his works. He is uncreated, and there cannot be a science of the uncreated creator who is his own creation. (The sociology of philosophy would come up against an even greater obstacle, because, being the creator who conceives his own creation, the philosopher cannot be the object of thought for any kind of scientific approach; he claims to be able to think his way through any thought that would take him as its object; he claims to be able to found himself in his thought better than any other thinker.) That having been said, once we have sidestepped the defensive–offensive professional ideology which the artist uses to constitute himself as artist (and the philosopher as philosopher), it is very amusing to see how far the material offers itself up almost structured in advance.

Let me take, for example, the enquiry led by Huret, recently reissued.[10] Huret was a journalist. In 1891 he published the 'Huret enquiry', which consisted in questioning for a journal all the writers who mattered at the time. He starts with naturalism, which was both dominant and despised, and Zola; he declares that 'Naturalism is dead' (this has been a classic move by journalists since the intellectual field developed), and he goes on to question one after the other the representatives of the symbolist school, the neo-realists, the neo-naturalists, the surviving Parnassians, asking them each time: 'Do you think that Zola is really dead?' He interviews Zola himself – in fact, he interviews everybody – and in my opinion this journalistic document is a most interesting scientific document: instead of taking for its unit, as literary history usually does, one work by an author (such as *The Princess of Cleves*), or the complete works of an author, or an author and his work, it takes for its subject, in a journalistic logic, the whole of a space, all the people who matter, have a name, or are trying to make a name for themselves. The youngest and the most obscure are obviously under-represented; the sample is not perfect, but we get an overview of the space.

If you read between the lines and keep the notion of the field in mind, you will see that there is hardly a sentence that is not relational: even, and especially, when the writers are really talking about themselves, they are talking of nothing but the others. Of course the author of the enquiry garners this kind of commentary because he questions them systematically, at least on the main positions of their times; if he had asked them, 'May I respectfully ask, dear Sir, whether you tend to write mostly in the morning or rather at night?', it is likely that they would have thought in a less relational and structural way. That having been said, the questions are not particularly biased. He questions them on the naturalist and symbolist schools, the Parnassians, Verlaine, Mallarmé; they reply, 'Oh yes, they are obscure, I don't read them, I don't understand them', and there is a whole space that constitutes itself. You do not need very much more to construct the structure of the field and to understand, using this structure, what each writer is saying and how the structure comes to reveal itself. Here we obviously meet the classic hermeneutic circle: the better I know the position of each individual, the more I discover the structure, and the better I know the structure, the better I understand each agent's position – which is the antithesis of our ordinary situation where we imagine that we will get to know a particular individual by immersing ourselves in their particulars. In a word, social reality functions in such an obviously structural way that, as soon as we cultivate the right thoughts, it delivers itself up almost fully-fashioned.

(The profit from any kind of questioning of a social subject – conversation, open-ended interview, questionnaire, etc. – is enormously increased as soon as you start thinking structurally and read into what the social subjects are saying of themselves what they are saying about their position in their space. We are so accustomed to thinking in non-structuralist ways that it is very easy to hear the information without understanding it. When an OS [specialised workman] such as a boiler-maker discusses a boiler, he is in fact discussing the person installing it. He cannot discuss his own position without discussing the rest of the space. Paying attention to the structuralist manner of thinking is listening to information that is spontaneously structural, and it is also obviously knowing how to present the questions in such a way as to intensify this kind of mobilisation of experience that, once structurally constituted, emerges all the better and all the quicker if you consciously adopt a structural viewpoint – this is one of the problems of the well-conducted interview: we want to obtain the maximum information in the minimum time. If for example you are investigating teachers, you might start by asking, 'How do you see the role of the teacher?', but things will immediately work out better if you ask, 'What subject do you teach, and are there conflicting aims and struggles in your institution?', for instance. This is not provocation; it is just that reality works in a structural way. Taking note of this and understanding it can only increase the efficiency of the stimulus provided by any scientific procedure. The sociologist in his interview is undertaking an experiment, and his main goal is to stimulate his informant sufficiently to obtain the most information in the least possible time. Some interviews reveal nothing, because the questioner has somehow failed to stimulate the people to respond in terms of belonging to a 'field': if you go to see a publisher and you fail to ask him how he situates himself in relation to the other publishers, he will hold forth with the same general spiel as all the other publishers. I trust that you found this parenthesis on practice useful.)

Art versus method: charismatic ideology and the 'sociology of literature'

In the ordinary practice of literary history or criticism, in fact in everything concerning literary or artistic matters, the unit of study is nearly always a single producer or the singular product of a single producer. You can verify this statistically in libraries: the proportion of research devoted to a whole current or a whole period, compared to studies of individuals, is minimal. I can cite an important work by Cassagne dating from 1905 that has recently been reissued in Geneva. It deals with the genesis of the 'art for art's sake' theory.[11] Like Huret's book, it studies art for art's sake not through a singular individual (such as Flaubert) but through all the people who inhabit this position in the artistic space that is distinct from 'bourgeois art' and 'social art'. More than others – although maybe not as much as he should – he shows the space within which this position of 'art for art's sake' is situated. If literary terrains are particularly productive from the point of view of the exercise in method that I propose, it is because the scientific analysis is particularly improbable on account of the charismatic nature of the ideology of this field: the work of creation, grace and charisma has no explanation outside itself, and the charismatic character who is his own creation, born of himself or his works, cannot obey any determinants external to the reality that he constitutes. This is a dominant vision of the intellectual phenomenon, which is hardly less strong in the scientific world, for example, even if science of course in its modern avatar has become so obviously collective that the charismatic ideology has lost some of its powers of resistance. But it can emerge in different guises: I shall demonstrate this if one day I come to discuss the sociology of science. In any case, art remains the archetypal terrain of the charismatic ideology, the most antithetical to scientific method.

There are, however, complicated cases that I would like to mention in passing, such as Sartre's *Flaubert*, which presents a problem. Sartre obviously follows the logic that I have been describing: he takes as his object a singular author and looks for the final cause of a work in the singularity of the person.[12] He starts out then from a direction diametrically opposed to the one that I pursue.[13] In fact, if you have grasped what I mean by the notion of field, you will see immediately that the creator of Flaubert's works is Flaubert in so far as he is the site where a field of forces that is the true source of Flaubert's work has come to fruition. My method then consists in asking what Flaubert had to do in order to bring to fruition what was written into the position that he inhabited. I shall therefore proceed in the opposite direction from Sartre. I shall start by describing the space as a whole before coming to Flaubert's own position between social art and bourgeois art, but distinct from both, and it is only once I have described the position with all its properties and in all its complexity that I shall be able to turn back to his biography, his childhood and his first novels to ask myself what Flaubert had to be (the family idiot, the second child, his relations with his father and his elder brother, and so on) in order to be so well suited to do what he did – that is, to fill this central position in the field. The change of direction is no accident.[14]

We also need to situate the method in relation to the method we normally associate with the idea of the sociology of literature and which corresponds to the Lukács–Goldmann solution:[15] you concentrate on one producer (such as Flaubert, Debussy, Mallarmé, Heidegger or Adorno) and investigate the social group that produced them and for which they produce, making the hypothesis that this particular producer has expressed the unconscious expectations and experiences and the social vision of the group – usually doing it unwittingly and yet better than the group would have been able to. This functions marvellously well when you have, for example, a bourgeois author expressing the bourgeois group whose unconscious spokesman he is, with the group speaking through him without his realising it. You will recognise this immediately: it is the most idealist philosophy, simply inverted. I think of Hugo, the didactic poet invented by the nineteenth century, the poet who expresses some or all of his society. But here we have a materialist theory of art: we need to find the group concerned. This group is sometimes the final cause: it is the group for which the work is produced, and we are talking about commissions. Applied to the history of painting, this manner of proceeding is catastrophic, because it can only escape hagiography ('Da Vinci in his own words') by falling into its deliberate rejection, with the idea of commissions and patrons and the idea that reality lies in the commission. In his book on Florentine painting and its social background, Antal[16] tries to find from within the works the patrons' visions of the world, as if the truth of the works lay in the patrons' visions. This approach is very primitive and even phantasmagorical, because it constructs both terms of the relationship at once.

On the one hand, they construct the properties of the producer and the product; they will say that Mallarmé or Debussy, for example, had an enchanted view of the social world, that there was a sort of 'escapism', a desire to evade the social world by escaping into the past or adopting a regressive view of the social world, and so on. On the other hand, they construct the properties of the group: they refer to the Commune,[17] Fourmies,[18] Anzin,[19] the Confédération générale du travail and their struggles, and they say that the bourgeoisie, the salons and the aristocracy were asking for painting or music celebrating the delights of Cythera, a return to the past, escape to Couperin, and so on.[20] And the two poles meet. I think that this way of proceeding, which is so attractive for the sociology of art and literature, is a catastrophe.

The field as mediation

As is often the case on the terrain of social thought, the two polar positions reinforce each other mutually: we have a kind of eternal circular debate between those who call themselves 'formalists' in certain periods[21] and who say that you should study the works and nothing but the works, that the truth lies in the work and nowhere beyond, and those who will cite the rising bourgeoisie, the 'Hidden God',[22] and the like. What gets entirely lost in both of these cases is the quite specific mediation that is also a social mediation: the artistic field, meaning a social space within which the activity of cultural creation is structured. In other words, between the salons that wanted Fauré to play his 'bagatelles' and the true music of Fauré, there is a whole history of music. The specialists do what they can to invoke the history of music, but the history of music is the cumulative history of specific struggles or rivalry between people who introduce new harmonies rejected by the Conservatoire, for instance. There is a sort of specific accumulation, and it is in this specific space that a form of cultural production is composed. Most often appearances unfortunately speak in favour of 'Goldmannism', since these people who, in establishing a crude relation with a group supposed to be patron or public, make what I call a 'short-circuit' eliminating all the specific history of art – that is, everything that happens in the field – for example, the fact that Debussy is situated at such and such an angle towards his contemporaries or predecessors, the fact that he does things differently, that he does more, or something quite other.

As soon as we read structurally, we see that the newcomers are often saying little more than 'we must do something different'. People who found reviews write manifestos, but nine times out of ten they say virtually nothing. Thus, in his study of the late nineteenth-century philosophical field, Fabiani shows that there is nothing new in the inaugural manifesto of the *Revue de métaphysique et de morale*.[23] In general, the practice of the newcomers consists in saying that they are inspired by the (sometimes desperate) concern to do something new. There are people who give themselves labels, hoping that they will stick, but their opponents are not fooled. Zola for example said, 'What are these nut shells dancing on Niagara Falls?'[24] These people want to exist at all costs, and to exist at any particular moment you need a label, so they invent labels. There is often a kind of will to differ, but it is rarely so clearly expressed as in the *Revue de métaphysique et de morale*, which was born of the will of three or four young unknowns to do something different from the *Revue philosophique*. They say that they want to do something different, but they don't say what.

The direct and immediate explanatory principle that allows us to account for the fact that people do this rather than that is to be found in the relatively autonomous space of the literary field. Sartre's solution was to delve deep down into Flaubert himself (in *The Family Idiot*, Sartre finds everything; he relocates in Flaubert everything that is present in the field, but he did not set himself the task of constructing the literary field as such). The concept of the field allows us to avoid a double danger: either we dig down desperately into the individual to find the explanatory principle, whereas the truth of what constitutes Flaubert, for example, is not to be found in Flaubert but in Flaubert's relation to everything else; or alternatively we completely squeeze the literary space containing Flaubert, and we say that Flaubert is the provincial bourgeoisie, unearned income, and so on. Both approaches dodge the issue of the literary space.

Literary field and intertextuality

I want to mention a third means of dodging the issue. I am not saying all this in order to vaunt my own proposal or to offer unfair competition to my fellow professors, who are not here to answer back. I respect the people greatly as individuals. I am making this criticism of their systematic approach reluctantly, because I think that otherwise you would not see how efficient my proposal is. Things would appear to be too simple.

There is a style of reading works of art which may be confused with what I am going to suggest, which is in general terms systemic or structural. I already mentioned this last time: they are people who are inspired either by the Russian formalists or the Saussurian tradition and try to consider literary works as systems. Their method postulates that a work does not contain its own explanation, for what is important is what some call 'intertextuality': a text speaks only with reference to other texts, or a system of texts, in fact. Some of them who follow in the wake of the Russian formalists arrive at a kind of destruction of the literary phenomenon, as I shall demonstrate. This is why I am obliged to mention them, not to detach myself from my markers, which is one of the rules of the intellectual field (or the football field), but to avoid misunderstandings that would interfere with your understanding of what I am about to explain.

Some of them, following the works of Tynianov, for example,[25] insist on the fact that the literary field changes according to relatively simple rules of automation and disautomation. Briefly, the dominant schools are supposed to impose a mode of thought and expression that becomes automatic, and therefore banal, obvious and repetitive; at a certain degree of automation of literary life, a sort of lassitude and distaste would provoke disautomation (these are my terms, but I believe that they faithfully reproduce their approach)[26] – that is, a kind of break creating a sort of astonishment. The literary dialectic then would consist in producing a shift away from what was currently being done. These two propositions – on the one hand, the literary work takes on meaning only in relation to other works; on the other hand, there is a kind of history of works that is a history of the confrontations between works – may seem to resemble what I am going to argue. The difference obviously is that, for me, the motor of change cannot be situated at the level of the works; nothing happens at the level of the works; the principle that generates the stances adopted, which in this case are the works themselves, is to be found on the level of the space of the positions.

We can make a link between the Russian formalists, who speak of disautomation, and Max Weber, who talks of 'deroutinisation' and 'dishabituation'. (Here I plead in favour of a methodological eclecticism that has nothing to do with a passive eclecticism: a broad culture can lead to scientific results by establishing communication between intellectual currents that do not usually communicate, by breaking down barriers between cultural spaces.) For Max Weber, charisma is extraordinary, beyond everyday life, governed by the non-quotidian; it transcends and rejects the ordinary, it is para-doxical, it attacks the self-evident and the routine. One of the problems of the charismatic leader is his succession:[27] Who will succeed the charismatic leader who is the inimitable creation of his own works? The problem of succession is that charisma becomes routine, the exceptional becomes the everyday; How can we replace the grandiose, eloquent, magnificent leader with someone who will not have his historical legitimacy and will not be perceived as legitimate? There will be a relapse into the routine and the everyday, one of whose forms is the bureaucratisation that enables us every day to do in an everyday way things that charisma can do only in an extraordinary way. Weber developed these concepts of the habitual and dishabituation above all in relation to religion, contrasting the routine of the priest, performing the miracle of the mass every morning, with the prophet, who performs extraordinary miracles three or four times in an extraordinary lifetime. The prophet then is the person who deroutinises, who upsets the routine. There is an opposition between social agents engaged in the same space, a space of mutual competition, and what happens at a textual level ('for the letter killeth, but the spirit gives life',[28] the prophet's criticism of the priests, right and wrong readings, Barthes against Picard,[29] for instance) is the product of struggles between people holding different positions; the

priestly position of the magisterial master guaranteed by a statutory
and institutional authority and the position of the charismatic but
marginal master, authorised by himself alone. Deroutinisation then
does not arise from a sort of general fatigue with the text. In fact, at
a certain moment people want to read texts differently and they find
something different. They will be excommunicated. A whole series of
things is written into this position.

   The notion of intertextuality then shows some sort of progress over
reading texts as isolated units. I think that for many problems we
could make a kind of Mendeleev table of possible errors. In the case
of the literary field, the systemic vision is the one that has most of the
outward signs in its favour. It says clearly that we are dealing with a
system, that works exist only in relation and in opposition to others;
you cannot understand them if you do not grasp the fact that to exist is
to differ, and so on. You might think that what I am saying is no different. And yet what I am saying is that, at the level of the works, things
do in fact happen like this, but only in so far as the level of the works is
the symbolic expression, transfigured and transformed, of a system of
positions. There is a transfiguration; the relation between the position
and the stance adopted is obviously not mechanical.

   The writer needs to work at his answers, for it is important to convince himself and others that the stance he adopts has nothing to do
with his position. When Zola says: 'You are a nut shell bobbing up and
down on Niagara Falls' it is not at all to defend naturalism. If this were
the case, the formula would lose half of its impact, which is based on
belief in its impact. Think of Hobbes's phrase 'Reputation of power is
power'.[30] Symbolic power exists in so far as we believe that the person
wielding it does actually possess it. Consequently, if Zola's judgement
of the neo-Romantics, the Parnassians or the symbolists were to appear
moved by resentment, by the defensive interests of the dominant on the
way out, he would lose much of his impact. Except in circumstances of
enquiry, polemics, and the like, the stances adopted, especially towards
others, will be strongly euphemised and retranslated, and a part of the
writer's competence consists in disguising the direct relation between
positions held and stances adopted. This is important, and once again
it undermines those theories that short-circuit the process, such as
reflection theory. The process is so elaborate and refracted that we can
no longer speak of reflection.

   This systemic theory (intertextuality and the like) is valid then if we
see it as a provisional and partial method of studying the texts: it is
better to study an ensemble of texts from the same period, and their
relation to each other, rather than to study a single text. But this theory

will not take us very far if we do not make it clear that the relation to be studied is an objective one, and if we do not keep in mind the fact that the space of relations between the stances adopted, or between the modes of expression, has its source in the space of relations between the positions. I have sketched out the two or three tendencies in relation to which I wanted to place my argument.

A chiasmatic structure

I shall now move on to make a tentative analysis of the genesis and operation of the literary field.

First point: the literary field is a relatively autonomous sub-space inserted in a wider space that I call the field of power, which is itself inserted within an overarching space that I call the 'space of class relations' or the 'social field'. This can be shown in a relatively simple table [*while he continues to talk, Bourdieu draws a table on the board*].[31] The 'social field' is at the same time a field of struggles between the classes. The field of power itself is by and large the field of struggle for power between holders of the capital that creates opportunities in the struggle for power; if you like, it is the 'dominant class', but I prefer to call it the 'field of power', where the different fractions of the dominant class are sub-fields that are themselves a site of struggle while they struggle between themselves for power. There is a third level: what I call the field of cultural production, which includes intellectual, philosophical, artistic and literary production, and the like. One important thing that will become clearer as I progress is that the structure as I am describing it is neither eternal nor universal; there has not always been a structure of this kind, and there is not one now in every society, which does not mean that we cannot draw valid laws of the constitution or genesis of this kind of structure and its laws of operation once it is constituted.

What I have just said is true. I think that this is the right way to raise the problem of the laws of social science. The literary and artistic field is enclosed within the field of power, although it enjoys a relative autonomy within it, in particular in relation to the economic and political principles of hierarchisation; this is something very important whose consequences I shall elaborate. To say that a field is autonomous in relation to another is to say that it will continue to feel the forces that are at work in the other, but in attenuated form. The greater the autonomy of the field, the more the forces will be attenuated. In the present case, one of the principles of hierarchisation within the field of power is economic capital and, as I argued in *Distinction*,

The field of cultural production
in the field of power and in the social space

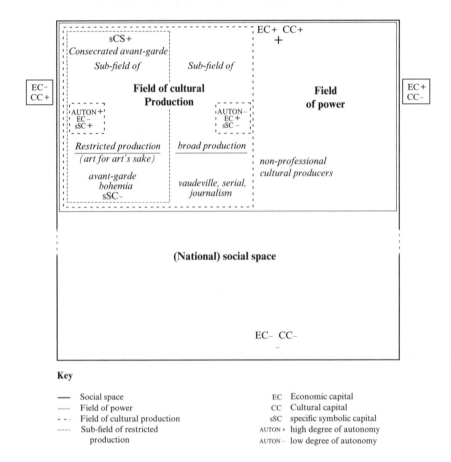

Key

—— Social space	EC Economic capital
—— Field of power	CC Cultural capital
- - · Field of cultural production	sSC specific symbolic capital
---- Sub-field of restricted	AUTON+ high degree of autonomy
production	AUTON− low degree of autonomy

on the basis of the most rigorous statistics available, the distribution of economic and cultural capital in the different fractions of the dominant class displays a chiasmatic structure (which is an index of the relative autonomy of the field of cultural production within the field of power).

There is a structure that everyone knows and finds obvious when it is explicitly commented on, but that strangely had never been highlighted in a scientific study. I shall remind you of this structure briefly: in the field of power, at the pole of the artists and intellectuals – that is, in the upper left-hand corner of my diagram – there will be less economic capital but, conversely, more cultural capital; we have then a chiasmatic structure, which gives rise to a number of properties.[32] This opposition will be retranslated on the ideological plane in the form of the opposition between 'in this world' and 'in the other'. This structure is an ideological matrix: for example, it will constitute the basis of the representation that artists will form of the ruling classes; when they say 'bourgeois', it will mean: 'You have the here and now, we have the beyond', or, again: 'You are powerful in this world but powerless in the next.'

This structure is historically variable. You have to constitute it as a structure in order to perceive variations. I am insisting on this point because the manner of thinking that I am promoting demands historicisation. You can only really work with it on historical material and on specific cases, but not in the same way as the historians (in their social definition; for, if the historians were as they should be, they would be no different from sociologists). This is another commonplace: Bachelard said that science is the art of treating particular cases as a 'particular case of the possible'.[33] These are things that are recited in lectures on epistemology, but I am in the process of putting them into action: I have this model in mind and, having constructed this space of the dominant class as such, I can ask myself what form this opposition will take in different societies and historical periods.

One of the properties of our own period in France, to take a precise example, is that this chiasmatic structure is less clear than it was at the end of the nineteenth century. The opposition between the artist or the writer rich in cultural capital but poor in economic capital is much less true today than it was in the nineteenth century, partly because our intellectuals are richer in economic capital, for complex reasons (they are closer to the university than to bohemia), and above all because, at the dominant pole of the dominant class, the accumulation of cultural capital is becoming greater and greater. In contrast, this presents intellectuals with a major problem. I will elaborate, so that you don't have only abstract models. In the literary and artistic field, there is a struggle for the monopoly of literary and artistic competence. The people there struggle to seize the monopoly of legitimate artistic competence – that is, the right to say 'I am an artist' and 'I can say who is an artist' and, at the same time, something essential, 'I can say who is not'. They are struggling then for the power to define a space of rivalry. If I am right, the traditional question posed by people who study intellectuals ('Whom do we call an intellectual?') has no sense, because it is a contentious issue within the very object of study. If I say, 'I am a serious historian and I shall call an intellectual . . .', I have already made up my mind. One of the things that are at stake in this space is to know who is an intellectual and who is not, and it is very important to be able to identify the people who are not. But when these people start to graduate from the École nationale d'administration, are awarded advanced academic diplomas and publish essays, they may be accused of unfair competition, of challenging the monopoly of legitimacy, of running an unlicensed business [*laughter*], which is a very important issue.

If we construct the division in this way, this leads us to ask quite a number of questions, for example: Will the transformation of the structures perhaps be one factor for change in this space? One considerable problem is that the statistics unfortunately do not confirm it: as soon as you construct the real social reality, the details belie it . . . this is why I was tortured by the problem that I have just mentioned. Historians have excuses because they are often obliged to construct their objects using only the documents available. And I think that, in fact, it would be better if they could admit that all documents suppose a preconstruction, because very often what we find in the documents is what people have placed there, with more or less sincere or suspect intent. It is, then, material that is already structured in such a way as to suggest a preconstruction. To take a famous case, the book by Darnton recently translated into French is based on the archives of a Genevan publisher who published not only the *Encyclopédie* but also erotica.[34] It is fine to study his archives, with his customers' orders, and so on. However, the object is largely prefabricated by the way the material is offered as given. In fact what this kind of exercise requires is for us to trace a dotted line around the space within which this material takes on meaning.

I keep repeating the same things, but the example of the *grandes écoles* is significant: if for example I isolate the archives of the École polytechnique, I am disposed to consider that these archives contain the essential material and the explanatory principle of what I am looking for. For a positivist, appearances are immaculate: I have my material, fairly, squarely and neatly selected, I discuss only the data given. But in some cases it may contain nothing at all. If we are looking at a phenomenon 95 per cent of whose explanation is to be found outside the space, it is the worst kind of fraud. Now in the social sciences we very often find ourselves in the situation of having to choose, on the one hand, between material that is impeccable from a positivist viewpoint but scientifically vacuous and, on the other, some scientifically rigorous material (meaning, 'constructed according to the model that I propose') that is weak from a positivist point of view, because the material is not in the right place. I maintain for posterity that, from a scientific point of view, it is better to proceed in this way, reconstructing the whole space, even if we have to guess the outlines, rather than choose the alternative of restricting ourselves to a prefabricated corpus in order to gain the approval of our contemporaries. I must insist: I think that it is better to appear to fail the test of positivist proof than appear to be right only by recording an artefact that may have been palmed off on the uncritical researchers (this is not always the case, but it often is – think for example of police archives).

The ideal would be to construct series – for example, to take the ruling class in 1900, 1930, 1950 and 1980 and compare the structures according to diplomas, gender, age, and so on. But in the first place the figures do not always exist; and then the comparison poses formidable problems because the indices themselves are structurally defined and may take on an entirely different meaning if the structure has changed. Which means that we are faced with a very difficult problem. That being said, I think that it is better to formulate insoluble problems clearly than successfully to resolve false problems [*laughter*]. I am declaring this forcefully, because unfortunately very few people are prepared to say it at all. Sociology is a dominated science. It is subjected to the stupidest forms of scientific demand. They require false mathematics and fake empiricism, and then they will leave us in peace. In fact what science should demand, especially given the stage that sociology has reached, is the rigorous construction of the object rather than insistence on proof. That said, what I am about to demonstrate is a form of proof. I think that it is valid and possesses both coherence and *self-probation*.[35]

Automation, hierarchisation, institutionalisation

The literary or artistic field enjoys a relative autonomy within the space of this field of power, and one of the questions that we might ask is how autonomous it is in relation to the forces that are active in this field. Anticipating a little, I want to say that one of the laws of this space is to be structured according to the dominant principle of hierarchisation, the economic principle: the more money and political power you have, the more powerful you are – this is a crude definition, but you must allow me it. The more money and/or political power you have, the more you find yourself in the right-hand part of the literary space. However, since I argue that the literary space has a relative autonomy, this relation will be less true the more autonomous the literary space. We might even imagine that, if the literary field were totally autonomous, there would be a total inversion: the less power and money you have, the more prestigious you will be. In the publishing market, for example, there will be a sub-space which will be a world upside down: it will function according to laws that will tend to be the inverse of the surrounding universe. But the other laws will continue to function. One of the questions will be to determine the degree of autonomy of this literary space in relation to the space of the field of power; the greater the autonomy, the less this general law will apply. This autonomy means that the boundary between the literary field and the field of power will become stronger and stronger, which raises the questions: Are artists bourgeois? Do the artists struggle against the bourgeoisie?

What is at stake is the definition of the intellectual, the refusal to submit to the general rule, the refusal to equate success, as measured in number of volumes published or in financial profit, with literary value; it is then a struggle to impose a relatively autonomous sub-universe whose rules are not the general rules of the field in which it is inserted and where we cannot say: 'It is because X is a member of the Académie française, or because he sells 800,000 copies of a book, that he is a philosopher and a good writer.' This then is autonomy from politics, economics and, ultimately, all external powers. Of course this model obliges us to question the variations that will occur in relation to the nature of the external powers. This is what we mean by a 'particular case of the possible': if the external power is 'right-wing' or 'left-wing' (if I may be so bold as to make a contemporary allusion),[36] it poses problems. How will things change depending on whether the intellectuals are faced with the Académie française or the Academy of the Soviet Union? If I wanted to give my imagination free rein, I would ask a whole lot of questions that objectively are bound to arise, for example, when someone enrols for a doctorate on writers in France between 1930 and 1940 or on the relations between writers and the Chinese Communist Party between 1924 and 1960. At the first level, the field studied is inserted in the space of the field of power and, even if part of the heteronomy remains invariant, we can investigate the changes that this part of heteronomy undergoes according to the power in opposition to which it is defined. I think that there are invariant laws and that the tendency towards dependency on power obeys universal laws, whatever the power, but we can nonetheless suppose that, if we proceed to make an empirical comparison, the form of the effects of dependency will change according to the form of the power. Being dependent on a Caesarean or a papal power is not the same as being dependent on a democratic type of power.

The literary field is enveloped within the field of power, where it enjoys a relative autonomy, which is also a relative dependency: it continues to be determined partly by the general laws of the field. In this space, it inhabits a dominated position: it is in the 'negative' pole (in terms of the dominant principle of hierarchisation) of the space of the field of power. The artistic field is enveloped within the field of power, and, although it enjoys a relative autonomy in relation to the economic and political principles of hierarchisation of this field, it holds a dominated position in the field. I forgot to point out that the field of power itself is situated at the dominant pole of the space of the social classes. As a result, this artistic field is the site of a dual hierarchy. On the one hand, a principle of heteronymous hierarchisation remains in place. It would impose itself totally if the autonomy of the artistic field disappeared; if the field lost its autonomy, this principle of hierarchisation would be all-powerful. This principle of hierarchisation is based on economic and political criteria – that is, according to success in terms of numbers of volumes published, numbers of editions, financial returns, and so on. On the other hand, there is the principle of autonomous, internal hierarchisation that the field enjoys in its own right, so to speak. There are continuous variations, and the degree of autonomy may constantly vary: if the degree of heteronomy becomes very strong, the principle of economic hierarchisation becomes dominant and the best writer is the one who sells the most copies; if the autonomy principle – that is, the internal law of the milieu – becomes dominant (and these internal laws, as I shall hope to show, are constituted in opposition to the overall laws of the field of power, in opposition to the bourgeois, the economy, profit, and so on), then what will impose itself will be the degree of recognition, of symbolic consecration granted in terms of recognition by the other members of the autonomous field.

In this space, then, there will be two possible principles of hierarchisation. If the external one comes to dominate, the field of cultural production becomes a field like the others, and we ultimately measure cultural production by the same criteria and standards as any other production. This is why, when people discuss for example the price of the book,[37] they will say: 'But you can't treat the market for books like all the others; they are not pots and pans.' By invoking this, they are defending a specific resistance based on irreducible autonomous criteria. There are authors who just will not sell, which does not mean that they are worthless, and an avant-garde publisher will point out that it is not because nobody buys their books that they are worthless. But does this automatically mean that they must have value?

This is a problem ... The dominated in this field in fact have an interest in this structure. They have an interest in saying that, the less success you have, the better you are, and that all those who succeed or who accumulate awards are corrupt and compromised, and so on. The properties of the positions in this field are very interesting. For example, one of the laws of ageing in literary circles or among intellectuals in general is that you can defer until very late the discovery of the law of prices. You can believe in fairy tales until an advanced age. In a manner of speaking, the whole argument about bohemia concerns only one subject: you can delay for an awfully long time the moment when you ask the question whether failure is the promise of success in the afterlife or just failure. You might think of the forms taken by the crises in the intellectual world, with the consequences that I shall try to analyse later, for example, the sudden reconversions – which take a political form – operated by people who, being really low down in the hierarchy of economic profit, are at the same time very high up in the hierarchy of the symbolic profits of consecration. There are for example certain frequently encountered types of trajectory, as shown in Flaubert's magnificent example of experimental sociology in *Sentimental Education* through the character of Hussonnet, who, after harbouring unsuccessful ambitions as writer and critic, carves out a grand career for himself in the administration of literature and the arts thanks to the 1848 Revolution.[38] Thus there are trajectories where people pass from the far left to the far right. The pre-fascist period is very interesting in this respect: it is a period of crisis in self-evaluation accompanied by dramatic reconversions that lead from bohemia, over there [on Bourdieu's diagram], to the boundaries of the political field, over here, where we find a servile type of pen-pusher, hawking his wares as peddler of symbolic services.

To resume: this sub-field is then the site of two hierarchies that are in competition with each other. There is on the one hand an external hierarchy: this is the common law, which is in a way what the cultural producers fear the most, and all the more so the more autonomous they are. This external law is not only publication figures, it is also (things are always more complicated in the intellectual and artistic field) a form of institutionalised consecration granted by a power acting within the field but very much linked to powers external to the field. The Académie française represents the paradigm, where there is an effective power of consecration different from the internal one. With variations according to the period, avant-garde writers cannot accept this kind of consecration without losing respect.

Briefly, there is first the principle of economic hierarchisation. From this point of view, the highest genre in the nineteenth century is the theatre. This is what brings in the most money: a play earns as much as a hundred thousand copies of a novel and thousands of times more than a volume of verse published in an edition of a hundred copies. In terms of the economic hierarchy, a dramatist such as Ponsard[39] would be very high up and Mallarmé very low down. The other hierarchy, the internal one, is based on the specific principle of consecration, on the fact of being recognised by those most recognised, by the elite of those able to grant recognition.

The history of the literary field in the nineteenth century, whose lineaments I shall sketch later, is the history of a process of autonomisation whereby this second hierarchy becomes objectively affirmed in the form of institutions (and not simply in the representation of a few young hotheads, such as Nerval, for example, who got arrested for shouting 'Kill the powerful!' in the street). These institutions may not be very institutionalised in the literary field, which is one of the universes where the degree of institutionalisation is weakest: there is no career path traced in advance, no conclusive title, no straightforward transmission of power and privilege. The modalities of succession are not clearly defined. There are classic moves, such as when a consecrated author writes a preface for a young author who will write a flattering review of that author's work, but these things are relatively uninstitutionalised.

In spite of everything, as history progressed, there came to be more and more mechanisms in the objective world that sanctioned the efficiency of the autonomous principle of hierarchisation against the heteronymous principle: this history of the nineteenth-century field may be described as a sort of progressive conquest of autonomy that translates as the increasingly clear appearance of market mechanisms within which emerges a pure, anti-economic value. As the century progresses, the author who turns his back on the strictly economic market will increasingly find objective support in the laws of operation of the field itself. For example, this anti-economic discourse against the vile and mercenary bourgeoisie, which was a theme in Vigny's *Chatterton*,[40] becomes something quite real. Writers know that they have to reject the Nobel Prize. Since Zola, intellectuals know that there are certain things that have to be denounced, and that this will bring its rewards, which is very important because it would be impossible to be a hero on every occasion. Thus, with the passing of time, a process of institutionalisation that initially required considerable imagination and courage requires less, simply because someone has already done it before. I find it very difficult to say these things because everyone knows them, but I do believe that we need to think of them in terms entirely different from those we normally use.

The literary and artistic field, then, is defined in its specificity by the fact that it tends to suspend or invert the dominant principle of hier-archisation, and it does so all the more fully the more autonomous it is – that is, the more accomplished it is as a field; but, however liberated it is, it remains traversed by the laws of the field enclosing it, those of economic and political profit. The greater the autonomy of the field, and the more the balance of symbolic power favours the more autono-mous producers, the more the restricted field of production, which is another sub-space of this space, tends to be cut off from the rest of the field. The restricted field of production is the field of producers for pro-ducers, those people who have no rivals other than their rivals – that is, the other producers of the restricted field of production. Advanced mathematics is thus a field where you can only be read by people who have the least interest in agreeing with your conclusions, which causes scientific progress. This is something very simple but very important. In the poetic market place throughout the nineteenth century the greatest symbolic successes were rewarded with sales of the order of a hundred copies. In other words, the divide between the two types of production (on my diagram, the sub-field of restricted production and the sub-field of major production) is extraordinary. Ultimately, the people who have great symbolic capital and very little economic capital are strikingly opposed to the people here, in the sub-field of major production. Over there, in the sub-field of restricted production, you will find the long-haired bohemians who hang around the cafés, who give themselves really weird and decadent names, who talk slang all the time, who are extremists and anarchists, and the like. Over here, in the sub-field of major production, you have Sacha Guitry, to take a recent example: he is the incarnation of those boulevard theatre actors who are really at home in the bourgeois world; they have a life absolutely like the life they portray in their plays and have the moral and politi-cal dispositions that you need to be immediately understood by the bourgeois theatre-goer. One of the reasons why people without bour-geois origins cannot succeed in the theatre in the nineteenth century is that theatre is based on immediate understanding, for example when it stages life in comic fashion: you laugh on the basis of an immediate participation in a shared system of references, which is often a shared moral code. There needs to be an almost perfect orchestration of the habitus of the producers and the habitus of the audience, which, except in the virtually impossible case of outright cynicism, is in fact achieved only when producers and audience belong to the same milieu. This is a case where Goldmannism works: the producer belongs to the milieu that he produces for, and he stages this milieu in its own setting.

The intellectual in the field of cultural production

Ultimately, the people who are over here, in the sub-field of restricted production, and the people who are over there, in the sub-field of major production, may have practically nothing in common apart from belonging to the same field. This is very important in order to see what a field is: they have nothing in common apart from the fact that they insult each other ('But he is not an artist!') and the fact that, if you put them in a room together, they will have quite fundamental things to say to each other. Thus the writer who calls into question the status of Robbe-Grillet as a writer is the Romantic novelist Guy des Cars – Claude Simon does not question him. These are people who have the same activity: they write things, have them printed and get people to read them, but nothing calls into question the unsellable writer producing only for other producers more effectively than the best-selling writer who has all appearances on his side, particularly in the eyes of those in power (this is important: he could be a member of the Académie française . . .). At the same time, in the eyes of the writer producing for producers, the best-selling writer has none of the qualities that define the writer for producers, since the writer for producers defines himself as wanting to have nothing to do with the best-selling writer. This best-selling writer is doing something that the writer for producers refuses to do by definition, which is to offer the public what it wants.

You can transpose that for example onto the plane of journalism, which is part of this space. This manner of thinking enables you to make phrases where you replace the word 'writer' with the word 'artist', 'intellectual' or 'journalist', asking yourself each time what the principle of variation is. One of the interesting things that you will discover if you carry out this kind of exercise is that, according to which aspect of the model you activate and which sector of the field of cultural production you consider, certain properties show up more than others, which raises a question: Why do some spaces present more of certain general properties than others? This is something very important for research in the social sciences: just as there are respondents to an enquiry who make quite general properties easier to see, so there are terrains which share affinities, and we need to know why. I shall give you an example. Just now I referred to the property whereby the definition of the field (in the sense of marking out its limits) is called into question in the field; in the intellectual field, and therefore in particular in the journalistic field, the question is: Who is, or is not, an intellectual?

But why does this question come more easily to mind when we think of intellectuals? Why, if we conducted an enquiry, would the question of the definition of an intellectual arise more often than the question of the definition of an artist? I think that this is the case above all in societies where you can no longer belong to the dominant fraction of the dominant class without having a high intellectual level (the level of the baccalaureate, the ability to write or make people believe that you can write, and the like). If this problem arises, it is because intellectuals are much more exposed to the threat of unfair competition on the level of writing than in the realm of mathematics, or even painting, or, even more so, music (where, apart from the case of concrete music where the profane may gain entry – but with difficulty – the entrance fee is very high). This is why, when I try to study the problem of the field as a field of struggle whose stake is the very existence of the field, I think more readily of the intellectual field. In this particular case, the question is inevitable: for intellectuals (if we understand by 'intellectual' someone who writes essays and is discussed in the press, and so on) the threat of unfair competition is infinitely greater than for painting or music and the like. We shall then find this question permanently asked in the field itself, with critical periods when the question is put more than in others – and, there, we need to know why. But, as I realise that I have outrageously overrun my allotted time [*laughter*], I shall leave it there.

Lecture of 18 January 1983

The world upside down – Field of power and field of cultural production – Conservative intellectuals – The law of symbolic legitimation – Return to the struggles within the field of cultural production – The genesis of the invariants – The adaptation of offer to demand through homology of structure – The conquest of autonomy – The hierarchy of productions and the hierarchy of publics

As you will have realised, one of the problems with the analysis that I am proposing is that you have to combine two principles of explanation that constantly tend to diverge: explanations in terms of field and explanations in terms of habitus. Thus, when we want to account for the production of a particular writer, we will constantly be torn between the temptation to explain everything through their position or to explain everything through the dispositions that the writers concerned import into the given position. I say 'torn', but if we were simply torn it would be too good to be true: in reality, depending on the particular configuration of the problems posed, we will tend to think in terms of one logic rather than the other. Even in the exemplary research that inspires my own work, that of Charle or Ponton and others trained to think in this way, we often see an oscillation between these two emphases.[1] And, as I develop my argument, I shall not myself be able to avoid wavering between the two, the reason being, I think, that social reality often presents itself with an inclination or an 'urge to exist', as Leibniz would say.[2] In my experience of research, as I have already told you, I have often had the feeling that a particular object calls out for a particular approach. The need to control these effects of the object is one of the reasons that justify the comparative method: it is extremely important for a researcher to work on several objects at once, for it is a way of building comparison into your experience in practice, because you are constantly led to submit object A to the same questions that arise in the case of object B. The fact of working in a group where others ask questions about different objects has the same effect.

I have made these preliminary remarks because I am going to start today by thinking in terms of the field. As my argument progresses and I turn to look at individual producers, the manner of thinking in terms of the habitus will increasingly prevail. This is partly on account of the logic of my exposition, for the method I adopt obliges me to invert the usual order completely. Rather than start out from the singular individual in order (sometimes) to ask questions about the space where they are inserted, I shall in fact start out from the most overarching framework, the social structure, and question the position of the field of power within that structure, then question the position of the intellectual field within that structure, and go on to question the position of the field of intellectuals, or writers producing for writers, and then finally turn to the position within this sub-space of one writer in particular, Flaubert, or another. This procedure leads us to think at first in terms of what we might call macrosociology and global relations, and then to move increasingly towards singular individuals.

The world upside down

I pointed out that the field of cultural production had its own particular structure. It was organised according to two contradictory hierarchies: one truly economic, that can be measured from the economic profits produced by the activities in question, and another that is specifically cultural, in the opposite direction, measured in terms of both symbolic profit and lack of economic profit. An important question was to know if the lack of economic profit was a necessary but also a sufficient condition of symbolic profit. In other words, is it enough to be a doomed poet in order to be consecrated? Might the doomed poet not be a failed poet? This question constantly arises in the process of human activity, and, as I said last time, it is sometimes put in dramatic fashion at certain crucial biographical moments, when the ambiguity that the milieu helps to perpetuate suddenly collapses. The Goncourts' novel *Manette Salomon* is a particularly interesting document for what I am saying here.[3] It provides a biography: a painter who starts as a *rapin*[4] finds himself suddenly starving, which leads him to wonder if he is doomed as well as starving, and therefore liable to be recognised in the afterlife, or if he is simply starving and a failure. This biographical career is structured by the very space in which it unfolds. The logic of the sub-field of cultural production is quite special: it is a universe where, as I said last time, the external forces – that is, the external laws of economics – continue to rule, but with less and less effect the further we move away from this pole to go towards the more or less autonomous pole of art for art's sake, producers producing for producers, whose rule of conduct is to suspend the ordinary laws of the social world.

We could say that this universe is the economic world upside down, the social world inverted: the ordinary laws of the economy (the more you work, the more profit you make) or the ordinary laws of the political world (the more powerful and important you are, the more honours you attract) are inverted.[5] These matters are entirely tacit: Sartre refusing to accept the Nobel Prize is an economic act adapted to this economic space whose economy is based on being anti-economic. In other words, it is a space where people play 'loser takes all'. It is a space where, the less you have, the more you win. But, if it is certain that you must have nothing if you are to win, is it enough just to have nothing in order to win? The logic of this universe is that of prophecy as I have described it: the pursuit of temporal goods contradicts the objective intentions of this universe.

On this point I must say straight away that we are still dealing with a hierarchy among people who cast off economic imperatives. As I said last time, the question is whether this '+' is a '+' for the whole of the space, or if there might not be another hierarchy at right angles to it. This is the problem of bohemia: having nothing, they are *eo ipso* rich in symbolic profit, since they obey the fundamental law of their universe, which is to reject the ordinary gratifications that motivate ordinary people; but in other cases having nothing really is having nothing, not even symbolic capital. This is the opposition between people who are simply dispossessed by being deprived and people who are dispossessed by their rejection, with the strategies of the dispossessed tending to transform privation into rejection, both for themselves and for others – that is, to make a virtue of necessity. The polemic between the two is never-ending. For example, during the Second Empire people such as Flaubert or the Goncourts ceaselessly directed their sarcasm at the dispossessed, attacking their logic of 'making a virtue of necessity':[6] 'You describe as elective poverty what is enforced poverty, you describe as a curse to be exorcised by salvation through art something that is quite simply an intellectual and existential failure.' There is then a very violent attack on bohemia and bohemians, which is moreover a response to the attack by bohemia on those who, holding a dominant position in the literary field, are described as rich, bourgeois manda-rins. I shall return to this point.

In this type of space there are several competing principles of legitimacy. The dominant principle of legitimacy is ultimately to make bourgeois success (for example in the theatre, with the forms of conse-cration usually associated with it, such as the Académie française) the principle of the position in the hierarchy. For the rival principle, we might invoke the debate that I have just touched on between those who will say that failure to succeed is *ipso facto* a guarantee of (future) elec-tion, and those who maintain the opposite. In this space, the horizontal opposition that I have indicated between the two principles of legiti-macy will then be crossed in both cases by a vertical opposition that will correspond roughly to the opposition between the professionals and the bohemians and to the opposition between those who are suc-cessful with the bourgeoisie and those who, having their success mostly with other classes, will claim a principle of popular legitimation.

Briefly, we might say that there are four principles of legitimation in competition. There are what we might call the bourgeois principle and the popular principle, which I think Zola invented – please excuse any historical errors. Since from this point of view success brings discredit (it is damning, since it can only be obtained through concessions to a public all the more shameful when it is more numerous), the riposte has to be: 'But this public is a popular public', with the word 'popular' being pronounced with a laudatory air, and being opposed to those writers whose only public is a handful of fellow bookworms – writers are horribly mean. 'True success' is failure to succeed, or success with those who are worthy to be considered pure: it is the legitimation principle of the desperate. Confronted by people who are no better endowed than they are, who ask them: 'Are you really sure that you don't regret your lack of means?', they fall back on the legitimation principle that you might call revolutionary, which is another, very different, manner of imposing the popular: I say this with some hesita-tion, but at a certain moment in time with certain inventors of realism such as the writer Champfleury or the painter Courbet, there is a refer-ence – an outright fantasy, of course – to the people.

I would like in passing to make a remark that I find important for the sociology of the people: in this space, 'the people', sometimes called 'the public', are constantly referred to, but obviously what is said about them is always filtered through their relation to other inhabitants of the field. In fact the people are rarely discussed as such: 'the people' is only a slogan used to maximise the force of their dismissal of their intel-lectual opponents. This is very important: if it is so difficult to make a sociological study of what we call 'the people', 'popular language',' popular culture' and, in fact, everything qualified by the adjective 'popular',[7] it is because, before you even meet the people, you have to sieve through four or five layers of discourse on the people that do not in fact discuss the people at all, but discuss only those who discuss the people and their positions in the space where the people are discussed. This is obviously complicated by the various rival interpretations of the word 'popular', and the fact that it also changes its sense as the field changes and the iron filings are drawn towards the left or the right, which is a very striking phenomenon. Although I may be expressing a bias, I have to say that what strikes me in the social history of art or literature, considered in this light, is the degree to which, within the limits of its relative autonomy, the space is transformed along the lines of any changes to the relation between the relatively autonomous sub-field and the field of power. For instance, the 1848 Revolution was accompanied by a general move towards social art:[8] there was no one who didn't found a journal dedicated to the people and who didn't say, to keep up with everyone else, that 'art must serve the people'; but afterwards, as soon as the structure of the field of forces changed, everything headed towards 'art for art's sake'.

Field of power and field of cultural production

Now that I have made this point, I intend to develop what it is that we can understand of what happens in the field of cultural production. Given the logic of the procedure that I shall follow, what I have to say may appear formal and abstract; afterwards things will become more concrete and I will move more and more to consider the singularity of individual writers.

One of the stakes in the field of power (we could call it 'the field of the dominant class', but I think that calling it the 'field of power' marks an advance in theory)[9] is, as in any field, the dominant and legitimate principle of domination: people fight to establish in whose name it is legitimate to dominate. The symbolic struggle (which is obviously not the only struggle; there are others, such as the economic struggle, for instance) is a fight to establish the dominant principle of domination, which is not identified as such, but is recognised and therefore legitimate. In this struggle, the two camps are *grosso modo*, in the terms of the nineteenth-century artists themselves, the artists versus the bourgeois. Overall, this struggle between artists and bour- geois ought theoretically to oppose the whole of the political-cultural field to the whole of what we might call the dominant fractions of the dominant class, those that are dominant according to the principles that really dominate the field of power (economic capital and political capital); there should be a simple struggle between those who, from the perspective of the structuring principles of the field, are on the '−' side and those who are on the '+' side. In fact the whole difficulty of this struggle derives from the fact that it is situated inside the field of cultural production. The producers in the sub-field of restricted production, whose economy is one that inverts economics, attack in the name of 'art for art's sake', or other principles of legitimacy, the hold of the 'bourgeois' over their cultural production; they reject the subordination of art to a function. One of the difficulties of their struggles is that they are situated inside a field of struggles where their opponents, although they are cultural producers, agree to conform to the general rules of the field of power. The more autonomous the field, the more the rule is not to follow economic laws. Now there are in this field people (those who produce for the theatre, some of those who produce novels, and the like) who recognise the laws of economics and who submit their production to the sanctions of the market. The struggle against the 'bourgeois' will then in fact be a struggle against the 'bourgeois artists'. Baudelaire put it very well: the true enemy is not the bourgeois but the 'bourgeois artist':[10] although he is a cultural producer, he denies what should be the law of the field – that is, the law of negation and denial of economics. This struggle within the field of power for the dominant principle of domination takes place, then, in fact inside the field of cultural production in the form of a struggle between 'art for art's sake' (or pure art) and art subordinate to external conditions.

We can grasp the opposition in the domain of art and literature, but the problem is posed much more clearly on the wider terrain of intellectual production, in so far as, the more we move towards the purer arts – moving from the theatre to the novel, from the novel to poetry, and from poetry to music – the more this relation to external functions dissolves; essay writing, for instance has an even higher degree of reference to the social world than does the theatre that speaks of the social world. The closer we approach the forms of cultural production that deal with the social world, the more the conflict within the universes of cultural production over the struggle for the legitimate principle of evaluation becomes visible, and it is in the intellectual field containing the producers of essays that the struggle will become clearer.

Conservative intellectuals

How will this pole, subordinate to external conditions, be expressed in the symbolic struggle to impose the dominant principle of legitimation? Firstly, in what Comte would have called an 'organic' period,[11] its discourse will be characterised by an absence of discourse: the discourse of the dominant on the social world is a non-discourse or a discourse of defence against discourses raising questions that by definition the dominant exclude. The dominant discourse may be silence, and – a property that I find important for understanding the functioning of the field – there is a degree zero of the discourse of legitimation, a kind of tacit conservatism which does not even need to express itself in words. Secondly, there is a discourse that we might term 'political' in the widest sense – that is, a first-degree, naïve conservative discourse, addressed for example to people who occupy different positions in the social world. I could put names to this: I am referring to a tradition that has developed among historians, especially American ones, over the very special historical problem posed by the naïve; their ambition is to understand the genesis of conservative thought and the very particular form of conservative thought taken by the naïve.[12] They have tried to analyse, in particular in the Germany of the 1830s, the move from a silent conservatism, born of a class *ethos* that has no need to be expressed, to a professional conservatism.

This approach has been used in several studies of one of the founders of conservative thought – whom I shall describe in a moment – who differed from the more or less bourgeois writers, who are amateurs. There are writers who are not professionals, and it is worth noting that in France more than half of what is published is written by people who belong to the dominant fractions of the dominant class. This is important because, when we study intellectuals or cultural production, apart from an exceptional case like the one that I want to mention, we compose a sample that omits people such as Marcel Dassault[13] and all the people like him who write books. There is then, as well as silent conservatism, what we might call the naïve, first-degree conservatism of those who make explicit something that is so self-evident that there is no real need to discuss it. What is interesting is that they come to speak of it by holding an imaginary dialogue with the space of the field of cultural production.

Further, there is another category of people, typified by the early nineteenth-century conservative writer Adam Müller;[14] they are professional producers who raise conservative discourse to a very special level of expression, who change its nature, although this often passes unnoticed, by the simple fact of thinking of it with reference to the producers in the sub-field of restricted production. These are people who do not reply directly to political objections such as 'You govern, but by what right? You govern, but have you been authorised to govern? Is it enough to invoke race and blood in order to govern legitimately? etc.', but reply to the questions as they are reformulated in this space. This means that their language, their social position and, in fact, all their positions in the space are transformed. These people are *gatekeepers*[15] who guard the frontier that divides up the intellectual field, and they will constantly import into the intellectual field (over here) problems which have come from the dominant fractions of the dominant class (over there). In this case, we could take the analysis further and, starting out from the structural analysis of the position, go on to study the properties of the agents who inhabit it. Schumpeter is an interesting person to study in this perspective.[16] He is an example of the typical intellectual who has emerged from the dominant fractions of the dominant class; they have left through the fact of having become intellectuals – their career takes them from the dominant fractions of the dominant class towards the dominated fractions of this class – and from this position they turn back towards their original starting point. Their biography is a two-way trip, and their contradictory dispositions, as intellectuals who are intellectuals in their relations with the bourgeois and bourgeois in their relations with the intellectuals, are written into both their positions and their dispositions.

(I don't want to launch into a detailed demonstration, but I shall return to Schumpeter's case, where we can show the redundancy of properties associated with the position and the individuals who inhabit it. This is a parenthesis, but it plays an important part in the work of research. If we bear in mind that, in many cases, position and disposition are basically two translations of the same term, to use Spinoza's metaphor,[17] this will enable us to find in the description of the positions questions that we can ask of the dispositions, and vice versa. We can set up a kind of fast shuttle service in our research: as soon as we discover something about a position, we should look into the texts to see if it relates to the product of a disposition or, starting out from the position, ask questions that we wouldn't have thought of asking, about the trajectory taken, for example.)

Returning to the theatre for a moment: in his book *Théorie de l'art pour l'art*, Cassagne, whom I have already quoted several times, says that people spoke of a 'school of good sense' when discussing a theatrical school that emerged from Romanticism with Ponsard, Augier, and the like.[18] These people adopted from the Romantics' attacks on what were seen as normal matrimonial relations what could fit within the limits of bourgeois ethics, and according to Cassagne they created a moderate form of Romantic theatre, founding what we now call the 'right bank' bourgeois theatre.[19] In the intellectual field, the people who play the part of go-betweens[20] between the dominant and the dominated fractions are in a way the messengers of good sense. They accuse the producers for producers of obscurity, in asking questions that there is no need to ask, for instance in poetry. They rely on the intellectual competence granted by membership of the intellectual field, where they have obtained specific tokens of consecration, to reassure the bourgeois about any intellectual audacity. This is very apparent in theatre criticism, for example (I refer you to my comparative analysis of theatre criticism according to the distribution of the critics in the space);[21] the role of the *Figaro* critic, speaking of Arrabal,[22] for instance, addressing the people in the dominant fractions of the bourgeoisie (over here): 'I am well placed to understand this audacity, and as an intellectual I can tell you that there is nothing extraordinary there.' In other words, his function is to use his intellectual authority to reassure them. This kind of deeply divided character can only make his reassurance effective for these people if he is disturbed and disturbing (that is to say, intellectual), because he must be able to say, 'since I am an intellectual', in order to say: 'I can tell you that there is nothing there to understand.' He must be the person who would understand if there were anything to understand, otherwise his exorcism would have no effect. By the same token, he disturbs, all the more so because his intellectual point of honour in his relations with the pole of the field of restricted production obliges him to be disturbing. In particular, if only because he is defending his monopoly, he has no pity for naïve, first-degree conservatism.

This part is increasingly difficult to play, particularly because of the general rise in the level of education that I mentioned last time. In fact, thirty years ago far more people in the dominant fractions of the dominant class were educated in private schools, whose function for the bourgeoisie was to teach as little as possible – that is, to teach without producing intellectuals.[23] There was a kind of anti-intellectualism that was the tacit basis of the educational contract signed by the bourgeois parents with the private education sector. The equivalent today would be that, in order to accede with all the trappings of legitimacy to the dominant positions of the dominant class, people need to have graduated from a *grande école*, which encourages people in this position to choose their own ideology and in fact to be their own ideologists and interpreters of symbols, and thus to dispense with those professional ideologists who were situated in key positions.

The law of symbolic legitimation

What will always save the men who hold this position is one of the laws of legitimation on which I must insist, because otherwise you will not fully understand what I am suggesting; it is what I call, in my shorthand, 'the Napoleon paradigm'.[24] In crowning himself, Napoleon made a mistake from the point of view of symbolic logic, for if there is one domain where the maxim that 'a man's best servant is himself' is not true, it is consecration; if there is one thing that we are unable to do on our own, it is to legitimate ourselves. If your brother consecrates you, there is a relationship pre-existing the act of consecration and he will be suspected of being over-indulgent. This is a parenthesis that I do not wish to prolong, but legitimation is all the stronger when the circuit of consecration is longer.[25]

Intimate mutual admiration societies have a weak legitimation effect because it is all too easy to see when X writes a review of Y's work and Y returns the favour. You only have to read the weekly journals: A writes a review of B in journal X, and B writes a review of A in journal Y. If you don't read both journals, you will miss this exchange of courteous compliments. The circuit becomes more complicated if A writes a review of B, who writes a review of C, who writes on A. This is one consequence of the general law of the symbolic economy (the symbolic economy is the antithesis of the economic): whenever there is an economic relation between, for example, the person celebrating and the person celebrated, the celebration loses value because it is suspected of being interested. (We could establish a theory of the ways in which relations are euphemised so that the symbolic efficiency requiring this dissimulation can function, but I shall not take this further; this is just a parenthesis.)

The people over here in the diagram, holding dominant positions in the dominant class, would like to crown themselves as Napoleon did, and say: 'It is good to be what we are.' Max Weber claimed to found a law that I believe to be true when he said that the dominant require an ideology to provide a 'theodicy of their own privileges'.[26] Basically, they expect to be justified in existing in the way that they exist – that is, as dominant. They want it to be said that it is right for them to dominate, and that the world is made to be dominated by them. We could make a vast comparative sociological study of sociodicies. It seems to me that, the function of sociodicy being constant, this would show that what varies in reality is the principle of legitimation invoked, which is itself linked to the principle of domination: this is how an aristocracy can seek the principle of their legitimacy in earth and blood. This is why Simone de Beauvoir, seeking in the 1950s to isolate the essence of conservatism, rooted it in the conservative ideologies invented in Germany in the 1830s largely to justify the domination of the Junkers.[27] That said, when the dominant class changes, the principle of its domination and thereby its legitimating discourse changes. Briefly, the greater the part of cultural capital in the principles of domination in the name of which the dominant classes dominate, the more the meritocratic principle will serve as a principle of legitimation, for example with the ideology of the gift.

I propose the following hypothesis: if you ask nothing of this dominant fraction, it will make no reply; when nothing happens, silence is the dominant ideology. This is very important: orthodoxy exists only when the *doxa* is broken; there has to be heresy for the orthodox discourse to intervene. Thus this fraction breaks silence only when ordered to do so by being questioned. They then claim to justify themselves, drawing on their own resources spontaneously to invent a sociodicy reflecting the principle of legitimation that underpins them. However, if the rule that I enunciated just now is true, it is a mistake for the dominant class to create their own legitimation, dispensing in a way with ideologists, because in good symbolic logic, where legitimacy is concerned, a man's best servant is other people.

Return to the struggles within the field of cultural production

The ideologist then is a character whose mission is to reply to the questions put to the dominant class, and he will reply no longer naïvely, but in the second degree; he will recognise the questions he has to answer, which means that his discourse will have a quite distinctive style. It will contrast for instance with those of the intellectuals: he will be urged to affect simplicity, clarity and the *doxa* as opposed to the para-dox of the intellectuals. I spoke just now of good sense: 'good sense' means silence. The *doxa* is silent, whereas the paradoxicals put impossible questions: they call things into question; they upset styles of theatrical staging,[28] attack rhyme schemes that are generations old and start to call for free verse. They ask the questions that nobody asked, and the dominant fractions of the dominant class stay speechless while the ideologist continues to speak and produce ortho-dox discourse. He must respond to the heretical provocation, but in a language that is the antithesis of this barbed heretical discourse, which looks for problems, uses German concepts, and so forth. He must respond simply and clearly, in good French. But if the ideologist ventures too far down the path of clarity and good sense, he trips over: he loses his intellectual properties, he has crossed the boundary and he is banished. Now one of the fundamental stakes in the struggle is to be able to say where the boundary lies. (Think of the philosophers, find your own examples . . . I am wary of offering any myself, because an example would weaken my more general model; yet, at the same time, if we don't think of any example, this will seem to be merely a formal exercise. So I leave it up to you to do the necessary to make it work.)

The struggle focuses on the place of this boundary, since the producers for producers have as their rule to exclude those whose productions are commissioned, arguing that one of the weak points in the struggle between the artist and the bourgeois is the existence of bourgeois artists, who use their prime position to call into question the existence of artists as artists. We could talk for hours about these bourgeois artists and ideologists; it would be easy to give thousands of examples. If they venture too far in the direction of simplicity and good sense ('let me explain', 'there's no need to worry', 'there is nothing very complicated in Sartre', and so on), they run the risk of being purely and simply rejected. Among the dominated fractions of the dominant class, people will say that 'they don't understand a thing', or that they are 'vulgarisers', which is a manner of expelling them from the field: the 'vulgariser' (the word deriving from *vulgus*) is disqualified by the very audience that he addresses. In this case, these bourgeois artists and ideologists lose their specific efficacity. It is important to realise that they were not officially mandated in the first place.

The sociology of intellectuals that I mentioned the other day[29] commits a basic error by establishing direct relations between the producer and the social group for whom he writes, by trying to describe the producers with reference to the class that they spring from or the class that consumes their products: this sociology forgets that the symbolic effect I describe would not be produced if the producer were an instrument, if he were writing for someone. You should re-read the passage in *Distinction* on the drama critics: the drama critic of the *Figaro* says explicitly that he has never, ever been inspired by the idea of addressing the readers of the *Figaro*. Similarly, the 'ideologist' (an unfortunate word that I use only as a kind of shorthand to avoid losing contact by having to keep repeating 'the holder of this symbolically dominated and economically dominant position in the cultural field') can only fulfil his symbolic function if, when he formulates criticism of the people over there, the bourgeois, he does so on his own account, to save his skin and serve his own personal interests, without ever considering those people. If the latter are pleased, that is a bonus, and they are all the more pleased if he has not acted on purpose. I had read declarations by Jean-Jacques Gautier, a very influential drama critic whose word we can believe, who said that he had never written a critique intended for his editor or his readers; he merely wanted to annoy the critic of the *Nouvel Observateur*, whom he took for the representative of the opposite pole.[30]

Anticipating once more what I shall be arguing in a moment, I want to say how important it is that what we may call the ideological effect ('I shall say what will appeal to the people inhabiting the dominant position in the field') is achieved only as a side-effect. It is not sought for in its own right, and it is all the better fulfilled if it is less sought for in its own right. It is fulfilled on the basis of a homology of positions: the petit-bourgeois intellectual is to the bourgeois intellectual what the petit-bourgeois is to the bourgeois. By defending his position in the relatively autonomous field where he finds himself, he automatically defends, within the limits of homology – which, we should note, is never identity – the position of the people in whose name he is supposed to speak, without being their spokesman. The image of the spokesman is catastrophic, and that would still be true in the case of the field of trade union organisations or the field of political parties; in the political field you can have a spokesman, but, in both cases, the direct relation between the speaker and the group in whose name he is supposed to speak hides the fact that, as soon as you are in a field, you speak primarily against, for and with the people who are in the field, and you speak on behalf of those people who hold homologous positions in this field [over here], the social space, only as an extra. The idea of the wordsmith as hired hack and 'lackey of the bourgeoisie' is extremely naïve and is one of the great obstacles to making a rigorous sociological study of cultural production. Obviously this direct, mechanical relation, although scientifically and politically false, is as always more simple and straightforward than the much more complicated relation that I am suggesting.

If the agent [over here], the bourgeois intellectual, is led by the logic of his position in the field to go too far towards importing into the field values and representations of the other field [over there], that of the dominant fractions of the dominant class (such as good sense, virility, seriousness and economic realism), he loses all credit in his space; he disqualifies himself from being able to achieve his principal effect, which depends on his being different from the spontaneous producer and ideologist. Moreover – and I do no more than describe the contradictions attached to this position – in the relation with the dominant fractions for which he is supposed to speak, he can only defend his intellectual honour by importing the characteristic demands and values of the intellectual, attacking primary conservatism and giving lessons in politics to the politicians as well as lessons in conservatism to the conservatives. Since, given his profession, he cannot be content with the silence of the *doxa*, another of his temptations is to speak of things that had better remain silent and offer explanations of strategies that were better disowned. He is then in an awkward position in his relation to the dominant, and this role of the intermediary is in a way the role of a priest. In so far as he legitimates what in the last resort has no need of legitimation, he is suspected of needing the principles of legitimation for himself. Here, again, my demonstration is abstract. I could illustrate it, but I shall leave this theme here for the moment.

To recapitulate: the struggle internal to the field of cultural production is the form taken by the struggle within the dominant class, within the field of power. It is then a struggle for the principle of legitimate legitimation, or, more precisely, a struggle for the legitimate manner of being a man: the dominant principle of domination states what a man must be in order to be legitimated to govern, dominate and rule. For example in recent times, in the 1960s, intelligence was one of the most frequent themes referred to in the discourse of legitimation.[31] Remember what I was saying just now about the tacit contract between the bourgeoisie and Catholic education. To simplify somewhat, there was a drive to substitute sport for Latin translation (which had enabled the petit-bourgeois to rise from the ranks), and there was the debate in the nineteenth century over what should be taught in the *grandes écoles*. This kind of visceral suspicion of intelligence was expressed quite unambiguously then. But since then the principles governing access to the dominant class and the dominant fractions in the field of power have changed; intelligence, and differences in talent, and so on, have featured in ideological discourse as one of the principles of legitimation – which has in a way changed the whole structure of the field of struggles for the principle of domination and, by the same token, the defensive strategies that the dominated could adopt.

It is very important to reflect in the light of this logic on what happened in May 1968 and the counter-ideological discourse that was devised then against diplomas and exams: I think that this was a collective effort by the intellectual fraction to establish a counter-discourse against a dominant class that was no longer content with dominating in the name of economics and power, but wanted to dominate also in the name of what the intellectuals habitually used against them – that is, educational qualifications. In particular – if I may be brutal and political – we can draw on this logic to understand a certain form of left-wing anti-intellectualism. This kind of ideological slippage, which has recently turned many of the arguments sustained by the right between the wars into left-wing arguments, is a result of the structural effects of the changes in this space. A very important thing, which is self-evident but which perhaps needs spelling out in this case, is that the pairs of opposites that frame the construction of identities and the ideal ways of being a man (reason vs. passion, and the like) have no content other than their relationship.

Again, these seem quite trivial matters, but I want to underline them, because these pairs of opposites are rationalised and eternalised by the educational system. We should analyse all the mechanisms that tend to eternalise these pairs of opposites. These pairs eventually function independently of the social conditions in which they were engendered and, thereby, independently of the space where they were founded and where their reality was constituted. In fact, they have hardly any substance other than that given them by the fact that they were borne by such and such a group, to such an extent that you discover for example that there was a moment when it was psychoanalysts who defended rationalism against Taine and Renan.[32] In other words, one of the only ways of writing the history of the struggles within the dominant class is to write the history of their struggles over ideas. Now the whole logic of the history of ideas and intellectuals studying ideas leads us to act as if our ideas could exist on their own (there is liberalism, there is neo-liberalism, and so on), as if it all happened in a pure heaven of ideas. But the pairs of opposites are in reality social spaces channelled into language, and to assign a real substance to these seemingly eternal or ahistorical opposites we must first reconstitute the space within which they really functioned. That is the first thing. The second is that the process obviously works both ways. When we set all these opposites, such as 'nature and history', as topics for dissertations, we are in fact taking a short cut and imposing an after-image. For example, opposites that in their original usage and for eight or nine generations corresponded to oppositions between the left and the right can exchange places in the present generation, or even an earlier one. We align them all in the same direction, but their polarity may have shifted, and we forget that these terms take on meaning only in relation to each other, which may seem obvious – but is not so obvious when you start to study the history of liberalism or positivism.

To start with, it is easy to forget that each term can exist only within a space and in relation to other terms and, secondly, that, every time that this space is upset, the directions of the two terms of the relationship are upset. No need to insist, but this is I think one of the important things that ensues from the little model that I wanted to show you. Some of the problems raised by what the manuals used to call 'moral' philosophy are in fact problems which create an important division within the dominant class. Within the field of cultural production, one of the terms of the relationship in fact expresses the dominant position, whereas the other expresses the dominated position, given that both of them are always defined by their mutual struggle. This is my first point, which could be developed further.

Of course, on the plane of the field of cultural production in its literary form – so far I have been taking it in its more or less philosophical, theoretical and political form – the opposition will concern the definition of the legitimate artist and be translated into the struggle between the two forms of legitimate art; art with no message and functional art; art with no moral and moral art; art that transgresses everything, including morality, and art which respects it; bourgeois theatre and symbolist poetry; and so on. This conflict over the legitimate and successful way of being an artist is one of the ways of fighting for the legitimate way of being human. For example, the debates on rationalism and irrationalism, which are constant debates in the dominant class, will take on forms transformed by the logic of the field.

To recapitulate: the internal struggles in the field of cultural production have as their stake the legitimate manner of being an artist, writer or intellectual and enact in sublimated form the struggles within the dominant class over the legitimate manner of being dominant and the legitimate manner of dominating. In these struggles, one of the stakes is the boundary of the intellectual field: Is the intellectual field limited to the producers for producers, producers recognised as legitimate by the legitimate producers or recognised as legitimate by the most legitimate of the legitimate producers, or does it include all the people who make it their business to produce, whatever the destination of their products?

Let us pass on to another point: How can we arbitrate in this struggle between the two rival principles of legitimation? The formula 'the most legitimate of the legitimate producers' implies that there is a circle: Who is to choose the legitimate producer when, as I showed some time ago, there is no apparatus to legitimate the agencies of legitimacy? Who will say, who can say who is a writer? Who has the legitimate status to say who is a legitimate writer?[33] Given that every writer claims legitimacy and the power to possess the legitimacy to decree which publishing house marks the last frontier beyond which nobody is a writer, this struggle over the boundaries of the field of cultural production is the form that the symbolic struggle within the field of power will assume.

The genesis of the invariants

Before taking this point further, I wish to make a remark in response to an objection concerning the historical value of my description. This is a problem that I face and that you also face: it is obvious that I constantly pass from one period to another, from the present to the past, from one period in the past to another, from a generalised nineteenth century to a more specific nineteenth century, and so on. I think that this is one of the effects of an oral delivery and the fact that, to try to display the properties of the model as fully as possible, I am led to exaggerate this aspect of my method that enables me to ask general questions about historical meaning. Having said that, this is how things function in the practice of research: what I have to offer is something that has no historical truth; it is a series of snapshots that intermingle certain states of the structures of the field. In truth, I should say: 'I am going to study the structure for the period from 1880 to 1890.' For example, the books by Charle and Ponton, among others that I have been quoting, are focused on this period, for reasons that I shall try to explain next time: it seems to me that this is the moment when these spaces tend to take on the structure that has remained theirs since then. These structures then are not eternal; they have a genesis, they are linked to a history, and you could for example describe the whole history of the image of the artist in the nineteenth century – if I have time I shall do this briefly – as the history of the atomisation of the space of the artistic and literary field. It is the gradual conquest of autonomy,[34] a sort of liberation war, a kind of very long-drawn-out struggle, which started very early with the painters and was continued by the writers, who acted as their ideologists and took them as examples: it is the *rapin* who incarnates the sacrifice for the sake of art, who dies for the love of art, and who clears the way for the subsequent exchange of roles.

This struggle for liberation was obviously necessary. This manner of thinking is not the way historians usually think, and it may shock them, but it is in fact eminently historical. For example, for a writer to be able to settle into a professorial chair entitled the Nouveau Roman[35] without creating a sensation, it needed people literally to die of hunger (you don't have to die to write a Nouveau Roman, even if it can be painful – but some of its birth pangs linger on). I am putting this rather dramatically, but there is an anecdote in one of those novels that nobody reads (because they do not belong to the corpus that the instances of consecration have declared to be survivors): three *rapins* go to bury their comrade and, as they set out they get drunk and so don't have a penny left to give to the grave-digger, who says: 'That's all right, you'll be back!' [*laughter*]. These painters in a way died in order to incarnate the fact that you can die for art, that art is a value that transcends economics. They served as an exemplary figure that the writers exploited in the same way. The image of the artist that they projected enabled the artist to stand up to the academies and the scholars and their like.

In order to think of all that in historical terms (I am going to confuse the issue even more, but I need to say this to justify myself): the history of this field is the history of a permanent struggle, which we must keep in mind, between these producers for producers and the academic producers. This is one of the reasons why I started with this point: for example, it did not exist to the same degree in every historical period, and we can well imagine that this field could disappear (this is very important; I did say at one point that we should abandon linear models and irreversible developments). Ten centuries of struggles for an artistic economy can be erased, and even this room in the Collège de France can also disappear. These are the products of a historical struggle, with progress and regress, changing boundaries, and so on. Similarly, the people listening to these lectures are themselves the products of a history. The habitus is a history; the field is a history; and each state of the field is the product of a previous history.

For example, one very simple thing is to replace the notion of bohemia by the notion of the avant-garde, in terms of a conquest. This field is constructed as anti-economic, against the economic economy but also against the political economy, against power and consecration. It was constructed against institutionalisation and reminds us of the paradox of the Reformed Church as stated by Troeltsch:[36] how can the Reformed Church, which was set up in opposition to the Churches, avoid becoming a new Church and provoking the need for a new Reformation? The problem of heresies is that, in order to constitute themselves as a serious and organised instrument of revolt against domination, they have to establish an apparatus. Similarly, one contradiction of this sub-field is that, since it was set up in opposition to the institution, it is very under-institutionalised. Nonetheless, we do not start afresh with each generation. There are achievements, but these do not include the Académie française, the École des beaux-arts or the Légion d'honneur. They are little reviews, the word 'avant-garde', all sorts of little things that prevent the newcomers from having to start from scratch: they know that the publishers who encourage you to found a new review constantly come and go, but that there is a publisher who, believing in a certain idea of the great publisher, is prepared to publish works that matter at a loss. And then there are the great predecessors: Hugo, Renan and the generation who were twenty years old in 1840, then, in a later period, Verlaine and Mallarmé. Each of these configurations will leave at least an image, and this is a considerable advantage: you don't have to start from scratch, you don't have to reinvent the wheel, and you can use their reputation as a weapon. Another very interesting thing (that everyone understood but nobody thought): one of the extraordinary benefits that contemporary painters inherit from the painters of the past is the idea that there have been many misunderstandings, that clients got things wrong and did not buy the canvases that they should have bought. The fear of making mistakes is nowadays an important factor in the economy of the painting market.

I must emphasise that all this has to be thought through in a histori-cal logic. If I have time in my next lecture I will explain that at every moment history is present in two forms. On the one hand history is there because we have the Académie française, and there are two thea-tres now where there was only one, and it is an extraordinary change to be able to say 'the theatres', which was unthinkable in the times when there was only one of them; these are things that exist, that are inscribed in our memory, and the educational system reproduces them or their memory. On the other hand there are people who are shaped by what they have been told, by their fantasies. There is another mag-nificent passage in *Manette Salomon* where the young painter gives his basic reason for becoming a painter: because when his friends saw him drawing on scraps of paper they said: 'Hey, that's fun, you're going to be a painter', and then because he had fantasies about studios, models and freedom, and so on.[37] In every period, if you analyse it, among the things that help to constitute the dispositions that will enable people to fill the positions, there is the more or less fantasised effect of the posi-tions. So, I insist, we must take into account the relation between the two kinds of history: history objectified in the form of institutions, even if they are not strongly institutionalised, and history incorporated in the form of dispositions (the desire to become a painter, for instance).

(I shall finish with this point here, but it remains the case that my exposition tends to present you with a sort of description of the transhistorical invariants of the structure of the intellectual field and the field of power. But what I say is possible since there are nonetheless invariants: when an intellectual field has attained a sufficiently advanced degree of autonomy, we have a structure of this kind. In other words, the process of autonomisation of the intellectual field tends towards such a structure; this is why it seems to me to represent the ideal-typical invariant.)

The adaptation of offer to demand through homology of structure

After this parenthesis, I come to my second point. Having described in general terms the struggle between the intellectual field and the field of power, I shall briefly describe the struggle within the intellectual field. The model that I shall propose, which is based to a considerable extent on the work of Ponton and Charle that I mentioned just now, is especially relevant to the period between 1880 and 1900. I situate my analyses in the space of this field of cultural production, with this sub-field of restricted production, which we may say represents the truth of the field of cultural production.

In this space there are two rival principles of hierarchisation: one economic and one cultural. We have then the chiasmatic structure, which as you may remember also characterises the field of power as a whole, and we shall find a homology between the structure of the field of cultural production and the structure of the surrounding field. I mentioned this effect of adaptation by homology just now. I am repeating myself because I did not explain it fully then. It is customary to describe this relation between the intellectual field and the field of power, or the field of classes as a whole, as a relation of service: 'He writes for this or that fraction.' Or it may be described as a relation of transaction – this would be Max Weber's model: in the case of religion Weber describes the relation between the rival religious agents and the laity as relations of transaction and exchange, in the economic sense. For example he explains that, in the competition for access to the laity, the priests and the sorcerers are led to make concessions to them, to negotiate with them in order to keep their clientele.[38] We could apply this model of negotiated transaction here and say: 'The people who write boulevard theatre, for example, are in a quasi-permanent state of negotiation with their audience; if it doesn't succeed, they change their product and adapt it to suit their clientele.'

This purposive and functionalist model is I think particularly false, and it is all the more false because within the field of cultural production we move away from the economic pole and towards the intellectual pole. That is what I meant just now in my analysis of the ideologists and my rejection of the idea of the intellectual lackey and hired hack of the bourgeoisie. I wanted to say that, even in the case that is apparently most favourable for them, where the writers accept Légions d'honneur, prizes and profits, the model of the transaction and the analysis of cultural production in economic terms are only very partially true; it is on the basis of a homology of position that the adaptation between production and demand occurs. To phrase it differently: even in this case, we cannot understand the whole of cultural production in terms of the hypothesis of a conscious search for an adaptation of offer to demand, and, if my model is right, there is an effect of automatic adaptation of offer to demand which springs from the homology of structure. It is then because the academic producers are producing partly or wholly in opposition to the producers for producers that, in so doing, they produce for the dominant fraction of the dominant class, who do not ask for this explicitly. Similarly, if the best-selling producers serve the dominant fraction of the dominant class, it is because in serving them they serve themselves, and they serve so well only because they are serving themselves at the same time, and their service to others is an extra. I am insisting on this model, because I think that it is realistic and because it goes against the grain of political ways of thinking (in terms of attack, and the like).

This homology of structure is established between the right and the left of the fields (I always put the '−' sign on the left because it is an opposition between dominant and dominated). The homology between, on the one hand, the fact of being on the side of the dominated in a field and, on the other hand, the position of the dominated in the field of classes is the source of political encounters that, like all encounters founded on homology rather than identity of position, are only partial encounters. Zola has explained clearly that one run of a bourgeois play (I don't know of what importance) could earn its author what a novelist would need to sell 200,000 copies to earn,[39] with the same novelist earning in a year more than a poet could earn in three lifetimes. Within this structure, some writers make large profits, others middling ones, and obviously the groups are more or less dispersed: one of the properties of the position in the sub-field of restricted production is that it brings in large profits but only to a small number of people – this is very important – whereas the position in the sub-field of mass production brings in large profits to quite a large number.

The conquest of autonomy

This hierarchy obviously imposes itself in economic terms all the more strongly the more one recognises the dominant values and, by the same token, the less relative autonomy the field enjoys. The more the independence of this sub-field grows in relation to the surrounding field, the more the artists in the artistic field will defeat the bourgeois and the more the specific law of the artistic field will assert itself. I should have spoken just now of the law of the artistic field: Max Weber said more or less that the economy is constituted as economy when the tautologous axiom 'business is business' (or 'there is no place for sentiment in business') becomes the law of business;[40] we could say that art is constituted when the axiom of 'art for art's sake' is asserted as such. The assertion of 'art for art's sake' is one of the conquests that I mentioned just now when I was saying that the modern artist is the product of a struggle for liberation. We are particularly dominated by the retrospective illusion: we see this history from the viewpoint of the end of a process where many things that were only imaginary conquests have come to seem self-evident, even to those who have benefited most from them; they realise that they have fought against the preceding generation but are unable to see what they have inherited (and even used as arms in their struggle) from the work of all the generations of the past (including the preceding one). This retrospective illusion is very important. We do not realise what an extremely difficult conquest was this apparently quite banal idea of 'art for art's sake', an artistic activity that has no aim other than to exist. It is difficult to imagine now, and you can completely disconcert an artist by asking him: 'What use are you?'

To give you another analogy (but one that I intend to limit), I believe that, to understand this, we need to refer to the social sciences and the situations where people ask social scientists: 'What use are you?' It is very difficult to reply: 'I am useful for studying the social sciences' [*laughter*] – just try it and you will see. If it is difficult to say, it is because of another very important social law: there are things that are sayable and thinkable because as soon as you say them they are accepted, you are sure that there is a market for them; and there are things that are unspeakable and therefore unthinkable, because the person who utters them seems peculiar and unjustified. These matters play an important part in the process of conquest. The further the process of autonomisation advances, the clearer it becomes that the pole of producers for producers is symbolically dominant and the less artistic the best-selling authors feel; if they are left out of a survey, they are unhappy. This seems naïve but is in fact very important; in the 1860s and even the 1880s it was still possible to be a best-selling author and feel satisfied overall – that is, both crowned by success and relatively artistic. The change is a result of the process of symbolic imposition.

It is also important to note that you have in a way won a symbolic struggle when you impose your own categories of perception on your opponent. The dominant dominate symbolically when they impose on the dominated their own categories of perception, so that the dominated see themselves as the dominant see them or see themselves through the spectacles the dominant use to look at them. I always use the example of intimidation: the symbolically dominated person is the one who loses his grip when in the presence of the dominant. They can resist the dominant but their body language gives them away: they blush, panic and stammer, for instance. In the procedure of symbolic domination, the dominated assume as their own the dominants' principles of perception. In other words, victory here is not simply saying: 'The theatre is rubbish, it's only good for the bourgeois'; it is making the economically dominant, with their Légion d'honneur, their theatre, audience and applause, feel ill at ease and perhaps lead a double life and start to write other things.

There is a case study in *Actes de la recherche en sciences sociales*: Cécil Saint-Laurent, who is at the same time Jacques Laurent.[41] This is a typical case, a kind of experimental proof: he could have been perfectly satisfied to be typified by this definition: 'He has a lot of money' (films were made of *Caroline chérie*, and so on); yet he went to some lengths to live a double life and have an honourable career; he used two names. He personifies this space: he is the illustration of this space where we distinguish between things that are easy or difficult, clear or obscure, meretricious or pure; he wants to try to be at both poles of the space, which is I think impossible. In this space you cannot be in two places at once, even if only because the duplication is never perfect. It is interesting to note that he uses a pseudonym: the pseudonym is a way of recognising that there is something shameful in doing what you are doing. It is a way of disguising and therefore recognising legitimacy, as Max Weber notes when he says that the thief recognises legitimacy by hiding in order to steal[42] (even if it is more complicated than that).

In this space where there are two principles of hierarchisation competing (one economic, the other symbolic), one part of the process will consist in establishing this principle of symbolic legitimation as the dominant or sole principle, thereby constituting this sub-field as an artistic or literary universe, by saying that outside this sub-field there are no more writers but only 'wordsmiths' or 'hired hacks', and the like – that is, by discrediting people through the simple act of attributing a function to their practices. This is what I was saying just now: I think that the theory of art for art's sake is to the artistic field what the formula 'business is business' is to the economic field: it expresses its truth, and the people who struggle for this position do in a way have the logic on their side that enables them to say to others: 'What you are doing is producing something, like everyone else.' This will be the opposition between the pure and the commercial. I could continue . . .

The hierarchy of productions and the hierarchy of publics

A second opposition linked to this, but not entirely dependent on it, lies in the fact that we evaluate acts of position not only by their social intentions but also by their social destination. This is another way of looking at the external constraints in this field, which aspires to autonomy. As I have always maintained, this autonomy is relative, and the forces of the surrounding field continue to operate, particularly because we judge a production by the social quality of the public we assume to be addressed, because it is affected, since we obviously tend to see a mechanical logic in the internal struggle of the field. If I have returned yet again to the idea that we should not think in terms of function, that we should not explain an artist by the group that he is supposed to serve, it is because one of the weapons used in the field is the insult that reduces a production to its function: 'You only write for women's magazines.' They reduce the artistic quality of a work by assigning it a function ('You do industrial art') and they reduce it all the more (reducing it twice over, so to speak) the lower in the social hierarchy the group that the work is supposed to serve is placed. In the theatre, between the facile, gross comedy of the eternal triangle and the more noble boulevard, there will be an opposition based on the social hierarchy of the audience.

For the hierarchies concerning the novel, I can draw on Rémy Ponton's analyses while telescoping the periods, but there is another interesting element there: poetry is the speciality whose autonomisation is the most ancient even if still today the popular representation of literature is associated with poetry. When it happens exceptionally that people from the lower or middle classes write, they write poetry rather than a realist novel describing what they see before them.[43] But, contrariwise, poetry is historically the sector that gained its autonomy first, partly from necessity (lacking a public), partly by choice, and therefore in a dialectic of necessity made virtue. In poetry the struggle within the pure sub-field between the old and the new, orthodoxy and heresy, was established long ago. Ponton shows clearly how the idea of literary revolution that we associate with the idea of the artistic field was taken from the case of poetry. The idea of a permanent revolution, where one school drives out another (the Parnassians overthrow the Romantics, and so on), is exemplified by poetry, and when we look for the model of this revolution we think of poetry, because it has spent more time pursuing the logic of the struggle for difference, for a purely symbolic economy – I shall return to the symbolic economy, which is the economy of distinction. As the field gradually becomes autonomous, all the positions in the field, even including those least autonomous from the world of economics, will partake of the logic illustrated here: there will be vertical oppositions that will no longer be simply hierarchised with oppositions reflecting the quality of the public.

Here I need to introduce a later period, with its tradition of avantgarde theatre in the théâtre Antoine, and the right-bank versus left-bank forms of theatre (which I described in a paper)[44] that reveal an opposition between the theatre with a bourgeois public and the theatre whose audience is made up of students and teachers, and the like. This opposition started to form at the end of the nineteenth century for the theatre and for the novel, where we find the opposition between the experimental novel and the utilitarian novel. But, before this sector became autonomous, the hierarchy of practices corresponded to a hierarchy of the audiences affected.

Following Ponton, if we make the schools overlap a little, we can say that there are largely the psychological novel, the society novel, the naturalist novel (Zola), the *roman de moeurs*, the popular novel and the rural novel: the hierarchy of genres corresponds roughly to the hierarchy of their publics. I am anticipating the result here, and, as Ponton clearly shows, the hierarchy of the genres corresponds to the hierarchy of the authors' social origins:[45] there is a sort of homology between the degree of social exclusiveness of a genre and the degree of social exclusiveness of those who practise it. The psychological novel, for instance (Paul Bourget, among others), was produced by migrants from poetry – that is, by people who came from a nobler genre, according to the laws that I showed working in the scientific field, by people who come from a higher discipline and bring to a less prestigious region the prestige that they earned in their original discipline;[46] to operate this conversion, they need to have properties associated with high social origins (the courage to make a break, a feel for the strategies of adaptation, and so on). These writers are going to offer a product which will present a social milieu that is itself higher in the hierarchy, and this

gives rise to some amusingly explicit debates: Are the emotions of a
chambermaid as interesting as those of a duchess? (This is spelt out in
detail in certain debates.) It even happens that the relation between the
hierarchy of genres and the hierarchy of the groups shown in the novel
is openly questioned.

To conclude: in the space thus hierarchised there gradually formed
an autonomous hierarchy, as the hierarchy according to genres tended
progressively to make way for the appearance around 1900 of a single
opposition between avant-garde poetry, fiction and theatre as opposed
to bourgeois poetry, fiction and theatre. The transition was gradual.
This is why, as I said just now, repeating Charle's very sound argument, this period 1880 to 1900 is so interesting:[47] it was the moment
when the structure took shape, and we can see the two principles of
hierarchisation. The hierarchical principle based on economic strength
remained in force while already the other hierarchical principle, which
had been in force for poetry for some time, started to establish itself in
the whole of the field.

Having described the space, I shall finish now, in order to attempt
next time to give an overall sense to my analysis. I would like simply
to say, as I have said so often in my previous lectures, that this field
will be the site of a struggle to transform the field. There will be two
axes of struggle: firstly, the struggle that I have just mentioned between
the economically dominated and the economically dominant poles,
the struggle being nothing less than the form taken in this field by the
struggle within the dominant class; and, secondly, the struggle that
gradually takes over to the point of overshadowing the first, a struggle
within each genre between a utilitarian art with immediate profit and
an art which serves only itself and whose profit is deferred. In other
words, two different economies will be established: an anti-economic
economy and an economic one, which will correspond to two antagonistic types of artist. What I would like to do next time is try to show
in what manner the newcomers, depending on their dispositions – that
is, the properties they import into the field – enter this space: any newly
arrived artist will have to situate themselves in this space; they will
be manipulated by the forces at work in the field, and their fate will
depend on the relation between these forces and the dispositions that
they import.

Lecture of 25 January 1983

The economic logic of cultural enterprises – The truth of practice – The deferred profits of disinterestedness – The ambivalent profits of the market – The subversion of the rules of the field – Time-scales and 'personalities' – Clients and rivals: the mediation of the education system – Generations and revolutions – Modes of ageing and eternalisation – Overthrowing for the sake of overthrowing – Orientating the self in the space of possibilities – Trajectory and habitus – The impious dismantling of the fiction

I think that you are entitled to feel dissatisfied, and I want you to know that I understand. I want to tell you what I feel is missing from what I have been saying. I would have liked to take my explanation of the logic of a field to its conclusion. To do so, I would have had to broach a problem that I did not have time to deal with in the few sessions remaining: the problem of the relation of the notion of the field to the notion of capital. In fact you have heard me constantly using the notion of capital – whether cultural, economic or social – and you might have felt that I used these different concepts somewhat vaguely or approximately, whereas I believe that they can be clarified and situated in relation to each other. Similarly, I ought to have provided more details on the problem of the field of social classes, particularly because all the arguments that I have formulated seem to me to reveal their full force and logic when applied to this problem, which I believe to be one of the worst formulated in the sociological tradition, perhaps because it was one of the first to be formulated.

But this will have to wait for another year, when I will recapitulate briefly what I have established on the notion of the field in order to try to show how it is inseparable from the notion of capital and how the distribution of the different kinds of capital, and the struggles over its distribution, perpetuation and transformation, can enable us to revise completely the way we think of class and, in particular, free us from the realist way of thinking so often associated with the notion of class.[1] I am saying this in order to voice your dissatisfaction, and I would like at least to give you an idea of all that I had to say. In this respect, I think that those among you who would like to take this further will find yourselves very well placed to read what I wanted to say. That having been said, I would not want you to feel that I have said my last word on all these topics because otherwise all your reproaches would be justified.

The economic logic of cultural enterprises

I shall now return to the point in my last lecture where I left my analysis of the intellectual field, or the field of intellectual production, and try to take it a little further, moving on from what was a description of the structure of the intellectual field at one particular moment to an attempt to construct a model allowing us to explain this description. In other words, I constructed, as I think we must try to do in the social sciences, a sort of descriptive model – which was summarised in the schema that I showed you – but that model could appear to be constructed in order to adapt to a reality known in advance. Very often people proceed in this way, and not only in the social sciences: they speak of a model, whereas in reality, since they know a distribution, they have constructed the formula that allows them to trace the points that represent that distribution. This is the archetype of the false model, of the *ex post* model that describes while pretending to explain.

The model that I have to offer should escape this reproach in so far as it is based on the concept of the field that I have described and tries to account for the structure revealed by a historical analysis showing how the different genres of literary production are distributed according to two inverse and chiasmatic hierarchies: one following the degree of economic profit procured and the other, conversely, following the degree of specific consecration. At one pole the theatre, at the other, poetry. And I think that, in order to account for this distribution, we need to take into account two extremely simple factors. I already suggested one of these last time, which is that, the more the field of cultural production affirmed its autonomy, the more it established itself as having its own economy whose logic was the negation of economics in the ordinary sense of the word. The fundamental tenet of this singular universe ('art for art's sake') is the antithesis of the fundamental tenet of economics ('business is business'): the tenet of the cultural universe is the antithesis of the fundamental tenet of the economic universe. Having established this, we see that, the more profit an artistic genre or practice generates, the more it will tend to be discredited symbolically. There will then be a negative correlation between the ability of a genre, manner or style to generate economic rewards as rapidly as possible – which is an aspect to which I shall return – and the ability to generate symbolic rewards.

My second proposition is that we can treat the different genres, manners or schools as business enterprises and investigate the conditions under which they generate profit. We shall see that these businesses may be studied from three distinct angles: 1) the price of the item produced (to simplify); 2) the range and number of the clientele; 3) the length of the economic cycle. We may then use these three categories to contrast the three genres that I have been considering – poetry, the

The literary field at the end of the nineteenth century (detail)

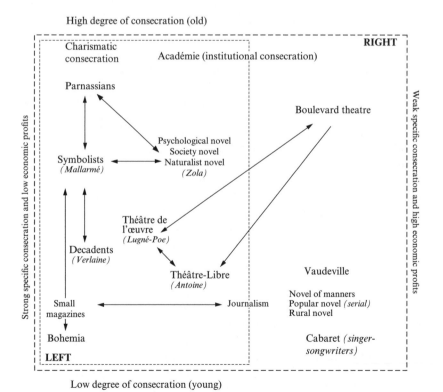

novel and theatre – treating them, in an exercise in methodological abstraction, as economic entities.

From the point of view of the unit price, we can see that there is not much difference between poetry and the novel: what will vary in these two cases, generally speaking, is the print run. That being said, the comparison between theatre on the one hand and poetry and the novel on the other shows that a play, as a written unit, can generate much more profit with a much smaller number of performances. I reminded you last time that writers themselves became aware of this colossal difference. For an identical investment – if, once again, we are prepared to view the cultural enterprise as a business like any other – the profit per unit will be incomparably greater for one than for the other.

The second angle, which correlates with the former: the size of the public that a given work can attract. We see that, to obtain the same profit – which depends on variations in the unit price – it takes an infinitely greater number of units for the novel than for the theatre, and consequently, if you combine the consequences of this proposition with the proposition that I advanced to start with – that is, that there is a negative correlation between economic rewards and symbolic rewards – novelists will need an infinitely greater public to earn the same economic profit as a playwright; which means that they will be much more vulnerable to the discredit linked to the size of the public.

The third property, which is very important because it will form the basis of the fundamental opposition in the field of cultural production, as I see it: the opposition between a business with a long circuit and one with a short circuit. For specific illustrations, I refer you to the article that I wrote on the production of belief, where I gave the sales figures for a novel that won the Goncourt prize on the one hand and a work by Beckett on the other: in accumulated sales after twenty years, the Beckett and the Goncourt were roughly equivalent; Beckett sold as many copies as this now forgotten author.[2] That being said, the latter had all his readers, and therefore his profits, in one year, whereas it took Beckett twenty years. This means that the economic enterprise is going to be completely different even if the results in accumulated profits are identical. In fact, in one case the investment can be experienced as a loan without security; it is only with hindsight that we know that it is a productive investment. For a long time the publisher has to accept the risk of never being able to balance the books and the author to accept working in conditions where he is never sure of making ends meet. There are then two completely antagonistic relations to the economy: one located in a logic of fair exchange, where a piece of work gives an immediate result; the other following a logic analogous to the exchange of gifts – that is, with an interval of time, where the interval imposed is very important, as in all systems of exchange founded on the denial of economics.

The truth of practice

I refer you to an argument in *The Logic of Practice*, where I showed how the structural analysis of the exchange of gifts as described by Lévi-Strauss omitted a very important dimension of the exchange of gifts – that is, the temporal gap between the moment of giving and the moment of receiving the counter-gift.[3] I don't know if you remember the argument: Lévi-Strauss showed that Mauss had offered a naïve analysis of exchange in the sense that it was only a scholarly transcription of the indigenous experience. Mauss's description turned the exchange of gifts into a discontinuous series of acts of generosity: I give as if I shall never receive anything in return, and the recipient returns a gift as if he had never received anything, and so on. And in a famous analysis Lévi-Strauss showed that this semblance of irreversibility concealed a structure of reversibility, an *a priori* model whereby the donor is assured of receiving in return because the very mechanism of exchange implies that there is no gift without a counter-gift, and the counter-gift attracts a gift, and so on.[4] I pointed out simply that these two apparently contradictory analyses are not contradictory at all: in reality, both are true. The donor can make his gift as if not expecting a return even though a model that obeys the logic of reversibility governs his act, which enables the exchange of gifts to be experienced as described by Mauss – whereas in reality it needs the time lag that Lévi-Strauss describes. In almost all societies, there are two rules: you never give back exactly the same thing as you received, and you don't give back immediately – moreover, giving back immediately would be precisely giving back the very same thing that you had received. This model erases the gap, the temporal aspect. In fact mechanist models typically tend to abolish time, which would justify us applying to them Bergson's critique of science as destructive of the essential – that is, of time.[5] In this particular case, I think that the economic model of exchange eliminates the essential – that is, the disjunction of the two experiences that is made possible, among other things, by the fact that they are not simultaneous.

(I need to open an important parenthesis: I think that scientific work often uses a simple effect of simultaneity to enable us to grasp the model: all the operations that the researcher performs when he draws schemas and establishes chronologies or genealogies consist in rendering simultaneous certain things that are only viable because they are successive. There are things that are so full of contradictions that they would be unbearable if they were simultaneous and are only bearable because they happen in separate phases, moments and places, and because nobody is there to act the Leibnizian God able to totalise things that are not totalisable. This is an illustration of something that I keep repeating: reflecting on the nature of scientific practice always means also reflecting on what makes the difference between scientific practice and practical practice.)

In this particular case, the distance between the donor and the experience of the analyst is crucial: if things happened as the analyst says, they would not work. So it is very important in the human sciences to make models that include the conditions of functioning of the models. There have always been retrograde and obscurantist debates comparing the human sciences with the natural sciences. I think that the analyses that invoke the specificity of the human sciences are in general very archaic and serve to defend the spiritual *point d'honneur* of humanity or the interests of the philosopher reflecting on the human sciences. The real point of difference between the human sciences and the natural sciences lies in the aspect that I have just mentioned: the human sciences are sciences like the others but have to include in their model the fact that real life does not conform to the model. These are simple things but they are important: to borrow from what Marx said of Hegel, we should not confuse the things of logic with the logic of things.[6]

In other words, the fundamental anthropological error – my lectures are in fact a long variation on this theme – consists in placing inside the minds and practices of agents the models that we have to construct in order to understand their practice. We should understand that, to understand these practices, we need to construct things that explain the truth of practice but are not contained in the truth of practice. In fact people live exchange objectively, in the way that Lévi-Strauss says, but it needed Lévi-Strauss to discover this truth that people are unaware of or, more often, prefer not to know. If I have time, as I hope I will, you will see that, in the case of art, this distinction is extremely important because what makes the sociology of art difficult (especially for people like intellectuals for whom art is their religion) is that it objectifies things that are antithetical to the experience of the work of art. This is why the sociologist is denounced both as the clumsy character who says what everyone knows already and as someone telling lies and talking rubbish; he is reproached both with telling lies and with repeating the obvious. If he is reproached with both at once, it is because he says things that in a way everyone knows but does not wish to know. This would be true also for the exchange of gifts: as soon as you work on any particular society, you will find that there are some proverbs saying that nothing is finer than people's generosity and others saying there is nothing worse than receiving a gift; in other words, a lucid vision does exist. On the work of art – as I shall show you – sociology carries out work that in a way nobody else does, especially not artists.

The deferred profits of disinterestedness

As I return to my argument, you will find that I have not deviated from my line at all. I was speaking of a temporal gap, since after twenty or thirty years Beckett's profit is the equivalent of what it is for some other writers in the space of a single year. The most disinterested businesses, the avant-garde enterprises that produce for a market they have to create themselves, take the risk of never retrieving the funds they have invested, but they can, in a certain number of statistical cases, earn similar or even greater profits – think of the classics: if Racine had earned royalties . . . It remains the case that these absolutely fantastic profits figure in a deferred and therefore different form. The acts that produce these deferred profits can be experienced as radically disinterested. I would even say that they could only earn these deferred profits if they are really experienced as disinterested: disinterestedness is one of the conditions of success in this economy of disinterest. This being so, the difference between the theatre, which reaps its rewards much more quickly, and poetry, which brings in very little but will bring in a lot in the long run, or between the immediately profitable novel bought at the station to read on the train and the avant-garde novel that sells thirty copies in its first year – as is often the case for the avant-garde novel – but then has a rising curve of sales, consists in a temporal gap which is absolutely vital because it makes all the difference to the author's experience. This is what allows the avant-garde author to radically despise the best-selling author. All the logic of the field is based on this opposition.

This detour is important for understanding what I wanted to say the other day when I was opposing an economic economy to the anti-economic economy of art. The different genres – to take only the three principal ones: theatre, fiction and poetry – are then fundamentally distinct from each other in terms of the profits that they earn and the ways in which they earn them. The theatre brings in large economic profits with a relatively limited and bourgeois public; the novel brings in large profits, but with a broad public, and it earns a very large profit, equivalent to that earned by the theatre, only on condition that it reaches out beyond the bourgeois public. I remind you of one of the propositions that I introduced last time: the autonomy of the field of production is always a relative autonomy. Principles of evaluation external to the field continue to function within the field, even if retranslated in euphemised and disguised forms: the value attributed to a success depends on the size of the public, but the size of the public indicates the social quality of the public. There is a feeling, although it is not explicitly formulated, that as the public grows so the social quality of the clientele declines, and so the value of the consecration bestowed by purchase of the work diminishes. Consequently, an art form such as the novel, which can earn economic profits only by enlarging its clientele and reaching out to a very vast public (which, according to Christophe Charle's analyses, includes the top of the working classes for certain novels by Zola), contains for the producer the threat of discredit, if it is true, as I have argued, that there is this negative correlation between the amount of economic profit and the amount of symbolic profit. The whole problem of the novel will be that it has large profits and a large public, whereas the theatre has large profits but not a very large public. The novel has a large public, but one that is suspect. Poetry, however, is perfect in every respect: it has neither profits nor public, and therefore can reap only deferred rewards.

The ambivalent profits of the market

We should take this analysis further. I think that the comparison between the genres is interesting (just think of the status of painting), and obviously what I am saying helps us to understand what artists of the different genres say about their relation to the public; when they speak of the public, they express this contradiction. For example, the avant-garde painter today can be satisfied with five clients if three of them are museums; and this means that he has no need to deliver apocalyptic tirades on the masses or the people: in any case his prices are so high . . . We see then that an avant-garde painter will not develop the same fantasy of success and the same professional ideology as an avant-garde novelist. He can dream of selling a single work, whereas a novelist, however clever (and there are some), cannot live off the sales of five signed copies. The very different economies of cultural products are retranslated into totally different relations to the profession, the critics, the public and the market.

This logic is well explained in Raymond Williams's famous analyses in *Culture and Society*: he shows how the English poets developed their Romantic ideology of the charismatic poet as a reaction to their confrontation, however imaginary, with the market.[7] The analysis is in fact more subtle and detailed, but I will give you the outline: he shows that the representation of the artist besieged by the masses, forced to construct a charismatic persona and capable of fighting against the surrounding forces trying to absorb him, is constructed in parallel with the development of an anonymous market and develops at the same time as the writer's dependence, no longer on a few chosen sponsors assuring his livelihood but on an anonymous market that assures his livelihood only if he sells well to a number of strangers, whose approbation becomes more and more dubious the more numerous they become. The antinomic relation to the public, which you might see as cynicism, is written into this particular form of profit, as described in rigorously economic terms.

If you will allow me the axiom according to which there is a negative correlation between symbolic profit and strictly economic profit, you will see how the different genres, given that they yield profits of very different value, will lead to inverse hierarchies. Using these analyses, we can even understand something bizarre: the theatre, which earns large profits with a relatively large public and is socially inferior from the artists' point of view (but less so than the novel), will procure a form of bourgeois consecration. In my diagram it is situated on the upper right,[8] on the side where I indicated the Académie française, the side where the writers earn major economic profits, that are relatively unembarrassing and are accompanied by rewards from the bourgeoisie and the state – that is, the forms of official consecration whose paradigm is the Académie française. For poetry, things are clear, since there are no profits. With a few rare exceptions (it does happen that a poet such as François Coppé, for example, writes verse drama, which means that they become playwrights), poets are positively rewarded from the point of view of the anti-economic economy found in the field of restricted production, and they are therefore consecrated, which may allow them at the end of their lives – as I shall explain in a moment – to find themselves in the Académie française alongside the dramatists. As for the novelists, especially the naturalists, they present quite a special problem, since they can achieve very large profits, which is a fault, for they are dubious profits, obtained by going too far: these novelists transgress social boundaries and, especially with the naturalist novel, reach the upper echelons of the lower classes. Which explains – here I cut some corners – all of Zola's problems with the Académie française, where he was often a candidate but always beaten by dramatists or psychological novelists, and the like.

The naturalist novel could have no kind of legitimacy: neither the pure legitimacy accorded to art for art's sake – that is, art for the artist, the art whose sole market is its competitors – nor 'bourgeois' academic legitimacy; whence the need for this art to found a new legitimacy, and it is no accident that this fiction claims to be popular, using a common strategy of stigmatised groups, raising the stigma as their banner. Success, previously a flaw, becomes subject to approval and praise when, instead of being a vulgar success, it is a popular success. There is a whole struggle to replace the vulgar with the popular, the popular being a select form of the vulgar. (This might cause us to reflect and discuss: the fact of calling 'vulgarisation' 'popularisation' changes everything. Depending on who does the vulgarisation . . . we should think about this, but it would take me too far from my argument.)

The subversion of the rules of the field

This ambiguous and contradictory position of the novel is written into its economy and, briefly, Zola's very complex strategy is characterised by the fact that, being in a central position in the field, he tried to hold together two normally self-exclusive things – that is, on the one hand, a sort of literary and political dignity which meant that he could not be dismissed as a vulgar novelist, like the regional or populist novelists, and, on the other hand, an undoubtedly popular public.[9] It is no accident that naturalism was at the heart of a particularly violent struggle.

I think – as I shall try to show later – that naturalism was a specific revolution. As I have already argued, one of the properties of fields lies in the fact that they are a site of struggles for subversion. All fields are places of revolution: there are as many forms of revolution as there are fields; there are for instance revolutions in mathematics and physics. These partial revolutions bear the same relation to general revolution as each relatively autonomous field does to the field of fields. This is important: most often partial revolutions within a field are presented as general revolutions because there are people in these fields whose interest is to universalise their revolution. I have said it time and again: there are specific revolutions (I think that the use of this word is absolutely justified) – that is, actions tending to subvert and overthrow the balance of power that constitutes a given space, as well as the structure of distribution that structures this space. One problem with these specific revolutions is that they can, under certain conditions, become general revolutions. I shall not elaborate on the problem of the relation between revolutions in a more or less autonomous sub-field and revolutions that gradually take hold of all the fields – that can wait until next year. But I shall have it in mind.[10]

To return to Zola, I think that he represents a specific kind of revolution in so far as he introduces a principle of legitimation that is not recognised by any of those who dominate according to the principles of legitimation that are dominant in the field: he is recognised neither by the proponents of pure economics nor by the upholders of the bourgeois economy. He seems to scandalise symbolist poets as much as he does bourgeois dramatists. Huret's enquiry is very typical: you have only to note the number of references to Zola, who is the public enemy at the heart of the investigation.[11] The enquiry in fact is asking, 'What do you think of Zola?', and everyone speaks and situates themselves in relation to Zola. This is because Zola introduced something that profoundly subverted the economy of the field of cultural production. He introduced a principle of legitimation that was to discredit the proponents of art for art's sake, since they lacked a popular public, dismissing them as hard-hearted, self-regarding, gratuitous, useless and empty, while the others were dismissed as bourgeois.

This partial subversion had some impact on the naturalist revolution: it was a failed revolution. To refer to the diagram: we had poetry, Zola's novels and the bourgeois theatre, and then the psychological novel – called the 'analytical novel' at the time – whose subjects came from the bourgeois class, made its appearance. Referring to the Huret enquiry once more, the strengths and weaknesses of the psychology of chambermaids and priests are compared on two occasions, as well as the question as to whether it is more interesting to describe a washerwoman or a duchess. The debate, which is formulated very naïvely in these terms, raises the question of the quality of the work according to the social quality of the public: Is the value of the work not equivalent to the social value of its public? This polemical debate grasps something essential – that is, the kind of correspondence, due to an absolutely extraordinary series of homologies, that constitutes the complexity but also the simplicity of these fields: the social qualities of the characters, the authors (voicing their characters) and the publishers will match, and the heroines of the psychological novelists will bear the same relation to Zola's heroines as the psychological novelists and their publishers do to Zola and his editors.

The psychological novelists come from symbolism, bringing with them a specifically symbolic capital, earned on the terrain of poetry. They lose some of their capital by entering the inferior field of the novel, but they import into this inferior genre a capital borrowed from a superior genre, so that they enhance the genre and make it tolerable to a homologous public in the ruling class: this novel will have a public equivalent to that of the bourgeois theatre. The novel will have a bourgeois public, whereas it was unthinkable – according to Huret's enquiry, once again – for there to be salon conversations discussing Zola's *Earth*, which had created a scandal and provoked the rejection of the naturalist school by the bourgeois, with its descriptions that shocked intellectual opinion. The psychological novel on the other hand was a product that respected the bourgeois milieu and its values, as was the case with the bourgeois theatre, whose circumscribed but faithful (as long as its values were respected unconditionally) audience was one of the unspoken causes of its success. Obviously what we are saying here is limited to what we can say on the plane of the literary field, for at the same time there was the end of the Empire, with the Commune, and so on, and we might say that Zola failed because at the same time in the political field there was the Commune, etc. I shall return to this absolutely crucial problem of the coincidence between fields.

Time-scales and 'personalities'

To get to the heart of the matter, it seems to me that the oppositions between the genres can be understood on the basis of my propositions concerning the economic logic of the field and the economies specific to each of the genres. Starting out from analyses of the specific economies, we understand that the opposition between the two economies that I described three lectures ago – the ordinary economic economy whose law is 'business is business' and the anti-economic economy of the field of restricted production – started to take the form of an opposition between the genres, largely between poetry and the theatre. What I started to describe rather clumsily last time is the sort of schism that would occur within all the genres: in the theatre, between bourgeois and avant-garde theatre; in fiction, with the oppositions between the psychological, naturalist and regional novels and the novel of manners. Concerning the novel of manners, there is a splendid text by Flaubert, who tells his friend Feydeau rudely, 'I have been trying to save you from decline for years',[12] as Feydeau gradually succumbed to the risqué novel, a kind of elegant pornography. The novel of manners is a lesser breed of the psychological novel.

Little by little, the opposition between the two economies that was originally articulated between poetry and theatre came to be mirrored in a way within each of the genres: in the guise of the opposition between a noble, bourgeois novel that became the Proustian novel (I must avoid anachronisms; I've already confused the periods too much) and an ignoble novel, a novel that sells in the market place. In the theatre there also came a break, with a right-wing theatre of moral conformity and an avant-garde theatre where the producer becomes the main character. At the same time the space became structured in a simple way between two oppositions: a principal, horizontal opposition on the one hand, setting poetry, the experimental avant-garde novel and theatre against their bourgeois rivals, and a second opposition, at right angles to the former, between – as I shall explain in a moment – the left bank and the right bank. I refer you again to my article 'The production of belief',[13] where I analysed the painters according to whether their galleries were situated on the left bank or the right bank (where the painters were more well-to-do).

All the indications converge to show that there are two economies: on the one hand, long-term economies – that is, non-economic economies ('I sell thirty copies in the here and now, but I will have salvation in the beyond'); on the other hand, a short-term economy, with books commissioned and written in response to demand, completely subject to wage labour – in fact, a universe answerable to economic analysis. It would be a mistake to say that it is no longer literature, and I shall not forget to place it in my analysis of the intellectual field. As soon as somewhere people produce following the logic of art for art's sake, as soon as institutions recognise this logic, and as soon as there are all sorts of sanctions, the producers for a wider public cannot help feeling that, in this perspective, their lives are crippled compared to those of the producers for a restricted public. I am prepared to try the experiment tomorrow: if we could ask a television producer to get all these producers round the table together, I think that we would be able to predict their attitudes quite easily – the producers for a wider public cannot ignore the producers for a restricted public, who can, however, pretend to ignore their rivals. I shall not return to this point, but I think that it was important to recall it.

This then is the kind of space that we find, and the structure of the literary and artistic field is constituted by this double opposition, which is at once the structure of the field at a given moment and the principle for change. This is important for those who keep in mind the opposition between structure and history. In fact the principle of the structure itself is the very principle of the field. The description that I made of the state of the field around the 1880s corresponded therefore to a phase of transition. There will be, generally speaking, two economies face to face: one ordinary economy and one anti-economic economy. There will be two time-scales: a short one, for a type of economy with a rapid turnover, a life expectancy of six months per book, which supposes a certain kind of bookseller, and press attachés, because they are short-lived products which need to be sold quickly; and an economy which counts on the long run, with long-term returns on book sales, and supposes a different type of investor and bookseller. This is another law of the fields – I keep repeating it, but it is very surprising to see it at work so often in the space of publishers.[14]

Because there is a field, we can always postulate that there will be a homology between publishers and authors: avant-garde publishers will be related to arrière-garde publishers as avant-garde producers are to arrière-garde producers. For example, Fabiani shows in his work on philosophers that Félix Alcan, the founder of the publishing house of the same name, showed affinities with the authors that he published (École normale graduates, and so on);[15] he possessed properties that helped him enter into the logic of an anti-economic economy, accepting which supposed a strong symbolic investment.[16] We could describe the time-scales of these two spaces, and, in so far as our temporal structures and our relation to the future are among the most fundamental structures of what we call 'personality', they would correspond to quite different personalities: long-term investors as opposed to short-term investors, for instance.

Clients and rivals: the mediation of the education system

Obviously, if we consider the struggles of this period from the point of view of the public, the people who are on the side of the pole of restricted production have a shared interest with the young, with students and bohemia. They also include their rivals among their public, for – an important point that I want to repeat – the more autonomous a market, the more the producers have no clients but their challengers; this is true for strongly esoteric scientific milieux but also for the majority of avant-garde literary or artistic experiments. What is more, these progressive positions often have students and the young as their public, which is one of the channels of mediation through which the field of cultural production is dependent on changes in the education system. The education system is one of the most important forces of mediation to understand what happens in the literary field, for two reasons.

Firstly, it can be the source of a profound change in the producers' mode of production. The change represented by the naturalist novel is thus linked to the formidable growth in secondary schooling pouring out onto the market a mass of producers coming from milieux that were not previously included in the education system and did not subscribe to the conventional values. As they were hostile to the dominant values, they accepted things considered dishonourable (this was the period when the press was beginning to take shape). Major changes in the field of production, especially changes creating a specific revolution, are often linked to important social changes mediated through changes in the education system. We might think for example of changes in the history of German philosophy. This very general model enables us to understand many things: I think that the history of ideas is beholden to the history of the education system in this respect.

Secondly, the education system also intervenes by producing the consumer. Ian Watt has written a classic book on the birth of the novel in England, relating it to the schooling of women.[17] This very fine book shows the link between the genre of fiction and the emergence of a new public of female consumers. To anticipate the development of my argument a little, I think that the struggles that occur within the field between, for example, those who want to start a revolution by imposing a new style of writing and those who support tradition depends to a great extent on the public: it is the public that decides. True ideas have no intrinsic power, as Spinoza said:[18] even in the purest and most scientific of scientific struggles, truth cannot impose itself unaided. It is always good to remember that the history of science is paved with discoveries ignored and discoveries discovered in retrospect, largely because it was in the interest of the scientists' rivals to misunderstand them. As I said just now, this is because the market condemns producers to have their rivals as clients, and all the more so, the more autonomous the producer. The sanction of the market does not always conform to what it should be if the law of the market were the law of the truth. That being said, the fact of having only your rivals for clients is also a fantastic control mechanism: the fact that your rival has the wherewithal to understand but is not motivated to understand (or in any case is not motivated to sympathise without understanding) is a protection against charisma, magic, and all the effects of this kind.

(Another parenthesis in passing, but I do believe that it is important. We might judge these two propositions to be normative, but they are presented here in terms that treat them as positive propositions. I don't know if you see what I mean: I have taken two laws of the functioning of the scientific field, and everything derives from properties that you might call normative. You could say 'Through its very logic, the more autonomous the scientific field, the more resistance it offers to the effects of symbolic and charismatic imposition.' This is important because a sociology that strives to be positive is often understood to be enunciating normative propositions. Although these propositions can sound normative, it still remains the case that, when they are engendered in conformity with the specific logic of scientific production, they are not normative; they report the logic of functioning of the field. To continue for a moment with the scientific field: if there is progress towards truth in the scientific field, it is because the scientific struggle is becoming more and more scientific: the scientific field is continually becoming more autonomous, entry to the field is becoming increasingly demanding, the weapons needed to triumph in the field are becoming increasingly sophisticated, the mechanisms required to demolish your opponent's theory are increasingly subtle and specialised. This could be better expressed, but there is then a progress of reason that is founded in a social logic that has nothing to do with reason. This means that I do not need a rationalist postulate in order to ground my judgement, as long as under certain conditions in certain fields at certain moments the logic of change follows the direction of a superior reason. There is then a progress that we can acknowledge without accepting any kind of idealist philosophy. I am going to return to my lecture plan, because here I think that I have really wandered off the track [*laughter*]. To conclude on this point, I have said that this progress of reason is not a Hegelian type of linear progress but one depending on conditions and terms of entry that have changed. End of parenthesis.)

Generations and revolutions

The emergence of a new public can help to change the balance of power in the field, but the principle of the efficiency of the public can only be found in the public itself; the specific principle of efficiency (that is specifically intellectual, cultural or artistic) of the public can only be found in the logic of the field itself at a certain moment. This means for example that we need to understand what was taking place between Zola and Bourget, for instance, to understand that the emergence on the education market of less well-educated social strata who can find fulfilment in what Zola has to offer gives a positive sanction to Zola and reinforces his position in triggering a revolution. That being said – and to return to what I was saying before – Zola can only win this race if he knows how to profit from his success (he needs to be able to say: 'It is not *vulgar*, it is *popular*'), since the others will want to discredit him. Approval by a public is a very ambiguous thing: one kind may grant prestige, another may bring disrepute. This means that naïve statements of relation such as 'the emergence of new social strata produced Zola who expressed them' are virtually meaningless.

We shall then find an opposition between two economies, two time-scales and two publics, and here the student public plays an important part. I think for example that we would not understand a word of what has happened in the intellectual field in France since 1945 if we did not take into account the changes in the education system and its twin effects on producing the producers on the one hand and producing the consumers on the other, as I have shown. Obviously this does not mean that they can be considered to be determining factors: they are not a necessary but they are an enabling cause; in other words, a certain type of struggle will develop and allow positions having very little chance of success in the internal struggles – or only in the very long term – to surface as something that at least needs discussing, that has to be discussed because it is backed by social forces.

Of course this varies considerably according to the nature of the genres. I was considering the genres just now as economic affairs, but we also need to consider them from the point of view of the subjects they discuss and the ways in which they speak of the social world. One of the pertinent oppositions in this respect – I add this briefly since it helps us gain a fuller understanding – is the one that arose between theatre and music, which is to a certain extent much more liable to solicit a 'transclass' affiliation because it does not speak of the social world; it is the most socially negative art.[19] In the logic of the construction of our model, this degree of explicit or implicit reference to the social world is an important property. I have described this opposition enough for now, and I shall not continue.

The second opposition, relatively independent of the first, may be observed within the sub-field of production for producers. It can be found within each genre: there will be a consecrated avant-garde theatre and an avant-garde avant-garde theatre, a consecrated avant-garde novel and an avant-garde avant-garde novel, and so on. Basically it is an opposition deriving from the degree of specific consecration and seniority in the field between the young avant-gardists and the old avant-gardists. Rémy Ponton was the first to have drawn attention to this property, with poetry providing the richest ground for its study, since it is here that were constituted this model of permanent revolution and this idea of an artistic generation and school, etc. With poetry, there is also a longer time-scale and there are more revolutions. Rémy Ponton notes that this model of permanent revolution opposes people who are distinguished as 'neo-' (new schools are in fact most often called 'neo-': 'neo-naturalists', 'neo-Marxists', etc.). This opposition between the 'paleo-' and the 'neo-' is almost meaningless from the point of view of formal content: in an article on the Parnassian movement[20] Ponton shows that the motivating principle of the opposition between the discourse of the most and the least specifically consecrated people can be reduced to the opposition between the 'young buck' who wants to be noticed – Zola speaks contemptuously of the young symbolists in these terms: for him, they do not exist or are only pretentious pretenders – and the corrupt *parvenu*, the 'traitor' who has made concessions to the material world.

This is where the opposition between heresy and orthodoxy and the logic of the return to the sources of purity come to fruition: the old are confronted with what they once stood for when they confronted their even older seniors. As Huret's enquiry once more shows, this surfaces in individual minds when the older generation says in its defence: 'They are doing to us what we did to the others', 'They are accusing us of doing what we accused the others of doing.' This is not an opposition between two visions of the world, between art and money, artist and bourgeois, disinterest and interest, purity and impurity, political indifference and political commitment, against all political self-interest or interested politics (the Légion d'honneur, for instance). This is not the relevant opposition, although re-enacting it may have its objective grounds and suit the agents' strategy; as I was saying just now, the Académie française, for example, in the period of the 1880s studied by Charle could include people who had joined it after very different careers.

We should then distinguish between two oppositions that underlie two struggles for change. The opposition that I am discussing now is one that engenders permanent revolution, for the breaks defining the changes of literary generations can be extremely frequent. People can in fact belong to two different literary generations only ten years apart – it quite often happens that two literary generations are separated by less than ten years. In a very different perspective, an American author (whose name I forget) studied the emergence of the idea of generation in the 1880s and the growing influence of this manner of thinking in terms of generation,[21] and it is important to note that the birth of the theme of generation, or the emergence of a theoretical construction of generation, coincides with the generalisation in objective reality of a structure of division that was until then reserved for poetry but became that of the whole literary field, and thereby became a system for the student world. This opposition according to artistic generation is of a very different order from the opposition between the artist and the bourgeois. It opposes incumbents to pretenders and orthodoxy to heresy; the law driving the change is the permanent revolution that operates within the limits of the field in the name of the principles of the field and the fundamental law of the field that condemns success. The problem of the initial accumulation (How do people who have nothing start to possess something?) arises in every field, but the law of the literary field is that you should possess nothing. It is an anti-economic economy where the wretched and dispossessed can make a virtue of necessity. They can say that they have chosen to possess nothing and to exploit their wretchedness as a weapon against the well-provided, the consecrated who have more readers – as their sales numbers rise – and who have already won signs of consecration.

Another property noted by Ponton is that this opposition, having no formal content other than the formal structure of 'before' and 'after' or 'veteran' and 'newcomer', is quite vacuous; the invectives that the authors exchange are based on formal oppositions that are quite empty. In fact the consecrated say that the young avant-gardists are obscure, which is a positive property, since the anti-economic law condemns the producers to produce their own market. Consequently they will produce products structured according to the categories of perception that they must produce. In other words, they must produce their consumers, which takes time; the consumers see red, they don't understand; as seen by the Parnassians, the symbolists are indeed obscure. The 'clear' will be opposed to the 'obscure', 'clear' in fact meaning 'bourgeois' ('clear enough to appeal to the bourgeois'). One of the elementary strategies will consist in transforming the effects of structure into effects of strategy. I think that it is possible to explain the essence of what takes place by using the entirely formal structure that opposes the newcomers lacking capital to the consecrated incumbents.

Modes of ageing and eternalisation

Among the properties that oppose these two poles of the intellectual space, it would be important to analyse the modes of ageing. The authors and their works do not age in the same way at the different poles of the field. Social ageing is defined by the specific law of the changes in the corresponding social universe; social ageing and this law of change are obviously the same thing twice over. Briefly: ageing will be the product of this struggle. Every time that a claimant manages to gain recognition and make a mark, they will relegate to the past those who preceded them. Every time that a school manages to gain recognition, it relegates the preceding school to the past. The time-scale then is a struggle. The history of the field is the struggle itself, and there is no history outside this struggle. It is the old formula: 'History is the history of the class struggle', but only if we take the saying in a very banal sense, which is, however, the sense given by Marx (he said that there had always been class struggles throughout history, which is not strictly true, but never mind . . .).[22] All that I am saying is that it is conflict that makes history: it is by struggling to relegate to the past the people who themselves struggled to relegate others to the past that I make a space, and therefore a time, the very time of this space.

The consecrated authors struggle to be eternal, to last forever, to become classics, or at least to avoid being downclassed. They struggle to pass from being downclassed (which means absent from history, time and the field) to the status of classic, which, being both dated and transhistorical, is one of the proofs of eternalisation, since a classic author remains an object of conflict. The education system is the site of the eternalisation of the classics, which, as the word implies, are linked to the social classes. But the education system, where academic celebration endows the works with a rather special eternity, is the writers' inferno, and there is another form of existence more sought after by the people who struggle in this space: it consists in existing eternally as a subject of conflict in the field – Marx, for instance, lives on as a subject of conflict in these struggles. I often quote this phrase 'To quote is to bring back to life';[23] every time that we quote someone, we resuscitate them, we bring them back to life, since being alive in this field is to be a subject of conflict and continue to participate in the struggle or arbitrate between struggles. This struggle has its own logic and time-scale: we see in passing that the fields have the property of having a structural duration, a time that is their own and that is nothing less than their law of change. If, for example, nothing happened for a period of time, if fifty years passed without any new school being created, people would not grow old; they would be provisionally eternalised, they would remain in their position, still dominant. As I was saying just now, the opposition between young and old, paleo- and neo-, is an opposition between something overtaken and relegated to the past and something still active and operational. My analysis has been rather hasty and inexplicit, but it is developed further in the article I have already mentioned, 'The production of belief', where I describe this specific time-scale of the field. I shall not repeat these rules, which are closely linked to the opposition between the long run and the short run.

Overthrowing for the sake of overthrowing

Social agents are historical agents – that is, agents who can relate consciously to history. According to Marx's oft-cited example of modern revolutionaries re-enacting the Roman revolution,[24] the writers struggling today are eternally re-enacting the literary revolutions of the past, for example the battle of *Hernani*. An effect of the historicity of the field of struggles is the fact that we know that to make our mark we have to have a revolution, we have to overthrow. In the struggles within the field, the incumbents opposed the pretenders, denouncing the aim to overthrow for the sake of overthrowing, and this started as early as the 1880s. It is in fact the eternal problem of privation or rejection: to those who have nothing and draw strength from their weakness, it is always possible to say: 'If you have nothing it is perhaps because you are worth nothing.' For the people over here at the avant-garde pole, one strategy would be to say, 'You are old, you are out of date', and the dominant and consecrated would reply, 'You are trying to overthrow for the sake of overthrowing.' For example, the great increase in the number of schools in the 1880s, the emergence of an abundance of neo-styles, seems to me very striking in that it represents the practical effect of a sort of consciousness awakening to the law of change in the field as a place in which you change things by moving them and overthrowing them and by establishing the emergence of a new manner of being or doing. And the consecrated authors over here will say: 'It is not a genuine overthrow, they are not overthrowing in order to say something new, you need to have something to say if you want to overthrow, they are just overthrowing for the sake of overthrowing.' This is what I would call the *Tel Quel* effect . . .[25]

That being said, people who are contemporaries are nonetheless situated differently in time. One of the great problems in analysing these phenomena is what we call the question of generations: people who from the point of view of literary generations are not contemporary were biological contemporaries; contemporary people can live in different times. If the law of change is perpetual overthrow and relegation to the past, the corresponding model of change is not far from the model of fashion. There exist for example in painting all sorts of neo-realisms, and one problem is to know what makes the difference between the grandfather and the grandson (who takes on the name of the grandfather), between degree-zero realism and realism as recurrence. The profane viewer who does not see the difference between one neo-realism and another kind of realism scandalises the specialists. A field endowed with such a law of change supposes producers who internalise history into their own production – it is Merleau-Ponty's metaphor of the telephone number: when you dial 6 after dialling 3 and 2, it is not the same as dialling it after 1 and 2. The historical time of the artistic field is of this nature: the recurrence is never a true repetition. In 'The production of belief' I quote an extraordinary text by Duchamp.[26] It's a shame that he's called Duchamp [the field] . . . [*laughter*], but he is the first artist who understood in practice the laws of the field; he spends his time explaining these laws and people's denials of them to critics who only half-understand them.[27] He wrote a brilliant piece on these recurrences that are never identical (he says they are like double-barrelled guns). He makes a fine analysis of this property of fields in virtue of which history never repeats itself, because it is a history whose very nature is non-repetition.

We find another very interesting example in the naïve painters. Le Douanier Rousseau had a whole history behind him when he entered the field, and he became a sort of painter-object:[28] he set off to do something without knowing what it was. The other painters treated him like a plaything, organising bogus consecration ceremonies, for example. Rousseau was a sort of experimental character. He copied the paintings of academic realist painters and what he did took on a meaning that escaped him completely in a history of which he was unaware. In front of his own paintings he was like a spectator who, unaware of this history, cannot perceive them adequately – that is, historically. This is very important from the viewpoint of the sociology of perception of the work of art: in the artistic field you can only understand the works of the period $t + 1$ if you know all the history. You have to know that the painter in $t + 1$ has painted in relation to the painter who painted in t, who painted in relation to the painter painting in $t - 1$, who did the same in respect of $t - 2$; and if the painter painting in $t - 1$ paints like the one painting in $t - 2$ it is not the same, because he does it afterwards. I shall say no more about this, but I believe that it is important for understanding many things.

Orientating the self in the space of possibilities

I come to my last point, without being able to do it justice for want of time, although it is surely the most difficult and subtle point, which would require the most evidence (it deserves a better analysis than mine). What I have described up to now, while anticipating what I shall go on to say, is a space of positions, and ultimately I could have given the whole description without introducing the agents, the writers, and the like: everything takes place more or less between positions. What I have described – to return to the theoretical analysis that I gave of the notion of the field – is a space of positions and oppositions between the positions, a space of possible, antagonistic and incompatible positions so arranged that you could almost deduce from the positions what would be the stances adopted; thus you could draw on tracing paper the space of stances adopted and place it over this space of positions,[29] and say that the bourgeois theatre stands over to the right, or that it tends to support conformity and the moral order. So you can in a way predict from the positions alone the stances adopted without needing to refer to the agents who fill those positions. Now, as I said when I presented the notion of the field in the abstract, the field can be described both as 1) a space of positions whose structure matches the distribution of specific capital and as 2) a field of struggles to transform this space. I distinguish between these two descriptions – which are not at all incompatible – for reasons of method and theory, in order to maintain the material priority of the positions over the practices: it is in the space of positions that lies the explanatory principle of what people will do.

Having explained that, I come to the second phase of my explanation in terms of fields. Since this space is a space of possibilities, we cannot derive the stances from the positions as a simple mechanical reflection or a carbon copy: there is an important mediation through the habitus of the agents who inhabit the different positions. At the same time a fundamental question arises. You have to imagine the space organised like a game. There are people already playing there, and there are new people arriving at every moment, for example the young Flaubert, who has just finished his studies in Rouen. How will he enter the field? How does the field appear to the new entrant? Will his perception of the field depend on things that are not written into the field? For the field will in fact be perceived very differently by different people depending on their habitus. Given that the habitus is a general system of schemes of perception and appreciation that finds a particular terrain of application in art, it will function, to use a classic metaphor, like a set of lenses, and, seen through these spectacles, the same objective reality, the space of positions, will be perceived differently.

But, having said that, a problem arises. The statistical analysis undertaken by Rémy Ponton shows that there is in general a match between the properties of the agents inhabiting the lower positions and the properties of those positions. Positions that are socially lower will then welcome people who are lower; and, given two genres, one more bourgeois and the other more popular, we will always find the petit-bourgeois on the more bourgeois side. It is almost self-evident to associate the positions with the characteristics of the holders of those positions, but it is much to the credit of Ponton to have demonstrated it in detail. At a given moment there is a match between the positions and the holders of those positions. Briefly, in all periods, one position is related to another position as the holders of the first are to the holders of the second, and the more we enter into detail the more this can be verified – say, by taking three ordinary people in a small group in a very small sector. We might ask by what miracle this is achieved and how it comes to pass. It is not mechanical, and there are people out of place, outside their proper place, for example those who have a petit-bourgeois capital and who for a while (before being put in their place) write psychological novels.

How should we account for this match? If we think of the field as a field of forces that attracts the iron filings in a differential fashion, we can of course imagine that, the higher the origins of the people, the more they will resist the attraction of a lower pole – and in fact this is not entirely false. We are obliged to take into consideration the perception of the field that the social agents possess at any moment and have possessed at different strategic moments in their career. In other words, to account for the statistical relations observed for writers in the 1880s, you have to place yourself in that space. You start by analysing the properties of the positions using a certain number of objective criteria: the writers' professions, the genres they practise, their styles of writing, and so on. After the description of their employment, you make a description of their properties, with classic points such as social origins, father, grandfather, mother, son-in-law, and the like. Then you superimpose the two images; you see what matches and what does not – and they tend to match both *a priori* and *a posteriori*.

How has this encounter come about? This is where we run into complications. Unless we hypothesise a process of mechanical adaptation, we are obliged to ask how the different agents have been led to the position that they hold at a given moment in time, which may or may not be their definitive position. One of the difficulties with this analysis is that in certain positions we find people with very different dispositions, some being permanently in the position and others just passing through – and likewise in the social space. Among the people who are permanently there, some are there because they have been relegated there for good and others because it is truly their place of election.

Those who are only passing through are often there because they have made some blunder, because they have failed to use their practical common sense.

I think that I have now explained the essence of my model. To account for the relation observed at certain moments between the space of positions and the space of dispositions, we need to posit agents who are not all at the end of their journey but, rather, find themselves at different points in their trajectory which confront them with alternatives: after the baccalaureate, should they go for the arts faculty or for law (this was a very important choice in the nineteenth century)? Then, should they write fiction or poetry, naturalist novels or journalism? At every moment in their trajectory they are guided by something that is not full awareness but is a kind of obscure relation to themselves, a sense of orientation as a particular dimension of the feel for practice. It would be even better to speak of a feel for 'placing' – in the sense both of 'placing' a financial investment and of 'placing' yourself on the sports field, leading you to move to one position rather than another. The opposition between Paris and the provinces plays an enormous part in the history of art, but there is also the opposition between masculine and feminine and the opposition between different social origins: these will all be retranslated in terms of the specific logic of the field, through the mediation of this sense of placing.

To recapitulate once more, in simple terms: we need to have understood the notion of the field and the specific law of the field to know how the social origins will take effect. Usually scholars do exactly the opposite; they start out from some individual and their habitus. This is a mistake. In fact, you need to know what a field requires in terms of its general law in order to understand which elements of the class habitus will provide the payoff (payment is I think a very pertinent term) and what will be positively or negatively sanctioned. Let us suppose for example that Zola had triumphed: after this popular revolution, every popular habitus would gain a surplus value and, as we have seen in certain post-revolutionary situations, the social handicaps would be overturned for a time, and people might even (for a time) go so far as to put on popular accents. The value of what the newcomer has to offer will then depend on the field. Consequently, trying, as Escarpit did, to draw up tables and statistics of the number of sons of workmen or whatever down the ages and centuries is meaningless (at best the statistics do produce results here and there, but they would have to be interpreted at several mental removes). What is important is that, every time that the market and the field change, the benefit to a writer being, say, the son of a peasant farmer from the Quercy region[30] may be everything or nothing. One of the things at stake in the struggle among people in the field is to create a field where they are able to hold a dominant position. This is why the struggles in this field are absolutely mortal. They are mortal because what is at stake is designing a game where you are the winner. The mechanistic vision whereby social origins or position in the field determine the stances adopted is catastrophic, because it does not take the habitus into account.

Trajectory and habitus

In the model that I am offering, there are two things, the field and the habitus, and it is by knowing the laws of functioning of the field that we shall be able to understand what happens to the habitus. To take one out of a thousand examples: the example of Courbet, or of Champfleury, who is considered to be the theoretician of the realist novel. Courbet's biographers say that he would take on the appearance of a peasant and assume a Besançon accent (I could give more details, but as I am running out of time I will just tell you enough to enable you to take the analysis further yourselves).[31] It was in a particular field that Courbet became aware of his social origins and his provincial accent: it was in his relations with the other artists, the painters he met in the bars, that he heard his accent as an accent compared to non-accents, or accents that do not count as accents. Under these conditions he had no choice: there are only two possibilities – either lose your own accent or you accentuate it. Accentuating your accent is realism. But imagine that the others also go in for realism . . . [*silence*]. You cannot just make a simple correlation as the contemporaries of Champfleury and Courbet did: 'Yes it's easy for them, they are sons of peasants, they speak like peasants, so they do realism, they paint peasants and farm scenes, they paint with a heavy touch, like peasants.' In fact Courbet did act the peasant, and he fought in the Commune, but this was in a determined space.

One important thing that helps explain the specific efficiency of the habitus is the fact that people carry their habitus around with them; they are so tied up with it that they cannot shake it off – which gives it a mysterious quality. We need to make these theoretical analyses work in practice: the habitus is that part of capital that is incorporated. Now, as everyone knows, what is incorporated cannot easily be detached: one great difference between cultural capital and economic capital is this, that cultural capital (like linguistic capital) is incorporated, is embodied in its bearer. Since it is, as it were, grafted onto the skin of its bearer, this capital will be a living obstacle at every moment in the struggle to obtain a maximum return from capital. But what is interesting is the considerable importance that scientific or artistic struggles attach to the image of their opponents' habitus, in so far as it is revealed through their bodily *hexis*. One example (which once again ought to be developed) is the case of Ingres: Ingres was despised by almost everyone in his generation because he approached the Salon in an arrogant way, but more fundamentally because he had a formidably bourgeois habitus. He looked like a banker or one of the landed gentry, and in people's judgements of him there was a kind of permanent intuition of the social person apprehended by the sort of spontaneous character-reading that people use, which is in fact a spontaneous sociology. I think that, if later generations judged him very differently from the way his contemporaries did, it is particularly because posterity did not know the person physically (except through portraits), and so their judgement was socially neutral. This is an effect analogous to that of the translation: when Heidegger is translated into French you lose a lot of connotations that you can hear only in the German; he is dissocialised and becomes a philosophical author with no reference to the social world, whereas in fact he is full of it. Similarly, in the case of a dead author, posterity no longer feels the presence of a real person, as they have become reduced to a position in a space. In the case of Ingres, it became possible to rediscover him when the critics no longer saw him in person, and the qualities that went unnoticed by the contemporaries who opposed him because he was so unpleasant became visible.

I shall finish on this point, with a feeling of embarrassment: to understand what people are, at every moment of their career, you need to know their habitus. One of the difficulties is that, when we study the social history of painting or literature in the nineteenth century, we know how the story ends. This is a banal remark that the slightest reflection on history requires us to make. But there is a further point to make: for the purposes of a study, we can imagine that the positions held at successive dates (1880, 1890, etc.) are represented by a series of points. The genres will then start to move. Similarly, painter X, who was represented by one particular point, will be represented ten years later by a slightly different point. These gradual movements trace a career. They have nothing to do with biography. They are moves across a space that can be perceived only if you construct it – that is very important. Everything that I have said means that the biography of Hugo, for instance, is not a succession of chronological events but the series of the pertinent moves in the space; of course, as long as I have not constructed this space, I cannot construct Hugo's trajectory. These infinitesimally small displacements are very important. For example, Champfleury, who started as a populist, was finally decorated with the Légion d'honneur by Napoleon III in a kind of populist National Socialism *avant la lettre*. This is a fine career, and quite a classic one, that of the intruder in the intellectual field who, because of their relation to the artists of bourgeois origins who are more successful according to the laws of the field, is at first relegated to populism but, failing in populism as well, is driven towards national-populism, its aggressively right-wing version. Grasping these trajectories at different moments is to grasp the successive realisations of a kind of little programme that is the habitus, which is engaged in a constant relation with a field that is itself in a state of constant change. Some historians may be aware of the fact that Champfleury's realism was not the same at the beginning as at the end of his career, but often the historians know the final term, and that solicits a philosophy of history that prevents them from asking the extremely complicated questions of how and why at every moment and every turn the individual in question finds themselves in one position rather than another. We need to enquire into the development of the position and the perception that he could have of the state of the field at every point of decision: How at every moment did he perceive the space of possibilities? Thus someone who entered as a poet in the 1880s immediately saw two figures, Verlaine and Mallarmé, and had to compose himself in relation to them.

The impious dismantling of the fiction

To conclude, since this is the last session, I shall read you a passage from Mallarmé which asks a question that you have no doubt been asking yourselves:

> We know, captives of an absolute formula, that, indeed, there is only that which is. Forthwith to dismiss the cheat, however, on a pretext, would indict our inconsequence, denying the very pleasure we want to take: for that *beyond* is its agent, and even its engine, as I might say were I not loath to perform, in public, the impious dismantling of the fiction and consequently the literary mechanism, to display the principal part or nothing. But I venerate how, by a trick, we project to some forbidden – and thunderous! – height the conscious lack in us of what is bursting up there.
> Why should we do this?
> It is a game.[32]

Roughly speaking, Mallarmé is saying, in an obscure and hermetic manner – that is, in a way that does not say it – what I have been saying to you. He says why he does not want it said. He says that people would like there to be a transcendental, inaccessible beauty existing in the absolute, but that we must not be deluded: it is a lure. However, it is impossible to say this and deconstruct the literary mechanism. 'Forthwith to dismiss the cheat, however, on a pretext, would indict our inconsequence, denying the very pleasure we want to take': in other words, art is a fetish, it is the product of a collective work of creation, but to say so is a problem in so far as it destroys a pleasure that we wish to enjoy. This is the question that I have never stopped asking of the function of sociology: Is sociology something that destroys the pleasure of literature?

Appendix

Summary of lectures, published in the Annuaire du Collège de France

For the social scientist, the object of study is neither the (biological) individual nor the group as a set of individuals but the relation between these two manifestations of the social in bodies (or biological individuals) and in things; that is, the obscure, dual relation between the *habitus* – as a system of schemas of perception, appreciation and action produced by the socially instituted body – and the field as a system of objective relations produced by socially instituted things or mechanisms that are almost as real as physical things. It is also everything engendered by this relation – that is, social practices and fields when they appear in the shape of realities perceived and appreciated, and hence form fields of action and fields of struggle.

The relation between the habitus and the field is a two-way process: it is on the one hand a relation of conditioning, where the field structures the habitus, which is the product of the incorporation of the requirements of a field (or set of fields); it is also a relation of knowledge, with the habitus helping to constitute the field as a world that is endowed with meaning and value and is worth investing in. It follows from this that, on the one hand, a part of the relation of knowledge depends on the prior relation of conditioning that fashions the structures of the habitus. And, on the other hand, that science is in this case knowledge of a kind of knowledge and must make room for a sociologically orientated phenomenology of the experience of the field, or, more precisely, of its invariants (including, for example, analyses of everyday practice and doxic experience, as well as crisis and criticism) and of the variations in the relations between the different habitus and the different fields. In short, the specificity of social science lies in the fact that it takes as the object of its knowledge a reality that encompasses agents who take this same reality as the object of their own knowledge. We need, then, to elaborate a theory of practice as practice and also a theory of the mode of practical knowledge that this implies.

If we need to attempt an adequate description of the specific logic of practice and of practical knowledge, it is not in order to respect some spiritual point of honour but in order to produce scientific results: in fact, the confusion of scholarly knowledge and practical knowledge, as practised by the scholar or the agent, is at the root of a whole cluster of common errors, in sociology as much as in economics. Such an analysis, as conducted today in a quasi-independent manner by the most advanced currents in the social sciences – interactionism, ethno-methodology and cognitive anthropology – is made difficult, as so often in the social sciences, by formidable social obstacles: from the divine philosopher of the classic theory of knowledge to the magiste-rial sociologist of the classic theory of social knowledge, by way of all the theories of absolute knowledge, objective meaning and bad faith or false departures, contempt for what Alexander Baumgarten called the *gnoseologia inferior* has never abated. And yet, although it is certain that the sociologist must break with our spontaneous knowledge of the social, he must nonetheless include within his theory the knowledge in opposition to which he has constructed his scientific knowledge and which, come what may, continues to orientate people's practice. This supposes overturning the common arguments for and against in a way that the great objectivists who were responsible for the most decisive breaks with ordinary knowledge, Marx and Durkheim, were not able to accomplish. Apart from all these social obstacles, the science of *gnoseologia inferior* sets some extremely difficult problems: it means, in fact, establishing a science of the confused and the vague without being confused or vague oneself and without, as frequently happens, destroying the object of study with the tools that have usually been constructed in opposition to it – that is, in opposition to the inclina-tions of practical logic and the *perceptio confusa* that Baumgarten says we apply to the object (a problem that arises most acutely whenever we want to account for so-called natural logics).

The relation of practical knowledge is not a relation between a subject and an object constituted as such that sets some particular problem. With its incorporation of the social, the habitus participates in the social world and is directly present in the field that it inhabits, where it feels quite at home and free to grasp things instinctively as endowed with meaning and interest. Successful practical action may be described in the terms of Plato's *orthe doxa* (*Meno*, 98c): the opinion that is right or appropriate, the coincidence between disposition and position, between the game and the feel for the game, mean that the agent does 'what needs to be done' without positing it explicitly as a goal, without calculation or even awareness. The theory of the habitus allows us to escape a whole series of alternatives that usually constrain our reflections on action. For example, the alternatives of awareness and the object: the habitus as feel for the game produces actions adapted to the objective demands of the game without needing to posit them as such – that is, as ends, which would give the illusion of purposiveness. Likewise the alternatives of mechanism and purposiveness (under different guises): agents are neither things passively submitted to mechanisms nor subjects setting consciously calculated goals; in the ordinary course of practice they act neither under mechanical causal constraint nor in full awareness. Also the alternative of subjective teleology, which (like all theories of rational choice) implies utilitarian individualism, and objective teleology, whose best- or worst-case functionalism ascribes intentions and projects to personified collectivities. It is impossible to produce a theory of the practical mode of knowledge without producing by the same process a theory of the scholarly mode of knowledge, which, unless it is conceptualised as such, tends to contaminate the analysis of practice. This substitution of the scholarly subject for the practical subject is particularly visible in the philosophy of action to which most sociological or economic theories subscribe, explicitly or implicitly – that is, the representation of the agent as a rational calculator guided by his well-understood interest, capable of choosing and deciding perfectly lucidly, reducible in the last analysis to a utilitarian function and thus totally deprived of properties linked to an individual or collective history (precisely those that are housed in the habitus). We see in passing that this agent who acts with full awareness, measuring his expectations and investments against the odds of reaping benefits, is no more than the purposive version, based on the projection of the scholarly subject onto the active agent, of the agent mechanically led by causal constraints (which are also known only to the scholar). Beyond the imaginary anthropology of the rational calculator we encounter the frankly mythological, with theories of action and history that play games with language in order to be able to treat grammatical subjects as knowing subjects and personified collectivities, populating the social world with personified collectivities setting their own goals (e.g. the School eliminates . . ., the School serves to . . ., etc.).

The theory of the habitus explains why the purposive theory of the individual or collective rational or reasoning agent, although anthropologically false, may appear founded in empirically observable reality.

Individualist purposiveness, which assumes that action is determined by the conscious targeting of explicitly formulated ends, is a well-founded illusion: the feel for the game that anticipates and encourages the adaptation of the habitus to the needs and possibilities inscribed in the field assumes the appearance of a successful targeting of the future. Likewise, the structural affinity between habitus of the same class which, being the product of the same conditions and the same conditioning, can engender convergent and concerted practices independent of any conspiracy, explains the quasi-teleological phenomena that we may see in the social world (for instance, in the reactions of the professorial body to the increase in the number of teachers imposed by an increase in the number of students) and that we are often tempted to interpret either through the logic of individualist purposiveness (and conspiracy theory) or through organicist metaphors (such as *homeostasis*).

Having recalled the theoretical functions of the notion of the habitus and shown how the habitus only really operates and reveals its potential in relation to a field, we can attempt to establish the general properties of fields. To speak of the field is first of all to break with the substantialist mode of thinking, which is spellbound by the directly visible – individuals, groups or interactions, material and symbolic exchanges, etc. – and ignores the invisible relations between the positions, relations that are irreducible to the interactions in which they are displayed and which they structure. Sociology in its objectivist phase is an *analysis situs* – that is, an analysis of a space of objective relations between positions (or posts), relations that are relatively independent of the agents who occupy those positions and of their intentions and aims (and are also irreducible to a *network* of 'relations'). And we can show that a knowledge of positions constructed, and therefore of the global space within which each position is defined (as high, low or intermediate, dominant or dominated, etc.), entails a knowledge of the stances adopted by their inhabitants.

Apprehended at any given moment in time, the field appears to be a relatively autonomous space of possible forces that affect everyone who enters it – the structure of the field being no more than the structure of distribution of the specific kind of power at work in the field in question, with a position in the field being defined by the position held in this structure. As a field of possible forces, the field is also a field of possible actions and, in particular, a field of struggles aiming to preserve or transform the field of forces. In other words, it is the field as network of objective relations between positions of force that – through the intermediary of dispositions constituting the habitus

– founds and orientates the strategies that the occupants of these positions, whether singular agents or groups, whether on their own behalf or in the name of an institution, engage in their (patent or latent) struggles to defend or improve their position; in return, the struggles through which the agents strive to preserve or transform the network of objective relations are determined in their strength and direction by their position in the balance of power. Or, to be more concrete, by the trumps that they hold – that is, by the specific capital they can deploy as a source of strength in a given game.

Leaving for another year the study of the relations between the habitus and the field (which enables us to articulate the two definitions of the field as a field of forces and a field of struggles), the analysis of the relation between field and capital in its different guises (with the theory of power that this implies), and the search for the formal laws or the invariants of the functioning of the fields, we have concentrated on the analysis of a particular case, that of the literary and artistic field in France at the end of the nineteenth century (which will be the object of a forthcoming publication).

Notes

Editorial Note

1 Bourdieu, *Science of Science and Reflexivity* (Cambridge: Polity, 2004).
2 Bourdieu, *On the State: Lectures at the Collège de France, 1989–1992*, trans.
   David Fernbach (Cambridge: Polity, 2014); *Manet: A Symbolic Revolution:
   Lectures at the Collège de France, 1998–2000*, followed by an unfinished manuscript by Pierre and Marie-Claire Bourdieu, trans. Peter Collier and Margaret
   Rigaud (Cambridge: Polity, 2017).
3 The first volume appeared as *Classification Struggles: General Sociology,
   Volume 1*, trans. Peter Collier (Cambridge: Polity, 2018).
4 Bourdieu, *On the State*, pp. xi–xii.
5 [Where the sense is evident, I have translated the wording supplied without
   square brackets. – Trans.]

Lecture of 5 October 1982

1 See Bourdieu, 'La lecture de Marx ou quelques remarques critiques à propos
   de "Quelques remarques critiques à propos de *Lire le Capital*"', *Actes de la
   recherche en sciences sociales*, nos. 5–6 (1975): 65–79.
2 Bourdieu develops this point in his last lecture course at the Collège de
   France, published as *Science of Science and Reflexivity*, trans. Richard Nice
   (Cambridge: Polity, 2004).
3 In information theory, 'originality', as opposed to 'redundancy', is one of
   the parameters of the value of a piece of information (see Abraham Moles,
   Information Theory and Esthetic Perception (Champaign: University of Illinois
   Press, 1966).
4 Bourdieu may have a specific quotation in mind, or he may be thinking in
   general terms of the criticism that Socrates levels at the Sophists in a number of
   Plato's dialogues. In the *Phaedrus*, for example, he launches a long attack on
   a speech by the Sophist Lysias, where 'the various parts of his speech give the
   impression of being thrown together at random', and criticises other Sophists
   who saw that 'probability is to be rated higher than truth and who could make
   trivial matters appear great and great matters trivial simply by the forcefulness

of their speech, besides discovering how to clothe new ideas in fine old language and to refurbish old thoughts by novel treatment'. Plato, *Phaedrus and Letters VII and VIII*, trans. Walter Hamilton (Harmondsworth: Penguin, 1986), § 264, p. 78; §267, p. 84.

5 Karl Popper, *The Logic of Scientific Discovery* (London: Routledge, [1934] 2002).
6 Bourdieu develops this analysis in *The State Nobility*, trans. Lauretta C. Clough (Cambridge: Polity, 1966), in particular, pp. 131–2.
7 On this point, see Bourdieu, *Outline of a Theory of Practice*, trans. Richard Nice (Cambridge: Cambridge University Press, 1977), pp. 22–5.
8 The *Cours de linguistique générale* by Ferdinand de Saussure (1857–1913) was published in 1916 by two of his pupils, Charles Bally and Albert Sechehaye, using his notes. Subsequent editions varied as new sources were incorporated, particularly during the 1950s and 1960s. Robert Godel in particular published *Les Sources manuscrites du cours de linguistique générale* (Geneva: Droz, 1957). In English, see *Course in General Linguistics*, trans. Wade Baskin (New York: Columbia University Press, 2011). On the comparison of Saussure with Durkheim, see Witold Doroszewski, 'Quelques remarques sur les rapports de la sociologie et de la linguistique: É. Durkheim et F. de Saussure' [1932], in Jean-Claude Pariente (ed.), *Essais sur le langage* (Paris: Minuit, 1969), pp. 97–109.
9 Clyde Kluckhohn and William H. Kelly, 'The concept of culture', in Ralph Linton (ed.), *The Science of Man in the World Crisis* (New York: Columbia University Press, 1945), pp. 78–105. (The article expounds different positions on culture, including that of Edward Sapir.)
10 Luc Boltanski, 'Pouvoir et impuissance: projet intellectuel et sexualité dans le *Journal* d'Amiel', *Actes de la recherche en sciences sociales*, nos. 5–6 (1975): 80–108.
11 Ralph Linton, *The Study of Man* (New York: Appleton-Century, 1936), p. 91.
12 Gaston Bachelard, *The Formation of the Scientific Mind* (Manchester: Clinamen Press, 2002), ch. 1.
13 For a critique of the notion of 'the masses', see Pierre Bourdieu and Jean-Claude Passeron, 'Sociologues des mythologies et mythologies de sociologues', *Les Temps modernes*, no. 211 (1963): 998–1021.
14 For Goffman, a '*working consensus*' is an agreement or '*modus vivendi*' that those participating in an interaction undertake to realise; it 'involves not so much a real agreement as to what exists but rather a real agreement as to whose claims concerning what issues will be temporarily honoured.' Erving Goffman, *The Presentation of Self in Everyday Life* (Harmondsworth: Penguin, 1969), p. 21.
15 In fact, photos of this kind figure on the covers of the books by Erving Goffman published by Bourdieu with Éditions de Minuit in the collection 'Le sens commun': *Les Relations en public* (*La Mise en scène de la vie quotidienne*, vol. II, 1973), *Façons de parler* (1981) or *Les Rites d'interaction* (1974): men at a café terrace, a still from a film where a croupier signals to gamblers in a casino.
16 See Émile Durkheim, *The Rules of Sociological Method*, trans. W. D. Halls, ed. Steven Lukes (New York: Free Press, [1895] 1982), and, on the illusion of transparency, see Pierre Bourdieu, Jean-Claude Chamboredon and Jean-Claude Passeron, *The Craft of Sociology: Epistemological Preliminaries* (New York: de Gruyter, 1991), pp. 109–17, where they refer in particular to *The*

Rules of Sociological Method [although Durkheim himself does not use these exact terms – Trans.].

17 Bourdieu often uses this image of spectacles (particularly in 'Éléments d'une théorie sociologique de la perception artistique', *Revue internationale des sciences sociales*, 20/4 (1968): 642, or Pierre Bourdieu and Alain Darbel, *The Love of Art, European Art Museums and their Public* (Cambridge: Polity, 1997), p. 141. It owes something to a quotation from Martin Heidegger: 'When, for instance, a man wears a pair of spectacles which are so close to him distantially that they are "sitting on his nose", they are environmentally more remote from him than the picture on the opposite wall. Such equipment has so little closeness that often it is proximally quite impossible to find.' *Being and Time*, trans. John Macquarrie and Edward Robinson (Oxford: Blackwell, 1962), p. 141.

18 See Martin Heidegger, 'What calls for thinking?' in *Basic Writings*, ed. D. F. Krell (London: Routledge, 1978). Bourdieu often practises this kind of questioning; see for example: 'Qu'est-ce que faire parler un auteur? À propos de Michel Foucault', *Société et représentation*, no. 3 (1996): 13–18; 'Le mystère du ministère: des volontés particulières à la "volonté générale"', *Actes de la recherche en sciences sociales*, no. 140 (2001): 7–11 (where he explicitly proposes to transfer Heidegger's question 'What does thinking mean?' to the question of voting: 'What does voting mean?'); or, again, in 'Some questions on the gay and lesbian movement', in *Masculine Domination*, trans. Richard Nice (Cambridge: Polity, 2002), pp. 118–24.

19 Durkheim defined sociology as 'the science of institutions': 'In fact, without doing violence to the meaning of the word, one may term an *institution* all the beliefs and modes of behaviour instituted by the collectivity: sociology can then be defined as the science of institutions, their genesis and their functioning.' *The Rules of Sociological Method*, preface, p. 15.

20 This is no doubt a reference to the principal course of lectures given by Maurice Merleau-Ponty as part of his teaching for the Collège de France in the year 1954–5 under the title of '"L'institution" dans l'histoire personnelle et publique' (transcription in Merleau-Ponty, *L'Institution, la passivité: notes de cours au Collège de France, 1954–1955* (Paris: Belin, 2003), pp. 31–154).

21 Ernst Hartwig Kantorowicz, *The King's Two Bodies: A Study in Medieval Political Theology* (Princeton, NJ: Princeton University Press, 1957), p. 412.

22 *Le Matin de Paris* was a daily newspaper associated with the *Nouvel Observateur* and the Parti Socialiste that was then in power. It was founded in 1977 and ceased publication in 1988.

23 This formula, which gave rise to numerous debates among anthropologists, is taken from the ethnographer Karl von den Steinen (1855–1929) who, in *Unter den Naturvölkern Zentralbrasiliens* (Berlin: Reiner, 1894, pp. 305–6), reported that the Amazonian tribe of the Bororó identified with their totem, the Arara parrot. Lucien Lévy-Bruhl writes:

> 'The Bororó . . . proudly claim to be red araras (parrots).' That does not mean only that after their death they become araras, and that araras are metamorphosed Bororó, and must be treated as such. It means much more. 'The Bororó', says Mr von den Steinen, who would not believe it, but had to give in to their explicit affirmations, 'give one rigidly to believe that they are araras *at the present time*, just as if a caterpillar declared itself to be a

butterfly.' It is not a name that they give themselves, nor a relationship that they claim. What they want people to understand is an essential identity. Mr von den Steinen judges inconceivable that they could be at one and the same time both the human beings that they are and birds with red feathers. But for a mentality governed by the law of participation, there is no difficulty. All societies of totemic formation include collective representations of the same order, implying a similar identity between the individuals of a totemic group and their totem. (Lucien Lévy-Bruhl, *How Natives Think*, trans. Lilian Ada Clare (London: Allen & Unwin, 1926), pp. 77–8)

24 François Simiand, for example, writes: 'The clergy represents an organ of the body that is the Church; it does itself suffer the action of this body much more than it acts on it. In fact the body of the Church, or a religion, can exist without that organ, without a clergy. We would then be refusing to understand a whole part, perhaps the major part of the social phenomena of religion if we were to reduce the Church *arbitrarily* and *a priori* to the clergy.' ('Méthode historique et sciences sociales' [1903], *Annales ESC*, 15/1 (1960): 91.)
25 Max Weber, *The Sociology of Religion*, trans. Ephraim Fischoff (Boston: Beacon Press, [1920] 1993). On this point (and more generally on Bourdieu's reading of Weber's sociology of religion), see Bourdieu, 'Genèse et structure du champ religieux', *Revue française de sociologie*, 12/3 (1971): 295–334; 'Une interprétation de la théorie de la religion selon Max Weber', *Archives européennes de sociologie*, 12/1 (1971): 3–21.
26 See Howard S. Becker, *Art Worlds* (Berkeley: University of California Press, 1982). The book had not yet appeared at the time of Bourdieu's lectures, and Bourdieu is referring to one of the articles which had preceded its publication, probably 'Art worlds and social types', *American Behavioral Scientist*, 19/6 (1976): 703–18.
27 Georges Gurvitch was, with Raymond Aron, one of the two professors of sociology at the Sorbonne at the time of the creation of the degree in sociology in 1958. His lectures were followed by the majority of the sociologists trained in Paris at the end of the 1950s and the beginning of the 1960s.
28 Antoine de Saint-Exupéry (1900–1944) was a French writer and pioneering aviator. He is best remembered for his children's story *The Little Prince* and for his lyrical accounts of adventures as a pilot, in *Wind, Sand and Stars* and *Night Flight*. In 1940 he joined the Free French Air Force in North Africa, and in July 1944 he disappeared over the Mediterranean on a reconnaissance mission. After his death he became a national hero in France. His 1939 philosophical memoir *Terre des hommes* (Man and his World) became the name of an international humanitarian group. Bourdieu's ironic aside suggests something of his cult status (Trans.).
29 This church, situated in the Vth arrondissement of Paris, was much in the news from 1977 onwards; it was home to traditionalist Catholics, some of whom sympathised with the far right.
30 Situated on the left of the Parti Socialiste and reputedly close to intellectual milieux, the PSU (Parti Socialiste Unifié) closed down in 1989.
31 For the critique of the 'scholastic alternative of permanence and change', see Bourdieu, *Distinction*, trans. Richard Nice (London: Routledge, 1984), p. 164.

Lecture of 12 October 1982

1 Ernst Hartwig Kantorowicz, *The King's Two Bodies: A Study in Medieval Political Theology* (Princeton, NJ: Princeton University Press, 1957), p. 101, and 'Mysteries of state: an absolutist concept and its late mediaeval origins', *Harvard Theological Review*, 48/1 (1955): 65. Bourdieu was to develop this analysis in particular in 'Le mystère du ministère: des volontés particulières à la "volonté générale"', *Actes de la recherche en sciences sociales*, no. 140 (2001): 7–11.

2 Johan Huizinga, *The Autumn of the Middle Ages* (Chicago: University of Chicago Press, 1997).

3 Bourdieu, 'La maison ou le monde renversé', in Jean Pouillon and Paul Maranda (eds), *Échanges et communications: mélanges offerts à Claude Lévi-Strauss à l'occasion de son 60e anniversaire* (The Hague: Mouton, 1970), pp. 739–58; repubd in *Outline of a Theory of Practice*, trans. Richard Nice (Cambridge: Cambridge University Press, 1977), pp. 90, 110, 113.

4 Words wreak havoc when they happen to name something that is experienced but has not yet been named: they revive a complicit reflection by proposing a meaning for something when that meaning is, in fact, only a hypothesis of the future, only an extrapolation which cannot be accepted reflexively except by a vow. I have already cited that line of Mosca's referring to Fabrice and Sanseverina: 'If the word *love* is pronounced between them, I am lost.' Through this expression the collectivity affirms its right of surveillance over the most purely subjective intimacy, socializing the rather foolhardy tenderness the young aunt and her nephew feel for each other. (Jean-Paul Sartre, *The Family Idiot: Gustave Flaubert 1821–1857*, vol. 1, trans. Carol Cosman (Chicago: University of Chicago Press, 1971), pp. 127–8)

5 Pascal, *Pensées*, ed. Louis Lafuma, trans. John Warrington (London: Dent, 1960), §751, p. 211.

6 Durkheim approaches this question on many occasions. We might for example refer to his analysis of the clan (in *The Elementary Forms of Religious Life*, trans. Carol Cosman (Oxford: Oxford University Press, 2008)), which, 'like in any society ... can only live in and through the individual minds that compose it' (p. 167) and whose life expresses the alternating phases of dispersion and concentration of its members; the totemic emblem is for Durkheim one of the instruments that allows the clan to maintain a permanent identity: 'Generations may change but it remains the same' (p. 166).

7 Kantorowicz, *The King's Two Bodies*.

8 'For there are never two beings in nature that are perfectly alike, two beings in which it is not possible to discover an internal difference, that is one founded on an intrinsic denomination' (Gottfried Wilhelm Leibniz, 'The Monadology', in *Discourse on Metaphysics and Other Essays*, trans. Daniel Garber and Roger Ariew (Indianapolis: Hackett, 1992), §9, p. 69).

9 Bourdieu will return at length to consideration of the specific nature of the scientific field, particularly in his last lecture for the Collège de France, published as *Science of Science and Reflexivity*, trans. Richard Nice (Cambridge: Polity, 2004).

10 Pascal, *Pensées*, §217, p. 58.

11 An allusion to the debates that appeared in Germany at the end of the nineteenth century as a prolongation of the 'quarrel of methods' in economics and which became one of the central motifs of the epistemology of the human and social sciences, focusing on the distinction between 'sciences of the mind' that require hermeneutic understanding and 'natural sciences' that invite causal explanation. According to Wilhelm Dilthey, in particular, we can only 'explain nature, we understand psychic life'. (*Descriptive Psychology and Historical Understanding* (Leiden: Martinus Nijhoff, 1977), p. 27).

12 Martin Heidegger, *Being and Time*, trans. John Macquarrie and Edward Robinson (Oxford: Blackwell, 1962), p. 98.

13 Erich Auerbach, *Mimesis: The Representation of Reality in Western Literature*, trans. Willard A. Trask (Princeton, NJ: Princeton University Press, [1946] 1968). Auerbach's exact phrase is: 'Though the light which illuminates the picture proceeds from her [Emma], she is yet herself part of the picture, she is situated within it.'

14 Georges Poulet, 'La pensée circulaire de Flaubert', in *Les Métamorphoses du cercle* (Paris: Plon, [1955] 1961); repr. Flammarion, 1979, p. 386.

15 This qualification, taken from Roland Barthes ('Littérature objective', *Critique*, nos. 86–7 (1954): 581–91), relies on an analogy with a camera lens.

16 Maxime Chastaing, *La Philosophie de Virginia Woolf* (Paris: PUF, 1951).

17 Ibid., p. 86.

18 Bourdieu is alluding to Alain Touraine's sociology of action, which he had criticised as early as 1966. See 'Une sociologie de l'action est-elle possible?', *Revue française de sociologie*, 7/4 (1966): 508–17 (with Jean-Daniel Reynaud).

19 Bourdieu will devote several analyses to the authors of these two texts, James Joyce and Virginia Woolf, in *The Rules of Art*, trans. Susan Emanuel (Cambridge: Polity, 1996), and *Masculine Domination*, trans. Richard Nice (Cambridge: Polity, 2002).

20 No doubt Bourdieu is thinking of the analyses that Wittgenstein devoted to the experience of psychological incomprehension or opacity. We could quote in particular:

> And then there is what I should like to call the case of hopeless doubt. When I say, 'I have no idea what he is really thinking' – he's a closed book to me. When the only way to understand someone else would be to go through the same upbringing as his – which is impossible. Here there's no pretence. But imagine people whose upbringing is directed toward suppressing the expression of emotion in their faces and gestures; and suppose these people make themselves inaccessible to me by thinking aloud in a language I don't understand. Now I say 'I have no idea what is going on inside them', and there it is – an external fact. (Ludwig Wittgenstein, *Remarks on the Philosophy of Psychology*, trans. G. A. M. Anscombe (Chicago: University of Chicago Press, 1980), vol. 2, §568, pp. 99–100)

21 Bourdieu returns to this methodological requirement particularly in the chapter entitled 'Understanding', in Bourdieu et al., *The Weight of the World*, ed. and trans. Priscilla Parkhurst Ferguson (Cambridge: Polity, 1999), pp. 607–26.

22 An allusion to Socrates' maieutic, or 'midwifery' (Plato, *Theaetetus*, trans. Robin H. Waterfield (Harmondsworth: Penguin, 1987), §150b, p. 27).

23 For example, Edmund Husserl, 'Fifth meditation', in *Cartesian Meditations*, trans. Dorion Cairns (Dordrecht: Kluwer Academic, 1950), pp. 89–150.

24 See below, the lecture of 19 October 1982, pp. 50–1.
25 Bourdieu is quoting Karl Marx, from his 'Critique of Hegel's Philosophy of Right', *Early Writings* (London: Penguin, 1992), p. 244 [Trans.].
26 For the example of Quattrocento painting, see Pierre Bourdieu and Yvette Delsaut, 'Pour une sociologie de la perception', *Actes de la recherche en sciences sociales*, no. 40 (1981): 3–9.
27 Mikhail Bakhtin (V. N. Volosinov), *Marxism and the Philosophy of Language* (London: Seminar Press, 1973), p. 71.
28 See Bourdieu, *The Logic of Practice*, trans. Richard Nice (Cambridge: Polity, 1990).
29 Bourdieu will expound it later in 'Piété religieuse et dévotion artistique', *Actes de la recherche en sciences sociales*, no. 105 (1994): 71–4.
30 An allusion to the Saint-Sulpice or 'sulpicien' style of pious imagery (synonymous with 'kitsch'). The expression was coined by Léon Bloy with reference to the Saint-Sulpice quarter in Paris, known for its numerous shops selling religious items.
31 Jean Seznec, *La Survivance des dieux antiques* (Paris: Flammarion, [1939] 1980).
32 The manifestations of the aesthetic disposition in the museum are analysed by Bourdieu and Alain Darbel in the chapter 'Cultural works and cultivated disposition', in *The Love of Art: European Art Museums and their Public* (Cambridge: Polity, 1997), pp. 37–70.
33 In his later work, Bourdieu will call this phenomenon the 'scholastic bias' (see in particular the first chapter of *Pascalian Meditations*, trans. Richard Nice (Cambridge: Polity, 2000)).
34 Michael Baxandall, 'L'œil du Quattrocento', *Actes de la recherche en sciences sociales*, no. 40 (1981): 10–49 (this is the second chapter of Baxandall's *Painting and Experience in Fifteenth-Century Italy* (Oxford: Oxford University Press, 1972), later translated into French by Yvette Delsaut (Paris: Gallimard, 1985)).
35 Louis Gernet, 'La notion mythique de la valeur en Grèce' (1948), in *Anthropologie de la Grèce antique* (Paris: Maspero, 1968), p. 133.
36 Roger Chartier did not publish his study of this typical example of eighteenth-century pedlars' literature, from which this analysis is taken, until two years after these lectures ('Livrets bleus et lectures populaires', in Henri-Jean Martin et Roger Chartier (ed.), *Histoire de l'édition française*, vol. II (Paris: Promodis, 1984), pp. 498–511; Bourdieu had no doubt seen the work in progress).
37 The Collège de France format was supposed to be a one-hour lectured followed by a seminar, but Bourdeiu's audience was too numerous for the seminar, so he gave a two-hour lecture with a break in the middle.
38 See in particular the end of the next lecture (19 October) and the section entitled 'Critique of the scholarly relation', pp. 147–51, in the Lecture of 16 November 1982.

Lecture of 19 October 1982

1 Bourdieu develops this point in particular in *Algérie 60: structures économiques et structures temporelles* (Paris: Minuit, 1977), and takes it further in *The Social Structures of the Economy*, trans. Chris Turner (Cambridge: Polity, 2005), pp. 213ff.

2 Edmund Husserl, *The Crisis of European Sciences and Transcendental Phenomenology*, trans. David Carr (Evanston, IL: Northwestern University Press, [1936] 1970).

3 Jean-Paul Sartre, *Being and Nothingness*, trans. Hazel E. Barnes (London: Routledge, [1943] 2003), p. 83.

4 Husserl, *The Crisis of European Sciences and Transcendental Phenomenology*, p. 125.

5 See Gaston Bachelard, *The Formation of the Scientific Mind* (Manchester: Clinamen Press, 2002).

6 Alexander Gottlieb Baumgarten uses the expression in the very definition of the 'aesthetic', the notion that he was the first to introduce: 'L'Esthétique (ou théorie des arts libéraux, gnoséologie inférieure, art de la beauté du penser, art de l'analogon de la raison) est la science de la connaissance sensible' (*Aesthetica*, Frankfurt, 1750 [pubd in Latin]. This classic was only translated into French some years after Bourdieu's lectures: Alexander Gottlieb Baumgarten, *Esthétique*, trans. Jean-Yves Pranchère (Paris: L'Herne, 1988), p. 121. No English translation currently available.

7 Ernst Cassirer, *The Philosophy of the Enlightenment*, trans. Fritz C. A. Koelln and James P. Pettegrove (Princeton, NJ: Princeton University Press, [1951] 2009). For example: 'In the great metaphysical systems of that century – those of Descartes and Melbranche, of Spinoza and Leibniz – reason is the realm of the "eternal verities," of those truths held in common by the human and divine mind. What we know through reason, we therefore behold in God. Every act of reason means participation in the divine nature; it gives access to the intelligible world' (p. 13).

8 Gottfried Wilhelm Leibniz, *Nova methodus pro maximis et minimis*, 1684.

9 The principle of reciprocity theorised by Marcel Mauss in *The Gift: the Forms and Reason for Exchange in Archaic Society* (London: Routledge, [1923–4] 2001) was systematised by Claude Lévi-Strauss in his analysis of the rules governing matrimonial exchanges, *Elementary Structures of Kinship*, trans. Rodney Needham and James H. Bell (Boston: Beacon Press, [1949] 1971). Bourdieu mentions this critique in his Lecture of 25 January 1983, pp. 319–20.

10 For developments of this point, see Bourdieu, *Outline of a Theory of Practice*, trans. Richard Nice (Cambridge: Cambridge University Press, 1977), in particular 'From the mechanics of the model to the dialectic of strategies', pp. 3–9; *The Logic of Practice*, trans. Richard Nice (Cambridge: Polity, 1990), in particular the chapter 'The work of time', pp. 98–111; and 'The twofold truth of the gift', in *Pascalian Meditations*, trans. Richard Nice (Cambridge: Polity, 2000), pp. 191–202. See also below, the Lecture of 25 January 1983, pp. 319–20.

11 This phrase, often quoted by Bourdieu, is inspired by the following passage: 'a truly philosophical criticism . . . does not however consist . . . in discovering the concepts of logic at every point; it consists in the discovery of the particular logic of the particular object' (Karl Marx, 'Critique of Hegel's Doctrine of the State', in *Early Writings* (London: Penguin, [1843] 1992), pp. 158–9). One French translation is closer to the wording quoted by Bourdieu: 'Ce n'est pas la Logique de la Chose mais la Chose de la Logique qui est le moment philosophique' (Marx, *Critique du droit politique hégélien*, trans. Albert Baraquin (Paris: Éditions sociales, 1975), p. 51).

12 On this point, see Bourdieu, *Outline of a Theory of Practice*, in particular pp. 5–9, 171.
13 Georg Wilhelm Friedrich Hegel, *Lectures on the Philosophy of History* (Oxford: Oxford University Press, [1822–30] 2009).
14 On Paul A. Samuelson's *Economics* (one of the most authoritative manuals of economics in the world since its first edition in 1948), Bourdieu writes: 'Samuelson evokes the specific logic of practice only to reject it as unworthy. Denying the pretension of economic agents to possess adequate knowledge of economic mechanisms, the academic economist claims for himself a monopoly on the total point of view and declares himself capable of transcending the partial, particular viewpoints of particular groups and avoiding the errors that spring from the fallacy of composition' (*The Logic of Practice*, p. 28).
15 Durkheim for example, in his 1913–14 lectures on pragmatism, says:

> Each mind is free to choose the point of view from which it feels itself most competent to view things. This means that for every object of knowledge there are differing but equally justified means of examining it. These are probably partial truths, but all these partial truths come together in the collective consciousness and find their limits and their necessary complements. Thus intellectual individualism . . . becomes a necessary factor in the establishment of scientific truth, so that the diversity of individual temperaments can serve the cause of impersonal truth. Thus, on the one hand, scientific truth is not incompatible with the diversity of minds; and, on the other, as social groups become increasingly complex, it is impossible that society should have a single sense of itself. (*Pragmatism and Sociology* (Cambridge: Cambridge University Press, 1983), p. 92)

16 Spinoza set sensory perception and opinions derived from 'hearsay' (the first kind of knowledge), as well as objective knowledge based on the use of reason (the second kind), in opposition to a 'knowledge of the third kind' – that is, intuitive, and accessible only to the philosopher: 'This kind of knowing goes from an adequate idea of the formal essence of certain attributes of God to adequate knowledge of the intrinsic essences of things' (Benedict Spinoza, *Ethics Demonstrated in Geometrical Order*, trans. Jonathan Bennett, Part II, propositions 40–2, (pp. 40–1), www.earlymoderntexts.com/assets/pdfs/spinoza1665.pdf).
17 Bourdieu often refers to this 'geometral', or 'geometrical point or place', which corresponded for Leibniz to God's viewpoint (see, for example, *Science of Science and Reflexivity*, trans. Richard Nice (Cambridge: Polity, 2004), p. 95), using Maurice Merleau-Ponty's interpretation:

> Our perception ends in objects, and the object, once constituted, appears as the reason for all the experiences of it that we have had or that we could have. For example, I see the neighboring house from a particular angle. It would be seen differently from the right bank of the Seine, from the inside of the house, and differently still from an airplane. Not one of these appearances is the house *itself*. The house, as Leibniz said, is the *geometrical plan* [le *géométral*] that includes these perspectives and all possible perspectives; that is, the non-perspectival term from which all perspectives can be derived; the house *itself* is the house seen from nowhere. (Maurice

Merleau-Ponty, *Phenomenology of Perception*, trans. Donald A. Landes (New York: Routledge, [1945] 2012), p. 69)

18 Pierre Rosanvallon, 'Hegel, de la main invisible à la ruse de la raison', in *Le Capitalisme utopique: critique de l'idéologie économique* (Paris: Seuil, [1979] 1999), pp. 162–78. (The analysis in question is based more on a reading of Hegel's *The Phenomenology of Spirit* (Cambridge: Cambridge University Press, [1807] 2018).)

19 It is often alleged against monarchy that it makes the welfare of the state dependent on contingency, for, it is urged, the monarch may be badly educated, he may be unworthy of the highest position in the state, and it is senseless that such a state of affairs should be regarded as rational. But all this rests on a presupposition that is nugatory, namely that everything depends upon the monarch's particular character. In a completely organised state, it is only a question of the culminating point of formal decision (and a natural bulwark against passion). It is wrong . . . to demand objective qualities in a monarch; he has only to say 'yes' and dot the 'i'. (Georg Wilhelm Friedrich Hegel, *Outlines of the Philosophy of Right* (Oxford: Oxford University Press, 2008), Addendum to §280, p. 272)

20 See Max Weber, 'Science as a vocation', in *The Vocation Lectures* (Indianapolis: Hackett, [1919] 2004), in particular pp. 17–22.

21 Sigmund Freud, 'Fragment of an analysis of a case of hysteria' ('Dora', in *Case Histories I: 'Dora' and 'Little Hans'*, trans. Alix Strachey and James Strachey (Harmondsworth: Penguin Freud Library, vol. 8, 1977).)

22 An allusion to the theme of the 'epistemological break' introduced by Louis Althusser in 1965 as identifying the passage from ideology to science in the thought of Marx in 1845–6 (Althusser, *For Marx* (London: Verso, [1965] 2005).)

23 A formula used by Pascal on the subject of the imagination: 'It is that dominant part of man, that mistress of error and falsehood, the more of an imposter in that she is not always so; for were she the touchstone of falsehood, she would be likewise an infallible guide to truth' (Pascal, *Pensées*, ed. Louis Lafuma, trans. John Warrington (London: Dent, 1960), §81, p. 25).

24 Joseph Ben-David and Randall Collins, 'Social factors in the origins of a new science: the case of psychology', *American Sociological Review*, 31/4 (1966): 451–65. On this point (and also for Bourdieu's commentaries on his own scientific trajectory), see also Bourdieu, *Science of Science and Reflexivity*, pp. 67–8.

25 None of his works had yet been translated into French at the time of these lectures (a collection of some of his articles was published a few years later under the title *Le Chercheur et le quotidien*, trans. Anne Noschis-Gillieron (Paris: Klincksieck, 1987)). However, a study devoted to Husserl, which Bourdieu refers to implicitly later, had been published two decades earlier: Alfred Schütz, 'Le Problème de l'intersubjectivité transcendentale chez Husserl', trans. Maurice de Gandillac, in M.-A. Béra (ed.), *Husserl: Troisième Colloque philosophique de Royaumont* (Paris: Minuit, 1959), pp. 334–81.

26 'In short [Husserl's] enterprise is fairly close to that of Hegel, as is suggested by Husserl's use of the word "phenomenology". . . . If it is true that Husserl sought through the study of phenomena to find the roots of experience, we should not be surprised that his phenomenology ended with the theory of a "reason hidden

in history"' (Maurice Merleau-Ponty, *Phenomenology and the Sciences of Man* (Evanston, IL: Northwestern University Press, 1973), vol. 1, pp. 57–8).

27 'It is a possible and highly important task to project ourselves into [*einzufüh-len*] a human community enclosed in its living and traditional sociality, and to understand it insofar as, in and on the basis of its total social life that human community possesses the world, which is not for it a "representation of the world", but the real world' ('Sur la mythologie primitive: lettre d'Edmund Husserl à Lucien Lévy-Bruhl', trans. Philippe Soulez, *Gradhiva*, no. 4 (1988): 63–72). Bourdieu could have seen this letter, dated 11 March 1935, mentioned by Maurice Merleau-Ponty in 'The philosopher and sociology', in *Signs*, trans. Richard C. McClearly (Evanston, IL: Northwestern University Press, 1964), pp. 107–8, or quoted (as above) by Jacques Derrida, *An Introduction to Edmund Husserl's Origins of Geometry*, trans. John P. Leavey (Lincoln: University of Nebraska Press, 1989), p. 111.

28 Kant's aesthetics sees in form a 'purposiveness apart from any purpose' that is not dependent on a natural end or human understanding. Emmanuel Kant, *Critique of Judgement*, trans. James Creek Meredith and Nicholas Walker (Oxford: Oxford University Press, [1790] 2007), p. 83.

29 On this point, see in particular Pierre Bourdieu and Jean-Claude Passeron, *The Inheritors: French Students and Their Relation to Culture*, trans. Richard Nice (Chicago: University of Chicago Press, 1979).

30 This refers to Plato's 'The Meno', whose point of departure is the following question (Guthrie translates *arete* as 'virtue'): 'Can you tell me, Socrates, is virtue something that can be taught? Or does it come by practice? Or is it neither teaching nor practice that gives it to a man but natural aptitude or something else?' (Plato, *Protagoras and Meno*, trans. W. K. C. Guthrie (London: Penguin, 1986), p. 115).

31 'So that for practical purposes right opinion is no less useful than knowledge, and the man who has it is no less useful than the one who knows. . . . To recapitulate then: assuming that there are men good and useful to the community, it is not only knowledge that makes them so, but also right opinion, and neither of these comes by nature but both are acquired – or do you think either of them *is* natural?' (Ibid., pp. 156, 154–5).

32 Gottfried Wilhelm Leibniz, *The Monadology* [1714], in *Discourse on Metaphysics and the Monadology*, trans. George R. Montgomery (New York: Dover Press, 2005), §28, pp. 51–2:

> Men act in like manner as animals, in so far as the sequence of their perceptions is determined only by the law of memory, resembling the *empirical physicians* who practice simply, without any theory, and we are empiricists in three-fourths of our actions. For instance, when we expect that there will be daylight tomorrow, we do so empirically, because it has always happened so up to the present time. It is only the astronomer who uses his reason in making such an affirmation.

33 A reference to the use of the term 'apparel' in the fragment 'Imagination'.

> Our magistrates clearly understand this mystery. Their red robes, their ermine in which they wrap themselves like furry cats, the courts in which they administer justice, the fleurs de lis – all this august paraphernalia [apparel] was most necessary. Again, if the physicians had not their cassocks

and their mules, if the doctors had not their square caps and their robes four times too wide, they would never have duped the world, which cannot withstand such an impressive display. If the magistrates dispensed true justice, if physicians exercised the true art of healing, they would have no need of square caps; the majesty of these sciences would of itself be sufficiently venerable. But having only imaginary knowledge, they must employ these silly tools that strike the imagination with which they have to deal, and thus they do actually inspire respect. (Pascal, *Pensées*, §81, pp. 26–7)

See also Bourdieu, *Pascalian Meditations*, p. 168.

34 See Edmund Husserl, 'Fifth meditation', in *Cartesian Meditations*, trans. Dorion Cairns (Dordrecht: Kluwer Academic, 1950). For the Lacanian formula 'it speaks, and no doubt, where it was least expected', see Jacques Lacan, 'The Freudian thing, or the meaning of the return to Freud', in *Écrits: A Selection*, trans. Alan Sheridan (London: Tavistock, 1980), p. 125. (Lacan's 'Ça parle' is also translated as 'the "id" speaks'. Here it is Bourdieu who diverts it rather towards the notion of a social unconscious [Trans.].)

Lecture of 2 November 1982

1 See the passage in the previous lecture (pp. 58–9) on the 'universal class', identified by Hegel with the bureaucracy and then by Marx with the proletariat. In the 1960s, some critics spoke of the formation of a 'new working class' – for example, Serge Mallet, *La Nouvelle Classe ouvrière* (Paris: Seuil, 1963); and, in the 1970s, the student, ecological or feminist movements, for instance, inspired the sociologist Alain Touraine with the hypothesis that 'new social movements' could emerge and play in determining the major social orientations a role comparable to that which had previously been played by the 'workers' movement'.

2 On this point, see Bourdieu, 'Le mort saisit le vif: les relations entre l'histoire réifiée et l'histoire incorporée', *Actes de la recherche en sciences sociales*, nos. 32–3 (1980): 3–14.

3 Such [instruments] naturally in the kind of sound they produce are further removed from the soul's direct expression; they are in relation to that of an external object, a piece of dead mechanism, and music is essentially a spiritual movement and activity. When we find, therefore, this externality of the instrument vanishes altogether, in the case, that is, where the music of the soul breaks right through this alien crust of mechanism, by means of such virtuosity, even an instrument of this character is transformed into one as fully adapted to express the soul of the artist as it is possible to conceive. (Georg Wilhelm Friedrich Hegel, *The Philosophy of Fine Art*, trans. F. P. B. Osmaston (London: Bell, 1920), vol. 3, pp. 428–9)

4 On these points, see in particular Bourdieu, *Distinction*, trans. Richard Nice (London: Routledge, 1984), in particular the passages on the 'new professions' in chapter 6, 'Cultural goodwill'.

5 See, for example, Michel Crozier, *Le Phénomène bureaucratique* (Paris: Seuil, [1963] 1971), in particular the passage on 'La personnalité bureaucratique', pp. 243–56.

6 Erving Goffman, 'Role distance', in *Encounters: Two Studies in the Sociology of Interaction* (Indianapolis: Bobbs-Merrill, 1961), pp. 85–132.

7 The unconscious ceases to be the ultimate haven of individual peculiarities – the repository of a unique history, which makes each of us an irreplaceable being. It is reducible to a function – the symbolic function, which no doubt is specifically human, and which is carried out according to the same laws among all men, and actually corresponds to the aggregate of these laws . . . The unconscious, on the other hand, is always empty – or, more accurately, it is as alien to mental images as is the stomach to the foods which pass through it. As the organ of a specific function, the unconscious merely imposes structural laws upon inarticulated elements which originate elsewhere – impulses, emotions, representations, and memories. (Claude Lévi-Strauss, *Structural Anthropology*, trans. Claire Jacobson and Brooke Schoeff (New York: Basic Books, 1974), p. 200)

8 Erwin Panofsky, *Studies in Iconology* (Boulder, CO: Icon, [1939] 1972), pp. 3–4.

9 An allusion to the formula that Jules Michelet used as the epitaph on his gravestone: 'History is resurrection'.

10 On this point, see Bourdieu, 'Le mort saisit le vif: les relations entre l'histoire réifiée et l'historie incorporée', *Actes de la recherche en sciences sociales*, nos. 32–3 (1980): 3–14.

11 Karl Marx, *Capital* (New York: International, 1975), Section VII, chap. 24, 3, p. 806.

12 'The language itself is not a function of the speaker. It is the product passively registered by the individual. It never requires premeditation, and reflexion enters into it only for the activity of classifying. . . . Speech on the contrary is an individual act of the will and the intelligence' (Ferdinand de Saussure, *Course in General Linguistics*, trans. Wade Baskin (New York: Columbia University Press, 2011), p. 14).

13 The term *Träger*, which Marx happened to use on occasion, was used (like the expressions 'productive forces' or 'production relations') by the French neo-Marxists grouped in the 1960s around Louis Althusser and Étienne Balibar: *Reading Capital* (London: Verso, [1965] 2015); their aim, in an 'antihumanist' perspective, was to 'dispense with the theoretical services of a concept of man' entirely: social agents are only the instruments or bearers (*Träger*) of the tasks assigned to them in the process of production.

14 See the Lecture of 12 October 1982, pp. 31–3.

15 Gaston Bachelard, *The Poetics of Space* (Boston: Beacon Press, 1994).

16 Martin Heidegger, 'Building, dwelling, thinking', in *Basic Writings* (London: Routledge, [1954] 2010), pp. 239–56.

17 Bourdieu, *The Political Ontology of Martin Heidegger*, trans. Peter Collier (Cambridge: Polity, 1991).

18 Huizinga writes that the spoilsport 'robs play of its illusion, *inlusio* – a pregnant word which means literally "in-play" (from *inlusio*, *illudere* or *inludere*)' (Johan Huizinga, *Homo Ludens: A Study of the Play-Element in Culture* (London: Routledge, [1944] 1949), p. 11). 'In his well-known book, *Homo Ludens*, Huizinga says that, through a false etymology, one can make *illusio*, a Latin word derived from the root *ludus* (game), mean the fact of being in the game, of

being invested in the game, of taking the game seriously' (Bourdieu, *Practical Reason: On the Theory of Action* (Cambridge, Polity, 1998), p. 76).

19 See Edmund Husserl, 'Second meditation', *Cartesian Meditations*, trans. Dorion Cairns (Dordrecht: Kluwer Academic, 1950), §15, p. 35.

20 Georg Wilhelm Friedrich Hegel, *The Philosophy of History*, trans. John Sibree (New York: Prometheus Books, [1837] 1991), p. 23.

21 Although Durkheim may not have used this particular expression, he did write that 'this [religious] delirium . . . is well founded' (Émile Durkheim, *The Elementary Forms of Religious Life*, trans. Carol Cosman (Oxford: Oxford University Press), 2001, pp. 171–2). Durkheim develops the idea at greater length in a passage at the start of the conclusion to the book, where he explains that sociology owes it to itself to

> postulate that this unanimous feeling of believers across time cannot be purely illusory . . . religious beliefs rest on a specific experience whose demonstrative value is, in a sense, not inferior to that of scientific experiments, while being quite different . . . But, given the fact that, if you will, 'religious experience' is grounded in some way – and what experience is not? – it does not in the least follow that the reality that grounds it must objectively conform to the idea that believers have of it. (Ibid., p. 312)

22 This expression does not figure in *The German Ideology*. On the other hand, there is in Seneca a similar critique: 'You must not at this point imagine that I mean meals like Timon's or "the poor man's room" or anything else to which the extravagance of wealth resorts to amuse away its tedium' (Seneca, *Letters from a Stoic*, trans. Robin Campbell (London: Penguin, 2004), p. 67).

23 The family fantasy designates a genealogical history, a process whereby, 'as images of ghostly relations under the operation of projection, we induce others, and are ourselves induced, to embody them: to enact unbeknown to ourselves, a shadow play, as images of images of images . . . of the dead, who have in their turn embodied and enacted such dramas projected upon them, and induced in them, by those before them' (R. D. Laing, *The Politics of the Family and other Essays* (London: Routledge, 1999), p. 78).

24 Bourdieu, *Distinction*, pp. 372–4.

25 Paul E. Willis, *Profane Culture* (London, Routledge & Kegan Paul, 1978). Bourdieu returns to this book in 'Vous avez dit "populaire"?', *Actes de la recherche en sciences sociales*, no. 46 (1983): 102.

26 See above, Lecture of 19 October, note 14.

27 Jeremy Bentham, *Deontology: Or the Science of Morality* (Charleston, SC: Scholar's Choice, [1834] 2015).

28 See Adam Smith, *The Theory of Moral Sentiments* (New York: Gutenberg, [1759] 2011), p. 75.

29 John Harsanyi, *Morality and the Theory of Rational Behaviour* (Cambridge: Cambridge University Press, 1977), p. 42.

30 See Max Weber, 'Some categories of interpretive sociology', trans. Edith Graber, *Sociological Quarterly*, 23/2 (1981): 151–80.

31 'On Hare's view, the correct principle should be based not on actual preferences of agents, but on their "perfectly prudent preferences" – what someone would desire if fully informed and unconfused' (Amartya Sen and Bernard Williams, 'Introduction', in Sen and Williams (eds), *Utilitarianism and Beyond* (Cambridge: Cambridge University Press, 1977), p. 9).

32   All we have to do is to distinguish between a person's manifest preferences and his true preferences. His manifest preferences are his actual preferences as manifested by his observed behaviour, including preferences possibly based on erroneous factual beliefs, or on careless logical analysis, or on strong emotions that at the moment greatly hinder rational choice. In contrast, a person's true preferences are the preferences he would have if he had all the relevant factual information, always reasoned with the greatest possible care, and were in a state of mind most conducive to rational choice. (Harsanyi, *Morality and the Theory of Rational Behaviour*, p. 55)

33   See Bourdieu, *Algérie 60* (Paris: Minuit, 1977), and *Algerian Sketches*, trans. David Fernbach (Cambridge: Polity, 2013).

34   Frantz Fanon, *The Wretched of the Earth*, trans. Constance Farrington (Harmondsworth: Penguin, [1961] 2001).

35   On this point, see Bourdieu, *Algerian Sketches*.

36   Max Weber, *The Protestant Ethic and the Spirit of Capitalism*, trans. Talcott Parsons (London: Routledge, [1930] 1992).

37   Bourdieu draws on work conducted in his research centre in the 1960s on banking and credit (with Luc Boltanski and Jean-Claude Chamboredon, *La Banque et sa clientèle*, Paris: Centre de sociologie européenne, 1963). Bourdieu returned to these questions at the end of the 1980s in his study of private housing (*The Social Struuctures of the Economy*, Cambridge: Polity, 2005).

38   Bentham, *Deontology: Or the Science of Morality*.

39   Durkheim, *The Elementary Forms of Religious Life*, Book III, chap. 1, 'The negative cult and its functions. ascetic rites', pp. 221–42.

40   See, for example, *Critique of Pure Reason*, trans. Mary Gregor (Cambridge: Cambridge University Press, [1781] 1997), 'The transcendental doctrine of method', first chapter, first section, 'The discipline of pure reason in dogmatic use', which starts thus: 'Mathematics gives the most resplendent example of pure reason happily expanding itself without assistance from experience' (p. 63).

41   Bourdieu takes this reference from Ernst Cassirer, who points out that 'the thinkers of the Cambridge school speak of the "mathematical sickness" (*morbus mathematicus*) of Descartes, and they look upon this sickness as a fundamental flaw in his doctrine of nature' (*The Philosophy of the Enlightenment*, trans. Fritz C. A. Koelln and James P. Pettegrove (Princeton: Princeton University Press, [1951] 2009), p. 82).

42   On the 'Gerschenkron effect', see also *Choses dites* (Paris: Minuit, 1987), pp. 51–3; 'Le champ scientifique', *Actes de la recherche en sciences sociales*, nos. 2–3 (1976): 101–2. The book by Alexander Gerschenkron is *Economic Backwardness in Historical Perspective* (Cambridge, MA: Harvard University Press, 1962).

Lecture of 9 November 1982

1   Edmund Husserl, *Experience and Judgment: Investigations in a Genealogy of Logic* (Evanston, IL: Northwestern University Press, [1939] 1973), p. 52.

2   Edmund Husserl, *Cartesian Meditations*, trans. Dorion Cairns (Dordrecht: Kluwer Academic, 1950), §32, 'The Ego as substrate of habitualities', p. 66,

and §33, 'The full concretion of the Ego as monad and the problem of his self-constitution', pp. 67–8.

3 Maurice Merleau-Ponty, 'The body as object and mechanist physiology', *Phenomenology of Perception*, trans. Donald A. Landes (London: Routledge, 2012), pp. 84–102.

4 Ellery Eells, 'The philosophical and psychological significance of Bayesian decision theory', in *Rational Decision and Causality* (Cambridge: Cambridge University Press, 1982), p. 24. (Bourdieu refers on several occasions to the 'authors', in the plural, of the 'article' – whereas it is a collection of texts by the same author – no doubt in order to do justice to the range of sources cited.)

5 Ibid., p. 33.

6 Bourdieu is probably applying this reading to Noam Chomsky and Morris Halle, *The Sound Pattern of English* (Cambridge MA: MIT Press, [1968] 1991).

7 Eells, 'Common causes, reasons and symptotic acts', in *Rational Decision and Causality*, p. 149.

8 Proposition XXVIII of 'Concerning God', in Baruch Spinoza, *Ethics Demonstrated in Geometrical Order*, trans. Jonathan Bennett, Part I, proposition 28, p. 13, www.earlymoderntexts.com/assets/pdfs/spinoza1665.pdf.

9 An allusion to the book by Christian Baudelot and Roger Establet, *L'École capitaliste en France* (Paris: Maspero, 1971).

10 An allusion to an essay by Louis Althusser on 'Idéologie et appareils idéologiques d'État', *La Pensée*, no. 151 (1970); trans. as *On the Reproduction of Capitalism: Ideology and Ideological State Apparatuses*, trans. G. M. Goshgarian (London: Verso, 2014).

11 This traffic accident, which took place on 31 July 1982, had involved two coaches taking children to a holiday camp. There were fifty-three victims, mostly children. The collective emotion caused by the crash led to a series of measures regulating the speed limits of large vehicles and the transport of children.

12   Again, how will you prove what something is? Anyone who knows what a man or anything else is must also know that it exists (of that which does not exist, no one knows what it is). You may know what the account or the name means when I say 'goat-stag', but it is impossible to know what a 'goat-stag' is. But if you are to prove what something is and also that it exists, how will you prove them by the same argument? Definitions make a single thing plain, and so do demonstrations; but what a man is and that men exist are different. (Aristotle, *Posterior Analytics*, trans. Jonathan Barnes (Oxford: Clarendon Press, 1994), p. 55)

'Thus names and verbs by themselves – for instance "man" or "white" when nothing further is added – are like the thoughts that are without combination and separation; for so far they are neither true nor false. A sign of this is that even "goat-stag" signifies something but not, as yet, anything true or false, unless "is" or "is not" is added (either simply or with reference to time).' (Aristotle, 'De interpretatione', in *The Complete Works of Aristotle*, ed. Jonathan Barnes (Princeton, NJ: Princeton University Press, 1995), vol. 1, p. 25)

13 Gottlob Frege, 'On *Sinn* and *Bedeutung*' [1892], in *The Frege Reader*, ed. Michael Beaney (Oxford: Wiley-Blackwell, 1977), pp. 151–71.

14 This example is used in an article by Bertrand Russell in 1905, 'On denoting', *Mind*, 14 (1905): 479–93.

15 Gilbert Ryle, *The Concept of Mind* (Abingdon: Routledge, [1949] 2009).

16 Ibid., chap.1, 'Descartes' myth', pp. 1–13.

17 For example, Saussure writes: 'Language exists in the form of a sum of impressions deposited in the brain of each member of a community, almost like a dictionary of which identical copies have been distributed to each individual. Language exists in each individual, yet it is common to all. Nor is it affected by the will of the depositaries' (*Course in General Linguistics*, trans. Wade Baskin (New York: Columbia University Press, 2011, p. 19). Or again:

> If we could embrace the sum of word-images stored in the minds of all individuals, we could identify the social bond that constitutes language. It is a storehouse filled by the members of a given community through their active use of speaking, a grammatical system that has a potential existence in each brain, or, more specifically, in the brains of a group of individuals. For language is not complete in any speaker; it exists perfectly only within a collectivity. (Ibid., pp. 13–14)

18 On all these points, see Bourdieu, *Distinction*, trans. Richard Nice (London: Routledge, 1984).

19 Saint-John Perse, author of *Anabase* (1924), translated by T. S. Eliot as *Anabasis* (London: Faber & Faber, 1930), was a particularly hermetic high modernist poet [Trans.].

20 This might refer to the mathematician René Thom, 'Les mathématiques "modernes": une erreur pédagogique et philosophique?', *L'Âge de la science*, no. 3 (1970): 225–42; trans. as '"Modern" mathematics: an educational and philosophic error?', *American Scientist*, 59/6 (1971): 695–9.

21 'The confusions which occupy us arise when language is, as it were, idling, not when it is doing work' (Ludwig Wittgenstein, *Philosophical Investigations*, trans. G. E. M. Anscombe (Oxford: Wiley-Blackwell, 2009), p. 104).

22 The sophism of the Indian consists in saying that the Indian who has black skin and white teeth is both white and non-white.

23 On these two examples, see Ryle, *The Concept of Mind*, p. 16. Ryle mentions them as 'category-mistakes' of the same type as the fallacy of 'the ghost in the machine' (see above).

24 See Émile Durkheim, *The Elementary Forms of Religious Life*, trans. Carol Cosman (Oxford: Oxford University Press, 2008), pp. 327–35.

25 Friedrich Engels, *Dialectics of Nature*, trans. Clemens Dutt (Moscow: Progress, [1883] 1974), p. 211.

26 Edmund Husserl, 'Philosophy and the crisis of European man', in *Phenomenology and the Crisis of Philosophy*, trans. Quentin Lauer (New York: Harper & Row, 1965), pp. 157–8.

27 Max Weber, *The Protestant Ethic and the Spirit of Capitalism*, trans. Talcott Parsons (London: Routledge, [1930] 1992). [Although in fact Weber credits Babylonia with astronomy and India with geometry, as well as with decimal and algebraic calculation; pp. xxviii, xxxvii (Trans.)].

28 Max Weber, *The Rational and Social Foundations of Music* (Eastford, CT: Martino, [1921] 2009).

29 Ernst H. Gombrich, *In Search of Cultural History* (Oxford: Oxford University Press, 1969).

30 See above, lecture of 2 November, pp. 74–6.
31 In English in the text (Trans.).
32 This is *Ce que parler veut dire: l'économie des échanges linguistiques* (Paris: Fayard, 1982). The book appeared in English translation with additional material in 1991 under the title *Language and Symbolic Power*, trans. Gino Raymond and Matthew Adamson (Cambridge: Polity, 1991), and was later published in this new form in French, as *Langage et pouvoir symbolique*, in 2001 by Éditions du Seuil. This summary corresponds to the chapter entitled 'The production and reproduction of legitimate language', pp. 43–65 in the English edition.
33 Michel Butor, 'Victor Hugo romancier', in *Répertoire II* (Paris: Minuit, 1964), pp. 215–42.
34 Ibid., pp. 216, 225, 228, 230.
35 *L'Héautontimorouménos* is a comedy by the Latin poet Terence; Baudelaire revived the title for one of the poems of *Les Fleurs du mal*.
36 'Empirical observation can confirm or refute our subjective belief in certain expectation values, which may or may not be expressed in numerical form. Even if our expectations are vague and confused, they are not unreal. It might even be possible to speak of "statistical causality"' (Gaston Bachelard, *The New Scientific Spirit*, trans. Arthur Goldhammer (Boston: Beacon Press, [1934] 1984), p. 118). See Bourdieu, 'Avenir de classe et causalité du probable', *Revue française de sociologie*, 15/1 (1974): 3–42.
37 An *agrégé* is someone who has passed the *agrégation*, a highly competitive postgraduate diploma that qualifies them for a teaching post in a top *lycée* or university.
38 Here Bourdieu may be conflating the principles to be inferred from reading Jean-Jacques Rousseau's *Émile, or On Education* (Harmondsworth: Penguin, [1762] 1991), Book III, with a quotation from one of André Gide's characters in *The Counterfeiters*, trans. Dorothy Bussy (Harmondsworth: Penguin, [1925] 1990), p. 342: 'Rather than incessantly repeat to a child that fire burns, let us consent to his burning his fingers. Experience is a better instructor than advice.'
39 On the greater or lesser distance from economic and social necessity according to social groups, see *Distinction, passim*.
40 David Hume, *A Treatise of Human Nature* (Oxford: Clarendon Press, [1739–40] 2011), p. 5.
41 Bourdieu is referring to his research in Algeria (see *Algérie 60* [Paris: Minuit, 1977], and *Algerian Sketches*, trans. David Fernbach [Cambridge: Polity, 2013]). He also mobilised this schema of objective probabilities and subjective expectations in his first sociological enquiries into culture and the education system.
42 See the chapter in *Distinction* entitled 'The choice of the necessary' and devoted to the dominated classes (pp. 372–96): 'The fundamental proposition that the habitus is a virtue made of necessity is never more clearly illustrated than in the case of the working classes, since necessity includes for them all that is usually meant by the word, that is, an inescapable deprivation of necessary goods' (p. 372).
43 In one of La Fontaine's fables inspired by Aesop ('The fox and the grapes'), this is the reason given by the fox when he realises that the grapes he wants to eat are too high for him to reach: 'Bah! Fit for boors! Still green!' *The Complete Fables of Jean de la Fontaine*, trans. Norman R. Shapiro (Urbana: University of Illinois Press, [1668–94] 2007), p. 67.

44 See Bourdieu, 'The rites of institution', in *Language and Symbolic Power*, trans. Gino Raymond and Matthew Adamson (Cambridge: Polity, 1991), pp. 117–26, and *Masculine Domination*, trans. Richard Nice (Cambridge: Polity, 2002).

Lecture of 16 November 1982

1 See above, Lecture of 12 October, pp. 31–2.
2 In *The German Ideology*, where he derides the idealism of young Hegelians such as Max Stirner, whom he caricatures as 'Saint Sancho'. Karl Marx and Frederick Engels, *Collected Works*, Vol. 5: *1845–47* (London: Lawrence & Wishart, 1976), especially pp. 436–7.
3 On the process of generational ageing, see Bourdieu, *Distinction*, trans. Richard Nice (London: Routledge, 1984), p. 296, and 'L'Invention de la vie d'artiste', *Actes de la recherche en sciences sociales*, no. 2 (1975): 67–93, in particular, pp. 75–81.
4 For development of this point, see *Distinction*, p. 374: 'parvenus generally take a long time to learn that what they see as culpable prodigality is, in their new condition, expenditure of basic necessity.'
5 See above, Lecture of 2 November, p. 362, note 22, on the formula 'rich man's privilege'.
6 The Marxist theoretician Henri Lefebvre is often considered the inventor of the notion of the 'consumer society', in *Critique de la vie quotidienne* (Paris: L'Arche, 1958), on which Jean Baudrillard wrote a celebrated essay in the wake of May 1968: *La Société de consommation* (Paris: Gallimard, 1970).
7 Roland Barthes writes, for example:

> If one looks at the normal practice of music criticism (or, which is often the same thing, of conversations 'on' music), it can readily be seen that a work (or its performance) is only ever translated into the poorest of linguistic categories: the adjective. Music, by natural bent, is that which receives an adjective. . . . No doubt the moment we turn a work of art into a subject (for an article, for a conversation), there is nothing left but to give it predicates. (Roland Barthes, 'The grain of the voice', in *Image – Music – Text*, trans. Stephen Heath (London: Fontana, [1972] 1987), p. 179.)

8 On this point, see Bourdieu, 'Questions de politique', *Actes de la recherche en sciences sociales*, no. 16 (1977): 55–89.
9 The theory of 'levels of aspiration', whose principle Bourdieu resumes in the next sentence, was developed by the psychologist Kurt Lewin in *A Dynamic Theory of Personality* (New York: McGraw-Hill, 1935).
10 Sigmund Freud, 'Formulations on the two principles of mental functioning', in *On Metapsychology* (Harmondsworth: Penguin, [1911] 1984) [Pelican Freud Library, vol. 11].
11 On this opposition between the fairy tale, 'where prayers come true', and the fable, whose truth 'is in the terrible image', see Alain [Émile Chartier], *The Gods* (New York: New Directions, [1934] 1974), pp. 66, 136.
12 A *polytechnicien* is a graduate of the highly selective École polytechnique, which produces France's top scientists and industrial managers.
13 Plato, *The Republic*, trans. Tom Griffith (Cambridge: Cambridge University Press, 2000), Book 2, §§369–70, pp. 50–53.

14 Ibid., Book 10, §§614a–621b, pp. 336–44.
15 Bourdieu, 'The rites of institution', in *Language and Symbolic Power*, trans. Gino Raymond and Matthew Adamson (Cambridge: Polity, 1991), pp. 117–26.
16 Arnold van Gennep, *The Rites of Passage*, trans. Monika B. Vizedom and Gabrielle L. Caffee (London: Routledge, [1909] 2004).
17 See Bourdieu, 'The functions of kinship', in *Outline of a Theory of Practice*, trans. Richard Nice (Cambridge: Cambridge University Press, 1977), pp. 33–8.
18 Bourdieu is referring here to the research that he undertook during the 1960s on the family system in the Béarn, republished in *The Bachelors' Ball*, trans. Richard Nice (Cambridge: Polity, 2007).
19 François Roustang, *Elle ne le lâche plus . . .* (Paris: Minuit, 1980).
20 The concept of the *double bind* was introduced in the 1950s by the anthropologist Gregory Bateson, in particular in his research into schizophrenia; see 'Toward a theory of schizophrenia', pp. 201–27, and 'Double bind 1969', pp. 271–8, in *Steps to an Ecology of Mind* (Chicago: University of Chicago Press, 2000).
21 See above, Lecture of 2 November, note 23, p. 362.
22 This is no. 46, March 1983, devoted to 'l'usage de la parole', which contains contributions by Pierre Encrevé, Michel de Fornel, Bernard Laks and an interview with the sociolinguist William Labov.
23 Pierre Bourdieu and Jean Bollack held a series of interviews with Gershom Scholem in 1978: 'L'identité juive', *Actes de la recherche en sciences sociales*, no. 35 (1980): 3–19.
24 In a period when the École normale supérieure had produced far fewer leading politicians than under the Third Republic, Georges Pompidou and Laurent Fabius are no doubt the ex-*normaliens* with the most successful political careers. The former was prime minister (1962–8), then president of the Republic (1969–74). The latter, at the time of Bourdieu's lectures, had just been appointed minister in charge of the budget at the age of thirty-five and was to become, from 1984 to 1986, France's 'youngest prime minister'. Both had come first in the *agrégation* competition in French literature.
25 Bourdieu cites this 'Pareto paradox' quite frequently (see, for instance, '"Youth" is just a word', in *Sociology in Question*, trans. Richard Nice (London: Sage, 1993), on the subjects of income and age (p. 94). Concerning the personification of collective entities (such as social classes or countries) and the temptation, faced with continuous distributions, to mark thresholds or to draw lines, Pareto writes for instance:

> The lines alluded to are not geometrical, any more than the lines that separate the land from the waters of the ocean are geometrical. Only a presumptuous ignorance can insist on an exactness that the science of the concrete cannot attain. The terms of such a science must correspond to reality, but that is possible only within certain limits. No rigorous definition of 'humus' or 'clay' can be given, nor can one tell the exact number of years, days, hours, that separate youth from manhood. But that does not prevent experimental science from using such terms, as qualified by the approximations to which they are subject. (Vilfredo Pareto, *The Mind and Society: Treatise on General Sociology*, trans. Andrew Bongiorno and James Harvey Rogers (San Diego: Harcourt Brace, [1912] 1935), chap. 13, §2544, pp. 1835–6)

26 See the question at the end of the Lecture of 12 October 1982, p. 46.

27 Husserl cites two books by Friedrich Eduard Beneke: *Lehrbuch der Logik als Kunstlehre des Denkens* (1832) and *System der Logik als Kunstlehre des Denkens* (1842). See Edmund Husserl, *Logical Investigations*, Vol. 1: *Prolegomena to Pure Logic*, trans. J. N. Findlay (London: Routledge, [1900] 2012), pp. 29, 31.

28 Bourdieu, then, understands the word in the sense that it has for Kant, and not in the sense, influenced by a Marxist interpretation, given by the 'critical theory' developed by certain thinkers of German origins (primarily Theodor W. Adorno and Max Horkheimer) united from the 1950s under the name of the Frankfurt School.

29 Bourdieu, *The Logic of Practice*, trans. Richard Nice (Cambridge: Polity, 1990), pp. 80–97.

30 But I am quite disgusted . . . with the difficulty that there is in general to write ten lines of common sense on the facts of language. Since I have been preoccupied for a long time with the logical classification of these facts, and the classification of the viewpoints from which we approach them, I increasingly see . . . the immensity of the task we face if we want to show the linguist *what he actually does.* (Ferdinand de Saussure, letter to Antoine Meillet of 4 January 1894, quoted by Émile Benveniste, 'Saussure après un demi-siècle', *Cahiers Ferdinand de Saussure*, no. 20 (1963): 13.

31 Laurent Thévenot, 'Une jeunesse difficile: les fonctions sociales du flou et de la rigueur dans les classements', *Actes de la recherche en sciences sociales*, nos. 26–7 (1979): 3–18.

32 The end of this conclusion to the lecture is missing from the recording.

Lecture of 23 November 1982

1 An allusion to the definition by Max Weber of the contemporary state as 'that human community which (successfully) lays claim to *the monopoly of legitimate physical violence,* within a certain territory' (Max Weber, 'The profession and vocation of politics', in *Political Writings* (Cambridge: Cambridge University Press, 1994), pp. 310–11).

2 See Bourdieu, *The Political Ontology of Martin Heidegger*, trans. Peter Collier (Cambridge: Polity, 1991), and *Classification Struggles*, the lectures for 26 May and 16 June 1982, p. 68. and pp. 118–19.

3 See Bourdieu, 'Post-script: towards a "vulgar" critique of "pure" critiques', in *Distinction*, trans. Richard Nice (London: Routledge, 1984), pp. 485–500.

4 See Bourdieu, 'Le Nord et le Midi: contribution à une analyse de l'effet Montesquieu', *Actes de la recherche en sciences sociales*, no. 35 (1980): 21–5; repr. as 'La rhétorique de la scientificité', in *Langage et pouvoir symbolique* (Paris: Seuil, 2001), pp. 331–42.

5 Pierre Gourou, 'Le déterminisme physique dans *l'Esprit des lois*', *L'Homme*, no. 3 (1963): 5–11.

6 Montesquieu's theory of climates is exposed principally in books 14 to 17 of *The Spirit of the Laws*, trans. Anne M. Cohler (Cambridge: Cambridge University Press, [1748] 1989), pp. 231–84.

7 Ibid., p. 233.

8 See above, Lecture of 19 October, note 33, p. 359.

9 The 'meeting of minds' is a traditional theological and philosophical theme. In

the post-war decades, it was often evoked in relation to phenomenology and the existentialist philosophers, because they were challenging the more solipsistic conception of mind that was privileged in the classic philosophy deriving in particular from Descartes.

10 Claude Lévi-Strauss, *The Savage Mind* (Oxford: Oxford University Press, 1996).

11 This is no doubt the manuscript of an article that was published after the lectures: Martine Dumont, 'Le Succès mondain d'une fausse science: la physiognomonie de Johann Kaspar Lavater', *Actes de la recherche en sciences sociales*, no. 54 (1984): 2–30.

12 The author of the volumes *L'Argot* (no. 700, 1st edn 1956) and *Le Français populaire* (no. 1172, 1st edn 1965) is Pierre Guiraud, a professor of linguistics at the University of Nice.

13 Some extracts from Lavater's German treatise (1775–8) were translated into French as early as 1797 'with observations on the characteristics of certain personalities who figured in the French Revolution', and the complete text was published as *L'Art de connaître les hommes par la physionomie* in 1806; Eng. trans.: Johann Kaspar Lavater, *Essays on Physiognomy* (London: Forgotten Books, [1789–98] 2016).

14 In Book IV of the *Republic*, Plato distinguishes between three major characteristics of the soul ('desire', 'reason' and 'will') with which men are unequally endowed and which determine the place that is best suited for them in the city.

15 Balzac was inspired by Lavater for the physiognomy of the characters of *The Human Comedy*. See Dumont, 'Le Succès mondain d'une fausse science', p. 29.

16 Bourdieu, *The Political Ontology of Martin Heidegger*.

17 See above, the passage on Marxist teleology in the Lecture of 9 November 1982, pp. 116–17.

18 Bourdieu, 'L'Invention de la vie d'artiste', *Actes de la recherche en sciences sociales*, no. 2 (1975): 67–93, and the development of this analysis in *The Rules of Art*, trans. Susan Emanuel (Cambridge: Polity, 1996).

19 See Jacques Lacan, 'Seminar on "The Purloined Letter"', in *Écrits* (London: W. W. Norton, 2007), pp. 6–48.

20 See Jean-Paul Sartre, *The Family Idiot: Gustave Flaubert 1821–1857*, trans. Carol Cosman (Chicago: University of Chicago Press, 5 vols, 1971–93).

21 In sociology, we may recall, for instance, the title of Raymond Aron's inaugural lecture at the Collège de France: *De la condition historique du sociologue: leçon inaugurale au Collège de France prononcée le 1er décembre 1970* (Paris: Gallimard, 1971).

22 An allusion to the success in the years following May 1968 within militant circles of formulae such as 'Where are you coming from, comrade?'

23 See above, Lecture of 16 November, note 30, p. 369.

24 Here we reproduce the schema that figures in *Homo Academicus*, trans. Peter Collier (Cambridge: Polity, 1988), p. 122; the one that Bourdieu actually drew in the lecture must have been the draft for it.

25 Pierre Bourdieu and Monique de Saint Martin, 'L'Excellence scolaire et les valeurs du système d'enseignement français', *Annales ESC*, 25/1 (1970): 147–75.

26 The *concours général* is a prestigious annual national academic competition between baccalaureate students in nearly all subjects. Gifted students are

selected to participate by their teachers and their school principal. Usually, no more than one student per *lycée* is allowed to participate in the competition.

27 Emmanuel Kant, *The Conflict of the Faculties* (Cambridge: Cambridge University Press, [1798] 1996). See Bourdieu, *Homo Academicus*, pp. 62–3.

28 In France the discipline of economics developed at first within the law faculties.

29 The formula 'The style is the man himself' is taken from the naturalist's speech of reception at the Académie française in 1753. Wolf Lepenies, 'Der Wissenschaftler als Autor – Buffons prekarer Nachruhm', in *Das Ende der Naturgeschichte: Wandel kultureller Selbstverstandlichkeiten den Wissenschaften des 18. und 19. Jahrhunderts* (Munich: Carl Hanser, 1976), pp. 131–68.

30 See Bourdieu and Saint Martin, 'L'Excellence scolaire et les valeurs du système d'enseignement français'.

31 This somewhat disenchanted remark was to lead to a major enquiry into social misery that was launched a few years later and published as *The Weight of the World*, trans. Priscilla Parkhurst Ferguson et al. (Cambridge, Polity, 1999).

32 See above, Lecture of 2 November 1982, p. 99.

33 A degree in sociology was created in the arts and social sciences faculties by a decree of 2 April 1958.

34 Sociology is at the head of the classification of the sciences proposed by Auguste Comte, in particular in the *Cours de philosophie positive*, trans. Harriet Martineau as *The Positive Philosophy of Auguste Comte*, 2 vols (New York: Appleton, [1830–42] 1858). The sciences, in this classification, occupy a position all the higher because their object is more complex and less independent (and because, correlatively, they acceded later to the 'positive state'). Thus Comte's hierarchy starts with mathematics, moves up to astronomy and physics, then chemistry and biology, and lastly 'social physics' (which he finally rebaptised as 'sociology', precisely to mark out its autonomy from physics and the other, older, sciences).

35 Jacques Derrida, *Of Grammatology*, trans. Gayatri Chakravorty Spivak (Baltimore: Johns Hopkins University Press, [1967] 1997); Michel Foucault, *The Archeology of Knowledge*, trans. A. M. Sheridan Smith (London: Routledge, [1969] 2002).

36 A reference to Charles Péguy's formula 'Kantianism has clean hands, but it has no hands.' Charles Péguy, *Victor-Marie, comte Hugo*, in *Œuvres*, vol. III (Paris: Gallimard, [1910] 1992), p. 331.

37 Bourdieu is referring to Claude Lévi-Strauss's importation of the word 'anthropology' from the English-speaking world. The discipline thus renamed was conceived by Lévi-Strauss as the culmination (or 'synthesis') of a search for 'a global knowledge of man', of which ethnography and ethnology were the preliminary stages (Claude Lévi-Strauss, *Structural Anthropology* (New York: Basic Books, 1974), p. 355). Kant gave a notable series of lectures on *Anthropology from a Pragmatic Point of View* (Cambridge: Cambridge University Press, [1798] 2008), of which a translation by Michel Foucault, *L'Anthropologie d'un point de vue pragmatique*, was published by Vrin in 1964.

38 Probably an allusion to a book by Kostas Axelos, *Vers la pensée planétaire: le devenir-pensée du monde et le devenir-monde de la pensée* (Paris: Minuit, 1964).

39 This formula, which Bourdieu quotes in different circumstances (see, for example, *Distinction*, p. 444), is in fact due to Maxime Chastaing in *La Philosophie de Virginia Woolf* (Paris: PUF, 1951), p. 48: '[They are] briefly,

general ideas. But these ideas are in fact generals' ideas.' The text by Virginia Woolf to which Chastaing refers has not been definitely identified, but it is most probably a passage from the short story 'The mark on the wall' (1917):

> these generalizations are very worthless. The military sound of the word is enough. It recalls leading articles, cabinet ministers – a whole class of things indeed which as a child one thought the thing itself, the standard thing, the real thing, from which one could not depart save at the risk of nameless damnation ... Generalizations bring back somehow Sunday in London, Sunday afternoon walks, Sunday luncheons, and also ways of speaking of the dead, clothes, and habits – like the habit of sitting all together in one room until a certain hour, although nobody liked it. (Virginia Woolf, *The Mark on the Wall and Other Short Fiction* (Oxford: Oxford University Press, 2008), p. 6)

40 In this formula, Bourdieu may be condensing a passage from Marx: 'We do not mean it to be understood from this that, for example, the rentier, the capitalist, etc., cease to be persons; but their personality is conditioned and determined by quite definite class relationships, and the division appears only in their opposition to another class and, for themselves, only when they go bankrupt' (Karl Marx and Frederick Engels, *The German Ideology*, in *Collected Works*, Vol. 5: *1845–47* (London: Lawrence & Wishart, 1976), p. 78.

41 On the 'morality of resentment' (or slave morality) that Nietzsche opposes to 'noble morality' (or master morality), see in particular *On the Genealogy of Morals*, trans. Michael A. Scarpitti (London: Penguin, [1887] 2013).

42 This is the baccalaureate option renamed 'ES' in 1995. The allusion here is to the fact that this option, characterised by its major subjects of economic and social sciences, and which dated only from 1968, found it difficult to compete, in terms of academic excellence and social recruitment, with the traditional prestige of the literary baccalaureates and the more recent prestige of the scientific baccalaureates.

43 See above, Lecture of 19 October 1982, note 24, p. 358.

44 An allusion to the principal Durkheimian sociologists (Émile Durkheim himself, Marcel Mauss, François Simiand, Maurice Halbwachs, etc.) who had graduated, often with top honours, with an *agrégation* in philosophy, who came from Jewish families and/or wrote for *L'Humanité*; Marcel Mauss combined all these different properties.

45 A concept used by Spinoza in his *Ethics* and which designates the fact of persevering in one's being.

46 Viviane Isambert-Jamati (with Régine Sirota) published a biographical article on Edmond Goblot that made use of the family correspondence (Goblot was her great-uncle): 'La Barrière, oui, mais le niveau?', *Cahiers internationaux de sociologie*, no. 71 (1981): 4–33; later she published *Solidarité fraternelle et réussite sociale: la correspondance familiale des Dubois-Goblot (1841–1882)* (Paris: L'Harmattan, 1995).

47 There is no biography of Hubert Bourgin. Bourdieu may be thinking of a book by Bourgin himself, which contains portraits of numerous *normaliens* of the period: *De Jaurès à Léon Blum: l'École normale et la politique*. The book, which was originally published by Fayard in 1938, was reprinted in 1970 (London: Gordon & Breach, 1970).

48 This might be an allusion to the debates provoked by an enterprise such as

the 'sociologie historique' of Charles Tilly (who did in fact present his work at one of Bourdieu's seminars in the 1970s); this differs from the more traditional history practised in the same period by Carl Schorske, for example, at Princeton. In the 1970s, the use of statistics or borrowings from the social sciences by history, which was commonly thought of as a 'branch of literature', was often debated in the *American Historical Review*. These discussions were particularly lively in the United States, where the relations between history and the social sciences (and philosophy) are looser than in France, the former being traditionally attached to the humanities, whereas the social sciences are studied in separate departments.

49 Bourdieu develops this point more fully in the Lecture of 11 January1983, pp. 271–2.
50 Bourdieu applies this analytical grid to his own trajectory in *Sketch for a Self-Analysis*, trans. Richard Nice (Cambridge: Cambridge University Press, 2008).
51 See above, Lecture of 16 November 1982, pp. 143–4.

Lecture of 30 November 1982

1 On colonialism, Sartre writes: 'The old violence is reabsorbed by the inertia-violence of the institution' (*Critique of Dialectical Reason*, trans. Alan Sheridan-Smith (London: Verso, [1960] 2004), vol. 1, p. 723).
2 Spinoza says of *obsequium* that 'obedience is the constant will to execute that, which by law is good, and by the general decree ought to be done' (*Tractatus politicus*, trans. R. H. M. Elwes (New York: Dover, 2004), p. 298). Alexandre Matheron presents *obsequium* and respect for justice as 'the end product of the conditioning which the state uses to shapes us to its ends and enable its preservation' (*Individu et communauté chez Spinoza* (Paris: Minuit, 1969), p. 349).
3 In 1981, *Actes de la recherche en sciences sociales* had published an article by Michael Pollak entitled 'Une sociologie en acte des intellectuels: les combats de Karl Kraus' (nos. 36–7, pp. 87–103). On Karl Kraus, see also Bourdieu, 'À propos de Karl Kraus et du journalisme', *Actes de la recherche en sciences sociales*, nos. 131–2 (2000): 119–26.
4 Pietro Aretino (1492–1556) was the author in particular of satires which mocked princes and noblemen.
5 Bourdieu may be thinking of Aristophanes' play *The Clouds* (423 BC), which, by representing the character called Socrates in a basket hanging up in the air, mocks his pretension to rise above the viewpoint allocated to mere mortals.
6 Bourdieu returns to this notion in his Lecture of 11 January 1983, pp. 266ff.
7 See above, Lecture of 23 November 1982, pp. 154ff.
8 Georges Canguilhem, *Idéologie et rationalité dans l'histoire des sciences de la vie* (Paris: Vrin, 1977), p. 44; Eng. trans. as *Ideology and Rationality in the History of the Life Sciences* (Cambridge, MA: MIT Press, 1988).
9 Gerhard Lenski, 'Status crystallisation: a non-vertical dimension of social status', *American Sociological Review*, 19/4 (1954): 405–13.
10 Here Bourdieu may be confusing an article that he had referred to previously (see above, Lecture of 23 November, note 29, p. 371) with another one, which he had had translated, and which was published a few months later: Wolf Lepenies, 'Contribution à une histoire des rapports entre la sociologie et la

philosophie', *Actes de la recherche en sciences sociales*, nos. 47–8 (1983): 37–44. But he may also be referring to a pre-print copy of a chapter of the first German edition of his *Les Trois Cultures: entre science et littérature, l'avènement de la sociologie*, trans. Henri Plard (Paris: MSH, 1990), which was published only in 1985 but is more pertinent to these reflections on style.

11 Pierre Bourdieu and Monique de Saint Martin, 'L'Excellence scolaire et les valeurs du système d'enseignement français', *Annales ESC*, 25/1 (1970): 147–75; see also the continuation of this analysis in Bourdieu, 'Academic forms of classification', in *The State Nobility*, trans. Lauretta C. Clough (Cambridge: Polity, 1966), pp. 7–70.

12 Fernand Braudel's concept of 'three historical levels of time' – short-term history of events, broader history of conjunctures, and long-term or structural history – is set out in particular in his *On History*, trans. Sarah Matthews (Chicago: University of Chicago Press, 1982), p. 74.

13 See above, Lecture of 19 October 1982, note 24, p. 358.

14 On the 'new professions', see Bourdieu, *Distinction*, trans. Richard Nice (London: Routledge, 1984), pp. 354–71.

15 See Francine Muel-Dreyfus, *Le Métier d'éducateur* (Paris: Minuit, 1983).

16 This may be an allusion to the famous controversy between Raymond Picard, an academic specialising in Racine's theatre, and Roland Barthes, after the latter's publication of *Sur Racine* (Paris: Seuil, 1963), seen as emblematic of the 'new criticism' that emerged during the 1960s and was fustigated by Picard in *Nouvelle critique ou nouvelle imposture?* (Paris: Pauvert, 1965). In his day, Jules Lemaître had savaged the 'historical criticism' developed by Hippolyte Taine in his *Nouveaux essais de critique et d'histoire* (1865), mocking its 'obsession with seeing nothing more in Racine's tragedies than a reproduction of Versailles' (Lemaître, *Jean Racine* (Paris: Calmann-Lévy, 1908), p. 227), and Lemaître's 'literary criticism' was demoted in its turn by Gustave Lanson's positivism.

17 See, for example, Harold L. Wilensky, 'The professionalization of everyone?', *American Journal of Sociology*, 70/2 (1964): 137–58.

18 See Alvin W. Gouldner, 'Cosmopolitan and locals: toward an analysis of latent social rules', *Administrative Science Quarterly*, 2/3 (1957): 281–306.

19 For these developments, see the lectures of 28 April and 5 May 1982 in Bourdieu, *Classification Struggles* (Cambridge: Polity, 2018), pp. 12 and 18.

20 An implicit critical allusion to the Marxist approach that systematically sees the economic means of production as the final cause ('in the last analysis'), which is a way, attacked by Bourdieu, of short-circuiting a detailed analysis of the mediations that are at work in the first analysis.

21 Pierre Bourdieu, Luc Boltanski and Pascale Maldidier, 'La Défense du corps', *Social Science Information*, 10/4 (1971): 45–86. This question will be developed in *Homo Academicus*.

22 The corps of *maîtres-assistants* (assistant lecturers), created in 1960 to cope with the influx of students, was integrated into the ranks of the *maîtres de conférences* (lecturers) in 1984.

23 Leibniz is often quoted on this point by Bourdieu: 'All things are placed in time as to order of succession; and in space as to order of situation' (in *The Leibniz–Clark Correspondence* (Manchester: Manchester University Press, 1998), p. 154).

24 This may be the article on 'Kingship under the impact of scientific jurisprudence',

in Marshall Clagett, Gaines Post and Robert Reynolds (eds), *Twelfth-Century Europe and the Foundations of Modern Society* (Madison: University of Wisconsin Press, 1961), pp. 89–111.

25 An oft-quoted formula by Marx that opposes the 'radical revolution' to the 'partial, *merely* political revolution, the revolution which leaves the pillars of the building standing' (Karl Marx, *A Contribution to the Critique of Hegel's Philosophy of Right: Introduction*, in *Early Writings* (London: Penguin, [1844] 1992), p. 253).

26 See Karl Marx, *The Eighteenth Brumaire of Louis Bonaparte*, in *Surveys from Exile* (Harmondsworth: Penguin, [1852] 1973), pp. 143–249.

27 See, for example, Émile Durkheim, 'Individual and collective representations' (1898), in *Sociology and Philosophy* (London: Routledge, 2009), pp. 1–34.

28 Michel Butor, 'Individu et groupe dans le roman' (1962), in *Répertoire II* (Paris: Minuit, 1964), pp. 73–87.

29 See *Classification Struggles*, Lecture of 2 June 1982, pp. 84–5.

Lecture of 7 December 1982

1 Ernst Cassirer, *Substance and Function and Einstein's Theory of Relativity*, trans. William Curtis Swabey and Marie Collins Swabey (NewYork: Dover, [1910] 2003).

2 Ernst Cassirer, 'Structuralism in modern linguistics', *Word: Journal of the Linguistic Circle of New York*, 1/2 (1945): 99–120.

3 Bourdieu, 'Structuralism and theory of sociological knowledge', trans. A. Zanotti-Karp, *Social Research*, 35/4 (1968): 681–706.

4 See Kurt Lewin, *Field Theory in Social Science: Selected Theoretical Papers*, ed. Dorwin Cartwright (New York: Harper, 1951).

5 Gaston Bachelard, *The New Scientific Spirit*, trans. Arthur Goldhammer (Boston: Beacon Press, [1934] 1984), chap. 1, 'Dilemmas in the philosophy of geometry', pp. 24–5.

6 Bourdieu (in 'Structuralism and theory of sociological knowledge', p. 690) quotes the physicist Hermann Weyl saying that the electron is not '*an element of the field but "a product of the field" (eine Ausgeburt des Felds)*'.

7 We can link this passage to the following quotation in *On Television and Journalism*, trans. Priscilla Parkhurst Ferguson (London: Pluto Press, 2011), p. 54: 'It is vital to understand that [Bernard-Henri Lévy] is only a sort of structural epiphenomenon, and that, like an electron, he is the expression of a field. You can't understand anything if you don't understand the field that produces him and gives him his parcel of power.'

8 See *Théorie de la littérature: textes des formalistes russes*, ed. and trans. Tzvetan Todorov (Paris: Seuil, [1966] 2001).

9 See in particular Itamar Even-Zohar, 'Polysystem theory', *Poetics Today*, 1/1–2 (1979): 287–310.

10 See Charles S. Peirce, *Peirce on Signs: Writings on Semiotic* (Chapel Hill: University of North Carolina Press, 1991).

11 The word 'orthodoxy' is derived from the Greek *orthos*, which means 'right'.

12 'If I were as famous as Paul Bourget I would perform in a cabaret with a G-string every evening and I guarantee that I would draw in the crowd' (Arthur Cravan, 'L'Exposition des indépendants', *Maintenant*, no. 4 (1914).

Bourdieu quotes this phrase in 'Le Marché des biens symboliques', *L'Année sociologique*, 22 (1971): 49–126, at p. 107).

13 After theorising the concept of *episteme* in *The Order of Things* (London: Routledge, [1966] 2001) and *The Archeology of Knowledge* (London: Routledge, [1969] 2002), Michel Foucault ceased to use it.

14 Émile Durkheim, *The Evolution of Educational Thought: Lectures on the Formation and Development of Secondary Education in France (Selected Writings on Education)* (London: Routledge, [1938] 2006).

15 Paul Bénichou, *Morales du Grand Siècle* (Paris: Gallimard, 1948); Eng. trans. as *Man and Ethics: Studies in French Classicism* (Garden City, NY: Anchor Books, 1971).

16 Vladimir Propp, *Morphologie du conte*, trans. Marguerite Derrida, Tzvetan Todorov and Claude Kahn (Paris: Seuil, [1928] 1958); Eng. trans. as *Morphology of the Folktale* (Austin: University of Texas Press, 1968).

17 On conservatism and the social trajectory, see Bourdieu, *Distinction*, trans. Richard Nice (London: Routledge, 1984), in particular pp. 453–65. On 'substantialism', see *Distinction*, p. 22 (Trans.).

18 At the time of the lectures, only a partial French translation of Karl Mannheim's book *Ideology and Utopia: An Introduction to the Sociology of Knowledge*, was available (trans. Pauline Rollet (Paris: Marcel Rivière, [1929] 1956); a complete French translation, by Jean-Luc Evard, was published by MSH in 2006. Mannheim speaks of a 'socially unattached' or 'free-floating' intelligentsia.

> Thus [unattached intellectuals] always furnished the theorists for the conservatives who themselves because of their own social stability could only with difficulty be brought to theoretical self-consciousness. . . . They likewise furnished the theories for the proletariat, which, because of its social conditions, lacked the prerequisites for the acquisition of the knowledge necessary for modern political conflict. Their affiliation with the liberal bourgeoisie has already been discussed. This ability to attach themselves to classes to which they originally did not belong was possible for intellectuals, because they could attach themselves to any viewpoint and because they and they alone were in a position to choose their affiliation, while those who were immediately bound by class affiliations were only in rare exceptions able to transcend the boundaries of their class outlook. (*Collected Works of Karl Mannheim*, trans. Louis Wirth and Edward A. Shils, Vol. 1: *Ideology and Utopia* (London: Routledge, [1936] 2002), p. 141).

The notion of the 'organic intellectual', which is set up in opposition to the former, is taken from Antonio Gramsci: 'Every social group, coming into existence on the original terrain of an essential function in the world of economic production, creates together with itself, organically, one or more strata of intellectuals which give it homogeneity and an awareness of its own function not only in the economic but also in the social and political fields' (from 'Prison notebooks', in *An Anthology of Western Marxism*, ed. Roger S. Gottlieb (Oxford: Oxford University Press, 1989), p. 113).

19 Often quoted in its Latin translation (the Dutch original has been lost), the formula '*determinatio negatio est*' is used by Spinoza within the limited framework of the figure:

As to the doctrine that figure is negation and not anything positive, it is plain that the whole of matter considered indefinitely can have no figure, and that figure can only exist in finite and determinate bodies. For he who says, that he perceives a figure, merely indicates thereby, that he conceives a determinate thing, and how it is determinate. This determination, therefore, does not appertain to the thing according to its being, but, on the contrary, is its non-being. As then figure is nothing else than determination, and determination is negation, figure, as has been said, can be nothing but negation. ('Letter L: to Jarig Jellis', The Hague, 2 June 1674, in Baruch Spinoza, *Correspondence* [1883], pp. 369–70; http://sacred-texts.com/phi/spinoza/corr/corr48.htm)

20 The *commune, canton* and *département* are three administrative divisions of France. The *département*, roughly equivalent to an English county, is administered by an elected *conseil départemental*. Local services of the state administration are traditionally organised at departmental level. The *départements* are divided up into *cantons*, whose main role is to provide a framework for departmental elections. The *commune* is the smallest unit, equivalent to a parish or a village, but nonetheless elects its own mayor.

21 On this point, see Patrick Champagne, 'La Restructuration de l'espace villageois', *Actes de la recherche en sciences sociales*, 1/3 (1975): 43–67; repr. in *L'Héritage refusé* (Paris: Seuil, 2002), pp. 51–95.

22 'Scientific observation is always polemical' (Bachelard, *The New Scientific Spirit*, p. 12).

23 For developments of the argument on the difference between field and apparatus, see Pierre Bourdieu and Loïc Wacquant, *An Invitation to Reflexive Sociology* (Cambridge: Polity, 1992), p. 102.

24 See Pierre Bourdieu and Luc Boltanski, 'La Production de l'idéologie dominante', *Actes de la recherche en sciences sociales*, 2/2–3 (1976): 3–73; repr. (Paris: Démopolis, 2007). (Funded in 1946 in order to direct France's economic planning, the 'Commissariat général au Plan' was replaced in 2006 by the 'Centre d'analyse stratégique' then, in 2013, by the 'Commissariat général à la stratégie et à la prospective'.)

25 An allusion to Proust's analysis, in *In Search of Lost Time*, of Mme Verdurin's salon, which 'did not invite you to dinner: you had, at their house, a "place set for you". For the soirée there was no programme, the young pianist would play, but only if he "fancied", because they did not force anyone and, as M. Verdurin said: "Anything for our friends, long live our pals!"' (*The Way by Swann's*, trans. Lydia Davis (London: Penguin, 2002), p. 192).

26 Bourdieu developed the analysis of the salons in *The Rules of Art*, trans. Susan Emanuel (Cambridge: Polity, 1996), in particular pp. 57–60, and the analysis of the struggles between fields at the heart of the dominant class (or the State), in *The State Nobility*, trans. Lauretta C. Clough (Cambridge: Polity, 1966), Parts IV and V.

27 This is the enquiry into bishops by Pierre Bourdieu and Monique de Saint Martin, published as 'La Sainte Famille: l'épiscopat français dans le champ du pouvoir', *Actes de la recherche en sciences sociales*, nos. 44–5 (1982): 2–53.

28 On the analogy between energy and capital as social power, see Bourdieu, *The Logic of Practice*, trans. Richard Nice (Cambridge: Polity, 1990), p. 300, where

Bourdieu reproduces and comments on a quotation from Bertrand Russell on this subject.

29 Gustav Fechner (1801–1887) was the creator of psychophysics, a science aiming to measure psychological phenomena almost mathematically.

30 On the 'entitlement effect', see *Distinction*, pp. 22–3 (Trans.).

31   When a man who is happy compares his position with that of one who is unhappy, he is not content with the fact of his happiness, but desires something more, namely the right to this happiness, the consciousness that he has earned this good fortune, in contrast to the unfortunate one who must equally have earned his misfortune. Our everyday experience proves that there exists just such a need for reassurance as to the legitimacy or deservedness of one's happiness, whether this involves political success, superior economic status, bodily health, success in the game of love, or anything else. What the privileged classes require of religion, if anything at all, is this psychological reassurance of legitimacy.

Weber contrasts this theodicy of 'good fortune' with the 'theodicy of disprivilege'. (Max Weber, *The Sociology of Religion*, trans. Ephraim Fischoff (Boston: Beacon Press, [1920] 1964), pp. 107, 113)

32 Bourdieu and Boltanski, 'La Production de l'idéologie dominante', in particular p. 8, n. 4.

33 An allusion to the definition by Max Weber of the contemporary State as 'that human community which (successfully) lays claim to *the monopoly of legitimate physical violence*, within a certain territory' (Max Weber, 'The profession and vocation of politics', in *Political Writings* (Cambridge: Cambridge University Press, 1994), pp. 310–11).

34 Montesquieu uses the procedure of the naïve gaze in the *Persian Letters* (Oxford: Oxford University Press, [1721] 2008): French society is evoked through the eyes of a foreigner, a Persian philosopher.

35 See Bourdieu, 'The forms of capital', trans. Richard Nice, in John G. Richardson (ed.), *Handbook of Theory and Research for the Sociology of Education* (New York: Greenwood Press, 1986), pp. 241–58.

36 See Bourdieu, *Distinction*, in particular pp. 71–2, 281–2, and *passim*.

37 See the developments on the importance of symbolic capital in Bourdieu, *The Logic of Practice*, pp. 112–21.

38 Émile Benveniste, *Dictionary of Indo-European Concepts and Society* (Chicago: Hau Books, 2016), pp. 105–11.

39 On these points, see also Bourdieu, 'Le Capital social: notes provisoires', *Actes de la recherche en sciences sociales*, no. 31 (1980): 2–3.

40 See Bourdieu, 'Les Stratégies matrimoniales dans le système des stratégies de reproduction', *Annales ESC*, 27/4–5 (1972): 1105–27; repr. as 'Matrimonial strategies in the system of reproduction strategies', in *The Bachelors' Ball*, trans. Richard Nice (Cambridge: Polity, 2007), pp. 131–59, in particular pp. 135–8.

41 Bourdieu reveals part of the 'genesis' of this idea in his *Sketch for a Self-Analysis*, trans. Richard Nice (Cambridge: Polity, 2007), p. 65:

As I have said elsewhere, it was no doubt a banal remark of my mother's, which I would not even have picked up if I had not been alerted to it ('they've become very "kith and kin" with the X's now that there's a *Polytechnicien* in the family') that, at the time of my study of bachelorhood, triggered the reflexions that led me to abandon the model of the kinship rule for that of strategy.

42 An isotropic scaling transformation.

43 Pierre Bourdieu and Yvette Delsaut, 'Le Couturier et sa griffe: contribution à une théorie de la magie', *Actes de la recherche en sciences sociales*, 1/1 (1975): 7–36.

Lecture of 14 December 1982

1 An ideograph is usually a symbol standing for an idea – here it is the equivalent of a monograph devoted to a single concept.

2 Bourdieu refers to this example again in *Masculine Domination*, trans. Richard Nice (Cambridge: Polity, 2002), p. 1.

3 On the logics that govern 'the right to speak', see Bourdieu, *Distinction*, trans. Richard Nice (London: Routledge, 1984), pp. 411ff. Bourdieu returns to this question on several occasions, in particular in *On Television and Journalism*, trans. Priscilla Parkhurst Ferguson (London: Pluto Press, 2011), 'In front of the camera and behind the scenes', pp. 13–38.

4 The 'Roudy Act', so-called after the name of the woman appointed minister for women's rights when the left came to power in 1981, which proposed to refund voluntary termination of pregnancy, was about to be adopted at the time of these lectures.

5 Kurt Lewin, pioneer in social psychology. See *Resolving Social Conflicts: Field Theory in Social Science* (Washington, DC: American Psychological Association, 1997).

6 'The scientific mind overcomes the different epistemological obstacles and constitutes itself as rectified errors' (Gaston Bachelard, *The Formation of the Scientific Mind* (Manchester: Clinamen, [1938] 2002), p. 237).

7 Bourdieu, 'Champ intellectuel et projet créateur', *Les Temps modernes*, no. 246 (1966): 865–906.

8 Bourdieu is referring in particular to the approach developed by Ronald S. Burt, *Toward a Structural Theory of Action: Network Models of Social Structure, Perception, and Action* (New York: Academic Press, 1982).

9 The sociogram is a technique used since the 1930s. In its simplest form, it consists in representing the members of a group by a cloud of points and in joining or not joining the different points with lines, according to whether the corresponding individuals are linked or not. Sociograms can represent, for example, the relations existing within a group constituted by pupils from the same class (whence the reference to children that figures in the next sentence).

10 The concept of relative autonomy is linked to the Marxist tradition. Although they wrote for example that, in their relation to the economic infrastructure, 'Morality, religion, metaphysics, all the rest of ideology and their corresponding forms of consciousness, thus no longer retain the semblance of independence' (Karl Marx and Friedrich Engels, *The German Ideology*, in *Collected Works*, Vol. 5: *1845–47* (London: Lawrence & Wishart, 1987), p. 47), Marx and especially Engels did draw attention to the relative autonomy enjoyed, despite everything, by the 'superstructure'. On this point, Bourdieu has several

times quoted a letter to Conrad Schmidt where Engels speaks of the relative autonomy of the corps of jurists. (Marx and Engels, *Collected Works*, Vol. 49: *Letters 1890–1892* (London: Lawrence & Wishart, 2010), pp. 60–61).

11 Talcott Parsons was the translator (with Alexander Morell Henderson) of the first volume of *Economy and Society* under the title of *The Theory of Social and Economic Organization* (Oxford: Oxford University Press, 1947).

12 On the sociological context of the period and the hegemony of Talcott Parsons and, more generally, what Bourdieu calls 'the little Parsons–Lazarsfeld– Merton triangle', see 'Landmark', in *In Other Words*, trans. Matthew Adamson (Cambridge: Polity, 1990), pp. 36–8; see also 'La Cause de la science: comment l'histoire des sciences sociales peut servir le progrès de ces sciences', *Actes de la recherche en sciences sociales*, nos. 106–7 (1995): 6; and *Sketch for a Self-Analysis*, trans. Richard Nice (Cambridge: Polity, 2007), p. 72.

13 Bourdieu develops this point in his last lecture at the Collège de France in 2000–1, devoted to the scientific field and published under the title *Science of Science and Reflexivity*, trans. Richard Nice (Cambridge: Polity, 2004).

14 Bourdieu, 'Une interprétation de la théorie de la religion selon Max Weber', *Archives européennes de sociologie*, 2/1 (1971): 3–21 (from which the figure on p. 241 is taken); 'Genèse et structure du champ religieux', *Revue française de sociologie*, 12/3 (1971): 295–334. These articles were incorporated into *Microcosmes* (to be published by Éditions du Seuil), his unfinished work on the theory of fields.

15 This enterprise took place within the framework of a seminar on the social history of literature, art and forms of domination given at the École normale supérieure by Bourdieu and Jean-Claude Chamboredon, starting in 1968. Among the articles arising from this seminar, see, in addition to Bourdieu, 'Champ du pouvoir, champ intellectuel et habitus de classe', *Scolies: Cahiers de recherche de l'École normale supérieure*, no. 1 (1971): 7–26; Christophe Charle, 'L'Expansion et la crise de la production littéraire (2e moitié du XIXe siècle)', *Actes de la recherche en sciences sociales*, 1/4 (1975): 44–65; Christophe Charle, 'Situation sociale et position sociale: essai de géographie sociale du champ littéraire à la fin du XIXe siècle', *Actes de la recherche en sciences sociales*, no. 13 (1977): 45–59; Jean-Claude Chamboredon, 'Marché de la littérature et stratégies intellectuelles dans le champ littéraire', *Actes de la recherche en sciences sociales*, 1/4 (1975): 41–3; Rémy Ponton, 'Naissance du roman psychologique', *Actes de la recherche en sciences sociales*, 1/4 (1975): 66–81; Rémy Ponton, 'Les Images de la paysannerie dans le roman rural à la fin du XIXe siècle', *Actes de la recherche en sciences sociales*, nos. 17–18 (1977): 62–71.

16 See in particular Robert Escarpit, *Sociologie de la littérature* (Paris: PUF, 1958), and Escarpit (ed.), *Le Littéraire et le social* (Paris: Flammarion, 1970).

17 Georges Canguilhem, *La Connaissance de la vie* (2nd enlarged edn, Paris: Vrin, [1952] 1965).

18 Karl Marx, *Grundrisse: Foundations of the Critique of Political Economy* (Harmondsworth: Penguin, [1857–61] 1993), pp. 106–7.

19 Marx often refers to Max Stirner by the nickname of 'Sancho', taken from *Don Quixote*:

Sancho wants, or rather *believes* he wants, that intercourse between individuals should be purely personal, that their intercourse should not be mediated through some third thing (cf. competition). This third thing here is the 'something special', or the special, not absolute, contradiction, i.e., the position of individuals in relation to one another determined by present-day social relations. Sancho does not want, for example, two individuals to be in 'contradiction' to one another as bourgeois and proletarian; he protests against the 'special' which forms the 'advantage' of the bourgeois over the proletarian; he would like to have them enter into a purely personal relation, to associate with one another merely as individuals. He does not take into consideration that in the framework of division of labour personal relations necessarily and inevitably develop into class relations. (Karl Marx and Frederick Engels, *The German Ideology*, in *Collected Works*, Vol. 5: *1845–47* (London: Lawrence & Wishart, 2000), pp. 436–7)

20 See in particular Bourdieu, *Distinction*, pp. 472–3.
21 An allusion to the interview with Michel Foucault published in the first issue of the review *Hérodote*: 'Questions à Michel Foucault sur la géographie', *Hérodote*, no. 1 (1976): 71–85.
22 According to an anecdote told with slight variants in different sources (for example: Groucho Marx, *Groucho and Me*, New York: Da Capo Press, 1995, p. 321), Groucho Marx replied towards the end of the 1940s to the invitation by a private club for celebrities: 'I don't want to belong to any club that will accept people like me as a member.'
23 Louis Pinto, 'Les Affinités électives: les amis du *Nouvel Observateur* comme "groupe ouvert"', *Actes de la recherche en sciences sociales*, nos. 36–7 (1981): 105–24. (This research was developed in *L'Intelligence en action: Le Nouvel Observateur* (Paris: Métailié, 1984).)
24 In October 1982 (that is, two months before this lecture), Régis Debray (the author a few years earlier of *Le Pouvoir intellectuel en France* (Paris: Ramsay, 1979), who was giving a lecture on literature in Montreal, had made statements that were repeated and commented on in several media: he criticised the journalist Bernard Pivot, the presenter of the principal literary broadcast of the period, for 'exercising a veritable dictatorship over the book market' and denounced the power that he had acquired in literary life, speaking of the 'arbitrary will of a single man'.
25 This is most probably Svend Ranulf (who was, however, Danish), *Moral Indignation and Middle Class Psychology* (Copenhagen: Levin & Munksgaard, 1938).
26 This point is developed in Bourdieu, 'Condition de classe et position de classe', *Archives européennes de sociologie*, 7/2 (1966): 201–23.
27 See above, Lecture of 23 November, p. 171.

28 It has no doubt been the taste for 'living all lives' that Flaubert speaks of, and for seizing every opportunity to enter into the adventure that opens up each time with the discovery of new milieux (or simply the excitement of starting a new research project), that, together with the refusal of the scientistic definition of sociology, has led me to interest myself in the most diverse social worlds. . . . And so I have been able to participate in universes of thought, past or present, very distant from my own, such as those of the aristocracy or bankers, dancers at the Paris Opéra or actors at the Théâtre Français, auctioneers or notaries, and work myself into them. (Bourdieu, *Sketch for a Self-Analysis*, pp. 65–6)

29 See above, Lecture of 7 December, note 18, p. 376.
30 See above, Lecture of 19 October, note 25, p. 358.
31 See in particular George Herbert Mead, *Mind, Self and Society* (Chicago: University of Chicago Press, [1934] 2015).
32 See in particular Barney Glaser and Anselm Strauss, *Awareness of Dying* (Chicago: Aldine, 1965).
33 See Erving Goffman, *Frame Analysis: An Essay on the Organization of Experience* (Cambridge, MA: Harvard University Press, 1974).
34 J. L. Austin, *How to Do Things with Words* (Oxford: Oxford University Press, 2009). See the arguments that Bourdieu devoted to him at the time of these lectures in *Ce que parler veut dire*, repr. in *Language and Symbolic Power*, trans. Gino Raymond and Matthew Adamson (Cambridge: Polity, 1991), in particular pp. 107–11.
35 Several fundamental works of the Palo Alto School had just been translated by Éditions du Seuil, including in particular Paul Watzlawick and John H. Weakland (eds), *Sur l'interaction: Palo Alto (1965–1974): une nouvelle approche thérapeutique* (Paris: Seuil, [1977] 1981). In English: *The Interactional View: Studies at the Mental Research Institute, Palo Alto, 1965–1974* (London: W. W. Norton, 1977).
36 Émile Durkheim, *The Rules of Sociological Method*, trans. W. D. Halls, ed. Steven Lukes (New York: Free Press, [1895] 1982), pp. 128–31.
37 In particular in the lectures for the year 1985–6, for which there is a manuscript version that has since been published: Bourdieu, 'Champ du pouvoir et division du travail de domination', *Actes de la recherche en sciences sociales*, no. 190 (2011): 126–39.

Lecture of 11 January 1983

1 Bourdieu develops all the issues raised in this lecture in *The Rules of Art*, trans. Susan Emanuel (Cambridge: Polity, 1996).
2 The *philosophia perennis* was a trend in Renaissance philosophy, epitomised by Marsilio Ficino, that argues for metaphysical unity behind apparent contradictions.
3 Émile Durkheim, *The Rules of Sociological Method*, trans. W. D. Halls, ed. Steven Lukes (New York: Free Press, [1895] 1982), p. 29.
4 Bourdieu returned in 1999 to the structure of the field of publishing and the paths of entry for new writers: 'Une révolution conservatrice dans l'édition', *Actes de la recherche en sciences sociales*, nos. 126–9 (1999): 3–26.
5 Bourdieu uses this analogy again in *Pascalian Meditations*, trans. Richard Nice (Cambridge: Polity, 2000), p. 214, with reference to Dostoevsky's *The Gambler*.
6 On this property of fields and the image of gambling and chips, see 'Some properties of fields', in *Sociology in Question*, trans. Richard Nice (London: Sage, 1993), pp. 72–7.
7 On the alternatives to private income or sales, see *The Rules of Art*, pp. 81–5. It is a remark by Théophile Gautier to Ernest Feydeau that is quoted here: 'Flaubert is cleverer than us, he was intelligent enough to come into this world with some sort of inheritance, a thing that is absolutely indispensable for anyone who wants to "go in for art"' (Feydeau, *Théophile Gautier: souvenirs intimes* (Paris: Plon, 1874), pp. 126–7).

8 See, for example, *Distinction*, trans. Richard Nice (London: Routledge, 1984), pp. 177–9, 243–4, 372–9.

9 'The German language has kept "essence" (*Wesen*) in the past participle (*gewesen*) of the verb "to be" (*sein*), for essence is past – but timelessly past – being' (Georg Wilhelm Friedrich Hegel, *The Science of Logic*, trans. George di Giovanni (Cambridge: Cambridge University Press, [1816] 2015), p. 337).

10 Jules Huret, *Enquête sur l'évolution littéraire* (Vanves: Thot, [1891] 1982).

11 Albert Cassagne, *La Théorie de l'art pour l'art en France chez les derniers romantiques et les premiers réalistes* (Geneva: Slatkine, [1906] 1979).

12 Jean-Paul Sartre, *The Family Idiot: Gustave Flaubert 1821–1857*, trans. Carol Cosman (Chicago: University of Chicago Press, 5 vols, 1971–93).

13 On Bourdieu's analysis of Flaubert, see *The Rules of Art*, pp. 3–43 and *passim*.

14 Bourdieu approaches himself in the same manner in his *Sketch for a Self-Analysis*, trans. Richard Nice (Cambridge: Polity, 2007), written towards the end of his life, where the order of exposition is also the contrary of that of traditional biographies.

15 See Georg Lukács, *The Theory of the Novel*, trans. Anna Bostock (Cambridge, MA: MIT Press, [1916] 1974); Lucien Goldmann, *Towards a Sociology of the Novel* (London: Routledge, [1964] 1977).

16 Frederick Antal, *Florentine Painting and its Social Background* (London: Routledge & Kegan Paul, 1948).

17 The Franco-Prussian War (1870–1), which caused the overthrow of Napoleon III and his 'Third Empire', ended with the French National Assembly, elected in February 1871, concluding a peace with Germany, but the republican Parisians feared that the National Assembly meeting in Versailles would restore the monarchy. To ensure order in Paris, Adolphe Thiers, leader of the provisional national government, decided to disarm the National Guard (composed largely of workers who had fought during the siege of Paris). Resistance broke out in Paris, and on 26 March, municipal elections, organised by the central committee of the guard, resulted in the formation of a Commune government with a revolutionary programme. The Commune of Paris then faced armed suppression by the Versailles government. During *la semaine sanglante* that followed, the regular troops crushed the opposition of the Communards, who in their defence set up barricades in the streets and burned public buildings. Subsequent killings, repression and exiles were widespread and ferocious.

18 On 1 May 1891, the first French and international celebration of International Workers' Day on May Day, troops shot at peaceful strikers in Fourmies in northern France, killing nine among the demonstrators and strikers.

19 Émile Zola set his novel *Germinal* in the important coal mines of the Valenciennes basin belonging to the Anzin Company. The novel dramatises pit disasters, exploitation of miners, and strikes. See Émile Zola, *Germinal*, trans. Peter Collier (Oxford: Oxford University Press, [1885] 1993).

20 These examples are taken from an article by Michel Faure, 'L'Époque 1900 et la résurgence du mythe de Cythère: contribution à l'étude des mentalités sociales à travers les *Fêtes galantes* de Verlaine et de deux de ses musiciens: Fauré et Debussy', *Le Mouvement social*, no. 109 (1979): 15–34. [François Couperin (1668–1733) was a French baroque composer, organist and harpsichordist (Trans.).]

21 On formalism, see above, Lecture of 7 December 1982, pp. 210–11.

22 An allusion to Lucien Goldmann, *The Hidden God: Study of Tragic Vision*

in the 'Pensées' of Pascal and the Tragedies of Racine, trans. Philip Thody (London: Verso, 2016).

23 The thesis by Jean-Louis Fabiani that Bourdieu refers to here (*La Crise du champ philosophique, 1880–1914: contribution à l'histoire sociale du système d'enseignement* [Paris, EHESS, 1980]) was published later with the title *Les Philosophes de la République* (Paris: Minuit, 1988); see in particular pp. 36–8. The manifesto included the phrase 'Here we would like to do something different.'

24 This formula is related in the 'Huret enquiry': 'As they ponder over such stupid and idiotic notions, at this critical moment in the evolution of ideas, all these young things in their thirties and forties make me think of so many nut shells bobbing up and down on their way over the Niagara falls!' (*Enquête sur l'évolution littéraire*, p. 158).

25 Iouri Tynianov, 'De l'évolution littéraire', in Todorov, *Théorie de la littérature*, pp. 120–37. Bourdieu returns to this question in particular in 'Le Champ littéraire', *Actes de la recherche en sciences sociales*, no. 89 (1991): 20–1.

26 In fact the Russian formalists tend to use the term 'defamiliarisation' rather than 'disautomation', but I have kept Bourdieu's pairing (Trans.).

27 Max Weber, 'Charismatic authority and charismatic community', pp. 241–5, and 'The routinization of charisma', pp. 246–54, in *Economy and Society* (Berkeley: University of California Press, 1978).

28 The Second Letter of Paul to the Corinthians, 3:6, The New Testament (London: Dent, 1998), p. 291.

29 See above, Lecture of 30 November, note 16, p. 374, and Bourdieu, *Homo Academicus*, trans. Peter Collier (Cambridge: Polity, 1988), pp. 115–19.

30 The phrase, which Bourdieu alludes to on several occasions, is no doubt: 'Reputation of power is power; because it draweth with it the adherence of those that need protection'. Thomas Hobbes, *Leviathan* (Cambridge: Cambridge University Press, [1651] 1996), chap. X, p. 62.

31 The figure on p. 278 is taken from *The Rules of Art*, p. 124.

32 For developments of this, see Bourdieu, *Distinction*, pp. 128–9, and *La Noblesse d'État: grandes écoles et esprit de corps* (Paris: Minuit: 1988), pp. 100–1, 152, 155, 269–70.

33 'With a mathematical organization of experimental possibilities in hand, it is but a short step back to the empirical. The real turns out to be a particular case of the possible' (Gaston Bachelard, *The New Scientific Spirit*, trans. Arthur Goldhammer (Boston: Beacon Press, [1934] 1984), p. 59).

34 Robert Darnton, *The Business of Enlightenment: A Publishing History of the Encyclopédie* (Cambridge, MA: Harvard University Press, 1987).

35 In English in the original (Trans.).

36 We should remember that these lectures were given in the context of the return of the left to power [with François Mitterrand's election as president of the Republic in 1981 (Trans.)].

37 The question of the price of books was a live issue at the time of these lectures: in August 1981, shortly after the election of a socialist government, the 'law concerning the price of books' was passed. To protect the small booksellers (seen as 'retailers of goods of an exceptional nature'), it prohibited any seller of a book in new condition from offering a discount of more than 5 per cent of the sale price fixed by the publisher.

38 For these developments, see the analysis of *Sentimental Education* in *The Rules of Art*, pp. 3–43.

39 Ibid., in particular pp. 70, 94.
40 This play dates from 1835. It was part of the Romantic movement that was just the start of a series of breaks that only really came to fruition with the generation of Flaubert and Baudelaire.

Lecture of 18 January 1983

1 Christophe Charle, *La Crise littéraire à l'époque du naturalisme: roman, théâtre, politique* (Paris: Presses de l'École normale supérieure, 1979); Rémy Ponton, 'Le Champ littéraire en France de 1865 à 1905', thesis, École des hautes études en sciences sociales, 1977; Rémy Ponton, 'Naissance du roman psychologique', *Actes de la recherche en sciences sociales*, 1/4 (1975): 66–81. See also Jean-Claude Chamboredon, 'Marché de la littérature et stratégies intellectuelles dans le champ littéraire', *Actes de la recherche en sciences sociales*, 1/4 (1975): 78–87.
2 Leibniz speaks of the '*praetensio ad existendum*', for example: 'We must first acknowledge that since something rather than nothing exists, there is a certain urge for existence, or (so to speak) a straining towards existence in possible things or in possibility or essence itself; in a word, essence in and of itself strives for existence' ('On the ultimate origination of things', in *Philosophical Essays*, ed. and trans. Roger Ariew and Daniel Garber (Indianapolis: Hackett, 1989), p. 150).
3 Bourdieu quotes from *Manette Salomon* (1867) later in this lecture, as well as in *The Rules of Art*, trans. Susan Emanuel (Cambridge: Polity, 1996), p. 238, and in *Manet: A Symbolic Revolution*, trans. Peter Collier and Margaret Rigaud-Drayton (Cambridge: Polity, 2017), pp. 20 and 75–6.
4 The name given by Théophile Gautier to the little group of painters never admitted to the Salon (the annual exhibition of works approved by the Académie des beaux-arts), musicians with no commissions and writers with no publisher who met at the café Momus and were preserved for posterity by Henry Murger, the author of *Scènes de la vie de bohème* (1851), and by Puccini's opera *La Bohème* (1896).
5 See *The Rules of Art*, in particular 'An economic world turned upside down', pp. 81–5.
6 Ibid., pp. 81–2.
7 See Bourdieu, 'Vous avez dit "populaire"?', *Actes de la recherche en sciences sociales*, no. 46 (1983): 98–105.
8 On these points, see *The Rules of Art*, pp. 57–8, 71–3, 80–1, 130–1.
9 For more details, see Bourdieu, *The State Nobility*, trans. Lauretta C. Clough (Cambridge: Polity, 1966), pp. 263ff; Pierre Bourdieu and Loïc Wacquant, *An Invitation to Reflexive Sociology* (Cambridge: Polity, 1992), pp. 94–114.
10 'There is one thing a thousand times more dangerous than the bourgeois, that is the bourgeois artist, who has been created to come between the public and the genius; he hides each from the other' (Charles Baudelaire, *Curiosités esthétiques* (Paris: Michel Lévy, 1868), p. 208).
11 Auguste Comte contrasted 'critical' periods with the 'organic' periods that came in the wake of passing revolutions. *The Positive Philosophy of Auguste Comte*, trans. Harriet Martineau, 2 vols (New York: Appleton, [1830–42] 1858, Book VI, *passim*).

12 Here Bourdieu is referring in particular to Hans Rosenberg, *Bureaucracy and Aristocracy: The Prussian Experience, 1660–1815* (Cambridge, MA: Harvard University Press, 1958), and John R. Gillis, *The Prussian Bureaucracy in Crisis, 1810–1860: Origins of an Administrative Ethos* (Stanford, CA: Stanford University Press, 1971). Later he added to this corpus Robert M. Berdahl, *The Politics of the Prussian Nobility: The Development of a Conservative Ideology, 1770–1848* (Princeton, NJ: Princeton University Press, 1988).

13 The industrial tycoon and press magnate Marcel Dassault had published a brief autobiography entitled *Le Talisman* (Paris: Éditions J'ai lu, 1970), whose aim he summed up in these words: 'In writing this book I was thinking of the young. I wanted to show that you don't need to inherit a fortune in order to succeed, you just need to persevere. Not everyone finds a four-leaf clover, but everyone has their star.' The book reputedly sold hundreds of thousands of copies.

14 For a development of this argument, see *The Rules of Art*, p. 222.

15 In English in the original (Trans.).

16 The economist Joseph Schumpeter (1883–1950), known in particular for a theory of 'innovative entrepreneurship' (which was accompanied by criticism of the surplus production of intellectuals), was the son of an Austrian manufacturer. Although he mainly pursued an academic career, he was also at times a barrister, a government minister and the director of a bank.

17 We probably owe this metaphor to Bergson's reading of Spinoza: 'With Spinoza, the two terms Thought and Extension are placed, in principle at least, in the same rank. They are, therefore, two translations of one and the same original, or, as Spinoza says, two attributes of one and the same substance, which we must call God' (Henri Bergson, *Creative Evolution*, trans. Arthur Mitchell (New York: Henry Holt, [1907] 1911), p. 35 [Project Gutenberg ebook]).

18 Albert Cassagne, *La Théorie de l'art pour l'art en France chez les derniers romantiques et les premiers réalistes* (Geneva: Slatkine, [1906] 1979), p. 65).

19 The Paris of the 'left bank' of the Seine, with the Latin Quarter and the Sorbonne, is seen as intellectual, the 'right bank', with its administrative institutions as well as the Opéra and the Comédie française, as bourgeois.

20 In English in the text (Trans.).

21 *Distinction*, trans. Richard Nice (London: Routledge, 1984), pp. 234–41.

22 Fernando Arrabal, born 1932, Spanish playwright and film director living and working in Paris. Creator of a violent theatrical collective called the Panic movement.

23 Bourdieu develops this question in *The State Nobility*, pp. 164–5, 290 and *passim*.

24 On this point, see also Bourdieu, *Classification Struggles* (Cambridge: Polity, 2018), Lecture of 2 June 1982, pp. 98ff.

25 See Bourdieu, 'The lengthening of the circuits of legitimation', in *The State Nobility*, pp. 382–9.

26 See above, Lecture of 7 December, note 31, p. 378.

27 See Pierre Bourdieu and Luc Boltanski, 'La Production de l'idéologie dominante', *Actes de la recherche en sciences sociales*, 2/2–3 (1976): 3–73, at p. 42. The article by Simone de Beauvoir, written in response to a book by Raymond Aron, appeared in two parts in *Les Temps modernes* in 1955 (nos. 112–13, pp. 1539–75, and nos. 114–15, pp. 2219–61). It was republished in *Privilèges*

(Paris: Gallimard, 1955), reissued as *Faut-il brûler Sade* (Paris: Gallimard, 1972), and translated as 'Must we burn Sade?', in de Beauvoir, *Political Writings* (Champaign: University of Illinois Press, 2012). Raymond Aron's book *The Opium of the Intellectuals* (New York: Routledge, [1955] 2007) is a highly polemical criticism of left-wing intellectuals in general and Sartre in particular. For Bourdieu's commentaries on this book, see *The Rules of Art*, in particular pp. 192 and 223.

28 An allusion to André Antoine, the founder of the Théâtre-Libre:

> In constituting as such the problem of *mise en scène* and in posing various stagings as so many *artistic games*, that is as *systematic* sets of explicitly *chosen* responses to a set of problems which tradition was not aware of or to which it responded without posing them, André Antoine questions a doxa that was unquestioned as such, and he sets the whole game in motion, to wit, the history of *mise en scène*. (Bourdieu, *The Rules of Art*, p. 119)

See also *Manet: A Symbolic Revolution*, pp. 89–90, 96, 165, 384–5, 452.
29 See above, Lecture of 11 January, pp. 271–2.
30 See the passage and the note on the critic Jean-Jacques Gautier in *Distinction*, pp. 163, 165.
31 See in particular Bourdieu, 'The racism of "intelligence"', in *Sociology in Question*, trans. Richard Nice (London: Sage, 1993), pp. 177–80, as well as Bourdieu and Boltanski, 'La Production de l'idéologie dominante'.
32 Hippolyte-Adolphe Taine (1828–1893), a positivist, empiricist, anti-clerical philosopher who founded historical literary criticism. He supported Zola and naturalism but was a conservative critic of the French Revolution. Ernest Renan (1823–1892), a philosopher of religion, was famous for his *Life of Jesus* (1863). He promoted ideas of racial supremacy (Trans.).
33 See Bourdieu, 'The hit parade of French intellectuals, or Who is to judge the legitimacy of the judges?', in *Homo Academicus*, trans. Peter Collier (Cambridge: Polity, 1988).
34 See 'The conquest of autonomy: the critical phase in the emergence of the field', in *The Rules of Art*, pp. 47–112.
35 This is most likely a reference to Roland Barthes, defender of the Nouveau Roman, who held a chair in literary semiology at the Collège de France, 1977–80 (Trans.).
36 Here Bourdieu is referring to Ernst Troeltsch, *Die soziallehre der christlichen Kirchen und Gruppen* (1912), in *Gesammelte Schriften*, vol. 1 (Aalen: Scientia, [1922] 1961).

37 At heart, Anatole was not so much summoned by art as attracted to the life of the artist. He dreamt of a studio. He aspired to it with a schoolboy's imaginings and the appetites of his nature. What he saw there were the horizons of bohemia enchanting when viewed from afar: the novel of Misery; the shedding of bonds and rules; the freedom, indiscipline and disorder, with every day filled with chance, adventure and the unexpected; the escape from the orderly and ordering household, from the family's doings and its tedious Sundays, the bourgeois jokes; the voluptuous mystery of the female model; work that entails no pain; the right to dress up all year round, a sort of eternal carnival – these were the images and temptations conjured up for him by a rigorous and austere career in art. (Edmond and Jules de Goncourt,

Manette Salomon (Paris: UGE, [1867] 1979), p. 32; trans. Susan Emanuel in *The Rules of Art*, p. 238)

38 See in particular the section 'Religious congregation, preaching, pastoral care', in Max Weber, *The Sociology of Religion*, trans. Ephraim Fischoff (Boston: Beacon Press, [1920] 1964), pp. 60–79.

39   It is considered a good sale when three or four thousand copies are sold; this would make 2000 francs if we compute the royalty at 50 centimes a copy. . . . Thus for example suppose a play has a run of a hundred nights, which is the usual number today denoting success; the average receipts per night can be placed at 4000 francs, which brings into the box office 400,000 francs, and to the author a sum of 40,000 francs, if the royalties are ten percent of the profits. Now to earn the same sum by publishing a novel it would be necessary, putting the royalty at 50 centimes a copy, that 80,000 copies should be struck off, an output so extraordinary that I can only think of four or five examples during the last fifty years. And I am not speaking of its production throughout the rest of the country, of its reproduction in foreign countries, or of the revivals of the play. (Émile Zola, *The Experimental Novel* (London: Forgotten Books, [1893] 2012), pp. 183–4)

40   'Where the market is allowed to follow its own autonomous tendencies, its participants do not look toward the persons of each other but only toward the commodity; there are no obligations of brotherliness or reverence, and none of those spontaneous human relations that are sustained by personal unions. They would all just obstruct the free development of the bare market relationship' (Max Weber, *Economy and Society* (Berkeley: University of California Press, 1978), p. 636).

41 François de Singly, 'Un cas de dédoublement littéraire', *Actes de la recherche en sciences sociales*, no. 6 (1976): 76–86. A royalist and a member of Action française in the 1930s, Jacques Laurent-Cely (1919–2000) began his literary career after the Second World War. On the one hand he wrote mass-publication novels, in particular, under the pseudonym Cécil Saint-Laurent, *Caroline chérie*, whose success was amplified by a series of cinema adaptations in the 1950s starring the actress Martine Carol. On the other hand he published, under the name of Jacques Laurent, novels with a more limited readership that were part of the literary movement of the 'Hussards'; these had right-wing leanings and were precoccupied with questions of style and form. After ceasing his activities as a writer for a time, Jacques Laurent published *Les Bêtises* in 1971 and obtained the prix Goncourt. He was elected to the Académie française in 1986.

42   'A thief orients his action to the validity of the criminal law in that he acts surreptitiously. The fact that the order is recognized as valid in his society is made evident by the fact that he cannot violate it openly without punishment' (Weber, *Economy and Society*, vol. 1, p. 32).

43 Bourdieu provides more details on this point in *The Rules of Art*, p. 386, n. 47.

44 Bourdieu, 'The production of belief: contribution to a theory of symbolic goods', in *The Field of Cultural Producton* (Cambridge: Polity, 1993), pp. 74–111. See also *Distinction*, in particular pp. 19, 234–5, and *The Rules of Art*, Part I, chap. 3, 'The market for symbolic goods'.

45 See, in particular, Ponton, 'Naissance du roman psychologique', p. 68.

46 Bourdieu, 'La Spécificité du champ scientifique et les conditions sociales du progrès de la raison', *Sociologie et sociétés*, 7/1 (1975): 91–118, and 'Le Champ scientifique', *Actes de la recherche en sciences sociales*, nos. 2–3 (1976): 88–104. Bourdieu returns to these questions in *Science of Science and Reflexivity*, trans. Richard Nice (Cambridge: Polity, 2004).

47 'It is this period, in my opinion . . ., that inaugurates the structuring of the literary field in its present forms' (Charle, *La Crise littéraire à l'époque du naturalisme*, p. 16).

Lecture of 25 January 1983

1 See, for example, Bourdieu, 'Espace social et genèse des classes', *Actes de la recherche en sciences sociales*, nos. 52–3 (1984): 3–14.

2 Bourdieu, 'The production of belief: contribution to an economy of symbolic goods', in *The Field of Cultural Production*, ed. Randal Johnson (New York: Columbia University Press, 1993), p. 98 (the graph and its commentary are repeated, albeit rather differently, in *The Rules of Art*, trans. Susan Emanuel (Cambridge: Polity, 1996), pp. 143–5).

3 Bourdieu, *The Logic of Practice*, trans. Richard Nice (Cambridge: Polity, 1990), Book I, chap. 6, 'The work of time', pp. 98–111.

4 Claude Lévi-Strauss, 'Introduction à l'œuvre de Marcel Mauss', in Mauss, *Sociologie et anthropologie* (Paris: PUF, 1950), pp. ix–lii.

5 '[Science] always considers moments, always virtual stopping-places, always, in short, immobilities. Which amounts to saying that real time, regarded as a flux, or, in other words, as the very mobility of being, escaped the hold of scientific knowledge' (Bergson, *Creative Evolution*, trans. Arthur Mitchell (New York: Henry Holt, [1907] 1911), p. 337 [Project Gutenberg ebook].

6 See above, Lecture of 19 October 1982, note 11, p. 356.

7 Raymond Williams, *Culture and Society: 1780–1950* (London: Chatto & Windus, [1958] 1963).

8 See figure on p. 317.

9 For developments on Zola's strategy, see Bourdieu, *The Rules of Art*, pp. 127–31, 136–40.

10 On these questions, see in particular the analyses devoted to May 1968 in *Homo Academicus*, trans. Peter Collier (Cambridge: Polity, 1988), pp. 159–293, and *Manet: A Symbolic Revolution*, trans. Peter Collier and Margaret Rigaud-Drayton (Cambridge: Polity, 2017).

11 On the Huret enquiry, see above, Lecture of 11 January 1983, pp. 268–9.

12 Ernest Feydeau (1821–1873) was a stockbroker and a writer, linked in particular to Théophile Gautier and Gustave Flaubert. He found success with his novel *Fanny* in 1858. About his last novel, *Mémoires d'une demoiselle de bonne famille*, Flaubert wrote to him saying, for example, that he 'wouldn't say that there were too many romps and frolics, just that there was *nothing else*' (Letter of 21 September 1873, in *Correspondance*, Vol. II (Paris: Gallimard, 1991), p. 719).

13 'The production of belief: contribution to an economy of symbolic goods', in *The Field of Cultural Production*, pp. 74–111.

14 Bourdieu returns to this question later; see 'Une révolution conservatrice dans l'édition', *Actes de la recherche en sciences sociales*, nos. 126–7 (1999): 3–28.

15 Félix Alcan (1841–1925) was a *normalien* who came from a family of booksellers. The publishing house specialising in philosophy and social sciences that he
founded in 1883 was one of the four companies that merged in 1939 to create
the Presses Universitaires de France.

16 Jean-Louis Fabiani, *La Crise du champ philosophique, 1880–1914: contribution à l'histoire sociale du système d'enseignement* (Paris, EHESS, 1980); *Les
Philosophes de la République* (Paris: Minuit, 1988), pp. 104–9.

17 Ian Watt, *The Rise of the Novel: Studies in Defoe, Richardson and Fielding*
(Berkeley: University of California Press, 1957).

18 'A true knowledge of good and evil cannot restrain any emotion in so far as the
knowledge is true, but only in so far as it is considered as an emotion' (Spinoza,
Ethics Demonstrated in Geometrical Order, trans. Jonathan Bennett, Part IV,
proposition 14, p. 92), www.earlymoderntexts.com/assets/pdfs/spinoza1665.
pdf.

19   Music is the 'pure art' par excellence: it says nothing and has *nothing to say*.
      Never really having an expressive function, it is opposed to drama, which
      even in its most refined forms still bears a social message and can only be 'put
      over' on the basis of an immediate and profound affinity with the values and
      expectations of its audience. . . . Music represents the most radical and most
      absolute form of the negation of the world, and especially the social world,
      which the bourgeois ethos tends to demand of all forms of art. (Bourdieu,
      Distinction, trans. Richard Nice (London: Routledge, 1984), p. 19)

20 Rémy Ponton, 'Programme esthétique et accumulation de capital symbolique:
l'exemple du Parnasse', *Revue française de sociologie*, 14/2 (1973): 202–20.

21 This is no doubt a reference to Robert Wohl, *The Generation of 1914*
(Cambridge, MA: Harvard University Press, 1979).

22 An allusion to the first sentence of the 'Manifesto of the Communist Party'
by Marx and Engels (1848): 'The history of all hitherto existing society is the
history of class struggles' (*The Revolutions of 1848* (Harmondsworth: Penguin,
1973), p. 67).

23 Bourdieu quoted it in particular in his inaugural lecture at the Collège de
France ('A lecture on the lecture', in *In Other Words* (Cambridge: Polity, 1990),
p. 196), pointing out that it was a Kabyle proverb.

24 See *The Eighteenth Brumaire of Louis Bonaparte*, in *Surveys from Exile*
(Harmondsworth: Penguin, [1852] 1973), where Marx emphasises on several
occasions the inspiration that the French Revolution of 1789–1814 found in
the Roman Republic – in particular, pp. 147–8.

25 See Louis Pinto, '*Tel Quel*: au sujet des intellectuels de parodie', *Actes de la
recherche en sciences sociales*, no. 89 (1991): 66–77.

26   The characteristic of the century now coming to an end is that it is like a
      double-barrelled gun. Kandinsky and Kupka invented abstraction. Then
      abstraction died. No one was going talk about it anymore. It came back
      thirty-five years later with the American abstract expressionists. You could
      say that cubism reappeared in an impoverished form in the post-war Paris
      school. Dada came back in the same way. A second shot, second wind. It's
      a phenomenon typical of this century. You didn't find that in the eight-
      eenth or nineteenth centuries. After the Romantics, came Courbet. And
      Romanticism never came back. Even the Pre-Raphaelites aren't a rehash of

the Romantics. ('Interview' in *VH 101*, no. 3 (1970): 55–61; quoted in 'The production of belief', p. 109)

27 On Marcel Duchamp, as on Le Douanier Rousseau, whom he goes on to mention, see 'Reflexivity and "Naiveté"', in *The Rules of Art*, pp. 242–9.

28 A few years earlier Bourdieu had devoted an article to peasant farmers as an 'objectified class', 'obliged to form their own subjectivity out of their objectification' ('Une classe objet', *Actes de la recherche en sciences sociales*, no. 17 (1977): 2–5).

29 Bourdieu's idea is that a schema of the space of stances adopted, if reproduced on a transparent sheet, could be placed over the schema of the space of positions. He proceeds almost literally in this manner in a pre-publication of some chapters of *Distinction*: the schema of the life styles is accompanied by a sheet of tracing paper bearing the properties of the social groups that the reader can place over it. (See Pierre Bourdieu and Monique de Saint Martin, 'Anatomie du goût', *Actes de la recherche en sciences sociales*, nos. 2–3 (1976): 2–81.

30 Bourdieu must be thinking of Léon Cladel, whom he presents in *The Rules of Art*, pp. 262–3, as a 'classic case' of this mismatch.

31 On this aspect of Courbet, see *The Rules of Art*, in particular pp. 434–5, and *Manet: A Symbolic Revolution*.

32 Stéphane Mallarmé, 'La Musique et les lettres', in *Œuvres complètes* (Paris: Gallimard, 1970), p. 647. Bourdieu returns to this quotation and its commentary in *The Rules of Art*, pp. 274–7; see also *Manet: A Symbolic Revolution*, pp. 99, 516.

Index

and social mechanisms, 29
as space of constraint, 21, 46
as space of objective probabilities, 123
as space of possibilities, 336–42
and statistical aggregates, 235–7
struggles for domination of, 196, 197–8, 277, 293–4, 299–305
subdivision of, 38–9, 162–3, 198, 199
and the subject–object relation, 31–3
theoretical basis, 237–43
transformations of, 192–7
Flaubert, Gustave, 33–5, 158–9, 174, 222, 265, 271, 274, 284, 326, 337
forces, field of, 20–2, 39, 45–6, 165, 211–13, 226–7, 251–2, 257–64, 266–7, 338
Foucault, Michel, 90
Fragonard, Jean-Honoré, 35
Frankfurt School, 148
Frege, Gottlob, 109
French, as academic discipline, 162–3, 166
Freud, Sigmund, 58, 135, 140, 206, 223

gambling analogies, 226–7, 264–5
games
  feel for the game, 78–83, 126
  and *illusio*, 83–6
  investment in, 25, 82–6
  playing with rules of as indicator of excellence, 66, 76
  as social mechanisms, 25
Gautier, Jean-Jacques, 301
gender, 126, 138, 139, 145–6, 167, 170, 182, 193, 222, 247, 255, 329, 339
genealogical approaches, 6–7, 210, 239, 245
generational change, 332–6
geography, 162, 164, 167, 170, 171, 187
geology, 164
geometry, 204–5
The German Ideology (Marx), 131, 246
Gernet, Louis, 44
ghost in the machine, 111

gift exchange, 53–4, 319–21
Girl Reading (Fragonard), 35
gnoseologia inferior, 52, 60–4
Goblot, Edmond, 172
God-like knowledge, 52–3, 54–60, 62
Goethe, Johann Wolfgang von, 43
Goffman, Erving, 12–13, 63, 245, 252
Goldmann, Lucien, 272, 273, 287
Gombrich, Ernst, 117
Goncourt, Edmond de, 290, 307
Goncourt, Jules de, 290, 307
Gramsci, Antonio, 215
grandes écoles, 8, 46, 185, 217, 234, 237, 256, 280, 297–8, 302
graphology, 155
greetings, 77–8
groups *see* collectives; populations
Guitry, Sacha, 286
Gurvitch, Georges, 18

habituality, 25, 100–2, 275
habitus
  and adjustment to reality, 123–6, 127–9
  aesthetic habitus, 42–4
  classes of, 29–30
  and its clothing, 77–8
  defining concept of, 7–8, 29
  double relationship with the social, 122
  and economic theory, 96
  and experience, 101–2, 122, 123–5, 128
  in harmony with field, 14–15, 258–9
  Husserl's usage, 100–2
  and incorporation, 29–30, 32, 65, 122, 133–7, 342–3
  and memory, 21
  and motivation to action, 66–7
  and necessity, 124–5, 133–7
  and objectification, 25–6
  as *orthè doxa*, 67–9
  and positions, 337, 339–40
  and practical knowledge, 39–45, 64–9, 86–7, 101, 257–9

individuals
  classification of, 13, 29–30, 146–7
  individual representations, 199
  individual teleology, 65, 72, 89–99,
    105, 126, 149
  as object of sociological study, 11,
    12, 235, 256–7
  and personalist thinking, 205
  relation to society, 28–9
  social and economic conditions
    producing, 94–6, 128–9, 130
  as social institutions, 28
  see also social agents
individuation, 28
infinite regression, 46, 69–70, 118,
  147–8
infinitesimal calculus, 53, 54
information theory, 6
Ingres, Jean-Auguste-Dominique, 341
inhabitation, 81–2
inheritance, 188, 230, 255
institution, act of, 15–16, 137
institution, rites of *see* rites of
  institution
institutionalisation, 284, 285–6, 306–7
institutions *see* social institutions
insults, 190–1, 258, 287
intellectual determinism, 50, 89, 105–6
intellectual field, 15, 84, 161–75,
    177–81, 183–9, 192–202, 294–305,
    308, 316
intellectualist error, 49–54, 86–7, 96–8
intentionality, 22, 57, 64–7, 68, 89; *see*
  also purposiveness
interactionism, 12–14, 63, 83, 238,
    245–8, 249, 252–5
interactions, 12–14, 235, 236, 238–40,
    242, 245–8, 252–5
interest, 83, 85–6, 90–2, 96–7
intertextuality, 274–7
interviews, 143–4, 269–70
intuition, 187, 206, 247
invariants, 161, 173, 192, 241–2, 282,
    308
investment, 25, 82–6

Isambert-Jamati, Viviane, 172
Islam, 93

Jakobson, Roman, 76, 205, 206
journalism, 109, 110, 187, 268–9, 287–8
Joyce, James, 34, 35, 40, 121

Kabyle people, 26, 139, 170, 230
Kant, Immanuel, 65, 98, 115, 148, 153,
    157, 165, 167, 169
Kantorowicz, Ernst Hartwig, 16, 29,
    198
The King's Two Bodies (Kantorowicz),
    16, 29
kingship, 29
Kluckhohn, Clyde, 10
knowledge
  critique of, 147–51
  and feel for the game, 78–82
  gnoseologia inferior, 52, 60–4
  God-like knowledge, 52–3, 54–60, 62
  and habitus, 39–45, 64–9, 86–7, 101,
    257–9
  hierarchy of, 38, 52–3, 61–3
  historical contextualisation, 210
  modes of acquisition, 210
  practical knowledge, 33, 36–56,
    60–72, 78–82, 86–7, 147–9, 187–8,
    257–9
  relations of, 32–3, 36–9
  scholarly knowledge, 33, 36–46, 51,
    54–61, 69–72, 82, 86–7, 147–51
  scientific knowledge, 33, 36, 52–3,
    63, 147–8
  as technology, 148
  and truth, 67–8
  without consciousness, 47–9
Kraus, Karl, 177–8

Lacan, Jacques, 69, 159
Laing, R. D., 86, 141
language
  analytical philosophical approaches
    to, 109–12, 114–16
  and classification, 132–3, 156